MW01253073

FOCUS ON NONVERBAL COMMUNICATION RESEARCH

FOCUS ON NONVERBAL COMMUNICATION RESEARCH

FINLEY R. LEWIS

EDITOR

Nova Science Publishers, Inc.
New York

Copyright © 2007 by Nova Science Publishers, Inc.

NOTICE TO THE READER

Library of Congress Cataloging-in-Publication Data
Focus on nonverbal communication research / Finley R. Lewis, editor.
    p. cm.
Includes index.
ISBN 13: 978-1-59454-790-4
ISBN 10: 1-59454-790-4
1. Body language--Research--Methodology. I. Lewis, Finley R.
BF637.N66F63   2006
153.6'9--dc22   2005028273

Published by Nova Science Publishers, Inc. ✦*New York*

CONTENTS

PREFACE

Often defined as communication without words, nonverbal communication (NVC) refers to all aspects of a message which are not conveyed by the literal meaning of words. Both written and spoken communication can be nonverbal. The main types of NVC are chronemics, kinesics, paralinguistics, proxemics and semiotics. Culture, gender and social status influence nonverbal communication. NVC also includes object communication and haptics or touch. Paralinguistic mechanisms include intonation, stress, rate of speech, and pauses or hesitations; nonlinguistic behaviors include gestures, facial expressions, and body language, among others. This new book brings forth new and important research in this field.

Chapter 1 - Categorization is a fundamental property of the human brain. Studies of the categorical perception (CP) of sensory continua (colours, phonemes) have a long and rich history in psychophysics. In the last decade, developments in computer graphics have made it possible to explore categorical perception effects with multidimensional stimuli, such as faces, which defined an important substrate of nonverbal communication.

The aim of the present chapter is (1) to review the empirical data, collected up to now, relative to CP effects found on the different dimensions of faces; (2) outline for all of these different dimensions why the investigation of CP effects has been of the greatest conceptual relevance; and (3) put together empirical data collected with different techniques (experimental psychology, medical imagery) in order to provide a dynamic and functional view of CP of faces.

Chapter 2 - Sound spectrography has since the 1960s been used to objectively evaluate crying in neonates. The various cry characteristics used for scientific analysis are described. The crying of healthy infants has a mean fundamental frequency of 400-600 Hz most often with a falling or rising-falling melody contour. Prematurely born infants have the more high-pitched crying the more immature the infant. In impaired infants, and especially those with disorders involving the central nervous system, the cry has been abnormal; the fundamental frequency has been higher, the melody contour irregular and some cry characteristics very seldom seen in crying of healthy neonates has occurred more often.

Crying in newborn and small infants has been regarded as a graded signal, i.e. the cry indicates the degree of stress but does not change according to the cause of crying. In order to check the statement sound spectrographic characteristics in both spontaneous and pain induced cries were analyzed. Eighteen infants were followed from birth to the age of two months, and the cries were collected at six different occasions. A total of 1020 cries was analyzed. The results indicated a significantly higher pitch in pain induced than in spontaneous cries for the whole group. However, the differences between spontaneous and pain cries at the various ages were often marginal. The cry variables of spontaneous and pain cries did not change significantly with increasing age.

Many parents are upset about their infants' crying during the first month of life. Excessive crying is often called colic. Previous studies indicate that an organic cause for this type of crying is infrequent. A study of the amount and perception of crying in 281 infants in Finland and 97 infants in South America (Chile and Colombia) is presented based on parents' diaries. The results indicate that the crying and sleeping episodes in infants in both continents were similar and that a peak of crying occurred in the evenings for infants under the age of three months. The mean crying time per day for infants under the age of six months was 1.4 hours in Finland and 1.7 hours in South America. Crying for more than three hours per day in infants under the age of three months was observed in 12.4 % in Finland and 26.3 % in South America.

Chapter 3 - Several researchers have stated that facial expression recognition appears to play one of the most important roles in human communication. With regard to the basic cognitive structure of facial expression recognition, in this chapter, I would like to report and discuss the internal structure in terms of a dimensional account, which asserts that the structure of emotional facial expression recognition should be geometrically conceptualized in terms of two underlying bipolar dimensions—pleasure-displeasure and intensity of arousal. Significant advance in computer technology has enabled researchers to explore the cognitive structure of prototype facial expressions represented by not only still photographs but also computer-generated morphed facial expressions. Morphed facial expressions, in a sense, are complex and include diverse types of emotional information; therefore, discussing the structure of facial expression recognition appears to be extremely interesting and profitable for human nonverbal communication. First, I will briefly review earlier studies on facial expressions and major accounts of facial expression recognition. Second, I will discuss the internal structure of human facial expression recognition in detail as reported by some psychological experiments using morphing. Third, I will discuss the possibility of applying fractals, a concept of self-similarity, to facial expression recognition. Our experiment indicates that the structure of facial expression recognition definitely has a fractal aspect and a non-integer dimension of 1.18. The fact that the recognition system has fractal properties can perhaps be applied to not only psychology (nonverbal communication) but also various other domains of research.

Chapter 4 - Laughter is universal among humans. As an important part of life, few disagree with the statement: "Laughter is the best medicine." Even fewer would say laughter has no influence on the immune system, blood pressure, or cardiac output, which raises several questions: "What are the physiological responses during and following laughter?" Is laughter exercise and, if so, what are the health implications? Perhaps, the truth is somewhere in between the "best medicine" and the "promotion" of laughter as a business. The science of laughter is in its infancy. Hence, what is the physiology of laughter? What are the health benefits, given the interest in laughter as an alternative therapy? This chapter examines the cardiovascular responses to laughter. Cardiac output was measured during laughter to understand the role of the central (cardiac output) and peripheral (arterial-venous O_2 difference) components of oxygen consumption (VO_2) and its relation to energy expended. College subjects participated by sitting in a comfortable chair for 5 minutes, followed by viewing a videotape of a well-known comedian for 5 minutes, which was followed by sitting for 5 minutes. A repeated-measures ANOVA was used to analyze the data. During laughter, there were significant increases in stroke volume and cardiac output and significant decreases in arterial-venous O_2 difference and systemic vascular resistance. Following laughter, there was a significant decrease in oxygen consumption. More scientific research about laughter is needed to understand the healthcare implications. In the meantime, laughter is an important nonverbal communicative skill. It is fun to laugh, and it seems to decrease tension. People appear to feel good when they laugh, and maybe that is enough because it is pleasurable.

Chapter 5 - Electronic speech generating devices (SGDs) offer a vehicle for communicating with family and caregivers to hospitalized patients who lose the ability to speak during critical illness or following surgery. However, there is little empiric evidence regarding the abilities and preferences of nonspeaking, hospitalized older adults with regard to SGD use. This chapter presents a secondary analysis of data from two small pilot studies to explore the communication ability, frequency, content, method, SGD use, quality of SGD communication, and barriers to communication with SGDs among seriously ill hospitalized older adults. Both studies used a mixed methods, complementary design involving qualitative and quantitative data obtained by direct observation, survey, interview, and clinical record review. This analysis focused on the subsample of adult participants who were over 55 years of age. Eight patients, 66.4±8.5 years with 12.5±1.4 years of education and moderately severe illness (APACHE III= 39.2±14.5), had SGDs in their hospital rooms in the medical intensive care unit (n=4) or the otolaryngology surgical unit (n=4), for 1 to 13 (5.7±6.2) days. In total, 46 topics were recorded and categorized for the 32 observed communication events in this older adult sample. The greatest number of messages were about physical care and comfort. Seven (21.8%) of the observed communication events involved SGDs for message construction. SGDs were used by patients more often than other nonvocal communication methods to initiate communication and to construct messages about sentiments, emotions, home and family. Ease of Communication scores (ECS) showed improvement after use of the SGDs (23.3±9.7) when compared with pre-intervention scores (31.0±13.8) for older adults where lower scores indicate less difficulty with communication. This chapter includes descriptive observations of communication interactions involving SGDs and poignant quotations from patients, family members and clinicians about SGD use. In conclusion, SGDs can be used by nonspeaking seriously ill older adults for message building and as components of a comprehensive augmentative and assistive communication plan. The successful use of SGDs by acutely and critically ill older adults despite sedation and narcotic analgesia and in the absence of formalized education or feature matching is impressive. However, further research and development activities should be directed toward adapting SGDs for use by older adults and instructing communication partners on cueing and assistance strategies.

Chapter 6 - This chapter reports on a community-based participatory research (CBPR) strategy for collecting health related data from a linguistic minority in the United States: self-identified members of Deaf community. The literature available on deaf and hard of hearing persons' health and healthcare status suggests that these individuals rarely participate in surveys of citizens' well-being. Recent work assessing "health literacy" among hearing adults shows that obstacles to gaining healthcare information, including limited proficiency in English, impede healthcare knowledge, utilization, and costs, as well as health itself. Culturally identified Deaf individuals often view researchers from the "hearing world" with suspicion. Using CBPR and ASL-GLOSS (an American Sign Language—ASL—linguistics method) trained Deaf interviewers asked 130 Deaf senior citizens who depend on a signed language for communication about cultural practices and linguistic barriers to healthcare, focusing on end-of-life care information.[1] Interviews were videotaped, while a centrally located monitor received direct feeds from five enclosed interview booths allowed the research team to make adjustments to ensure consistency among interviewers during the study. A mirror placed behind the respondents enabled interviewer and respondent to be captured on the same videotape. The closed-ended questions of the half-hour interviews were coded on-site by the Deaf interviewers for statistical analysis. A team of Deaf interviewers reviewed the tapes to check the reliability of the initial coding and assign categories and codes to open-ended questions. A focus group comprised of expert Deaf interviewers, community leaders, and hearing researchers reviewed and interpreted the findings. The survey instrument and method revealed important findings concerning deaf senior citizens' perceptions about their end-of-life care needs, enabling the development of appropriate educational materials and information dissemination strategies. The research team concluded that the conceptual, sociocultural, and linguistic challenges of culturally identified deaf and hard of hearing persons can be addressed using CBPR strategies and ASL-GLOSS linguistic methods. These innovations in survey design and method can have a significant impact on collecting valid and reliable data from this underrepresented population. Moreover, the research experience speaks to the broader concern of health literacy among members of the Deaf community.

Chapter 7 - Among late-state dementia patients, depression and behavioral problems are both prevalent and highly difficult to treat. This paper offers a review of the literature in this area, interpreting findings in the light of dynamic systems theory and interpersonal process. It is argued that the cognitive disturbances present in late-stage dementia severely impair patients' ability to express emotions verbally, particularly depressed affect, though, as recent research has shown, non-verbal markers are patently in evidence. Caregivers have a great deal of difficulty accurately understanding and responding to dementia patients' emotions. If consistently misunderstood, dementia patients may try to communicate affects by increasing the intensity of their emotional behaviors. These are typically interpreted by caregivers as "behavioral problems," rather than emotional communications and caregivers tend to respond by becoming frustrated and critical. Patients then may feel more misunderstood and their behavioral disturbances may escalate. This vicious circle, it is argued, can be broken by educating caregivers about affect in late-stage dementia. An educative program developed by the authors is described.

Chapter 8 - Communication between subject and his close environment is a continuous and necessary condition for the organization and control of goal-directed actions. This includes the processing of various exteroceptive (visual, auditory, etc...) and interoceptive (proprioception, motor commands, etc...) information, in other words, the involvement of both internal and external communication. The continuous processing of multimodal and interdependent information, the so-called sensory or sensorimotor integration, is the basic mechanism for humans both to perceive themselves, their close environment and to interact with it. In this chapter, we argue these perceptuo-motor interactions are highly flexible (adaptation of integrative mechanisms to contextual conditions) and variable (differences in integrative mechanisms across subjects).

Chapter 9 - People are motivated to talk about emotional events with other people (Rime, 1994) and in these verbal interactions they frequently refer explicitly to emotional states ("I thought he looked quite annoyed with me"; "She looked jealous"). But accurately decoding emotional states is difficult; emotional expressions are often complex blends of a number of emotions (Scherer & Tannenbaum, 1986), and language may not be the best medium in which to disambiguate them. Indeed Halberstadt and colleagues have recently shown that explaining the emotional states of others, rather than improving emotion perception, can paradoxically impair it by biasing emotion encoding in the direction of the explanation (Halberstadt & Niedenthal, 2001; Halberstadt, 2003; Halberstadt, 2005). In these studies participants who explained why a target was feeling sad (for example) remembered her face as expressing more sadness than it actually did.

The purpose of the present chapter is to explore the implications of this "explanation bias" for emotion attributions themselves. The authors will first review the work done by Halberstadt and colleagues and Halberstadt's (2003; 2005) argument that explanation effects are due to a shift in processing strategy associated with verbalization. Next, they propose that social situations can be understood as configural stimuli and as such should be vulnerable to the same biases as facial expressions. They then report preliminary data that show an explanation bias for emotion attributions of gender-congruent targets in an ambiguous emotional situation. Finally, they explore the implications of these results in particular, and the importance of configural and featural encoding in social situations more generally.

Chapter 10 - Schizophrenics present attentional and emotional disorders. In particular, treatment of refractory schizophrenics (TRS) have shown larger deficits in logical-verbal memory and associative learning as well as in emotional recognition than in good responders. Some evidences point out that olanzapine (OLZ), an atypical neuroleptic, may induce an improvement of attention, memory and depressive symptoms, as well as on the interpretation of positive prosodic affective stimuli. Thus, the main purpose of this study was to determine if OLZ can improve the ability to recognize facial emotional expressions in TRS, regarding differences in performance and in the ERPs amplitude, using an "odd-ball" paradigm. Another objective was to determine the relationship between psychopathology and task performance and P3 amplitude before and after OLZ treatment.

14 TRS and 14 control subjects (CON) participated in the study. Patients were evaluated before (PRE-T) and after 8 weeks of OLZ treatment (POS-T). N2 and P3 were recorded during two "odd-ball" paradigm tasks, a typical attention task and a facial emotional recognition tasks with happiness as the target stimuli. N2 and P3 amplitude, as well as the performance measures were evaluated. Finally, correlations between psychopathology and task performance as well as P3 amplitude were performed.

OLZ did not induce changes in performance nor in ERPs amplitude. However, there were differences between TRS and CON, both on the attention and on the emotional task. TRS showed a lower number of correct responses and higher omissions, as well as a longer reaction time than CON. In addition, N2 and P3 amplitudes were lower in CON than in TRS. There was a correlation between performance and P3 amplitude of both tasks and symptoms related to thought disorders and poor rapport. In the POS-T there was also a correlation of performance with tension and depression in the emotional task. P3 amplitude negatively correlated with anxiety in the attention task and positive (excitement and hostility) and negative (emotional withdrawal) symptoms in the emotional recognition task in the POS-T.

Present results support other findings of attention and emotional disorders in schizophrenics. OLZ did not have a global effect on the performance of the attention nor on the emotional tasks, but there were changes in significant correlations between psychopathology, performance and P3 amplitude after OLZ. Event-related potentials are useful to evaluate deficits in attentional and emotional recognition processes, as well as the effects of neuroleptics in psychiatric populations.

Chapter 11 - Cross-fostered as infants in Reno, chimpanzees Washoe, Moja, Tatu, and Dar freely conversed in signs of American Sign Language with each other as well as with humans in Ellensburg. In this experiment a human interlocutor waited for a chimpanzee to initiate conversations with her and then responded with one of four types of probes; general requests for more information, on topic questions, off topic questions, or negative statements. The responses of the chimpanzees to the probes depended on the type of probe and the particular signs in the probes. They reiterated, adjusted, and shifted the signs in their utterances in conversationally appropriate rejoinders. Their reactions to and interactions with a conversational partner resembled patterns of conversation found in similar studies of human children.

In: Focus on Nonverbal Communication Research
Editor: Finley R. Lewis, pp. 1-29

ISBN 1-59454-790-4
© 2007 Nova Science Publishers, Inc.

Chapter 1

CATEGORICAL PERCEPTION OF FACES AND NONVERBAL COMMUNICATION

*Salvatore Campanella**

Cognitive Neuroscience Unit (NESC), University of Louvain-la-Neuve (UCL), Belgium
Psychiatry Service, Brugmann Hospital, Brussels, Belgium

ABSTRACT

Categorization is a fundamental property of the human brain. Studies of the categorical perception (CP) of sensory continua (colours, phonemes) have a long and rich history in psychophysics. In the last decade, developments in computer graphics have made it possible to explore categorical perception effects with multidimensional stimuli, such as faces, which defined an important substrate of nonverbal communication.

The aim of the present chapter is (1) to review the empirical data, collected up to now, relative to CP effects found on the different dimensions of faces; (2) outline for all of these different dimensions why the investigation of CP effects has been of the greatest conceptual relevance; and (3) put together empirical data collected with different techniques (experimental psychology, medical imagery) in order to provide a dynamic and functional view of CP of faces.

Key-Words: categorical perception, faces, behavioral data, brain imaging techniques, event-related potentials

* Address correspondence: Campanella Salvatore, PhD, UCL - Faculté de Psychologie - Unité NESC, Place du Cardinal Mercier, 10, 1348 Louvain-la-Neuve, Belgium; or CHU Brugmann, Service de Pychiatrie, Place van Gehuchten, 4, 1020 Brussels (belgium) ; e-mail : Salvatore.Campanella@psp.ucl.ac.be

INTRODUCTION

Non verbal behavior is generally considered as being informative regarding one's spontaneous thoughts and feelings. Today it is also suggested that nonverbal messages might play an important role in several clinical conditions (Philippot, Feldman & Coats, 2003). Indeed, as a major medium of social communication, nonverbal behavior is related to many aspects of affective experiences and emotional regulation. As a consequence, any nonverbal dysfunction might have an effect on the individual and interpersonal functioning. The study of nonverbal behavior is necessary to gain full understanding of clinical disorders. Inside the human visual environment, faces are fascinating stimuli, due to the amount of information they convey, and can then be considered as an important substrate of nonverbal communication. This can explain why, since the 1970s, face processing has become a field of intensive research (Bruyer, 2003). In the present chapter, we will focus on the phenomenon of *categorical perception* of faces.

The environment provides a large amount of various stimulations that the human brain cannot exhaustively process. One method to simplify our perception of events is to categorize stimuli. The categorization process is a highly complex cognitive function (e.g., Almassy, Edelman & Sporns, 1998), and its end-products, categories, are particularly important because they will determine how we will see and act upon the world. Indeed, if we looked at color categories, a continuous range of light frequencies represents the color spectrum. Nevertheless, we perceive bands of colors rather than a gradual continuum of color change. Categorization reflects a process by which linear physical changes of a stimulus have non-linear perceptual effects. Moreover, it appears that two colors straddling a category boundary (green-yellow) are easier to discriminate than two colors stemming from the same category (green-green), even though the physical differences in wavelength are identical within both pairs (Bornstein & Korda, 1984). This phenomenon, which consists in enhancing "between-category" differences while "within-category" differences are reduced, is known as the *categorical perception* (CP) effect (Harnad, 1987).

The CP effect was initially observed on unidimensional stimuli, such as speech sounds and color perception (Liberman, Harris, Hoffman, Griffith, 1957; Bornstein & Korda, 1984). Even if humans are confronted with physical linear changes, they perceive both phonemes and hues categorically. Accordingly, a physical change in a stimulus is taken into account when it occurs at the boundary between two categories while it is neglected when it occurs within a given category. This highly specific psychophysical phenomenon turns out to be of the greatest relevance as it may provide a representative model for the general categorization process. CP on speech sounds and color perception has thus been extensively explored, as illustrated and reviewed by Harnad (1987). Because this area of research has been already well documented, this kind of CP will not define the scope of the present paper. Identically, CP effects were also investigated in many others domains, such as with somesthesic stimuli (Romo, Merchant, Zainos, & Hernandez, 1997), musical patterns (Fiske, 1997), orientation of visual objects (Rosielle & Cooper, 2001), complex visual shapes (Livingston, Andrews, & Harnad, 1998), textures (Pevtzow & Harnad, 1997), familiar objects (Newell & Bülthoff, in press), and even in non human primates (Thompson & Oden, 2000). Nevertheless, these works were not considered in the present review, which will focus on a particular stimulus, for which all humans reached a high degree of expertise (Carey, 1992), i.e. human faces.

In the last decade, developments in computer graphics have made it possible to explore categorical perception effects with multidimensional stimuli, such as faces (see Figure 1 for illustration). Studying CP effects on face reveals to be of particular relevance because faces were particularly important in nonverbal social interactions, as they allow an observer to derive the identity, gender, age, emotional status, race of the face's bearer, influencing also the attribution of personality characteristics to persons (Schweinberger & Soukup, 1998).

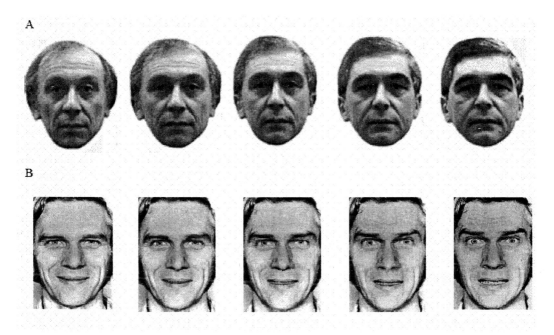

Figure 1. Illustration of two continua of morphed faces. The first one (A) shows morphed faces varying linearly from one identity to another one, while the second one (B) illustrates the manipulation of emotional information. These morphed faces are respectively constituted by 90%/10%, 70%/30%, 50%/50%, 30%/70% and 10%/90% of endpoint faces.

With this in mind, the aim of the present chapter is (1) to review the empirical data, collected up to now, relative to CP effects found on the different dimensions of faces; (2) outline for all of these different dimensions (expression, identity, ...) why the investigation of CP effects has been of the greatest conceptual relevance; and (3) put together empirical data collected with different techniques (behavioural, neuropsychological, neurophysiological and anatomical data) in order to provide a dynamic and functional view of what is known, at the present state of knowledge, about the mechanisms implied in the CP of faces.

CP OF EMOTIONAL FACIAL EXPRESSIONS

Behavioral Data

Facial expressions constitute an excellent way to explore the categorical perception with multidimensional stimuli (Calder, Young, Perrett, Etcoff & Rowland, 1996). First, people are very skilled at understanding other's facial expressions: even babies precociously respond to different facial expressions (Field, Woodson, Greenberg & Cohen, 1982). Second, it is nowadays largely accepted that some configurations of facial features, resulting from specific patterns of facial muscle movements, are perceived throughout the world as corresponding to particular basic emotions (Ekman & Friesen, 1971; Ekman, 1992, 1994). Third, (1) experimental studies on normal subjects showed that, when they were asked to make quick judgments of emotional expressions, reaction times were equal for familiar and unfamiliar faces (Bruce, 1988); (2) studies of patients with lesions affecting face perception have demonstrated that selective impairments in the recognition of facial expressions, sparing the ability to recognize identity, can occur after right temporoparietal lesions (Bowers, Bauer, Coslett, Heilman, 1985); (3) experiments with positron emission tomography (PET) and with functional magnetic resonance imagery technique (fMRI) have also shown the activation of different brain areas during the perception of facial identity and emotion (respectively, Sergent, Otha, McDonald & Zuck, 1994; Philipps, Bullmore, Howard, Woodruff, Wright, Williams, Simmons, Andrew, Brammer & David, 1998); and (4) neurons specifically responsive to facial expressions were found primarily in the cortex of the superior temporal sulcus (STS) of the macaque monkey (Hasselmo, Rolls & Baylis, 1989), while neurons responsive to identity were found in the inferior temporal gyrus (Young & Yamane, 1992). These results strengthened the hypothesis that functionally independent processes mediate facial identity and facial emotion (Bruce & Young, 1986), even if some interactions are possible (Schweinberger, Burton & Kelly, 1999). Moreover, selective impairments of specific emotions have been evidenced in Huntington's disease (Sprengelmeyer, Young, Sprengelmeyer, Calder, Rowland, Perrett, Hömberg & Lange, 1997) and different cerebral networks are thought to be implied in the recognition of different expressions (Adolphs, Damasio, Tranel & Damasio, 1996). With this in mind, it was interesting to investigate whether CP effect could be found for both processes (identity vs. emotion), and relies on identical neural substrates. We will focus on emotional data in a first step; then, the identity dimension will be considered.

The investigation of categorical perception of facial expressions turns out to be of the greatest conceptual relevance, as we know little about the *perceptual* representation of facial affect, and the mechanisms used to decode it (Calder et al., 2000). One of the fundamental issues that is still discussed concerns whether facial expressions are perceived as varying continuously along underlying dimensions or as belonging to qualitatively discrete categories, as one might use existing theories to argue either way (Calder et al., 1996). Indeed, the idea of basic universally recognized emotions would suggest categorical perception, whereas dimensional accounts would not.

Etcoff and Magee (1992) carried out the first study on categorical perception of facial expressions. They converted photographs from the Ekman and Friesen (1976) series of pictures of facial affect into line drawings and used a computer program to generate drawings of equal interpolated steps between two different facial expressions posed by the same individual. These authors used a two-step procedure. First, subjects were confronted with an ABX *discrimination* task, during which two drawings (A, B) were successively presented, followed by a third one (X). Subjects had to decide whether X was the same as A or B. Second, subjects were confronted with an *identification* task, during which they had to categorize all the randomly interpolated faces falling along a particular expression continuum (e.g., from happiness to fear). Although the expression information was linearly manipulated, sharp boundaries appeared in the subjects' responses between regions of each continuum perceived as corresponding to one expression, and a region corresponding to the other expression. Moreover, results of the ABX task showed that subjects discriminated more easily two pairs of drawings crossing a subjective category boundary (such as a drawing seen as happy in the identification task and one seen as fearful) as compared to pairs of drawings separated by an equal physical distance but laying within a category (e.g., two drawings identified as happy). This clearly demonstrated a categorical perception of facial expressions. By using photograph-quality morphed images of expression continua, Calder et al. (1996), Granato, Bruyer, & Revillon (1996), Young, Rowland, Calder, Etcoff, Seth & Perrett (1997), Bimler & Kirkland (2001) replicated Etcoff and Magee's (1992) findings in that field, these results being extended to 7-month-old infants and 9- to 10-year-children respectively by Kotsoni, de Haan & Johnson (2001) and de Gelder, Teunisse & Benson (1997). Moreover, it has been shown that high-functioning adolescents with autism do not perceive facial expressions categorically (Teunisse & de Gelder, 2001).

These results lead to two main considerations. First, the categorical perception effect needs two stages to be assessed: (1) *an identification task*, showing non-linear responses to linearly manipulated stimuli and allowing to define boundaries within each continuum, and (2) *a discrimination task*, defining the hallmark of categorical perception effect and which has to evidence an enhanced discriminability for BETWEEN- as compared to WITHIN-categorical differences. Second, findings of categorical perception of facial expressions were inconsistent concerning the emotion perception in terms of a two-dimensional model (such as pleasant-unpleasant and rejection-attention; e.g., Woodworth & Schlosberg, 1954) but provided strong evidence that facial expressions are perceived as belonging to discrete categories (Young et al., 1997; see also Calder, Burton, Miller, Young & Akamatsu, 2001 for discussion).

Neuropsychological Data

The above review shows that CP gives rise to the following phenomena: stimuli from the center of categories are classified faster than those at the edges (Bornstein & Monroe, 1980), discrimination of stimuli and same/different judgements are more accurate and faster across than within categories (Etcoff & Magee, 1992). Such an investigation has been extended to a neuropsychological case, patient LEW, who manifests a number of difficulties with naming and categorization judgements (Roberson, Davidoff, & Braisby, 1999). LEW was a 60-year-old man who suffered from a left hemisphere stroke that has left him with a right-sided hemiplegia. He was described as presenting no pre-semantic visual deficits, full visual fields, no neglect, performing excellently on Shape Detection, Object Decision and Position Discrimination and with no short-term spatial memory deficit (Roberson et al., 1999). LEW is an aphasic patient who has limited speech production, reading and writing, but excellent comprehension.

In a first experiment, Roberson et al. (1999) described LEW's difficulty in sorting visual stimuli such as colors and facial expressions. In other words, LEW has no difficulty in recognizing objects but he has marked difficulties in naming colors and expressions and he experienced great difficulty in sorting colors and facial expressions into groups. However, in a second experiment, LEW was confronted, for colors and emotional facial expressions, with an odd-one-out task where he has to select the most dissimilar of three stimuli (Laws, Davies,

& Andrews, 1995). In such a case, CP would lead subjects to select the two within-category stimuli as being most similar, or the cross-category stimulus as being the odd-one-out. Results clearly show that when judging similarity, LEW was able to make use of relatively unimpaired category boundaries as for colors than for facial expressions. In other words, LEW was able to make normal similarity computations between colors or facial expressions chips, even though he was unable to sort or name them successfully: Thus, there is an implicit knowledge about category boundaries available to LEW that was not used in explicit categorization task.

Considering this pattern of performance, Roberson et al. (1999) wonder what prevents LEW from having explicit access to his "intact" CP of colors and facial expressions. They argue that this was due to LEW's language impairment. Indeed, LEW has implicit access to the relevant information to make explicit categorizations, but, without language, LEW has only explicit recourse to similarity judgements that are insufficient to determine category membership.

At this point, we can suggest that: (1) the identification (explicit categorization) and discrimination tasks (implicit use of categorical boundaries knowledge) classically described in common CP paradigms are mediated by distinct neural systems; and (2) these different processing systems can independently be altered in brain-damaged patients. However, such firm statements should be made cautiously as "double dissociations" (a patient with intact explicit and altered implicit categorization abilities) are still needed. Moreover, Roberson et al. (1999) suggest that LEW's inability to use his implicit knowledge about categories is due to his language impairment. However, as outlined by the authors themselves, we can doubt the explanation based on naming because of some observations on patients AV, who showed perfect naming of prototypical colors but disastrous freesorting (Luzzati & Davidoff, 1994). In other words, the mechanisms that underlie implicit, rather than explicit, facial expressions categories presumably must be derived from perception (Roberson et al., 1999), but were still matter of debate.

Neurophysiological Data

With the growing area of cognitive neurosciences, the use of functional brain imagery techniques can help to solve many debates in the area of cognitive psychology.

The above review shows behavioral evidence for a better discriminability for two morphed faces showing two different expressions than for two morphed faces showing the same one (even if the physical distance inside each pair is identical). Moreover, it shows that this CP effect could be intact in brain-damaged patients while explicit categorization of facial expressions is altered. Due to its better temporal resolution (as compared to PET or fMRI), we used two separate ERPs experiments to assess where and mainly *when* does the categorical perception of facial emotional expressions occur (Campanella, Gaspard, Debatisse, Bruyer, Crommelinck & Guérit, 2002a; Campanella, Quinet, Bruyer, Crommelinck, & Guérit, 2002b).

ERPs allow us to investigate the temporal course and the various stages of cognitive processing (with a temporal resolution of 1ms). Most event-related brain potential (ERP) studies have used an " oddball paradigm ", in which subjects have to detect, amongst a series of standard stimuli, an infrequent deviant one (Garcia-Larrea et al., 1992). The detection of stimulus change may play a role in turning attention to events of biological importance (Halgren & Marinkovic, 1995). When subjects are placed in attentive conditions, deviant stimuli evoke a series of field potentials, the *N2/P3a*, called by Halgren & Marinkovic (1995) the *orienting complex*, because it subserves attention. Indeed, the orienting complex is defined as the mobilization of cerebral and somatic resources in order to effectively cope with a biologically important event. A *P3b* component, recorded maximally at parietal sites and functionally related to the conscious detection of change leading subjects to respond to deviant stimuli, has also been recorded (e.g., Campanella et al., 2000). In other words, the N2/P3a is a neurophysiological component functionally related to attention whereas the P3b component reflects decisional process. ERPs were recorded during repetitive stimuli representing a particular facial expression (e.g., sadness) and two different deviant rare stimuli, one showing the same emotion than the frequent stimulus, while the other one showed another facial expression (e.g., fear). Indeed, by using a morphing procedure, we generated triads of morphed stimuli, one used as frequent stimulus and two as deviants (one perceived as sharing the same emotion than the frequent stimulus, rare WITHIN; and the other sharing a different emotion, rare BETWEEN). Note that the physical distance separating the two rare stimuli from the frequent stimulus is always identical (30%). At a behavioral level, we found that subjects discriminated more easily (better performance and faster correct response latencies) deviant stimuli when they express a different emotion as compared with the frequent stimulus (rare BETWEEN), than when they express an identical one (rare WITHIN). These results are compatible with a CP effect of facial expressions (Campanella et al., 2002a). At a neurophysiological level, deviant stimuli evoked a N2/P3a complex that was delayed for deviant stimuli showing an identical emotion than the frequent stimulus, as compared with deviant stimuli showing a different emotion than frequent ones. The N2/P3a was thus implicated in the detection of physical facial changes, with a higher sensitivity to changes related to a new different emotional content, in order to lead to faster adapted reactions.

This study gives a first neurophysiological account for the CP effect described on facial expressions (higher correct response latencies for WITHIN differences as compared to BETWEEN ones). Indeed, categorical perception of facial expressions have received strong empirical support at a behavioral level (e.g., Etcoff & Magee, 1992; Calder et al., 1996; Young et al., 1997), suggesting that the discrimination performance is affected by category membership rather than by objective physical distance. In the present study, we showed that : (1) this latency effect was not specifically related to a decisional-motor response effect (which would have been indexed by a unique delayed P3b component); (2) it began at an earlier stage (around 270ms), as marked by the delayed N2 component; (3) it found its origin on supplementary visual areas (the latency effect being present over all posterior electrodes); and (4) it was correlated to the behavioral delay in response latencies, indexed by a delayed P3b component.

However, when reviewing the psychological and electrophysiological literature on emotions, a discrepancy emerges. In fact, if behavioral studies have demonstrated that emotions are extracted pre-attentively and influence subsequent perception (Kunst-Wilson & Zajonc, 1980; Murphy & Zajonc, 1993), only one study (Pizzagalli, Regard & Lehmann, 1999) has found neurophysiological correlates for these processes. Pizzagalli et al. (1999) showed that personal affective judgments of face images significantly modulated ERP responses at early stages, 80-116ms after right hemisphere stimulation and 104-160ms after left stimulation. Typical prior studies found emotion-modulated ERP components considerably later, typically between 250 and 600ms (Münte, Brack, Grootheer, Wieringa, Matzke & Johannes, 1998). Subjects of Potter & Parker (1989) had to decide whether the second face of a pair matched the first one in terms of expression. The ERPs showed a later difference in the 490-540ms time range, only for a right parietal site. Accordingly, Hautecoeur, Debruyne, Forzy, Gallois, Hache & Dereux (1993) showed a modulation of a parietal P400 when subjects were asked to look for emotional expression of the face (smiling or non-smiling) in comparison with a recognition task (known or unknown). Several studies, as ours (Campanella et al., 2002a) limited *a priori* their analyses around the P300 component by investigating emotional processing using oddball paradigms (e.g., Oroczo & Ehlers, 1998). Finally, by using intracranial recordings, Halgren & Marinkovic (1995) showed that significant differentiation among waveforms evoked by different facial emotions appears frontocentrally in the 400-600ms latency range. With this in mind, we wonder whether earlier modulations due to emotional categories could be found by using ERPs. This would suggest that our brain was able at early perceptual stage to discriminate between different facial expressions.

In a second separate ERP study (Campanella et al., 2002b), we created continua of morphed faces moving from one expression to the other (e.g., identity A " happy " to identity " A " fearful). Subjects were then confronted with three kinds of pairs of morphed faces: the BETWEEN pairs (a face perceived as happy and the other one as fearful); the WITHIN pairs (two morphed faces perceived as happy or as fearful); and the SAME pairs (two identical faces). Faces of WITHIN and BETWEEN pairs are always separated by a physical distance of 30%. The participants had to decide as quickly and as accurately as possible whether the second face of the pair was exactly the same as the first one (delayed same-different matching task). The results of this study showed that the perceptual categorization of happiness and fear facial expressions takes place early in the perceptual face processing system, at around 170ms following stimulus onset, in the bilateral occipito-temporal regions.

Indeed, several ERP visual studies have evidenced a negative occipito-temporal component, the N170 (e.g., Bentin, Allison, Puce, Perez, & McCarthy, 1996), recorded around 170 ms after stimulus onset. The N170 responds preferentially (and maximally at the right hemisphere) to faces as compared to objects and was functionally referred to the structural encoding stage of the Bruce and Young's model (1986). This stage was usually considered as allowing subjects to generate a configurational representation of the observed face. In their study, Campanella et al. (2002b) showed that following the second face onset in the pair, the amplitude of the bilateral occipito-temporal negativities (N170) was reduced for WITHIN and SAME pairs relative to BETWEEN pairs.

The higher amplitude of the N170 for the second face of BETWEEN pairs as compared to WITHIN and SAME pairs can be understood by the fact that subjects are confronted with two faces (in BETWEEN pairs) perceived as different expressions (happiness and fear) by the perceptual system. Two different configurational facial analyses have thus to be performed successively in the BETWEEN condition, whereas in the WITHIN and SAME conditions, the second facial expression belongs to the same expression as the first one. Several ERP studies have shown that successive repetitions of words, objects and faces lead to a reduction in ERPs amplitudes (Schweinberger, 1996; Paller & Gross, 1998). Concerning face processing in particular, repetition-priming effects on ERPs, indexed by a lower amplitude to the second face presentation, have already been observed (Begleiter, Porjesz & Wang, 1995; Ji, Porjesz & Begleiter, 1998; Henson, Shallice & Dolan, 2000).

Considering these evidences, we proposed that the striking reduction in the N170 amplitude to the second face of the SAME and WITHIN pairs reflects a *repetition priming effect*. In fact, BETWEEN pairs are constituted by two faces showing two different emotional expressions, while SAME and WITHIN pairs refer to the same one. These results indicate that the CP of human facial emotional expressions has a perceptual origin in the bilateral occipito-temporal regions, while typical prior studies found emotion-modulated ERP components considerably later.

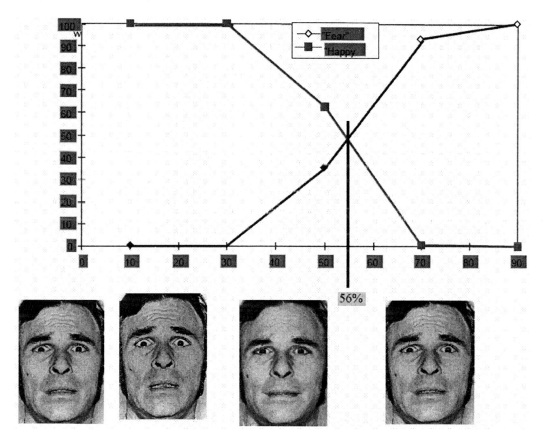

Figure 2. On the basis of the identification task, a categorical boundary can be computed for each single continuum. Then, pairs of morphed faces crossing (between) or not (within) this boundary are submitted to subjects in a discrimination task. Even if these pairs of faces are separated by an identical amount of physical distance, subjects discriminated more easily between-differences than within-ones.

Overview

The empirical data presented up to now show that subjects hardly discriminated two different morphed faces representing a same emotional expression as compared with two different faces representing two different facial expressions (the physical distance inside each pair being kept constant). This CP effect was both present for infants and adults, but can also be disrupted in some psychiatric disease such as autism. Moreover, a particular dissociation has been demonstrated in a neuropsychological study. Indeed, patient LEW shows intact CP effect for emotional expressions but is deficient when he has to explicitly categorize emotions. ERP studies were then performed in order to put light on the different mechanisms used in implicit (CP) and explicit emotion categorization.

In a first study, Campanella et al. (2002a) showed that CP of facial expressions - characterized by a latency delay in the discrimination of within-differences- does not only affect the P3b component, a neurophysiological component functionally related to a decisional-motor stage of subjects' response, but also an earlier component (around 270ms), the N2/P3a, which is more related to an attentional orienting complex (Halgren & Marinkovic, 1995). At this point, a question arises: could CP of emotional expressions affect early perceptive stages of face processing? In a second ERP experiment, Campanella et al. (2002b) showed that the temporal course of the perceptual categorization of happiness and fear facial expressions takes place early in the perceptual face processing system, at around 170ms following stimulus onset, in the bilateral occipito-temporal regions. However, whether the results so far suggest that face expression affects structural encoding if the task requires face emotional matching, we have to note that some ERP studies showed no perceptual priming effects, regardless of whether the task was a simple oddball or a speeded face recognition (Bentin & Deouell, 2000). In other words, tasks requiring explicit emotion identification involved later ERP components modulations. Then, we put forward the hypothesis that, unlike explicit identification, (implicit) emotional face matching is a shallow perceptual task that is probably based on shallow (structural encoding) processes.

If the first section of this review has been focused on emotional facial expressions, other facial dimensions have been concerned with CP studies. In the next section, we will consider what have been found about CP and face identity.

CP OF FACIAL IDENTITY

Behavioral Data

As with color categories, the perception of facial expressions appears to be universal. Facial expressions show consistency of labeling in cross-cultural studies (e.g., Ekman & Friesen, 1971; Ekman, 1994), very young infants show a sensitivity to facial expressions (e.g., Ainsworth, 1973), and, as reviewed above, higher level categories such as facial expressions can elicit CP effects (Stevenage, 1998). However, when considering CP effect of facial expressions, we can agree with Stevenage (1998) when she suggests that we are born knowing how to categorize such biologically prepared stimuli such as colors, phonemes and facial expressions. In this case, we can talk about "innate categorical perception". A question then arises: would CP effects be elicited with stimuli whose categories have to be learned and whose categories are not natural? This is of particular interest, because even though the ability to recognize specific individuals must be learned and the continua between individual faces are not naturally occurring, there might be general constraints on category formation that also apply to individual face recognition.

Beale & Keil address this question in 1995. By using a morphing technique, they created continua of morphed faces that moved linearly from one identity (e.g., Kennedy) to another one (e.g., Clinton). These authors used a two-step procedure. First, Beale and Keil (1995) confronted subjects with an *ABX discrimination task*, in which two morphed faces (A, B) were successively presented, followed by a third one (X=A or X=B). They had to match the X face to either A or B. Within-categorical (WITHIN) and between-categorical (BETWEEN) pairs were designed in such a way that two morphed faces attracted by the same prototype representation (the same representation, stored in long-term memory, of a known face) composed the WITHIN pairs and two morphed faces attracted by two different ones composed the BETWEEN pairs. Although the physical distance between the stimuli of each pair was constant (20%), subjects better discriminated BETWEEN pairs than WITHIN pairs. In other words, subjects discriminated more easily two morphed faces belonging to two different identities than two morphed faces belonging to the same one.

Second, subjects were confronted with an *identification task*, during which they had to categorize all the randomly presented morphed faces either as Kennedy or as Clinton. Although the identity information contained in the morphed faces was linearly manipulated, there were sharp boundaries in the subjects' responses. Indeed, the results show that the morphed faces situated close to the mid-point of the continua (50%) defined *the categorical boundary*, that is the point where 50% of the subjects answered "Clinton" while the other half answered "Kennedy". Moreover, morphed faces situated close to the endpoints of the continua were attracted by their respective prototype representations, stored in long-term memory. It was thus observed that the subject's responses do not follow the linear transformations of the facial morphed identities.

Thus, CP effects were found for both *innate* categorization of facial expressions and *induced* categorization of facial identity (Stevenage, 1998).

Many studies show that prior experience with stimuli can modulate how people will categorize and discriminate them. Indeed, for instance, Goldstone (1994), Livingston, Andrews, & Harnad (1998), and Goldstone, Lippa and Shiffrin (2001) showed that the discriminability of stimulus properties is altered by pre-exposure to different categorization tasks, whereas Schyns (1998) showed that different categorization tasks would lead subjects to use different relevant (diagnostic) information. All these works were then particularly relevant to the general question of how experience (learning) can influence categorization and discrimination. After the successful demonstration of CP for innately acquired facial expressions (e.g., Etcoff & Magee, 1992) and for overlearned familiar identities (Beale & Keil, 1995), Stevenage (1998) wanted to extend the Goldstone's works with natural stimuli, rather than artificial ones (such as squares of different size and brightness), by using faces. To do so, she used photographs of twin faces (Rosie and Elizabeth). Subjects had to rate the similarity of pairs of photographs (same: Rosie-Rosie; Elizabeth-Elizabeth; or different: Rosie-Elizabeth) before and after a category learning session. Stevenage found evidence for (1) a "compression effect", i.e., subjects judged the same-twin pairs as more similar after than before learning and for (2) an "expansion or separation effect", i.e., subjects judged the different-twin pairs as more different after than before the learning phase. These results clearly show that a CP effect does emerge for the perception of twin faces, with the same-twin pairs looking more similar and the different-twin pairs looking more different after category learning than before. The fact that CP can be demonstrated for previously unfamiliar categories of stimuli implies that the process of learning to categorize stimuli create a warping of their perception so that CP can emerge (Stevenage, 1998). This was congruent with Schyns's findings, suggesting that the way we categorize the world affect the way we perceive it (Schyns, 1998). Moreover, a recent study of Levin & Beale (2000), using unfamiliar facial identities, gave evidence for a CP effect. In their procedure, participants have some opportunities to learn the faces before the experiment. For instance, they viewed an instruction screen containing the two endpoints faces of each continua, each associated with an arbitrarily chosen name. Then, these data allow us to talk about categorical perception *of newly learned faces*. In other words, empirical data presented up to now, and concerning CP of facial identities, gave evidence for (1) a CP effect for overlearned familiar facial identities (Beale & Keil, 1995); and (2) an ability of CP effect to emerge through learning (Stevenage, 1998), even with a very rapid procedure (Levin & Beale, 2000).

With this in mind, it is important to outline that a common assumption underlies the works of Beale & Keil (1995), Stevenage (1998) and Levin & Beale (2000). Indeed, an important result of the Beale and Keil's study showed that the CP effect was correlated with face familiarity: a strong CP effect emerged for pairs of faces rated as highly familiar (for instance, Kennedy/Clinton), while this effect disappeared for pairs of faces rated as less familiar (Burns/Harris). According to Tanaka, Giles, Kremen, & Simon (1998), the morphed faces of between-categorical pairs are "attracted" by two different stored representations, while for the within-categorical pairs, the two faces are "attracted" by a single representation. Within-categorical pairs are thus more difficult to discriminate because the two different morphed faces activated a same stored facial representation. Considering this, the authors conclude that no categorical perception effect should be obtained by using unfamiliar faces, since, by definition, unfamiliar faces are not represented in memory. Identically, Stevenage (1998, p.46), presenting her data as providing a significant demonstration of induced categorical perception with natural stimuli, outlined that"...*it is unlikely that a categorical perception effect will emerge for participants who show no learning*...".

In a recent study, we suggest that the question of whether a categorical perception of totally unfamiliar identities exists or not remains unanswered and needs further empirical evidence (Campanella, Hanoteau, Seron, Joassin, & Bruyer, 2003). This question is of the greatest relevance because the discrimination of unfamiliar people plays a fundamental role in everyday life (Newell, Chiroro, & Valentine, 1999). Moreover, it could be argued that, even if unfamiliar faces have no stored representations in long-term memory, unfamiliar faces can still generate in short-term memory separate structural identities that might play a role in simple matching and discrimination tasks. The principal interest of that study is the CP effect found for unfamiliar facial identities by using a classical same-different matching task (e.g., Young et al., 1997). Two different groups of subjects were confronted with the same set of faces: one group is familiarized with these stimuli, the other not. Classical CP effect (found, for instance, for familiar faces) are evidenced by a better performance to discriminate between-differences as compared with within-ones, the correct between-responses being indexed by faster latencies. Here, we found that (1) if the general performance of familiarized subjects was better than the one of unfamiliarized subjects, both of them show a better discrimination for between-differences as compared with within-ones; and (2) if the familiarized group show faster correct response latencies for between-differences, no such a difference emerged in the unfamiliarized group. However, as a statistical difference (in %) emerged in the unfamiliarized group, so that unfamiliarized subjects - as familiarized ones - discriminated more accurately morphed faces belonging to two different categories than morphs belonging to the same one, we suggest that a CP effect (in performance but not in latencies) could be shown for totally unfamiliar faces (Campanella et al., 2003). As unfamiliar facial identities have no stored representations in long-term memory, we are aware that these results are particularly counterintuitive. Indeed, and contrary to familiarized subjects, how can these unfamiliarized subjects better discriminate two faces stemming from two different categories if these "identity" categories do not exist for these subjects? We propose that this specific CP effect for unfamiliar facial identities could be a consequence of the morphing procedure, which *reduced distinctiveness (or enhanced typicality) around the center of the continuum* (Busey, 1998; Levin & Beale, 2000; Campanella et al., 2003). As a consequence, when subjects have to discriminate two unknown faces, which are not represented in long-term memory, they would rely on other available cues such as (more importantly) *typicality and density*. CP of unfamiliar identities seems to arise from the fact that the morphed faces of between-pairs are more typical and lies in a denser region than the faces used in within-pairs. If these results could be interpreted as a consequence (an artifact) of the morphing procedure (see also Busey, 1998), it also demonstrates how the encoding of unfamiliar faces in memory would constrain our further discrimination performance. Indeed, faces are multidimensional stimuli, and subjects will use information that reveal to be the most relevant to perform the task (see for instance Schyns, 1998).

Overall, starting from the question "Do the rules implied in the generation of colors, phonemes and facial expressions categories also apply to categories which have to be learned and are not natural such as facial identities?", several behavioral studies showed that (1) a CP for overlearned familiar faces exists; (2) a CP for unfamiliar faces can emerge through a rapid or a deep categorization learning procedure; and (3) a CP effect with totally unfamiliar faces can be shown, suggesting that when people can't rely on stored facial representations (i.e., on the identity dimension), they will pick up other relevant facial cues, such as in this case typicality and density, to discriminate pairs of faces.

Brain Imaging Data

The question to know how the human brain is able to discriminate between familiar and unfamiliar faces was one of the most investigated question in face processing "neuroimaging" literature. However, despite a large amount of studies using cellular recordings in non human primates (e.g., Rolls, 1992), ERP recordings in humans (e.g., Bentin, Allison, Puce, Perez, & McCarthy, 1996), PET or fMRI (e.g., Sergent, Otha, & McDonald, 1992; Kanwisher, McDermott, & Chun, 1997; Gauthier, Tarr, Anderson, Skudlarski, & Gore, 1999 for PET; Katanoda, Yoshikawa, & Sugishita, 2000 for fMRI), the questions of where, when and how the brain operates to perform this discrimination remains largely unanswered (Haxby, Hoffman, & Gobbini, 2000).

For our purpose, one remaining question can be pulled out of functional models of face processing. A face is recognized as familiar if the perceptual representation matches a face representation stored in long-term memory (see the "face recognition unit" (FRU); Bruce & Young, 1986). In such a view, a face can be recognized as familiar if (1) an input beared sufficient resemblance to the stored unit: this will index an "all-or-none" process (Hay & Young, 1982); or even if (2) the unit will fire proportionally to the resemblance between the input and the stored representation, the familiarity decision being taken by a general cognitive system outside the face system per se (Bruce & Young, 1986). Then, the question to know whether the activation of the FRUs is an "all-or-none" (categorical) or a proportional (continuous) process was still matter of debate.

In order to solve this debate, Rossion, Schiltz, Robaye, Pirenne, & Crommelinck (2001) used the paradigm of CP in a PET study. Indeed, these authors familiarized 8 subjects with a set of 30 faces. Then, these 30 familiarized faces were morphed with other unfamiliar faces. First, in a pilot study, subjects were confronted with continua of "familiar to unfamiliar faces": as expected, a CP effect was found for face familiarity, i.e. a sharp boundary of familiarity decisions being present between the 40% and 60% morphed faces. Second, during the PET scanning, subjects were confronted with 6 conditions: 0% faces (totally novel faces), 20%, 40%, 60%, 80%, and 100% faces (totally familiar faces). The main result suggests that changes in brain activity were not linearly related to the physical information available in the continua, but rather to the CP shown by subjects. Indeed, when comparing the brain activity generated by 0% images and 40% images (both perceived as unfamiliar), no difference of brain activation emerged; however, if 40% images (perceived as unfamiliar) and 60% images (perceived as familiar) were compared, significant increases of activation were found in right occipito-temporal regions, even if the physical distance between 40% and 60% images is smaller than the one between 0% and 40% images.

At this point, we have to talk about a study of ours (Campanella, Hanoteau, Depy, Rossion, Bruyer, & Guérit, 2000) investigating ERP correlates of CP for familiar faces. We used the same method than the one described above with facial expressions (but by manipulating facial identity) (Campanella et al., 2002b): three kinds of pairs were presented in a matching task: (1) two different morphed faces representing the same identity (WITHIN), (2) two other ones representing two different identities (BETWEEN), and (3) two identical morphed faces (SAME). Following the second face onset in the pair, the amplitude of the right occipito-temporal negativity (N170) was reduced for WITHIN and SAME pairs as compared to BETWEEN pairs. We propose that the striking reduction in the N170 amplitude to the second face of the SAME and WITHIN pairs reflects an identity priming effect. Indeed, BETWEEN pairs are constituted by two faces belonging to two different identities, while SAME and WITHIN pairs refer to two same identities. According to this suggestion, the priming effect indicates that the perceptual system considered the two physical different faces of the WITHIN pairs as belonging to an identical facial identity. In other words, faces judged to be identical produce identity priming whereas faces not judged to be identical produce no (or less) priming. These results indicate that CP of familiar identities has a perceptual origin in the right occipito-temporal hemisphere, implying early (extrastriate) visual mechanisms.

Taken together, these data show that (1) right occipito-temporal regions rapidly (around 170 ms) and abruptly modify their level of activations when a perceptual boundary of identity (familiarity) is crossed; and (2) contrary to Bruce & Young's proposal, FRU activation is made in an all-or-none fashion (Rossion et al., 2001).

Overview

Empirical evidence has been presented as concerns the phenomenon of CP of facial identity. At a behavioral level, it has been shown that subjects discriminated more easily two morphed faces representing two different identities than two morphed faces representing the same person, even if the physical distance inside the pairs is fixed. Further evidence has also demonstrated that a CP effect can emerge through a learning procedure, this learning phase being deep or rapid. In other words, once a facial representation of identity has been created in long-term memory, the activation of two different representations lead subjects to be more efficient in discrimination than when an unique representation is activated.

Moreover, brain imaging studies show that (1) this activation of a "familiarity" feeling was an all-or-none process, *neuroanatomically* indexed by an increased activation of the right occipito-temporal regions; and (2) *neurophysiologically* indexed by a discrimination between two different identities beginning as early as about 170ms in these same occipito-temporal regions.

These data lead us to two main considerations. First, the exact mechanisms that allow these rapid and abrupt changes in occipito-temporal regions giving rise to the phenomenon of CP (i.e., the fact that a physical difference was taken into account when it occurs at the boundary between two categories, but not within a same category) are still unknown. In other words, further empirical evidence is needed to define which are the mechanisms underlying the "compression" and "separation" effects (e.g., Stevenage, 1998; Livingston et al., 1998) leading to the phenomenon of CP. Second, these data suggest that the phenomenon of CP seems to be an emergent property of any sufficiently powerful general learning system (Damper & Harnad, 2000). This explains why CP is shown for both innate (colors, phonemes, facial expressions) and induced (identity, familiarity) categories.

Finally, we have to note that a CP effect has been evidenced even for unfamiliar faces (significant better performance for between-differences as compared with within-ones, even if the general performance was worse than the one of subjects confronted with familiar faces; but no differences in correct latencies). Considering that unfamiliar faces do not have by definition any stored facial representation, we suggest that this counterintuitive result gives support to the claiming of Schyns (1998), showing that subjects will use the most relevant information to perform a definite task. In this case, faces are multidimensional stimuli, but gender, age, facial expressions and identity are non pertinent to perform the discrimination task. Subjects have then to rely on other pertinent facial cues, such as (in that case) typicality, because, as a result (artifact) of the morphing procedure, these parameters were different in between- and within-pairs (see Campanella et al., 2003, for discussion).

CP OF OTHER FACIAL DIMENSIONS

In face processing literature, a great deal of researches tended to show that independent processes mediated perception of facial identity and facial emotion. Due to developments of computer graphics, the investigation of CP effects for facial expressions and identities has been possible as shown by the pioneering works of Etcoff & Magee (1992) and Beale & Keil (1995). The major part of the works investigating CP effects with faces were focused on these two dimensions. Similarities and differences between these CP effects will be discussed in the Discussion section. However, last years have seen a growing interest for CP effects of other facial dimensions. In this section, we will then successively present behavioral evidence concerning CP effects for face-species, face-actions, gender and race.

First, humans are extremely good at identifying human faces, but they can also recognize individual monkey faces (Wright & Roberts, 1996). This begs the question to know what are the mechanisms underlying the human ability to recognize individual faces across species boundaries. On the one hand, it could be that face templates are species-specific. In other words, separate categories exist for different species' faces, as suggested by neuropsychological reports showing that brain lesions can selectively disrupt recognition for human and for animal faces in patients such as livestock farmers (Bornstein, Sroka, & Munitz, 1969; Bruyer, Laterre, Seron, Feyercisen, Strypstein, Pierrard, & Rectem (1983); Macneil & Warrington, 1993). On the other hand, it could be that a single template serves face perception across different species, by using the general architecture and properties of the upright face (Johnson & Morton, 1991). By using a CP paradigm, Campbell, Pascalis, Coleman, Wallace, & Benson (1997) tested these predictions. Indeed, if different prototypes exist for different species, then the discrimination of intermediate morphed images between faces of each species should be categorical. However, if a single prototype was used, there should be no systematic sharpening between species' faces. Several continua of morphed images were created between monkey-cow, cow-human and human-monkey faces. Subjects were confronted to the classical ABX discrimination and identification tasks. Results suggest that even if the identification task suggests sharply bounded categories for face images of each species, the distinction between primate faces and cow faces, and between cow faces and human faces, are categorically perceived, but not for human-monkey faces. This suggests that (1) correct identification is necessary, but not sufficient for CP; (2) most human viewers judged monkey faces by a human face criteria; and (3) as predicted by neuropsychological data, distinct cortical systems (and thus, different categorical representations) mediate the recognition of human (including primates) faces than those of other beasts. A CP effect for human-monkey faces versus other species' faces was then evidenced.

Second, as suggested in the introduction section, Liberman et al. (1957) were the first to investigate CP: they showed that the perception of acoustic tokens was categorical with respect to systematic changes in the physical dimensions of the sound stimulus. If CP of language has a long history, we presented here some relatively new data assessing CP effects even for faces. Hence, in British Sign Language (BSL), as in many sign languages of the deaf, the face is an important channel carrying information at all levels of language structure. For instance, Woll (1983) states that in BSL, for "yes-no" question " .. the eyebrows are raised, and chin, head, and shoulders are brought forward.." (p.149). By morphing the best exemplars of such relevant face actions, Campbell, Woll, Benson, & Wallace (1999) investigated whether these face actions, carrying significance within language, are perceived categorically by native sign-users. Indeed, it is well established that sign languages of the deaf are syntactically constrained, as are spoken languages. If native sign-users would perceived these relevant distinctions categorically, it could be proposed that CP is a necessary condition for language (Campbell et al., 1999). By using classical an ABX discrimination and an identification tasks, these authors showed that a categorical processing of face displays can be demonstrated for sign. The authors proposed that, as the classification of facial displays must be fast, efficient and predictive in oral conversation or/and in non verbal interactions, and many of the abstract representations for faces and their meaning may be structured in an image-based multidimensional feature space (O'Toole, Deffenbacher, Valentin, & Abdi, 1994), these images need to be caught "on the fly": this could be achieved by CP for face actions, as it may for speech.

Third, a further dimension of faces is gender. Contrary to the case with facial expressions (which can be accounted for by a number of 6 emotional categories, see Ekman, 1994) or facial identities (which are potentially defined by an infinite number), the categories implied in the gender discrimination process are limited to two. This could lead us to think that the perception of facial gender in necessarily categorical. However, we can imagine that, from a sexual reproduction viewpoint, the categories "attractive/unattractive" might be better psychological constructs than "male/female". With this in mind, it could be that the male/female distinction could as easily be continuous rather than categorical. Accordingly, different authors wonder whether subjects confronted with facial gender information that varies linearly will perceive it categorically or not. Bulthoff & Newell (2000) did not find any CP effect for face gender. However, because we were not convinced of their results (due to methodological purpose, such as for instance the small physical distance separating the presented faces (10%)), Campanella, Chrysochoos, & Bruyer (2001) generated continua of facial stimuli in which gender information was varied linearly across unfamiliar faces. By using a classical identification and "same-different" matching tasks, the results support the idea that there is categorical perception of gender information for unfamiliar faces. This meant that two unknown faces belonging to different gender are easier to discriminate than two unknown faces belonging to the same one (better performance and faster correct response latencies). This could be interpreted by the fact that, as it was the case for familiar identities and facial expressions, we dispose in long-term memory of different prototypes (or exemplars) of males and females, and that contrary to within-pairs, between-pairs activated these two different representations, facilitating our discrimination performance. However, we have also to outline, that, as it was the case for the above mentioned CP effect found for unfamiliar facial identities, the results of the present study also suggested interactions between the information demands of specific categorization tasks and the perceptual information available from the input stimulus. Indeed, moving from one gender to the other one necessarily implies the passage through one (here, unfamiliar) identity to another one. Then, we argued that, as unfamiliar faces have not available stored representations in memory, subjects rely on *diagnostic* cues (Schyns, 1998), i.e. the gender cues, to operate the discrimination task (Campanella et al., 2001).

Fourth, race is easily and quickly perceived (Levin, 1996), and the features specifying it are reasonably well understood by subjects (Sheperd & Deregowski, 1981). Levin & Angelone (2002) tested directly for CP of race (see also Levin & Beale, 2000) by comparing CP effects that do (white-black faces) and do not (white-white, black-black faces) cross race boundaries. By using classical ABX discrimination and identification tasks, these authors showed that continua running from a black to a white face do show stronger CP effects than continua between two black faces or two white faces. This suggests that (1) CP is also sensible to "social" categories, enhancing our perception of out-group members; and (2) the CP phenomenon can be extended to categories more like the "generic knowledge categories" discussed by Medin & Barsalou (1987). Faces represented a case where CP can be driven by a set of categories with varying levels of generality. A given face can serve as endpoint on different categorically perceived continua, so that it can be defined as transient and with no individual identity. For instance, sad and happy faces constitute categories that include a set of individual faces. However, in the case of race categories, both the category and the identity of the face refer to permanent features, thus allowing functions of generic knowledge such as induction over time (Gutheil & Rosengren, 1996).

GENERAL DISCUSSION

The first aim of the present chapter was to present the empirical data, collected up to now, for the phenomenon of CP of faces. Since the first investigations on CP were focused on unidimensional stimuli, such as phonemes and hues, the recent development of computer image-manipulations had made the investigations of multi-dimensional stimuli, such as the human faces, possible. Then, we concentrate the present review on the phenomenon of CP of faces. The classical method used to evidence such CP effects relies on (1) the generation, by means of a morphing technique, of continua of morphed faces, the intermediate morphed faces varying on one facial dimension (for instance, identity) between two endpoints faces; (2) the use of an identification task, showing sharp boundaries even if the physical changes between intermediate morphed faces are linearly manipulated; and (3) the use of a discrimination task, showing that two (physically) different morphed faces identified as representing a same category (for instance, the same identity) are harder to discriminate than two morphed faces representing two different categories, even if the physical distance inside the pairs is identical.

With this in mind, three kinds of studies were reported in the present manuscript. First, at a behavioral level, CP effects on faces were found for emotional expressions (e.g., Etcoff & Magee, 1992), overlearned familiar identities (e.g., Beale & Keil, 1995), unfamiliar identities through rapid or extensive learning (e.g., Levin & Beale, 2000; Stevenage, 1998), unfamiliar identities presenting changes in typicality or gender (e.g., Campanella et al., in press; Campanella et al., 2001), face-species (Campbell et al., 1997), face-actions (Campbell et al., 1999) and race (Levin & Angelone, 2002). Second, at a neuropsychological level, it has been shown that a dissociation between explicit identification and implicit CP effect can be observed (Roberson et al., 1999), suggesting that explicit recognition and similarity decision are mediated by different brain structures. Third, by using brain imaging studies (ERPs and PET), it has been shown that the phenomenon of CP of faces is indexed by abrupt changes in the activation of occipito-temporal neural structures, and that these regions were active as early as about 170 ms since faces' onset (Rossion et al., 2001; Campanella et al., 2000).

All these data lead us to the second aim of the present review: indeed, we can wonder, at the present state of knowledge, what are the mechanisms involved in this phenomenon of CP of faces. Broadly, we can consider that, in order to simplify the complexity of our environment, the principle scope of CP is to de-emphasize some physical variation while some other is enhanced. In other words, CP reflects a psychological remapping of physical variation into psychological categories (Levin & Angelone, 2002). These categories can be innate (phonemes, hues, and, for our purpose, emotional expressions), or induced through experience (i.e., after a learning phase, such as for familiar identities) or through social knowledge (such as for race). As a result, CP cannot only occur with biologically prepared stimuli that we are born knowing how to categorize. Several authors have then tried to propose different mechanisms accounting for effects of learning on CP (see Goldstone, 1998 for review). A first way to conceptualize how learning could lead to CP effects is the way of *differentiation*. Learning produced within-category compression effects (i.e., similarity inside a category increases) and between-category expansion effects (i.e., physical difference between categories is emphasized) (see, for instance, Livingston et al., 1998; Stevenage, 1998). These mechanisms seem to be implied in the CP effects found for familiar (learned) facial identities. Indeed, as suggested by Tanaka et al. (1998), we can consider that we dispose in long-term memory of different representations of all the different people we know, and that some minor physical variations can be accepted around these representations. This will allow us, for instance, to recognize someone 20 years after we had seen him for the last time, or that an intermediate morphed face (e.g., a morph 80%/20%) will be attracted by its endpoint face. Then, the learning of familiarity of faces can be considered as leading to accept some physical changes (with a specified threshold) around a particular facial representation (so that within-identity changes are neglected), whereas between-representations changes are emphasized. An alternative way to consider learning effect on CP is based on *selective attention*. CP effects are acquired by selectively attending to the relevant dimension along which the categories differ (Nosofsky, 1984) or to certain features by which they differ (Livingston & Andrews, 1995). This seems to be the case for CP effects found for unfamiliar faces (the identity dimension being irrelevant) presenting relevant changes in typicality or gender. What is then important to outline is that our perception of reality is mediated by categories, these categories being innately predefined or induced through learning. It is also important to note that categories seem to be flexible tools, the influence of learning extending from artificial rules (such as for identities) to more generic complex ones (such as social rules, see CP of race). This strengthens the idea that perception of reality and categorization processes are tightly anchored to subjects' environment. However, the exact nature of these mechanisms remains unanswered. Indeed, which are the mechanisms allowing us to enhance (or to reduce) physical variations through learning? How do we become able (through learning) to attend to a pertinent varying dimension of a stimulus? These questions need further empirical evidence in order to better delineate the grounding processes of induced CP effects. Nevertheless, if some questions remain, the present findings, coming from different areas of research (neuropsychology, experimental psychology, brain imagery), help us to draw two others principal considerations on the CP phenomenon for faces.

First, the identification of a known face can occur through a feature-based mechanism, i.e. the recognition occurs through information from local regions of the face (nose shape, eye color, ...), through a configuration-based mechanism, i.e. relying on the information integrated over all the face region, or both (Tanaka & Farah, 1993). Evidence have been gathered not only in favor of the superiority of the configural processing, but also in favor of a particular normative global structure (Valentine, 1991), corresponding to an upright face. Indeed, when faces are inverted, detrimental effects on performance are observed with both memory and perceptual tasks (e.g., Yin, 1969). Inversion has frequently been used in research on face perception as a control for the role of nonface-specific properties of the material (Campanella et al., 2001), because it is supposed to alter the perception of the configural information conveyed by faces (Valentine, 1991). Then, for our purpose, if inversion "disturbs" the CP effect evidenced with upright faces, the information relevant to induce this effect on upright faces should be carried by configural information and does not represent the result of, for instance, an artifact of the morphing technique. However, if the same categorical results are obtained in the UPRIGHT and INVERTED conditions, it would mean that the categorical perception effect is unrelated to configural cues and may rather be due to other local facial cues or to technical artifacts related to the use of the morphing procedure. At first sight, contradictory results were obtained about this topic: de Gelder et al. (1997), Campanella et al. (2001), and Campanella et al. (2003) showed no CP effect for inverted faces, contrary to Levin & Beale (2000). However, the relation between inversion, configural processing and CP has recently received a strong empirical support by McKone, Martini and Nakayama (2001). They showed that subjects familiar with endpoints faces could perceptually distort a continuum between these faces to form a categorical perception of identity, but only when the faces were presented upright. When the same faces were inverted or a single isolated feature was shown, no categorical perception effect was found, even with very large amounts of practice spread over several months. This was interpreted by the authors by a failure to learn configural processing for inverted faces, as we know that humans are experts in the recognition of upright faces (Carey, 1992) and that experts differ from novices in their enhanced sensitivity to the configural properties of a stimulus (Tanaka & Gauthier, 1997). As a result, a particular link seems to exist between the emergence of a CP effect and the ability of subjects to perform a holistic processing of the presented face.

Second, the emergence of cognitive neurosciences has led many researchers to link cognitive functions with particular cerebral structures. For instance, the PET technique has the ability to localize the neural structures involved in a specific cognitive function, while ERPs can define the timing of occurrence of these different activations. Although the phenomenon of CP of faces has been well documented in behavioral studies, only four studies (3 using ERPs and 1 with PET) have tried to define the neural basis of this phenomenon. By using ERPs, Campanella et al. (2002 a; 2002 b) investigated CP of emotional expressions, while CP of familiar identities was investigated as by PET (Rossion et al., 2001) than by ERPs (Campanella et al., 2000). Several considerations can be pulled out of these studies. First, the CP effect suggests that the discrimination performance is affected by category membership rather than by objective physical distance. Accordingly, brain activity is correlated with the subject's perceptual awareness of a difference, rather than with the physical continuum of information. Indeed, by investigating CP of familiar faces, Rossion et al. (2001) showed that occipito-temporal regions of the right hemisphere abruptly modify their level of activation when crossing a perceptual boundary. This suggests that the mechanisms implied in the CP of familiar faces took place in low-level and mainly high-level visual areas, so that neurons will correlate their activity with the subject's perception. Second, and despite the fact that the exact nature of these mechanisms were always unknown, Campanella et al. (2000) showed that this right activation begins as early as 170 ms. This confirms the idea that CP can be indexed by an early activity modulation, the N170 being related to the generation of a configural representation of the presented faces (e.g., Bentin & Deouell, 2000). Third, ERP studies concerning CP of emotional expressions (Campanella et al., 2002 a; 2002 b) also show that occipito-temporal regions modify their activity as early as 170 ms, but this time *bilaterally*. Bilateral activations in the occipito-temporal cortex during unpleasant emotions have already been observed (e.g., Lane, Reiman, Bradley, Lang, Ahern, Davidson & Schwartz, 1997). It is suggested that the amygdala may be playing some role in tuning the visual system to become more sensitive to threat cues (Davidson & Irwin, 1999) by means of efferent projections to primary sensory areas (Amaral, Price, Pitkanen & Carmichael, 1992; Ledoux, 1995). Moreover, a large variety of data (animal cells recordings, neuropsychological data, experimental psychology data, neuroimaging studies by means of PET, fMRI or ERPs) showed that facial identity and facial emotion are mediated by different cerebral mechanisms. This suggests that (1) the segregation of the neural mechanisms implied in facial identity and facial emotion discrimination began at early stages, around 170ms, in the occipito-temporal regions; and (2) the CP of facial identities and emotions reveal abrupt changes in occipito-temporal regions as early as 170 ms, but that these activations could be the result of top-down activities coming from a larger network (including, for instance for CP of emotional expressions, limbic structures such as amygdala). Overall, the exact mechanisms that allow these abrupt changes accompanying perceptual awareness must be clarified in future studies, as well as for CP effects obtained with other facial dimensions (e.g., gender, race).

CONCLUSIONS

Since the pioneering work of Etcoff & Magee in 1992, concerning the CP of emotional facial expressions, an increasing number of studies have been related to the topic of CP of faces. Faces communicate a great deal of social information, and they are broadly implicated in nonverbal communication: it is therefore particularly important to try to understand how they are categorized, discriminated and represented in memory. We tried in the present manuscript to present an exhaustive view of the works performed up to now on CP of faces. This allow us to draw some considerations about what is known on the cognitive mechanisms grounding such a phenomenon (principle of differentiation, principle of selective attention, need of a holistic processing) and about their neural implementation (abrupt changes in occipito-temporal regions as early as about 170 ms). But, more importantly, these data also allow us to point to the principal unanswered questions about this phenomenon. Indeed, it would be of the greatest importance to reveal in further studies which are the precise mechanisms allowing the enhancement or the deemphasization of physical difference, the focus of selective attention to a relevant stimulus feature, and their respective neural implementation. Moreover, and even if we tried to remain "objective", all these works have been interpreted according to our point of view (and our works), which cannot be shared by everyone. This seems to us to be benefic, as we hope that agreements and disagreements about our positions will lead to fertile discussions and to a better understanding of this phenomenon.

To conclude, we also think that the importance of an area of research is related to the fact that it can be extended to other domains of research. CP of faces has been, up to now, largely studied in order to understand how the different facial dimensions are categorized and discriminated by normal subjects. A great part of these studies have been related to CP of emotional expressions. A recent work of Teunisse & de Gelder (2001) has shown that high-functioning adolescents with autism do not perceive facial expressions categorically. This seems to us of the greatest relevance as several studies have shown deficits in recognizing emotional facial expressions in different psychiatric populations (Power & Dalgleish, 1997). For instance, *depressive patients* better encoded stimuli with a negative valence (Denny & Hunt, 1992), increasing the accessibility of "bad recalls" into consciousness (Ellis & Moore, 1997). Moreover, they also over-estimate the emotional facial expression of sadness (Hale, 1998). *Schizophrenic patients* are defined by the important heterogeneity of their troubles (memory, attention, executive function, see Frith, 1992 for example). Langdon & Colthaert (1999) suggested that schizophrenic patients are unable to perceive and to use "state of mind" (of themselves and of others) to choose an adapted behavioral reaction. As a matter of fact, it has been shown that these patients have a general deficit when they have to identify emotional facial expressions (Mandal et al., 1998). *Psychopathy* generally referred to antisocial behaviors, which are principally defined by DSM IV as agressive behaviors directed to animals or humans, aggravated theft and disrespect of the laws, and which is typically correlated to the ADHD deficit (Attention Deficit - Hypercativity Disorder) (Mc Ardle et al., 1995). Studies investigating the recognition of emotional facial expressions showed as main result that psychopathics have a reduced experience of the fear emotional expression (Ogloff & Wong, 1990). We suggest that studying CP effect in these psychiatric populations could help us to better understand the origin of their deficit in recognizing emotions. For instance, by creating continua of morphed faces going from an neutral state to a specific emotion (e.g., sadness, happiness and fear), and by using a simple identification task in psychiatric populations and in apparied (normal) control subjects, we know that normal subjects will show sharp boundaries, the categorical boundary indexing the amount of physical information necessary (on the basis of a neutral state) to pick up in the face the presented emotion. Then, we can put forward the hypothesis that the locus of this categorical boundary will move in psychiatric populations. Indeed, we can imagine that depressive patients will need less physical information than controls to detect sadness on a face (because they are over-sensitive to sadness), as we can imagine that they will need more information to perceive sadness, because they focused on their own sadness, neglecting the one of others. We think that such "intuitions" have to be empirically tested and that performing such studies could help us to make clear assumptions about the dysfunctioning of their recognition of facial emotions.

ACKNOWLEDGMENTS

We thank Professors Raymond Bruyer, Xavier Seron and Jean-Michel Guérit for their helpful suggestions and comments. We also thank all the students and PHD students who participated in our experiments.

The author was supported by the Belgian National Fund of Scientific Reserach (F.N.R.S.).

REFERENCES

Adolphs, R., Damasio, H., Tranel, D., & Damasio, A.R. (1996). Cortical systems for the recognition of emotion in facial expressions. *Journal of Neuroscience*, 16 (23), 7678-7687.

Ainsworth, M.D.S. (1973). The development of infant-mother attachment. In B.M.Caldwell & H.N. Ricciuti (Eds), *Review of Child Development Research*, Vol.3. Chicago: University of Chicago Press.

Almassy, N., Edelman, G.M., & Sporns, O. (1998). Behavioral constraints in the development of neuronal properties: a cortical model embedded in a real-world. *Cerebral Cortex*, 8(4), 346-361.

Amaral, D.G., Price, J.L., Pitkanen, A., & Carmichael, S.T. (1992). Anatomical organization of the primate amygdaloid complex. In *The Amygdala- Neurobiological Aspects of Emotion, Memory and Mental Dysfunction*, ed. J. Aggleton. Wiley, New York, pp 1-66.

Beale, J.M., Keil, C.F. (1995). Categorical effects in the perception of faces. *Cognition*, 57, 217-239.

Begleiter, H., Porjesz, B., Wang, W.Y. (1995). Event-related brain potentials differentiate priming and recognition to familiar and unfamiliar faces. *Electroencephalography and Clinical Neurophysiology*, 94(1), 41-49.

Bentin, S., Allison, T., Puce, A., Perez, E., McCarthy, G. (1996). Electrophysiological studies of face perception in humans. *Journal of Cognitive Neuroscience*, 8, 551-565.

Bentin, S., & Deouell, L.Y. (2000). Structural encoding and identification in face processing: ERP evidence for separate mechanisms. *Cognitive Neuropsychology*, 17 (1/2/3), 35-54.

Bimler, D., & Kirkland, J. (2001). Categorical perception of facial expressions of emotion: Evidence for multidimensional scaling. *Cognition & Emotion*, 15(5), 633-658.

Bornstein, M.H., Korda, N.O. (1964). Discrimination and matching within and between hues measured by reaction times : Some implications for categorical perception and levels of information processing. *Psychological Research*, 46, 207-222.

Bornstein, M.H., & Monroe, M.D. (1980). Chromatic information processing: rate depends on stimulus location in the category and psychological complexity. *Psychological Research*, 42, 213-225.

Bornstein, B., Sroka, II., & Munitz, H. (1969). Prosopagnosia with animal face agnosia. *Cortex*, 5, 164-169.

Bowers, D., Bauer, R.M., Coslett, H.B., & Heilman, K M. (1985). Processing of faces by patients with unilateral lesions. 1. Dissociation between judgments of facial affect and facial identity. *Brain and Cognition*, 4, 258-272.

Bruce, V., & Young, A.W. (1986). Understanding face recognition. *British Journal of Psychology*, 77, 305-327.

Bruce, V. (1988). *Recognizing faces*. Hove: Lawrence Erlbaum Associates Ltd.

Bruyer, R., Laterre, C., Seron, X., Feyereisen, P., Strypstein, E., Pierrard, E., & Rectem, D. (1983). A case of prosopagnosia with some preserved covert remembrance of familiar faces. *Brain and Cognition*, 2, 257-284.

Bruyer, R. (2003). Impairments of facial nonverbal communication after brain damage. In Philippot, P., Feldman, R.S., & Coats, E.J. (Eds.), Nonverbal behavior in clinical settings. New York: Oxford University Press.

Bülthoff, I., & Newell, F.N. (2000). There is no categorical effect for the discrimination of face gender using 3D-morphs of laser scans of heads. *Investigative Ophtalmology & Visual Science*, 41(4), S225.

Busey, T.A. (1998). Physical and Psychological Representations of Faces: Evidence from Morphing. *Psychological Science*, 9(6), 476-483.

Calder, A.J., Young, A.W., Perrett, D.I., Etcoff, N.L., Rowland, D. (1996). Categorical perception of morphed facial expressions. *Visual Cognition*, 3, 81-117.

Calder, A.J., Keane, J., Cole, J., Campbell, R., & Young, A.W. (2000). Facial expression recognition by people with Möbius syndrome. *Cognitive Neuropsychology*, 17 (1/2/3), 73-87.

Calder, A.J., Burton, A.M., Miller, P., Young, A.W., & Akamatsu, S. (2001). A principal component analysis of facial expressions. *Vision Research*, 41, 1179-1208.

Campanella, S., Hanoteau, C., Dépy, D., Rossion, B., Bruyer, R., Crommelinck, M., & Guerit, J.M.(2000). Right N170 modulation in a face discrimination task : an account for categorical perception of familiar faces. *Psychophysiology*, 37(6), 796-806.

Campanella, S., Chrysochoos, A., & Bruyer, R. (2001). Categorical perception of facial gender information : behavioral evidence and the face-space metaphor. *Visual Cognition*, 8(2), 237-262.

Campanella, S., Gaspard, C., Debatisse, D., Bruyer, R., & Guérit, J.M. (2002 a). Discrimination of emotional facial expressions in a visual oddball task: an ERP study. *Biological Psychology*, 59, 171-186.

Campanella, S., Quinet, P., Bruyer, R., Crommelinck, M., & Guérit, J.M. (2002 b). Categorical perception of happiness and fear facial expressions : an ERP study. *Journal of Cognitive Neuroscience*, 14(2), 210-227.

Campanella, S., Hanoteau, C., Seron, X., Joassin, F., & Bruyer, R.. (2003). Categorical perception of unfamiliar facial identities, the face-space metaphor and the morphing technique. *Visual Cognition*, 10, 129-156.

Campbell, R., Pascalis, O., Coleman, M., Wallace, S.B., & Benson, P.J. (1997). Are faces of different species perceived categorically by human observers? *Proceedings of the Royal Society of London*, B 264, 1429-1434.

Campbell, R., Woll, B., Benson, P.J., & Wallace, S.B. (1999). Categorical perception of face actions: their role in sign language and in communicative face displays. *The Quarterly Journal of Experimental Psychology*, 52 A (1), 67-95.

Carey, S. (1992). Becoming a face expert. *Philosophical transactions of the Royal Society of London*, B335, 95-103.

Damper, R.I., & Harnad, S.R. (2000). Neural network models of categorical perception. *Perception & Psychophysics*, 62(4), 843-867.

Davidson, R.J., & Irwin, W. (1999). The functional neuroanatomy of emotion and affective style. *Trends in Cognitive Sciences*, 3(1), 11-21.

De Gelder, B., Teunisse, J.P., Benson, P.J. (1997). Categorical perception of facial expressions : categories and their internal structure. *Cognition and Emotion*, 11, 1-23.

Denny, E.R., & Hunt, R.R. (1992). Affective valence and memory in depression: Dissociation of recall and fragment completion. *Journal of Abnormal Psychology*, 101, 575-580.

Ekman, P., & Friesen, W.V. (1971). Constants across cultures in the face and emotion. *Journal of Personality and Social Psychology*, 17, 124-129.

Ekman, P., & Friesen, W.V. (1976). *Pictures of facial affect*. Palo Alto, CA: Consulting Psychologists Press.

Ekman, P. (1992). Facial expressions of emotion: An old controversy and new findings. *Philosophical Transactions of the Royal Society, London*, B335, 63-69.

Ekman, P. (1994). Strong evidence for universals in facial expressions: A reply to Russell's mistaken critique. *Psychological Bulletin*, 115, 268-287.

Ellis, H.C., & Moore, B.A. (1997). Mood and memory. In T. Dalgleish & M. Power (eds), *The Handbook of Cognition and Emotion*. Chichester: Wiley.

Etcoff, N.L., Magee, J.J. (1992). Categorical perception of facial expressions. *Cognition*, 44, 227-240.

Field, T.M., Woodson, R., Greenberg, R., & Cohen, D. (1982). Discrimination and imitation of facial expressions by neonates. *Science*, 218, 179-181.

Fiske, H.E. (1997). Categorical perception of musical patterns: How different is "different". *Bulletin of the Council for Research in Music Education*, 133, 20-24.

Frith, C.D. (1992). *The Cognitive Neuropsychology of Schizophrenia*. Lawrence Erlbaum, Hove.

Gauthier, I., Tarr, M., Anderson, A.W., Skudlarsky, P., & Gore, J.C. (1999). Activation of the middle fusiform -face area- increases with expertise in recognizing novel objects. *Nature Neuroscience*, 3, 191-197.

Garcia-Larrea, L., Lukaszewicz, A-C., & Mauguière, F. (1992). Revisiting the oddball paradigm. Non-target vs. neutral stimuli and the evaluation of ERP attentional effects. *Neuropsychologia*, 30 (8), 723-741.

Goldstone, R.L. (1994). Influences of Categorization on Perceptual Discrimination. *Journal of Experimental Psychology : General*, 123(2), 178-200.

Goldstone, R.L. (1998). Perceptual learning. *Annual Review of Psychology*, 49, 585-612.

Goldstone, R.L., Lippa, Y., & Shiffrin, R.M. (2001). Altering object representations through category learning. *Cognition*, 78, 27-43.

Granato, P., Bruyer, R., & Revillon, J.J. (1996). Etude objective de la percpetion du sourire et de la tristesse par la méthode d'analyse de recherche de l'intégration des émotions "MARIE". *Annales Médico-Psychologiques*, 154 (1), 1-9.

Gutheil, G., & Rosengren, K.S. (1996). A rose by any other name: Preschoolers' understanding of individual identity across name and appearance. *British Journal of Psychology*, 14, 477-498.

Hale, W.W. (1998). Judgment of facial expressions and depression persistence. *Psychiatry Research*, 80, 265-274.

Halgren, E., & Marinkovic, K. (1995). Neurophysiological Networks Integrating Human Emotions. In *The Cognitive Neuroscience*, M.S. Gazzaniga (Editor), MIT Press, Cambridge, Massachusetts, pp. 1137-1151.

Harnad, S. (Ed.) (1987). *Categorical Perception : The groundwork of cognition*. Cambridge : Cambridge University Press.

Hasselmo, M.E., Rolls, E.T., & Baylis, G.C. (1989). The role of expression and identity in the face-selective responses of neurons in the temporal visual cortex of the monkey. *Behavioral and Brain Research*, 32, 203-218.

Hay, D.C., & Young, A.W. (1982). The human face. In Ellis, A.W. (Ed.). *Normality and Pathology in Cognitive Functions*. London: Academic Press.

Hautecoeur, P., Debruyne, P., Forzy, G., Gallois, P., Hache, J.-C., Dereux, J.-F. (1993). Potentiels évoqués visuels et reconnaissance des visages. Influence de la célébrité et de l'expression émotionnelle. *Revue Neurologique (Paris)*, 149(3), 207-212.

Haxby, J.V., Hoffman, E.A., & Gobbini, M.I. (2000). The distributed human neural system for face perception. *Trends in Cognitive Sciences,* 4, 223-233.

Henson, R., Shallice, T., & Dolan, R. (2000). Neuroimaging evidence for dissociable forms of repetition priming. *Science*, 287, 1269-1272.

Ji, J., Porjesz, B., Begleiter, H. (1998). ERP components in category matching tasks. *Evoked Potentials-Electroencephalography and Clinical Neurophysiology*, 108(4), 380-389.

Johnson, M.H., & Morton, J. (1991). *Biology and cognitive development: the case of face recognition*. Oxford, UK: Blackwell.

Kanwisher, N., McDermott, J., Chun, M.M. (1997). The fusiform face area: a module in human extrastriate cortex specialized for face perception. *Journal of Neuroscience*, 17, 4302-4311.

Katanoda, K., Yoshikawa, K., & Sugishita, M. (2000). Neural substrates for the recognition of newly learned faces: A functional MRI study. *Neuropsychologia*, 38, 1616-1625.

Kotsoni, E., de Haan, M., & Johnson, M.H. (2001). Categorical perception of facial expressions by 7-months old infants. *Perception*, 30(9), 1115-1125.

Kunst-Wilson, W.R., & Zajonc, R.B. (1980). Affective discrimination of stimuli that cannot be recognized. *Science*, 207, 557-558.

Lane, R.D., Reiman, E.M., Bradley, M.M., Lang, P.J., Ahern, G.L., Davidson, R.J., & Schwartz, G.E. (1997). Neuroanatomical correlates of pleasant and unpleasant emotion. *Neuropsychologia*, 35(11), 1437-1444.

Langdon, R., & Coltheart, M. (1999). Mentalizing, schizotypy, and schizophrenia. *Cognition*, 71, 43-71.

Laws, G., Davies, I., & Andrews, C. (1995). Linguistic structure and non-linguistic cognition: English and Russian blues compared. *Language and Cognitive Processes*, 10, 59-94.

Ledoux, J. E. (1995). In search of an emotional system in the brain: Leaping from fear to emotion and consciousness. In *The Cognitive Neuroscience*, M.S. Gazzaniga (Editor), MIT Press, Cambridge, Massachusetts, pp. 1049-1061.

Levin, D.T. (1996). "Classifying faces by race: The structure of face categories". *Journal of Experimental Psychology: Learning, Memory and Cognition*, 22, 1364-1382.

Levin, D.T., & Beale, J.M. (2000). Categorical perception occurs in newly learned faces, other-race faces, and inverted faces. *Perception & Psychophysics*, 62(2), 386-401.

Levin, D.T., & Angelone, B.L. (2002). Categorical perception of race. *Perception*, 31, 567-578.

Liberman, A.M., Harris, K.S., Hoffman, H.S., Griffith, B.C. (1957). The discrimination of speech sounds within and across phoneme boundaries. *Journal of Experimental Psychology*, 53, 368-385.

Livingston, K.R., & Andrews, J.K. (1995). On the interaction of prior knowledge and stimulus structure in category learning. *Quarterly Journal of Experimental Psychology; Section A: Human Experimental Psychology*, 48, 208-236.

Livingston, K.R., Andrews, J.K., Harnad, S. (1998). Categorical Perception Effects Induced by Category Learning. *Journal of Experimental Psychology : Learning, Memory and Cognition*, 24 (3), 732-753.

Luzzatti, C., & Davidoff, J. (1994). Impaired retrieval of object-colour knowledge with preserved colour naming. *Neuropsychologia*, 32, 933-950.

Mandal, M.K., Pandey, R., & Prasad, A.B. (1998). Facial expressions of emotions and schizophrenia: a review.*Schizophr-Bull*. 24: 399-412.

McArdle, P., O'Brien, G., & Kolvin, I. (1995). Hypercativity: Prevalence and relationship with conduct disorder. *Journal of Child psychology and Psychiatry*, 36(2), 279-303.

McKone, E., Martini, P., & Nakayama, K. (2001). Categorical Perception of Face Identity in Noise Isolates Configural Processing. *Journal of Experimental Psychology: Human Perception and Performance*, 27(3), 573-599.

MacNeil, J.E., & Warrington, E.K. (1993). Prosopagnosia: a face-specific disorder. *The Quarterly Journal of Experimental Psychology*, 46A, 1-10.

Medin, D.L., & Barsalou, L.W. (1987). Categorization processes and categorical perception, in *Categorical Perception: The Groundwork of Cognition*, Ed. S.Harnad (New York: Cambridge University Press), pp.455-490.

Münte, T.F., Brack, M., Grootheer, O., Wieringa, B.M., Matzke, M., & Johannes, S. (1998). Brain potentials reveal the timing of face identity and expression judgments. *Neuroscience Research*, 30, 25-34.

Murphy, S.T., & Zajonc, R.B. (1993). Affect, cognition, and awareness: affective priming with optimal and suboptimal stimulus exposure. *Journal of Personality and Social Psychology*, 64, 723-739.

Newell, F.N., & Bülthoff, H.H. (2002). Categorical perception of familiar objects. *Cognition*, in press.

Newell, F.N., Chiroro, P., Valentine, T. (1999). Recognizing Unfamiliar Faces : The Effects of Distinctiveness and View. *The Quarterly Journal of Experimental Psychology*, 52A(2), 509-534.

Nosofsky, R.M. (1984). Choice, similarity and the context theory of classification. *Journal of Experimental Psychology: Learning, Memory and Cognition*, 10, 104-114.

Ogloff, J.R., & Wong, S. (1990). Electrodermal and cardiovascular evidence of a coping response in psychopaths. *Criminal Justice and Behaviour*, 17, 231-245.

O'Toole, A., Deffenbacher, K.A., Valentin, D., & Abdi, H. (1994). Structural aspects of face recognition and the other-race effect. *Memory and Cognition*, 22, 208-224.

Orozco, S., & Ehlers, C.L. (1998). Gender differences in electrophysiological responses to facial stimuli. *Biological Psychiatry, 44*, 281-289.

Paller, K.A., & Gross, M. (1998). Brain potentials associated with perceptual priming vs. explicit remembering during the repetition of visual word-form. *Neuropsychologia*, 36(6), 559-571.

Pevtzow, R., & Harnad, S. (1997). Warping similarity space in category learning by human subjects: The role of task difficulty. In M. Ramscar, U. Hahn, E. Cambouropolos, & H. Pain (Eds.), *Proceedings of SimCat 1997: Interdisciplinary workshop on similarity and categorization* (pp. 189-195). Edinburgh, Scotland: Department of Artificial Intelligence, Edinburgh University.

Philippot, P., Kornreich, C., & Blairy, S. (2003). Nonverbal deficits and interpersonal regulation in alcoholics. In Philippot, P., Feldman, R.S., & Coats, E.J. (Eds.), Nonverbal behavior in clinical settings. New York: Oxford University Press.

Philipps, M.L., Bullmore, E.T., Howard, R., Woodruff, P.W.R., Wright, I.C., Williams, S.C.R., Simmons, A., Andrew, C., Brammer, M., & David, A.S. (1998). Investigation of facial recognition memory and happy and sad facial expression perception: an fMRI study. *Psychiatry Research: neuroimaging Section*, 83, 127-138.

Pizzagalli, D., Regard, M., & Lehmann, D. (1999). Rapid emotional face processing in the human right and left brain hemispheres: an ERP study. *Neuroreport*, 10, 2691-2698.

Podgorny, P., & Shepard, R.N. (1978). Functional representations common to visual perception and imagination. *Journal of Experimental Psychology: Human Perception and Performance,* 4(1), 21-35.

Potter, D.D., & Parker, D.M. (1989). Electrophysiological correlates of facial identity and expression processing. In: Crawford, J.R., Parker, D.M. (Eds), *Developments in Clinical and Experimental Neuropsychology*. Plenum Press, New York, pp 143-155.

Power, M.J., & Dalgleish, T. (1997). *Cognition and Emotion: From Oder to Disorder*. Hove: Psychology Press (Erlbaum, UK).

Rhodes, G., & Tremewan, T. (1996). Averageness, exaggeration, and facial attractiveness. *Psychological Science*, 7(2), 105-110.

Roberson, D., Davidoff, J., & Braisby, N. (1999). Similarity and categorization: neuropsychological evidence for a dissociation in explicit categorization tasks. *Cognition,* 71, 1-42.

Rolls, E.T. (1992). Neurophysiological mechanisms underlying face processing within and beyond the temporal cortical visual areas. *Phil. Trans. Roy. Soc.,* 335, 11-21.

Rolls, E.T. (1994). Brain mechanisms for invariant visual recognition and learning. *Behavioral Processes,* 33, 113-138.

Romo, R., Merchant, H., Zainos, A., & Hernandez, A. (1997). Categorical perception of somesthesic stimuli: psychophysical measurements correlated with neuronal events in primate medial premotor cortex. *Cerebral Cortex,* 7, 317-326.

Rosielle, L.J., & Cooper, E.E. (2001). Categorical perception of relative orientation in visual object recognition. *Memory & Cognition,* 29(1), 68-82.

Rossion, B., Schiltz, C., Robaye, L., Pirenne, D., & Crommelinck, M. (2001). How does the brain discriminate familiar and unfamiliar faces? A PET study of face categorical perception. *Journal of Cognitive Neuroscience,* 13(7), 1019-1034.

Schweinberger, S.R. (1996). How Gorbachev primed Yeltsin: Analyses of associative priming in person recognition by means of reaction times and event-related potentials. *Journal of Experimental Psychology-Learning, Memory and Cognition,* 22(6), 1383-1407.

Schweinberger, S.R., & Soukup, G.R. (1998). Asymmetric relationships among perceptions of facial identity, emotion, and facial speech. *Journal of Experimental Psychology: Human Perception and Performance,* 24(6), 1748-1765.

Schweinberger, S.R., Burton, A.M., & Kelly, S.W. (1999). Asymmetric dependencies in perceiving identity and emotion: Experiments with morphed faces. *Perception and Psychophysics,* 61 (6), 1102-1115.

Schyns, P.G. (1998). Diagnostic recognition : task constraints, object information and their interactions. *Cognition,* 67, 147-179.

Sergent, J., Otha, S., & McDonald, B. (1992). Functional neuroanatomy of face and object processing: A positron emission tomography study. *Brain,* 115, 15-36.

Sergent, J., Otha, S., McDonald, B., & Zuck, E. (1994). Segregated processing of Facial identity and Emotion in the Human Brain: A PET Study. *Visual Cognition,* 1(2/3), 349-369.

Sheperd, J.W., & Deregowski, J.B. (1981). Races and faces- a comparison of the responses of Africans and Europeans to faces of the same and different races. *British Journal of Social Psychology,* 20, 125-133.

Sprengelmeyer, R., Young, A.W., Sprengelmeyer, A., Calder, A.J., Rowland, D., Perrett, D., Homberg, V., & Lange, H. (1997). Recognition of facial expressions: Selective impairment of specific emotions in Huntington's disease. *Cognitive Neuropsychology,* 14(6), 839-879.

Stevenage, V.S. (1998). Which twin are you? A demonstration of induced categorical perception of identical twin faces. *British Journal of Psychology,* 89, 39-57.

Tanaka, J., & Farah, M.J. (1993). Parts and wholes in face recognition. *Quarterly Journal of Experimental Psychology: Human Experimental Psychology,* 46(A), 225-245.

Tanaka, J., & Gauthier, I. (1997). Expertise in object and face recognition. *The Psychology of Learning and Motivation,* 36, 83-124.

Tanaka, J., Giles, M., Kremen, S., Simon, V. (1998). Mapping attractor fields in face space : the atypicality bias in face recognition. *Cognition*, 68, 199-220.

Teunisse, J.P., & de Gelder, B. (2001). Impaired categorical perception of facial expressions in high-functioning adolescents with autism. *Neuropsychology of Developmental Cogntion, Section C Child Neuropsychology*, 7(1), 1-14.

Thompson, R.K.R., & Oden, D.L. (2000). Categorical perception and conceptual judgments by non human primates: The paleological monkey and the analogical ape. *Cognitive Science*, 24(3), 363-396.

Valentine, T. (1991). A unified account of the effects of distinctiveness, inversion, and race in face recognition. *Quarterly Journal of Experimental Psychology: Human Experimental Psychology,* 43(A), 161-204.

Woodworth, R.S., & Schlosberg, H. (1954). *Experimental Psychology: Revised edition.* New York: Henry Holt.

Wright, A.A., & Roberts, W.A. (1996). Monkey and human face perception: inversion effects for human faces but not for monkey scenes or faces. *Journal of Cognitive Neuroscience*, 8, 278-296.

Yin, R.K. (1969). Looking at upside down faces. *Journal of Experimental Psychology,* 81, 141-145.

Young, M P., & Yamane, S. (1992). Sparse population encoding of faces in the inferotemporal cortex. *Science*, 256, 1327-1331.

Young, A.W., Rowland, D., Calder, A.J., Etcoff, N.L., Seth, A., Perrett, D.I. (1997). Facial expression megamix : Tests of dimensional and category accounts of emotion recognition. *Cognition*, 63, 271-313.

In: Focus on Nonverbal Communication Research
Editor: Finley R. Lewis, pp. 31-64

ISBN 1-59454-790-4
© 2007 Nova Science Publishers, Inc.

Chapter 2

SOUND SPECTROGRAPHIC CRY ANALYSIS AND MOTHERS PERCEPTION OF THEIR INFANT'S CRYING

Katarina Michelsson
University Hospital, Helsinki, Finland
Helena Todd de Barra
Corporation for Child Development, Santiago de Chile, Chile
Oliver Michelsson
University Hospital, Helsinki, Finland

ABSTRACT

Sound spectrography has since the 1960s been used to objectively evaluate crying in neonates. The various cry characteristics used for scientific analysis are described. The crying of healthy infants has a mean fundamental frequency of 400-600 Hz most often with a falling or rising-falling melody contour. Prematurely born infants have the more high-pitched crying the more immature the infant. In impaired infants, and especially those with disorders involving the central nervous system, the cry has been abnormal; the fundamental frequency has been higher, the melody contour irregular and some cry characteristics very seldom seen in crying of healthy neonates has occurred more often.

Crying in newborn and small infants has been regarded as a graded signal, i.e. the cry indicates the degree of stress but does not change according to the cause of crying. In order to check the statement sound spectrographic characteristics in both spontaneous and pain induced cries were analyzed. Eighteen infants were followed from birth to the age of two months, and the cries were collected at six different occasions. A total of 1020 cries was analyzed. The results indicated a significantly higher pitch in pain induced than in spontaneous cries for the whole group. However, the differences between spontaneous and pain cries at the various ages were often marginal. The cry variables of spontaneous and pain cries did not change significantly with increasing age.

Many parents are upset about their infants´ crying during the first month of life. Excessive crying is often called colic. Previous studies indicate that an organic cause for this type of crying is infrequent. A study of the amount and perception of crying in 281 infants in Finland and 97 infants in South America (Chile and Colombia) is presented based on parents´ diaries. The results indicate that the crying and sleeping episodes in infants in both continents were similar and that a peak of crying occurred in the evenings for infants under the age of three months. The mean crying time per day for infants under the age of six months was 1.4 hours in Finland and 1.7 hours in South America. Crying for more than three hours per day in infants under the age of three months was observed in 12.4 % in Finland and 26.3 % in South America.

INTRODUCTION

In the far past, the newborn babies were claimed to cry at birth because they experienced a "loss of paradise" and "an overwhelming sense of inferiority at thus suddenly being confronted by reality without ever having to deal with its problems" (see Illingworth 1955). The first cry also represented mythological aspects; Mohammed and Saint Bartholomei were said to have cried already before birth (Parviainen 1948). The first cry has also been thought to have certain physiological usefulness in the early days of neonatal adjustment (Brazelton 1962), such as to increase body temperature (Watson & Lowrey 1951) and to improve pulmonary capacity during the first days of life (Long & Hull 1961).

Scientific studies about baby crying are found from the 19th century. Gardiner, in 1838, compared infant crying with musical notes. Darwin, in 1855, noted differences between crying for hunger and crying in pain. Flatau and Gutzmann (1906) found the basic pitch of normal neonates crying at middle A (440 Hz) and that crying of abnormal infants was one octave higher. In the 1940s cry studies dealt with auditory perception about when, why and how much babies cry (Aldrich et al. 1945). Several studies compared crying sounds with the symbols on the phonetic alphabet (Irwin & Chen 1943, Irwin 1948). Irwin and Curry (1941) implied that prelinguistic vocal sounds became meaningful speech and that infant sounds thus conform to the phonetic elements of adult speech. The alphabet was, however, developed to describe the sounds of adult speech and unsuitable for infant cry analysis which not resembles adult phonations

Progress in cry research was maintained in the beginning of the 20th century by the development of equipment which enabled permanent recording of the cry sound. The first studies used a graphophone (Flatau & Gutzmann 1906) and a gramophone (Fairbanks 1942). The development of tape recorders in the 1920s and the sound spectrograph in the 1940s enabled more accurate analysis of sound.

For objective analysis of acoustic signals the sound spectrograph became an important tool for permanent visualization of the cry sound. The sound spectrographic method, called ´visible speech´, has been used in phonetics since the mid 1940s (Potter et al. 1947). The apparatus was first intended for use in speech therapy for deaf-mutes but was found to be too slow in administration. The first investigation of baby crying with sound spectrography was performed by Lynip in 1951 analyzing the preverbal vocalizations of one infant. Ten years later, Wasz-Höckert et al. (1962) utilized the capacity of sound spectrography for objective and detailed analysis of crying, and they developed nomenclature for different cry characteristics to be used in cry analysis (Wasz-Höckert et al. 1968, Michelsson 1971). Later, several other studies have reported the use of the sound spectrograph in cry research (Oswald et al. 1968, Ringel & Kluppel 1964, Sedlackova 1964, Truby & Lind 1965, Hirschberg 196, Stark et al 1975, Hirschberg & Szende 1995, Hirschberg 1990)

Since the 1980s data based analysis of cry sounds have been undertaken. Golub and Corwin (1985) presented an automatic, computer based signal-processing system for cry analysis. Several studies describe acoustic features of neonatal crying (Lester 1976, Lester & Zeskind 1978, Zeskind & Lester 1978, Lester, 1987, Lüdge & Gibs 1989, Lüdge & Rothgänger 1990).

In cry analysis, there are some very basic differences between spectrographic measurements done by hand and automatic digital analysis. While the sound spectrograph enables an analysis of several different cry characteristics the data based cry analysis concentrates on a few acoustic parameters, duration of cry segments, fundamental frequency and percentage of time the cry is phonated, dysphonated or hyperphonated.

Many disciplines have been interested in baby crying because it can be dealt with from so many different perspectives: anatomical, physiological, phonetic, pediatric and psychological. During the last decades several researchers have been interested in different perspectives of crying as a means in the mother-infant interaction. In this respect, there are two different approaches, i.e. how the baby is crying and how the cry is perceived by the adult listener.

CRY RECORDING AND ANALYSIS

The cry sounds are produced by vibration of the vocal folds in the larynx. The number of times the sound wave repeats itself during a second is the fundamental frequency, F_0 (cycles per second, cps, Hz) and is what we hear as voice pitch. The higher the frequency the more shrill is the sound perceived. The vocal tract modifies the sound generated at the larynx producing resonance frequencies or formants.

Baby crying recorded for analysis has been defined as either spontaneous or pain induced. Spontaneous cries are most frequently heard when the infant is hungry but also at other times (Fairbanks 1942, Starck et al. 1975, Zeskind & Lester 1978). Pain cries have been collected during vaccination (Wasz-Höckert et al. 1968), blood test heels stick (Golub and Corwin 1985, Runefors et al. 2000), circumcision (Porter et al. 1986) or some other kinds of pain stimulus. These comprised a pinch or flick on the infant's biceps (Wasz-Höckert et al. 1968, Michelsson 1971, Thodén & Koivisto 1980) snapping the ear (Michelsson et al. 1977b) pulling the hair (Ringel & Kluppel 1964) and stimulus to the foot (Fisichelli & Karelitz 1966, Muller et al. 1974, Tenold et al. 1974, Murry et al. 1977). A rubber band apparatus has been used for a snap on the sole of the foot (Fisichelli & Karelitz 1963, Fisichelli et al. 1974, Murry et al. 1977, Zeskind & Lester 1978). The rubber band provides an audible snap from which the latency to the onset of crying can be measured. In the other provoked cries the latency has been measured from the middle of the word "now" uttered at the moment of the pain stimulus.

In the studies by Michelsson (1971), and Wasz-Höckert et al. (1968) usually only the first cry after pain stimulus has been analyzed in order to have the cry responses as similar as possible. The spectrographic analyses were at that time very slow in operation which also reduced the number of cries analyzed. In most other studies there has not been mentioned which type of crying was analyzed. The cries are, however, in a cry burst rather similar (Truby & Lind 1965, Thodén & Koivisto 1980, Runefors et al. 2000).

SOUND SPECTROGRAPHY

With the sound spectrograph the tape-recorded cries can be converted to visible spectrograms from which the different parameters used in cry research can be measured. The spectrograms display the time on the horizontal axis and the fundamental frequency on the vertical axis. Thus, the cry characteristics measured are related to either durational or fundamental frequency features. In infant cry studies, a certain terminology of the acoustic manifestations of the cry signal has been established. The nomenclature was mainly developed in the 1960s and 1970s, when characteristics for sound spectrographic analysis of infant crying were defined. (Wasz-Höckert et al. 1968, Michelsson 1971, Sirviö & Michelsson 1976, Michelsson 1980).

The sonagraph has two types of filters, the narrow band of 45 Hz and the wide band of 300 Hz. The narrow band filter displays the fundamental frequency and its harmonic overtones on the spectrogram as dark lines and is usually preferred in cry analysis. The lowest horizontal line in voiced cries is the fundamental frequency and represents the vibrations of the vocal folds, cycles per second (cps, Hz). The harmonics are seen as precise multiples of the fundamental.

Durational Features

The measure of time value of the acoustic characteristics is reported in seconds or milliseconds (0.001 sec). Detailed standardized methods for all cry characteristics are still missing, though much progress already has been achieved (Raes et al. 1991). Usually all durational features exceeding 0.1 sec have been included in the measurements.

Latency Period

The latency period is defined as the time from the pain stimulus to the onset of crying. The latency becomes shorter in repeated pain stimuli.

Sometimes the first sound emitted by an infant is a cough-like expiration, followed either by a longer "main" cry or an inspiration. Ringel and Kluppel (1964) took two measurements to determine the latency period: the time from the stimulus to the first response of the infant, and the time from the first expiration to the main signal. Karelitz and Fisichelli (1962) used the term cry threshold to describe the number of snaps required to elicit the cry.

Duration

The duration of a cry signal refers to all vocalization occurring during a single expiration or inspiration (Michelsson 1971, Sirviö & Michelsson 1977). In pain induced cries the first cry duration comprises the sound between the pain stimulus and the first inspiration.

When the vocalization consists of only one continuous phonation the duration of this is easily measured. Measurement problems occur when the signal is interrupted. Different opinions exist concerning how the silent parts should be handled. Wasz-Höckert et al. (1968) and Michelsson (1971) measured the duration from the onset of crying to the end of the last sound before inspiration irrespectively if the cry consisted of pauses or not. Several authors have not mentioned which cry segments have been included in the analysis; these seem to comprise the "main", i.e. the longest, phonation between two inspirations. Thus, it is difficult to compare durational features in different cry studies.

In the spectrograms, it is usually very easy to determine the onset of crying, because the intensity of the voice is at the beginning of the signal high. The end of the cry signal, however, can very often be characterized as a "fade out" where the intensity of the sound decreases gradually and the fundamental and the lower harmonics seem to have disappeared because they are not intense enough to be presented by the instrumentation. Though not visible on the spectrogram the sound is, however, audible on the tape.

Second Pause

Second pause is defined as the time interval between the end of the phonation to the next inspiration.

Crying Time

The crying time or cry duration is the total amount of time the infant is engaged in crying, for instance after a pain stimulus.

Fundamental Frequency Characteristics

The sound spectrogram, when using the narrow band filter, displays a voiced tone as dark lines on the sonagram. The fundamental frequency is the lowest line and the harmonic overtones are seen as parallel lines above the fundamental.

In cry research, the phonetic terminology has deviated somewhat from its original meaning. For instance, in phonetics, the term "pitch" generally refers to the sensation of the perceived differences in the fundamental frequency of the vocal folds. In cry studies, however, pitch has also been used to indicate the measurable height of the fundamental frequency as presented on a spectrogram.

The most common fundamental frequency characteristics used are the mean fundamental and the highest and lowest measurable points on the spectrogram. In the analyses with the old versions of the sound spectrograph a mean was not possible to acquire, in later versions and the computer versions, the mean fundamental is displayed automatically.

Maximum Fundamental Frequency

Maximum fundamental frequency, maximum pitch, refers to the highest point of the fundamental frequency measurable on the sound spectrogram.

Minimum Fundamental Frequency

This is the most low-pitched voiced part of the cry. On the spectrogram, it is the lowest measurable point in the fundamental frequency. In normal crying, the lowest part of the cry is sometimes difficult to measure at the end of the signal because of very low frequency, especially in cases when the fundamental turns into vocal fry.

Shift

This feature denotes a rapid abrupt increase or decrease in the fundamental frequency. In normal crying, the shift part is mainly seen as a high-pitched hyperphonation at the beginning of the phonations. In studies by Wasz-Höckert et al. (1968) and Michelsson (1971) the shift was considered to be sound emitted before the vocal folds had reached their crying state and was therefore measured separately. However, when cries of infants with central nervous system (CNS) diseases were analyzed, and more experience of baby crying was achieved, shifts were found to occur more irregularly. The primary definition of shift was that it comprised the shorter part of the fundamental and could therefore have a higher or lower pitch than the basic cry (Wasz-Höckert et al 1968, Michelsson 1971). In later studies, shift has been associated only with an abrupt change to high-pitched crying. Sometimes, however, high-pitched cries occur without any shifts. In data based computer analysis it is not possible to separate the shift parts and the mean value of the fundamental comprises the whole phonation. However, some studies have omitted the high-pitched parts from their measurements (Lester and Zeskind 1978).

Mean Fundamental Frequency

In the first sound spectrographic cry studies when all measurements were done by hand, it was not possible to measure a mean fundamental, and the term general pitch was used to describe the most common frequency (Wasz-Höckert et al. 1968). Nowadays, the computer analysis techniques enable measurements of the mean automatically.

As mentioned before, the end of the cry may fade out and the fundamental is not visible on the spectrogram because of the automatic gain control and limited dynamic range. Sometimes the upper harmonica are still visible. In these cases, the automatic display of the mean also gives a distorted value because the fundamental is measured from the upper harmonics that are still visible on the spectrogram.

Melody Type

The melody type has been classified as falling, rising-falling, rising, flat or no type, which means that the cry is very instable, consists only of voiceless sound or glottal plosives.

Continuity of the Signal

One cry is defined as the sound between two inspirations. It can be continuous, i.e. consist of only one signal, or be interrupted, i.e. consist of several parts separated by silence. In some studies the duration of the cries has been measured from the start of the signal to the end of cry sound before an inspiration irrespectively if the cry was continuous or consisted of several parts (Wasz-Höckert et al. 1968, Michelsson 1971). Many other studies have apparently used only the strongest signal between inspirations or analyzed all sounds separately irrespectively of inspirations.

Voice

Cries can be voiced or dysphonic. In a voiced cry the sound wave is periodic and the fundamental and its harmonics are clearly visible on the spectrogram. In voiceless dysphonic cries the spectrogram displays a blur of unperiodic noise turbulence and a fundamental is neither visible nor measurable. A half-voiced signal comprises both voiced and voiceless parts.

Vibrato

Vibrato is defined to comprise at least four up and down movements of the fundamental.

Glottal Roll

Many cries end with a sound of low intensity and decrease in pitch. In the glottal roll the fundamental and its harmonics are still visible but because of the low frequency range they are difficult to measure on the spectrograms. The lowest point of the fundamental has usually been measured from a point where the fundamental is still clearly visible. The glottal roll is sometimes preceded by vibrato.

Double Harmonic Break

The double harmonic break is seen between the fundamental frequency and its harmonics as parallel series of harmonics.

Biphonation or Diplophonation

Biphonation, also called diplophonation, is the result of two vibrating sound sources, i.e. a double series of fundamental frequencies. In comparison with the above mentioned double harmonic break, the two or more series do not have a parallel melody form. This feature, as most others in cry analysis, have been included if the duration exceeded 0.1 sec.

Gliding

Gliding is a very rapid continued increase or decrease of the fundamental frequency, and its duration is usually very short. In gliding, the change in the frequency has been defined to comprise at least 600 Hz in 0.1 sec, as measured from the fundamental, not its harmonics.

Furcation

Furcation is a term denoting a "split" in the fundamental frequency where a relatively strong cry signal suddenly breaks into a series of weaker ones, each of them with its own fundamental coutour.

Noise Concentration

Noise concentration denotes a high energy peak at 2000-2500 Hz found in both voiced and voiceless phonations.

Jitter

Jitter is the term for wave to wave variation in the fundamental frequency.

Glottal Plosive

A rapid open and closening of the vocal folds that results in brief production of air turbulence.

CRYING OF HEALTHY NEWBORN INFANTS

The modern era of cry research can be dated from the 1960s. In 1962, Wasz-Höckert et al. reported their first findings on sound-spectrographic cry analysis of four different types of infant crying: birth, pleasure, hunger and pain. Cry samples of newborn and small infants collected by Michelsson were analyzed with sound spectrography and published in 1968 (Wasz-Höckert et al.). The results indicated that the fundamental frequency of the cries of normal infants varied between 400 and 600 Hz, the melody type was mainly falling or rising-falling, and the mean duration of the signals varied between 1.2-2.6 seconds.

The mean fundamental frequency of cries of healthy newborn and small infants has also in several other studies been found to vary between 400 and 600 Hz (Ringel & Kluppel 1964, Oswald et al. 1968, Michelsson 1971, Tenold et al. 1974, Lester 1976, Kittel & Hecht 1977, Lester 1977, Murry et al. 1977, Lester & Zeskind 1978, Zeskind & Lester 1978, Thoden & Koivisto 1980, Michelsson et al. 2002).

Figure I presents the mean fundamental frequency of cries of 172 healthy full term 1-7 day old infants. For each infant a mean of 8-15 cries was calculated; a total of 1836 cries was analyzed. The figure shows that 88 % of the infants had cries with a mean fundamental frequency of 400-600 Hz, and 96 % between 350-700 Hz.

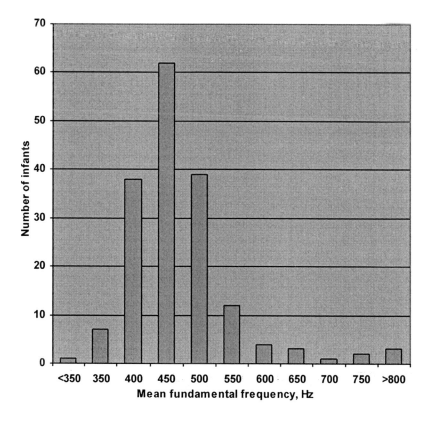

Figure I. Mean fundamental frequency in 1836 cries of 172 healthy full term 1- 7 days old infants. For each infant a mean of 8-15 cries was calculated, and the means of these cries are presented in the figure.

A variation in the duration of the latency period of cry signals has in studies of healthy infants varied considerably ranging from 0.6 sec to 3.6 sec (Fisichelli & Karelitz 1963, Michelsson 1971, Fisichelli et al. 1974, Lester 1977, Zeskind & Lester 1978). The variations in latency can be accounted for by individual variability, by the infants´ wakefulness or measuring techniques used. For instance, the first latency period is often longer than the latencies of immediately repeated pinches.

The duration of the phonations has also varied in different studies and is partly due to the measuring techniques used and the results can therefore not always be compared. The average duration has varied from 1.5 to 6.5 sec (Ringel & Kluppel 1964, Gleiss & Höhn 1968, Oswald et al. 1968, Wolff 1969, Michelsson 1971, Prescott 1975, Lester 1976, Lester & Zeskind 1978, Zeskind & Lester 1978). In studies by Wasz-Höckert et al. (1968) and Michelsson (1971) mainly the first phonation after pain stimulus has been used, but in most other cry investigations also other signals in the cry burst have been analyzed. In pain cries, the first phonation is often the longest in the cry cycle. Thodén and Koivisto (1980) measured values from 4.1 – 5.2 sec. in first cries of one day to six months old infants, and 1.2-2 sec. in the second and third cry after pain provocation. Also Runefors et al. (2000) reported that the first cry after pain stimulus was longer than the four next ones.

In some studies, the shift part has been calculated separately, in some studies the mean has been measured from the total phonation. Shifts are more common in pain cries than in spontaneous cries, and in cries during the first days of life shifts are very rare (Michelsson et al. 2002). The shift part, when present, occurs most often at the beginning of the signals in healthy infants.

The melody type in the crying of healthy infants is mainly falling or rising-falling and the fundamental frequency is quite stable. Biphonation, gliding and furcation do not occur or are extremely rare in the cries of healthy infants. Double harmonic break and glottal roll are fairly common (Wasz-Höckert et al. 1968, Thodén & Koivisto 1980).

Cries as produced by the same infant has not differed significantly from each other with respect to fundamental frequency, sound pressure and duration (Ringel & Kluppel 1964). In pain cries, when the vigor of the pain stimulus wore off the cries became lower in amplitude with more harmonic forms (Blinick et al. 1971). Thodén and Koivisto (1980) reported that the first cry after a pain stimulus was longer than the subsequent ones but that there were no other significant differences in the fundamental frequency characteristics. Runefors et al. (2000) reported that the fundamental frequency in five consecutive cries after a pain stimulus decreased but that the difference was significant only between the first and the fifth cry.

CRYING OF PREMATURES

In 1971, Michelsson reported data on crying in symptomless premature infants. She found that the differences in cry characteristics were comparable with the degree of prematurity. The cries were more high pitched the more premature the infant was. However, Michelsson noted in very small prematures considerable differences in the fundamental. The cries of some very premature infants were very short and shrill while others had a duration and fundamental frequency of the same range as seen in fullterm. This can be due to physiological reasons but might also have been caused by some disorders not detected because of lack of clear clinical symptoms and advanced equipment. For instance cerebral haemorrhage often detected in small prematures could not always be verified because ultrasound and other sophisticated investigation methods were not available in the 1960s when the infants were born. However, a change of cry variables with grade of prematurity seems to be the case as high pitched cries in small prematures also has been demonstrated in later studies (Thodén et al. 1980, Michelsson et al. 1983).

Figure II presents the mean value of maximum and minimum pitch of 302 cries of 48 premature infants born at 30-37 g.w.. The cries were recorded during the first week of life and then weekly until the infants were discharged from hospital. The results show that the cries were more high-pitched the more premature the infant. With the available equipment at the time of the study a mean value of the fundamental was not possible to measure. The maximum fundamental frequency was calculated both with and without the shift part. The smallest prematures presented shorter cries and more often biphonation and glide (Michelsson et al. 1983). The cry characteristics changed with increasing conceptual age and the older the infant the more the cry pattern resembled that of the fullterm.

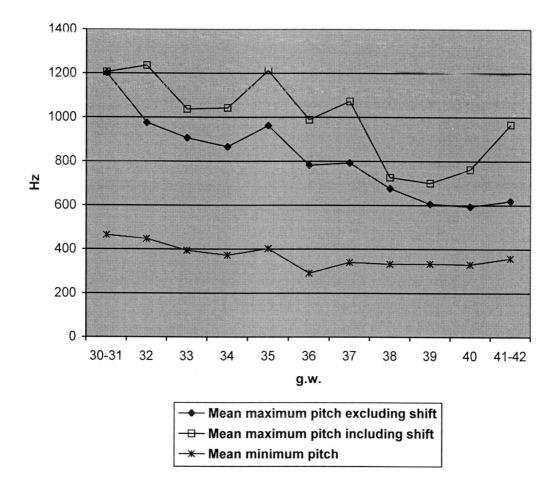

Figure II. Maximum and minimum fundamental frequency in 302 cries of 48 prematurely born infants according to conceptual age. The maximum fundamental is presented both including and excluding the shift part. The frequency is higher the more premature the infant.

Figure III presents a spectrogram of the cry of a two-week-old premature born at 30 g.w. The fundamental frequency and melody contour resemble that of a full term infant.

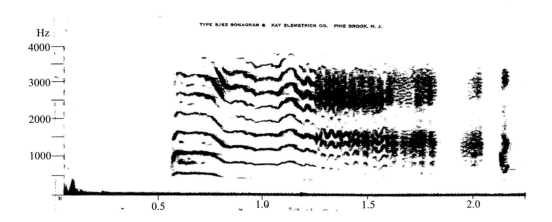

Figure III. A cry from a two-week-old infant born at 30 g.w. The cry has a normal range for full term of the fundamental, and vibrato and glottal roll at the end of the cry.

ANALYSIS OF CRIES IN ONE DAY TO TWO MONTHS OLD INFANTS

The study was undertaken in order to analyze differences and similarities in crying of infants from birth to two months of age, and to evaluate possible differences in spontaneous and pain induced cries. These results have not been reported previously.

Material and Methods

The series consisted of 18 newborn infants, born in 1997 in Chile at the regional hospital in Punta Arenas. All infants included in the study were born after a normal pregnancy. There were no complications during the delivery. All babies were born full term (mean 39.5 ± 0.8 g.w.), The mean birth weight was 3510 ± 360 g and the mean length 50.5 ± 1.6 cm. The Apgar scores were 9-10 at 1, 5 and 15 minutes of age. The babies had no problems in the newborn period.

The first cries were collected about 30 minutes after birth, and thereafter at the ages of 3, 24 and 48 hours, one week and two months of age. The cries from birth to the age of 48 hours were collected in the hospital, the cries at the age of one week at the outpatient clinic, and the ones at the age of two months in the babies' homes.

The recordings were made when the baby was fully awake and started to cry. Each sample comprised crying of at least 15 sec. When the baby had calmed after the spontaneous crying the pain induced cries were collected by running a finger along the sole of the infant's foot.

The cries were analyzed with a computer program (Babycry, Innomess). The program gives initially a data acquisition of up to 20 sec. of crying, from which 2 sec. parts can be chosen for the spectrographic analysis. The program calculates automatically the duration of the cry signals and the mean fundamental frequency. The highest and the lowest points on the spectrograms, i.e. the maximum and minimum fundamental frequency of the cries, were also calculated.

One cry was considered to be the sound produced during one expiratory phase. Ten cries, five spontaneous and five pain induced, were analysed from each infant from the recordings made at the various ages. Five consecutive cries with a duration of at least 0.5 sec were chosen for the analysis. When possible, in pain induced cries, the first five cries after the stimulus were selected for analysis.

The statistical measurements were performed with the SPSS statistical program using the t-test for means and for paired means.

Results

A total of 1020 cries were analyzed, 60 from each of 15 infants, and 40 from 3 infants from whom the recordings at the ages of one week and two months were missing. Ten cries, five spontaneous and five pain induced, were analyzed from each age sample. The mean values were calculated from each set of five cries and these values were used for the statistical analysis of the cry characteristics.

The fundamental frequency for the mean values for spontaneous and pain cries from each infant at various ages is presented in Table 1. The mean value for the spontaneous cries was 465 ± 106 cps and for the pain induced cries 502 ± 134 cps (p < 0.05). However, both high-pitched and low-pitched cries occurred in both groups (Fig. IV). Also the difference between the maximum fundamental frequency of spontaneous and pain cries was significant (p < 0.01). A mean fundamental frequency was noted. The cries had a duration of 1-2 seconds, the shortest cries were noted at birth. The melody contour was in almost all cries (97 %), falling or rising-falling.

Table 1 shows that when the spontaneous and pain cries were compared at the different ages the mean fundamental frequency was at all ages higher in the pain induced cries than in the spontaneous cries. The differences were significant at 3 and 48 hours of age. For the maximum values of the fundamental frequency of pain cries was significantly higher at all ages except birth and 24 hours of age. This was mainly due to an increase of the basic fundamental frequency because only 1% of the cries included a more high pitched shift part.

Figure V shows a spontaneous and a pain cry from a 2-day-old infant; the pain cry had a higher pitch and a shorter duration. In Figure VI both spontaneous and pain cries were high-pitched when the infant started to cry but changed towards the end of the sequence to a normal configuration. The pain cry signals have a higher fundamental and are shorter than the spontaneous cry.

Table 1. Spontaneous and pain induced cries in 15 infants from birth to the age of two months and 3 infants from birth to two weeks of age. Five spontaneous and five pain induced cries were analyzed from each infant at the different ages.

Age	Birth	3 h	24 h	48 h	7-15 d	2-3 m	Total
Number of infants	18	18	18	18	15	15	18
Number of cries	180	180	180	180	150	150	1020
Duration, sec.							
Spontaneous cries	1195 + 1216	1214 + 972	1087 + 520	1539 + 898	1323 + 1322	1333 + 688	1283 ± 995
Pain induced cries	1013 + 586	1385 + 1077	1386 + 883	1539 + 977	1378 + 787	1398 + 682	1349 ± 818
Mean fundamental frequency, Hz							
Spontaneous cries	471 + 96	452 + 119	483 + 103	454 + 108	448 + 93	476 + 121	465 ± 106
Pain induced cries	477 + 107	504*** + 105	496* + 114	518 + 132	479 + 108	561* + 216	502 ± 134
Maximum fundamental frequency, Hz							
Spontaneous cries	557 + 139	514 + 143	557 + 117	523 + 122	531 + 137	542 + 149	539 ± 133
Pain induced cries	583 + 163	615** + 182	569 + 146	631* + 188	60**5 + 164	663* + 283	600** ± 196
Minimum fundamental frequency, Hz							
Spontaneous cries	352 + 89	379 + 118	384 + 104	376 + 121	383 + 103	389 + 116	385 ± 110
Pain induced cries	399* + 96	401 + 120	428* + 111	396 + 122	387 + 107	431 + 186	391 ± 123

* $p < 0.05$

** $p < 0.01$

*** $p < 0.001$

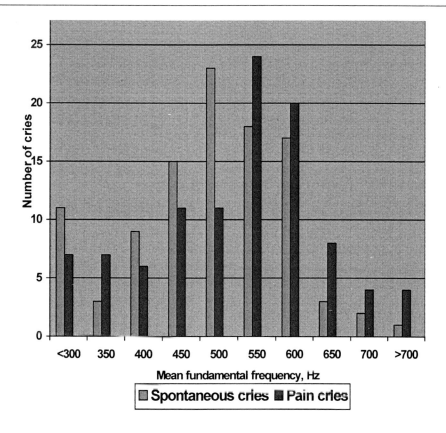

Figure IV. Mean fundamental frequency of spontaneous and pain induced cries in 18 one day to two month old. The results present 102 different recordings of spontaneous and 102 recordings of pain cry. From each recording a mean of 5 cries was analyzed and displayed in the figure.

Discussion

There were no significant differences noted between the spontaneous cries from birth to the age of two months. The same was true for the provoked cries. However, when the spontaneous cries were compared with the provoked ones significant differences were noted both concerning the mean and the maximum fundamental frequency. The pain induced cries had a higher fundamental frequency.

The provoked cries usually started abruptly indicating that the babies felt discomfort or pain. These cries often sounded more urgent and high-pitched than the spontaneous cries. This was also confirmed by the sound spectrographic analysis. However, the differences between the fundamental frequency characteristics between spontaneous and pain cries were more similar than beforehand was expected. This might be due to the fact that the spontaneous and pain cries actually are very similar, or that the stimulus was not painful enough to change the cry considerably, or because from each infant the mean of several cries were used for the statistical analysis. Runefors et al. (2000) have reported that effects of pain stimulus rapidly revert to a normal basic configuration. They analyzed in newborn infants the first five cries after blood sampling and found that the first cry signal after a pain stimulus was longer and more high pitched than the five consecutive ones. However the differences were significant only when the first cry was compared with the fifth one in the cry sequence. Neither Thodén and Koivisto (1980) noticed any significant differences in the three first cries after a pinch. Thus, the differences in our study between spontaneous and pain cries would apparently not have changed considerably if only the first cry after the pain stimulus would have been selected for analysis. Lind & Wermke (2002) analysed with sound spectrography the cries of one infant from birth to the age of three months, and found no significant differences in fundamental frequency characteristics.

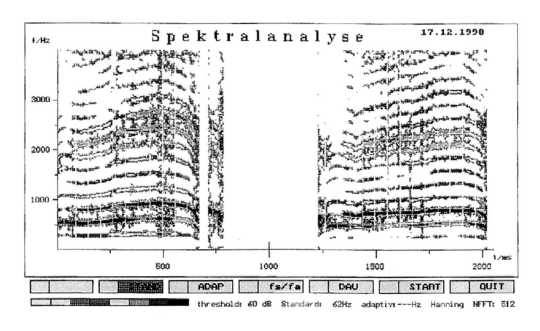

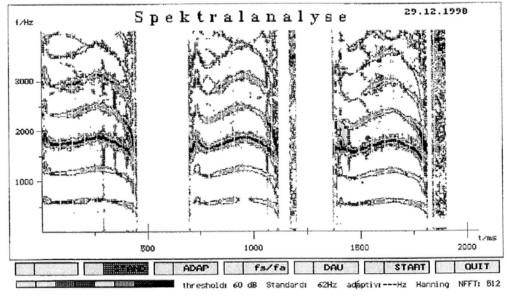

Figure V. A typical example of a spontaneous (upper curve) and a pain induced cry (lower curve) from a newborn full term infant. The pain cry is shorter and has a higher pitch.

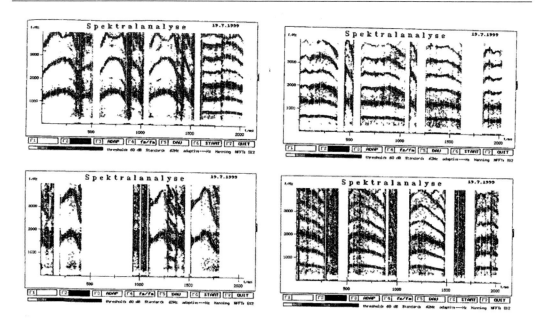

Figure VI. Spontaneous (upper curve) and pain induced (lower curve) cries of a two-week-old healthy infant. In both spontaneous and pain cries the start of crying is high-pitched and changes to a normal configuration at the end of the phonation. The pain cries have a higher pitch and are shorter than the spontaneous cries.

The present study reporting cry results from birth to two month of both spontaneous and provoked cries aims to contribute to the understanding of crying of healthy newborns. The results indicate that increasing age did not change the cry pattern but that the pain induced cries were more high-pitched. Consequently, when a spontaneous and a pain cry from the same baby are heard after each other a guess would be that the more high-pitched cry was caused by pain. However, as seen in Figure IV spontaneous cries might be high pitched as well as pain cries low-pitched. So, when only a spontaneous or a pain cry is heard it is obvious that it is not possible to specify which type of cry was produced. This gives support to the claim that infant crying is a graded signal and that the spontaneous and pain cries closely resemble each other. Neither Murry et al. (1977) found significant differences in hunger and pain cries and hypothesized that if cry types could be differentiated, the fundamental frequency appeared not to be a significant marker for this judgment. With more intensive pain stimulus, the effect on crying might be greater. Porter et al. (1986) that. during circumcision the cry cycles became shorter and briefer, more intense, were longer and had a higher pitch and less distinct harmonics.

CRYING OF NEWBORN INFANTS WITH DIFFERENT DISEASES

Crying of the human infant is a complex phenomenon and occurs during the expiratory phase of respiration and includes the production of sound of the vocal folds. Crying presupposes functioning of the respiratory, laryngeal and supralaryngeal muscles. The CNS controls the capacity, stability and co-ordination of the movements of these muscles. Hence it is assumed that crying provides information about how the CNS is functioning.

Most developmental disabilities result from a malformation or injury to the brain. The severity of involvement may range from mild to severe and depends on the anatomic location of the lesions. Many pediatric textbooks have mentioned that the crying of infants changes with the severity of the disease and that a high-pitched cry is a most indicative feature of an abnormal cry. Illingworth (1955) stated that "a clinician recognizes the hoarse, gruff cry of cretitinism, the hoarse cry of laryngitis, the shrill cry of hydrocephalus, meningitis, or cerebral irritability, the grunting cry of pneumonia, the feeble cry of amyotonia or a severely debilitated infant, and the whimper of a seriously ill child".

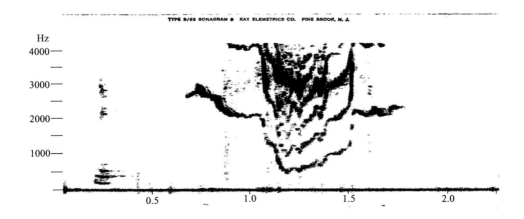

Figure VII. A high-pitched cry with a falling-rising melody contour of a 4-month-old infant with bacterial meningitis.

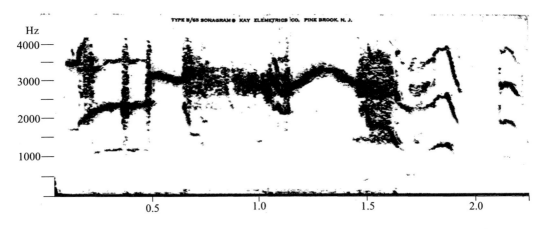

Figure VIII. Unstable high-pitched cry of a 3-week-old infant with severe asphyxia and brain damage.

Crying in infants with obvious brain damage often have cries that sound abnormal and the most striking feature is the fundamental frequency. The cries are high-pitched and show furthermore a variety of abnormal cry features, whether measured spectrographically or digitally. Spectrographic cry studies have comprised cry analysis of infants with various disorders, as meningitis (Michelsson et al. 1977), hydrocephalus (Michelsson et al. 1984), asphyxia (Michelsson 1971, Michelsson et al. 1977a), congenital abnormalities (Michelsson et al. 1975, Raes et al. 1982) chromosomal aberrations (Lind et al. 1970, Michelsson et al. 1980) and other disorders affecting the brain (Hirschberg & Szende 1982, Lester & Dreker 1989, Corwin et al. 1992), hypothyroidism (Michelsson & Sirviö 1976), and metabolic disturbances (Koivisto et al. 1974, Juntunen et al. 1978, Koivisto 1987). In all impaired infants the fundamental frequency has been abnormal when compared with normal crying. Especially high-pitched cries have been linked with cerebral involvement (Fig. VII-IX). Furthermore, other characteristics seldom seen in normal crying, as biphonation, furcation and gliding have been more common in cries of impaired infants. In the Cri-du-chat syndrome the cry was high-pitched and monotonous (Fig. X), while in infants with hypothyroidism the cry was low-pitched (Fig. XI). In abnormal infants, also the mean latency between pain stimulus and onset of crying has been longer and a greater stimuli to produce one minute crying was needed (Karelitz & Fisichelli 1962, Fisichelli & Karelitz 1963, Karelitz 1963).

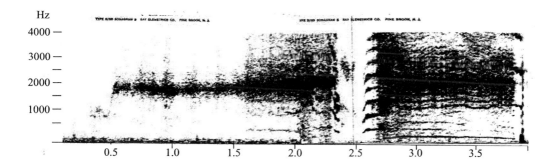

Figure IX. A cry of a two-week-old infant with herpes simples virus encephalitis, including both voiced and voiceless parts and noise concentration.

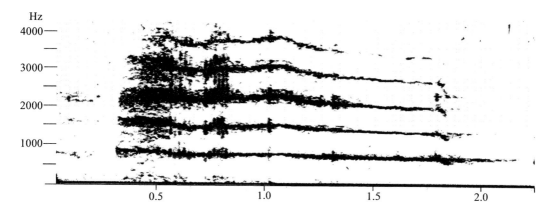

Figure X. A cry of a three-month-old infant with cri-du-chat syndrome. The cry is high-pitched with a rather flat melody contour.

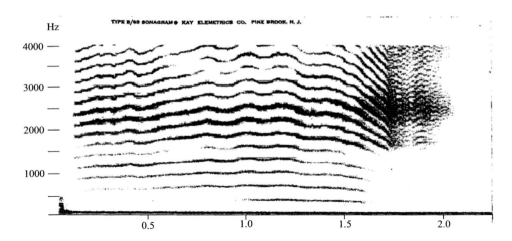

Figure XI. A low-pitched cry of a one-month-old infant with hypothyroidism.

Changes in the spectrographic cry characteristics have not, however, been clearly linked to specific types of brain damage. Some cries are extremely high-pitched and irregular but the spectrograms give no clue to possible reason for the odd cry features though in cries of infants with some specific disorders typical cry characteristics have been noted. In infants with exposure to marijuana the cries were shorter with a higher percentage of dysphonation (Lester & Dreker 1989). Also in newborn infants with herpes simplex virus encephalitis the cries were significantly more dysphonated and included more noise concentration than seen in cries of infants with other types of cerebral involvement (Fig. IX, Pettay et al. 1977). With the present knowledge, though these features were very common, it is impossible to conclude for certain if they really are specific for herpes simplex virus infection.

Studies on cry production imply that the vagal system is the primary sourse of variations in cry acoustics. Both respiratory and laryngeal functioning should be affected by changes in activity of the right branch of the vagus. Green at al (2000) have concluded, based on previous studies, that deficits in either brain stem functioning or higher brain functioning may affect vagal control of the cry, producing abnormalities in cry acoustics, especially fundamental frequency.

PERCEPTION OF CRYING

In auditory investigations, Wasz-Höckert at et al. (1964) found differences in birth, pain, hunger and pleasure vocalizations. The study has, however, been criticized because the listeners were in advance given the types of cries they were going to judge and might therefore have guessed which ones sounded most like pain, hunger or birth (Gustafson et al. 2000). Others have also claimed that acoustic characteristics of the cries of the normal infant appear to carry little perceptional information to the mother with respect to the cry evoking situation and that the cry only acts to alert the mother (Miller et al. 1974)

Several studies have reported that mothers can recognize the crying of their own infant on the basis of cries (Formby 1967, Green & Gustafson 1983, Valanne et al. 1967). Also many fathers and nonparents adults learn to recognize individual infants on the basis of cries (Sagi 1981, Green & Gustafson 1983, Gustafson et al. 1984)

Beyond alerting the caregiver the sounds of crying seem to convey more accurate information about level of distress and urgency of need than about specific causes. Lester & Boukydis (1992) and Zeskind et al. (1985) state that crying is a graded rather than a discrete signal. While in discrete signals the sound changes with the cause of crying a graded signal does not carry a unique symbolic meaning for receivers. They vary in duration and intensity across contexts but do not obviate the possibility of accurate interpretation. This does, however, not mean that differences in cry characteristics are not identifiable. A pain cry can sometimes reliably be distinguished from other types of cries because of an abrupt urgent start and a higher pitch. Important factors in cry perception are the fundamental frequency, sound quality and duration (Gustafson & Green 1989).

Lester et al. (1995) reported that mothers have negative perceptions of infants with high pitched cries. Frodi and Senchak (1990) examined responses to cries of atypical infants and found that the highest-pitched cries from asphyxiated infants with or without brain damage elicited more negative responses from listeners than the lowest-pitched normal cries.

PERSISTENT INFANT CRYING

The incidence of excessive crying in small infants is about 15-20 % (Illingworth 1955, Hide & Guyer 1982). In a study from England, St James-Roberts (1991) reported that during the first three months 20% of mothers were upset by their baby's crying and 11% had sought professional help. Excessive crying is usually called infantile colic and begins to increase at two weeks after birth, reaches its peak during the second month and subsides by the fourth month. Excessive crying is considered to be at one end of a continuum that includes sounds of lesser urgency often called fussing or fretting (Barr et al. 2000).

In the 1950s Wessel et al.(1954) and Illingworth (1955) defined colic as unexplained paroxysm of crying (violent screaming attacks) or fussing occurring usually between 6 PM and 10 PM, beginning between 3 days and 3 weeks of age, subsiding by 13-16 weeks. According to Wessel et al.(1954) a diagnosis of colic presupposes crying lasting for at least 3 hours a day for a minimum of three days a week for three weeks. Several studies have confirmed that healthy infants may cry for reasons that are far from clear for 2-3 hours per day at six weeks of age with a peak in the afternoon or evening (St James-Roberts & Halil 1991). In diagnosing colic, also other criteria have been used, as sudden onset of crying, perceived high pitch "pain" quality, resistance to soothing and behavior characteristics of hypertonia (Lester et al. 1990). The infant has been considered to have pain because he flexes his legs over the abdomen, has grimaces and is flushed. Crying is also said to be unpredictable and begin and end without warning (Lehtonen et al. 2000).

In clinical settings, a diagnosis of colic is often arbitrary and depends on the mothers' perception of her baby's crying. Some mothers are worried about the slightest amount of crying while others don't feel it problematic even if the baby cries excessively. It has, however, been reported that babies to parents seeking professional help for problematic crying behavior actually cry more than average (St James-Roberts et al. 1993).

For decades, clinicians have argued about the causes of colic. Colic has been considered to be caused by pain in the gastrointestinal tract because of protein allergy, abnormal peristalsis, excessive gas, increased sensitivity (neurolability or hypertonicity), maternal anxiety and tension, and infant temperament (Adams & Davidson 1987, Hewson et al. 1987). Recently Barr and Gunnar (2000) stated that colic is a "manifestation of individual differences is otherwise normal infants".

In a comprehensive study, Lehtonen et al. (2000) concluded, that only 5 % or less of babies crying excessively may have an organic cause. They searched Medline from 1966 to 1998 and PsychInfo from 1967-1997 to evaluate which organic causes have been found to explain excessive crying and if infants with an organic diseases could be identified. On the basis of what could be found in the articles they concluded that the evidence for an organic cause was strong, moderate or weak. Strong evidence was found for cows milk intolerance, isolated fructose intolerance, maternal drug effects, infantile migraine and anomalous left coronary artery. Moderate evidence was found for reflux oesophagitis and shaken baby syndrome. Weak evidence was found for lactose intolerance, eye pathology, central nervous system abnormalities and urinary tract infections.

Lehtonen and al. (2000) also searched for clinical clues to differentiate crying episodes caused by organic diseases but these were rare. They concluded that an organic disease may be present when the cry is high pitched, does not present a diurnal pattern and other signs and symptoms are present as well, as vomiting or diarrhea.

Persistent crying improves over time. Specific interventions have been no better than reassurance and support alone in decreasing daily hours of crying and maternal anxiety (Parkin et al. 1993). However, rapid response to crying was associated with significantly less crying overall (Baildam et al. 1995). By counseling parents they become more capable of meeting their infants needs and the amount of daily crying decreases significantly (Taubman 1984).

A STUDY OF MOTHERS' PERCEPTION OF CRYING

A study of perception of and feelings towards their babies crying was undertaken in Finland and South America (Colombia and Chile) in order to evaluate the amount of and feelings towards crying in two different continents. The results from Colombia have partly been presented previously (Rinne & al. 1990), the other results have not been reported earlier.

Material and Methods

The material was assembled in Finland in 1987-88 (K Michelsson), in Colombia in 1988 (AH Saenz) and in Chile in 1990-91 (H Todd de Barra). The series consisted of 378 infants under the age of one year; 281 were from Finland, 43 from Colombian and 54 from Chile. The mothers with children under the age of one year received an inquiry with questions about how and how much their baby cried and how crying was perceived. The mothers were also asked about their responses to crying and if they had felt a need of support because of their infants crying spells. Additionally, the parents were asked to fill in a 24-hour schedule indicating when the infant slept and was awake, as well as periods of feeding and crying.

The statistics were calculated with the BMDP statistical software, Chi-square and ANOVA.

Results

There were 55 % girls in the Finnish and 36 % in the South American material. All infants were healthy at birth and born fullterm with Apgar scores 8-10. There were no significant differences concerning the duration of breast feeding. The mean weight at the time of the study was 7.0 kg in Finland and 7.1 kg in South America, the mean lenth 65 cm in both countries.

Of the Finnish babies 47 % and of the South American babies 44 % were first born. The mean age for the mothers was 28 years in Finland and 26 years in South America. The mean age for the fathers was 30 years in both groups. The parents from South America were significantly from a lower social group than those from Finland. While 56% of the Finnish fathers belonged to well educated professionals including farmers, this was the case in 37% in South America (p < 0.001).

While 25 % of Finnish fathers helped with minding the baby during night time, only 2 % of fathers did this in Colombia. The percentage was 26% in Chile. In South America, in 4 % someone else than the parents took care of the baby at night. In Finland this was the case in one of the 281 families. During the day time, however, the mother had help in minding the baby in 26 % in South American families, and in only 1 % in Finland.

Table 2 presents the reports of the mothers´reports of baby crying in the two groups. About 14% of the mothers in both Finland and South America claimed that their baby cried much. The mean crying time was 1.4 hours in Finland and 1.7 hours in South America for infants under the age of 6 months. For the 6-12 month old infants the mean crying time was 1.3 hours for Finnish and 1.4 hours for South American babies. Babies under the age of 3 months cried more than the older ones (Fig XII). A peak of evening crying was noted in all age groups and was most pronounced among the youngest infants.

The mean sleeping time was 14-15 hours for babies under the age of 3 months in both continents, and decreased to 12-13 hours for infants with an age of 9 months or older. However, great individual differences were noted, and the infants in the youngest age group were said to sleep between 12 and 20 hours daily, and the oldest 9-16 hours daily. Figure XI shows a great similarity between the crying and sleeping patterns in Finnish and South American infants.

If crying more than 3 hours per day was used as a definition of infantile colic, then in the study 12 % of the Finnish and 26 % of the South American 0-3-month-old infants could be defined as colichy. A peak of crying was noted between 6 PM and 10 PM, as seen in Figure XI. Crying more than 3 hours daily was reported for babies 4 months or older in 3 % in Finland and 13 % in South America. About 3-4 % found their baby´s crying irritating.

In South America the mothers let their babies cry without intervention more often than the Finnish mothers. While 97 % of mothers in Finland reported that they always picked up the crying baby this was true in 74 % in South America.

Of the mothers, 18 % in Finland and 43 % in South America claimed that they would have wanted more help and support because of their babies crying spells (Table 3). These mothers reported that their babies cried more often than those not wanting help and that the excessive crying occurred especially during night time. Ten percent of the help wanting mothers were irritated and frightened and had feelings of failure. There was a great difference between the need of help in Chile and Colombia. While 59 % of the Chilean mothers wanted support this was the case for 24 % in Colombia.

Table 2. Mothers feelings towards and responses towards crying (in %) in 281 Finnish and 97 South American 0-12-month-old infants.

	Finland (n = 281)		South America (n = 97)		
	Never / Sometimes	Often / Very often	Never / Sometimes	Often / Very often	p
Amount of crying					
Cries much	86.1	13.9	86.3	13.7	
Cries a long time	98.6	1.4	92.5	7.5	**
In the morning	92.5	7.5	86.5	13.5	
During daytime	93.9	6.1	90.6	9.4	
In the evening	61.9	38.1	88.5	11.5	***
During night	92.8	7.2	84.4	15.6	*
Perception of crying					
High-pitched	95.6	4.4	90.2	9.8	**
Powerful	76.1	23.9	66.7	33.3	
Angry	94.1	5.9	81.7	18.3	***
Summoning	46.7	53.3	53.8	46.2	
Complaining	90.9	9.1	96.7	3.3	*
Feelings toward crying					
Irritates	95.7	4.3	96.7	3.3	
Exasperates	98.9	1.1	97.8	2.2	
Feeling of failure	96.8	3.2	93.4	6.6	
Management of crying					
Takes up baby	03.2	96.8	26.0	74.0	***
Gives a pacifier	60.4	39.6	74.7	25.3	***
Gives food	78.2	21.8	78.7	21.3	
Leaves to cry	96.4	3.6	93.4	6.6	
Cause of crying					
There is a cause	3.9	96.1	31.6	68.4	***
Cry is meaningful	6.2	93.8	21.1	78.9	***
Cry is natural	9.1	90.9	34.8	65.2	***
Expresses needs	11.5	88.5	15.8	84.2	
Hunger cry is recognizable	15.9	84.1	25.6	74.4	*

*   < 0.05
**   < 0.01
***   < 0.001

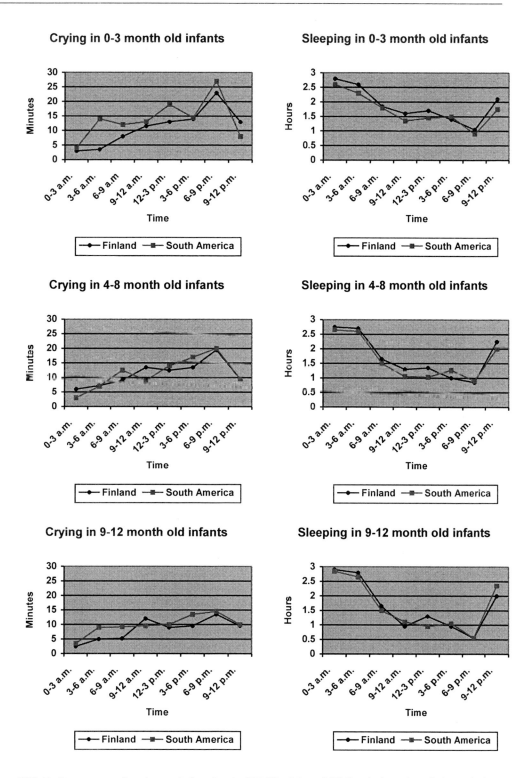

Figure XII. Daily amount of crying and sleeping in 281 Finnish and 97 South American infants during the first year of life.

Discussion

Crying can lead to positive response and increase the mother's need to care for the baby, as also found in this study. In Finland, the babies were almost always soothed and picked up when crying. In South America, crying was said to be a natural phenomenon and the babies were sometimes left to cry. This might be reflected by the higher prevalence of crying among 0-3 month old infants (Fig. XI). The tolerance against crying can, however, decrease if the baby cries a lot, and the crying is experienced as more and more irritating. The results give support to this assumption, as those mothers who wanted help because of their baby's crying spells were more angry, irritated, frightened and exasperated by the crying than those who not were in need of help. The mother became anxious and had feelings of failure.

The results indicate that mothers in both continents would benefit from more information and support. There was not only a need for medical advice but also a need of help with minding the baby and the household because of tiredness of the mothers. Surprisingly, medical advice was also needed in Finland where regular check-ups at baby clinics are well organized. This indicates that the infants might be difficult to soothe with any kind of help or a lack of knowledge among professionals about what advice should be given to calm babies and help families with excessively crying babies. Need of help with the daily care of baby and household was also wished-for not only in Finland but also in South America where in the daytime often another adult was helping with the household.

Table 3. The not help and help needing mothers' perception
of crying occurring often and very often on a five point scale in 281 Finnish and 97
South American of 2 month-old-infants.

	Mothers not needing help (n=285)	Mothers who wanted help (n=93)	p
Amount of crying			
Cries much	9.3	28.4	***
During the night	4.3	25.8	***
During meals	3.5	9.0	*
Perception of crying			
High-pitched	4.0	11.2	**
Powerful	21.9	40.4	***
Angry	7.0	14.6	*
Complaining	5.9	13.5	*
Lasts a long time	0.7	10.0	***
There is a cause for crying	90.5	84.4	
Feelings towards crying			
Irritates	2.5	9.1	**
Frightens	2.5	9.1	**
Exasperates	22.2	39.1	**
Feeling of failure	1.8	10.2	***
Awakes a desire to comfort	94.7	86.4	**

*   < 0.05
**   < 0.01
***   < 0.001

Early information about baby crying could act as a preventive and avoid irritability in families. The information should be available at maternity hospitals with a notification that allbabies cry sometimes and that a mean crying time of small infants is about 1.5 hours daily,and that crying time increases during the first week of life. It could also be important to point out individual differences in infants' voices. Some might have a peculiar high-pitched cry,, which is more irritating than the low-pitched. It may be possible that there exists several simultaneous reasons for the crying episodes. If some of the causes can be eliminated by support and help it may happen, that the baby can cope with the rest and stop crying. If a baby is soothed when crying he most probably develops other means of behavior apart from crying for communication with the adults.

CONCLUSION

All infants cry sometimes and it is their best way to achieve attention, consolidation and care. Sometimes, the crying can have opposite effect. Some parents feel irritated by the slightest amount of crying while others do not mind repeated crying bursts. Excessive crying can lead to frustration, neglect and maltreatment (Frodi 1985).

Infantile crying, called colic, increases from two weeks of age up to two months of age and subsides after three months of age. In only a minority of cases the crying has an organic cause, in most cases crying occurs in otherwise normal infants. A study of the amount and perception of crying in 281 infants in Finland and 97 infants in South America (Chile and Colombia) was analyzed based on parents' diaries. The results indicate that the crying and sleeping episodes in infants in both continents were similar and that a peak of crying occurred in the evening in infants under the age of three months. Infants under the age of six months cried for 1.4 hours per day in Finland and for 1.7 hours per day in South America. Crying for more than three hours per day in infants under the age of three months was observed in 12 % in Finland and 26 % in South America.

During the last decades discussions have emerged that the crying of newborn and small infants is a graded rather than a discrete signal. Discrete cries vary depending on the cause while graded indicate the degree of distress but not the cause. This does not mean that the cries are not identifiable. For instance, a pain cry is often, when compared with spontaneous crying, more urgent and high-pitched. In order to evaluate the possible differences in spontaneous and pain induced crying was 1020 cries analyzed from 18 infants recorded at six different occasions from birth to the age of two months of age. The results indicate a significantly higher pitch in pain induced than in spontaneous cries though the differences at the various ages often were marginal. Age had no influence on the fundamental frequency in neither spontaneous nor pain induced cries.

Sound spectrography has been used for objective analysis of the cry sound. A cry has been defined as the sound uttered between two inspirations. The first cry in pain induced cries is the sound from the pain stimulus to the first inspiration. The paper presents definitions for the different cry characteristics used in sound spectrographic analysis. Cries of normal infants have a mean fundamental frequency of 400-600 Hz. The crying between two inspirations is most often continuous and has a falling or rising-falling melody contour. Sometimes the cries includes high-pitched parts, hyperphonation.

Crying of sick and developmentally impaired infants is different from normal crying. The most abnormal cries have been found in infants with central nervous system (CNS) involvement. The cry has been more high-pitched and also other abnormal cry characteristics have been noted. However, some specific cry characteristics have not been linked with a specific disorder of the CNS, if not for instance the very common noise concentration in cries of infants with herpes virus encephalitis could point to some specificity for some disorders. A quite different low-pitched hoarse crying has been found in infants with hypothyroidism and Down's syndrome. Much research is still needed to clarify the associations between cry characteristics and various diseases.

Previous studies of cry characteristics in the newborn infant were aimed to determine if cry analysis could be successful in the early detection of the infant at risk for developmental difficulties and especially provide suspicion of CNS disorders. Studies of cry characteristics in infants with a variety of disorders was therefore undertaken. An abnormal cry may be a transient sign but may also indicate a more serious underlying problem. However, much research is still needed before it can be verified if some specific cry characteristic can be linked to a specific disease.

REFERENCES

Adams, L.M. & Davidson, M. (1987). Present concepts of infant colic. *Pediatric Annals 16*, 817-820.

Aldrich, C. A., Sung C. & Knop C. (1945). The crying of newly born babies. III. The early period at home. *Journal of Pediatrics 27*, 428-435.

Baildam, E. M., Hollier, V. F., Ward, B. S., Bannister, R.P., Bamford, F.N. & Moore. W. M. O. (1995). Duration and pattern of crying in the first year of life. *Developmental Medicine and Child Neurology, 37*, 345-353.

Barr, R. G. & Gunnar, M. (2000). Colic: the 'transient responsivity' hypothesis. In R. G. Rarr, B. Hopkins, & J. A. James (Eds.). *Crying as a sign, a symptom, & a signal. Clinics in Developmental Medicine* No. 152. Cambridge: Cambridge University Press.

Blinick, G., Tavolga, W. N. & Antopol, W. (1971). Variations in birth cries of newborn infants from narcotic addicted and normal mothers. *American Journal of Obstetrics and Gynecology, 110*, 341-348.

Brazelton, T. B. (1962). Crying in infancy. *Pediatrics, 19*, 579-588.

Corwin, M.J., Lester, B.M., Sepkoski, C., McLauglin, S., Kayne, H., Golub, H. L. (1992). Effects of in utero cocaine exposure on newborn acoustical cry chartacteristics. *Pediatrics, 89*,1199-1203.

Darwin, C. (1855). *The expressions of emotion in man and animals*. New York: Philosophical Library.

Fairbanks, G. (1942). An acoustic study of the pitch of infant hunger wails. *Child Development, 13*, 227-

Fisichelli, V. R. & Karelitz, S. (1963). The cry latencies of normal infants and those with brain damage. *Journal of Pediatrics, 62*, 724-734.

Fisichelli, V. R., Karelitz, S., Fisichelli, R.M. & Cooper, J. (1974). The course of induced crying activity in the first year of life. *Pediatric Research, 8*, 921-928.

Flatau, T. S. & Gutzmann, H. (1906). Die Stimme des Säuglings. *Archives Laryngology and Rhinology, 18,* 139-156.

Formby, D. (1967). Maternal recognition of infant's cry. *Developmental Medicine and Child Neurology, 9,* 293-298.

Frodi, A. (1985). When empathy fails: aversive infant crying and child abuse. In B. M. Lester, & C. F. Boukydis (Eds.), *Infant crying: theoretical and research perspectives* (pp 263-278). New York: Plenum.

Frodi, B. F. & Senchak, M. (1990). Verbal and behavioral responsiveness to the cries of atypical infants. Child Development, 61, 76-84.

Gardiner, W. (1838). *The music of nature.* Boston: Wilkings & Carter.

Gleiss, J. & Höhn W. (1968). Das Verhalten beim Schreien nach konstanter Schmertzreizung atemgesunder und atemgestörter Neugeborenen. *Deutsche Zeitschrift für Nervenheilkunde, 194,* 311-317.

Golub, H. L. & Corwin, M. J. (1985). A physioacoustic model of the infant cry. In B. M. Lester, & C. F Z. Boukydis (Eds.), *Infant Crying. Theoretical and Research Perspectives* (pp. 59-82). New York: Plenum Press.

Green, J. A. & Gustafson, G. E. (1983). Individual recognition of human infants on the basis of cries alone. *Developmental Psychobiology, 16,* 485-493.

Green, J. A., Irwin, J. R., Gustafson, G. E. (2000). Acoustic cry analysis, neonatal status and long-term developmental outcomes; in R. G. Barr, B. Hopkins, & J. A. Green J. A. (Eds.), *Crying as a sign, a symptom & a signal* (pp 137-156). Clinics in Developmental Medicine No. 152, London: Mac Keith Press.

Gustafson, G. E. & Green, J. A. (1989). On the importance of fundamental frequency and other acoustic features in cry perception and infant development. *Child Development, 60,* 772-780.

Gustafson, G. E., Green, J. A. & Tomic, T. (1984). Acoustic correlates of individuality in the cries of human infants. *Developmental Psychobiology, 17,* 311-324.

Gustafson, G. E., Wood, R. M. & Green, J. A. (2000). Can we hear the causes of infants' crying. In R. G. Barr, B. Hopkins, & J. A. Green (Eds.), *Crying as a sign, a symptom & a signal.* Clinics in Developmental Medicine No. 152, pp. 8-22. London: Mac Keith Press.

Hewson, P., Oberklaid, F. & Menahem, S. (1987). Infant colic, distress, and crying. *Clinical Pediatrics, 26,* 69-75.

Hide, D. W. & Guyer, B. M. (1982). Prevalence of infantile colic. *Archives of Diseases of Childhood, 57,* 559-560.

Hirschberg, J. (1967). Aphysiologische Stimmbildungen im Säuglingsalter. *Folia Phoniatrica, 18,* 269-279.

Hirschberg, J. (1990). The value of acoustic analysis of pathological infant cry and breathing noise in everyday practice. *Early Child Development and Care, 65,* 57-69.

Hirschberg, J. & Szende, T. (1985). *Pathological cry, stridor and cough in infants.* Budapest: Akadémiai Kiadó.

Hopkins, B., Green, J. A. (2000) (Eds): Crying as a Sign, a Symptom & a Signal. Clinics Develop Medic No. 152, Mac Keith Press, London, 2000, pp 8-22.

Illingworth, R. S. (1955). Crying in infants and children. *British Medical Journal I* :75-78

Irwin, O. (1948). Infant speech. Development of vowel sounds. *Journal of Speech and Hearing Disorders, 13,* 31-34.

Irwin, O. C. & Curry, T. (1941). Vowel elements in the crying vocalization of infants under ten days of age. *Child Development, 12,* 99.

Irwin, O. C. & Chen, H. P. (1943). Speech sound elements during the first year of life. J Speech Dis 8, 109-

Juntunen, K., Sirviö, P. & Michelsson, K. (1978). Cry analysis of infants with severe malnutrition. *European Journal of Pediatrics, 128,* 241-246.

Karelitz, S. & Fisichelli, V. R. (1962). The cry thresholds of normal infants and those with brain damage. *Journal of Pediatrics, 61,* 679-685.

Kittel, G. & Hecht, L. (1977). Der erste Schrei - frequenzanalytische Untersuchungen. *Sprache - Stimme - Gehör, 1,* 151-155.

Koivisto, M. (1987). Cry analysis in infants with Rh haemolytic disease. *Acta Paediatrica Scandinavica, suppl. 335.*

Lehtonen, L., Gormally, S. & Barr, R. G. (2000). 'Clinical pies' for etiology and outcome in infants presenting with early increased crying. In R. G. Barr, B. Hopkins, & J. A. Green (Eds.), *Crying as a sign, a symptom & a signal.* Clinics in Developmental Medicine No. 152, pp. 67-95. London: Mac Keith Press.

Lester, B. M. (1976). Spectrum analysis of the cry sounds of well-nourished and malnourished infants. *Child Development, 47,* 237-241.

Lester, B. M. (1987). Prediction of developmental outcome from acoustic cry analysis in term and preterm infants. *Pediatrics, 80,* 529-524.

Lester, B. M., Boukydis, C. F. Z., Garcia-Coll, C. T. & Hole, W. T. (1990). Symposium on infantile colic: Introduction. *Infant mental health journal, 11,* 320-333.

Lester, B. M. & Boukydis, F. Z. (1992). No language but a cry. In H. Papousek, U. Jürgens, & M. Papousek (Eds.). *Nonverbal vocal communication. Comparative & developmental approaches.* (pp. 145-173). Cambrudge: Cambridge University Press.

Lester, B. M. & Drekerm M. (1989). Effects of marijuana use during pregnancy on newborn cry. *Child Development, 60,* 765-771.

Lester, B. M., Zeskind, P. (1978). Brazelton scale and physical size correlates of neonatal cry features. *Infant Behavior and Development, 1,* 393-402.

Lester, B. M., Boukydis, C. F. Z., Garcia-Coll C. T., Hole, W. T. & Peucker, M. (1992). Infantile colic: acoustic cry characterisctics, maternal perception of cry, and temperament. *Infant Behavior and Development, 15,* 15-26.

Lester, B. M., Boukydis, Z., Garcia-Coll, C. t., Peucker, M., McGrath, M. M., Vohr, B. R., Brem, F. & Oh, W. (1995). Developmental outcome as a function of the goodness of fit between the infant´s cry characteristics and the mother´s perception of her infant´s cry. *Pediatrics, 95,* 51-57.

Lind, K. & Wermke, K. (2002). Development of the vocal fundamental frequency of spontaneous cries during the first 3 months. *International Journal of pediatric otolaryngology, 64,* 97-104.

Koiviso, M. (1987). Cry analysis in infants with Rh haemolytic disease. *Acta Paediatrica Scandinavica,* suppl. 335, pp. 1-73.

Koivisto, M., Michelsson, K., Sirviö, P. & Wasz-Höckert, O. (1974). Spectrographic analysis of pain cry of hypoglycaemia in newborn infants. *New Delhi: XIV International Congress of Pediatrics, 1,* 250.

Lester, B. M. (1987). Developmental outcome prediction from acoustic cry analysis in term and preterm infants. *Pediatrics, 80,* 529-534.

Lester, B. M. & Boukydis, C. F. Z. (1992). No language nut a cry. In H. Papousek (Ed.), *Origin and development of non-verbal communication*, pp. 145-173. Cambridge: Cambridge University Press.

Lester, B. M., Boukydis, B. R., Garcia-Coll, C. T., Peucker, M., McGrath, M. M., Vohr, B. R., Brem, F. & Oh, W. (1995). Developmental outcome as a function of the goodness of fit between the infant's characteristics and the mother's perception of her infant's cry. *Pediatrics 95*, 51-557.

Lind, J., Vuorenkoski, V., Rosberg, G., Partanen, T. J. & Wasz-Höckert, O. (1970). Spectrographic analysis of vocal response to pain stimuli in infants with Down's syndrome. *Developmental Medicine and Child Neurology, 12*, 478-486.

Long, E. C. & Hull, W. E. (1961). Respiratory volume flow in the crying newborn infant. *Pediatrics, 27*, 373-

Lüdge, W. & Gibs, P. (1989). Microcomputer-aided studies of cry jitter uttered by newborn children based upon high-resolution analysis of fundamental frequencies. *Computer Methods Programs in Biomedicine, 28*, 151-156.

Lüdge, W. & Rothgänger, H. (1990). Early diagnosis of CNS disturbances from computer analysis on infant cries. A new method of fundamental frequency jitter computation with high resolution in frequency and time. *Early Child Development and Care*, 65, 83-90.

Lynip, A. (1951). The use of magnetic devices in the collection and analysis of the preverbal utterances of an infant. *Gen Psychol Monogr, 44*, 221-262.

Michelsson, K. (1971). Cry analyses of symptomless low birth weight neonates and of asphyxiated newborn infants. *Acta Paediatrica Scandinavica, suppl. 216*, 1-45.

Michelsson, K. (1980). Cry characteristics in sound spectrographic cry analysis. In T. Murry, & J. Murry (Eds), *Infant Communication: Cry and Early Speech* (pp. 85-105). Houston: College Hill Press.

Michelsson, K. & Sirviö, P. (1976). Cry analysis in congenital hypothyroidism. *Folia Phoniatrica, 26*, 40-47.

Michelsson, K., Eklund, K., Leppänen, P. & Lyytinen, H. (2002). Cry characteristics of 172 healthy newborn infants. *Folia Phoniatrica and Logopaedica, 54*, 190-200.

Michelsson, K., Järvenpää, A-L. & Rinne, A. (1983). Sound spectrographic analysis of pain cry in preterm infants. *Early Human Development, 8*, 141-149.

Michelsson, K. Kaskinen, H. Aulanko, R. & Rinne, A. (1984). A sound spectrographic cry analysis of infants with hydrocephalus. *Acta Paediatrica Scandinavica, 73*, 65-68.

Michelson, K., Sirviö, P. & Wasz-Höckert, O. (1977a). Pain cry in full-term asphyxiated newborn infants correlated with late findings. *Acta Padiatica Scandinavica, 66*, 611-616.

Michelsson, K., Sirviö, P. & Wasz-Höckert, O. (1977b). Sound spectrographic cry analysis of infants with bacterial meningitis. *Developmental Medicine and Child Neurology, 19*, 309-315.

Michelsson, K., Sirviö, P., Koivisto, M., Sovijärvi, A. & Wasz-Höckert, O. (1975). Spectrographic analysis of pain cry in neonates with cleft palate. *Biology Neonate, 26*, 353-358.

Michelsson, K., Tuppurainen, N. & Aula, P. (1980). Sound spectrographic cry analysis of infants with karyotype abnormality. *Neuropediatrics, 11*, 365-376.

Michelsson, K. & Wasz-Höckert, O. (1980). The Value of Cry Analysis in Neonatology and Early Infancy. In T. Murry & J. Murry (Eds.), *Infant Communication: Cry and Early Speech* (pp. 152-182). Houston: College Hill Press.

Muller, E., Hollien, H. & Murry, T. (1974). Perceptual responses to infant crying; Identification of cry types. *Journal of Child Language, 1,* 89-95.

Murry, T., Amundson, P. & Hollien, H. (1977). Acoustic characteristics in infant cries: fundamental frequency. *Journal of Child Language, 4,* 321-328.

Ostwald, P. F., Phibbs, R. & Fox, S. (1968). Diagnostic use of infant cry. *Biology Neonate, 13,* 68-82.

Parkin, P. C., Schwartz, C. J. & Manuel, B. A. (1993). Randomized controlled trial of three interventions in the management of persistent crying of infancy. *Pediatrics, 92,* 197-201.

Parviainen, S. (1948) Vagitus uterinus. *Annals Chirurgie et Gynaecologie Fennica, 3,* 330-335.

Pettay, O., Donner, M., Michelsson, K. & Sirviö, P. (1977). New aspects on the diagnosis of herpes simplex virus (HSV) infections in the newborn. New Delhi: *XV Congress of Pediatrics, 5,* 235.

Porter, F.L., Miller, R. H., Marshall, R. E. (1986). Neonatal pain cries: effect of circumcision on acoustic features and perceived urgency. *Child Development, 59,* 495-505.

Potter, R., Kopp, G.-A. & Gren, H. C. (1947). *Visible Speech.* New York: van Nostrand.

Prescott, R. (1975). Infant cry sound; developmental features. *Journal Acoustic Society of America, 57,* 1186-1191.

Raes, J., Dehaen, F. & Despontin, M. (1991). Towards a standardized terminology and methodology for the measurement of durational pain cry characteristics. *Early Child Development and Care, 65,* 127-138.

Raes, J., Michelsson, K., Dehaen, F. & Despontin, M. (1982). Cry analysis in infants with infections and congenital disorders of the larynx. *Journal of Pediatric Otolaryngology, 4,* 156-169.

Ringel, R. L. & Kluppel, D. D. (1964). Neonatal Crying. A Normative Study. *Folia Phoniatrica, 6,* 1-9.

Rinne, A., Saenz, A. H. & Michelsson, K. (1990). Amount and perception of baby crying in Finland and Colombia. *Early Child Development and Care, 65,* 139-144.

Runefors, P., Arnbjörnsson, E., Elander, G. & Michelsson, K. (2000). Newborn infants´ cry after heel-prick; analysis with sound spectrogram. *Acta Paediatrica, 89,* 68-72.

Sagi, A. (1981). Mothers' and Non-Mothers' Identification of Infant Cries. *Infant Behavior and Development, 4,* 37-40.

Sedláčková, E. (1964). Analyse acoustice de la voix de nouveaunés. *Folia Phoniatrica,16,* 44-58.

Sirviö, P. & Michelsson, K. (1976). Sound spectrographic cry analysis of normal and abnormal newborn infants. *Folia Phoniatrica, 18,* 161-173.

Stark, R. E., Rose, S. N. & McLagen, M. (1975). Features of infant sounds: the first eight weeks of life. *Journal of Child Language, 2,* 205-221.

St James-Roberts, I. & Halil, T. (1991). Infant crying patterns in the first year. Normal community and clinical findings. *Journal of Child Psychology and Psychiatry, 32,* 951-968.

St James-Roberts, I., Hurry, J. & Bowyer, J. (1993). Objective confirmation of crying durations in infants referred for excessive crying. *Archives of Diseases of Childhood, 68,* 82-84.

Starck, R., Rose, S. N. & McLagen, M. (1975). Features of infant sounds: The first eight weeks of life. *Journal of Child Language, 2,* 205-221.

Taubman, B. (1984). Clinical trial of the treatment of colic by modification of parent-infant interaction. *Pediatrics 74*, 998-1002.

Tenold, J. L., Crowell, D. H., Jones, R. H., Daniel, T. H., McPherson, D. F. & Popper, A. N. (1974). Cepstral and stationary analyses of full-term and premature infants' cries. *Journal of Acoustics Society of America, 56*, 975-980.

Thodén, C-J., Järvenpää, A-L. & Michelsson, K. (1980). Sound spectrographic cry analysis of pain cry in prematures. In BM Lester & CF Boukydis (Eds.), *Infant Crying. Theoretical and Research perspectives* (pp. 105-117). New York & London: Plenum Press

Thodén, C-J. & Koivisto, M. (1980). Acoustic Analysis of the Normal Pain Cry. In T. Murry & J. Murry (Eds.), *Infant Communication: Cry and Early Speech* (pp. 105-118). Houston: College Hill Press.

Truby, H. M. & Lind, J. (1965) Cry sounds of the newborn infant. *Acta Paediatrica Scandinavica,* Suppl. 163, 7-59.

Valanne, E. H., Vuorenkoski, V., Partanen, T. J., Lind, J. & Wasz-Höckert, O. (1967). The ability of human mothers to identify the hunger cry signals of their own newborn during the lying-in period. *Experientia, 23,* 768-769.

Wasz-Höckert, O., Vuorenkoski, V., Valanne, E. & Michelsson, K. (1962). Sound spectrographic analysis of the infant cry. *Experientia 18*, 583-586.

Wasz-Höckert, O., Partanen, T., Vuorenkoski, V., Valanne, E. & Michelsson, K. (1964). The identification of some specific meanings in infant vocalization *Experientia, 20,* 154-156.

Wasz-Höckert, O., Lind, J., Vuorenkoski, V, Partanen, T. & Valanne, E. (1968). *The Infant Cry: A Spectrographic and Auditory Analysis.* Clinics in Developmental Medicine No. 29, pp. 1-42. London: Spastics International Medical Publications.

Watson, E. H. & Lowrey, G. H. (1951). *Growth and development of children.* New York, Year Book Publishers.

Wessel, M. A., Cobb, J. C., Jackson, E. B., Harris, G. S. & Detweiler, A. C. (1954). Paroxysmal fussing in infancy, sometimes called 'colic'. *Pediatrics 14*, 421-434.

Wolff, P. H. (1969). The natural history of crying and other vocalizations in early infancy. In B. M. Foss (Ed.), *Determinants of Infant Behaviour IV.* London, Methuen.

Zeskind, P. S. & Lester, B. M. (1978). Acoustic features and auditory perceptions of the cries of newborns with prenatal and perinatal complications. *Child Development, 49,* 580-589.

In: Focus on Nonverbal Communication Research
Editor: Finley R. Lewis, pp. 65-88

ISBN 1-59454-790-4

Chapter 3

DIMENSIONAL STRUCTURE OF EMOTIONAL FACIAL EXPRESSION RECOGNITION AND COMPLEX SYSTEM

Takuma Takehara
Hokusei Gakuen University, Sapporo, Japan

ABSTRACT

Several researchers have stated that facial expression recognition appears to play one of the most important roles in human communication. With regard to the basic cognitive structure of facial expression recognition, in this chapter, I would like to report and discuss the internal structure in terms of a dimensional account, which asserts that the structure of emotional facial expression recognition should be geometrically conceptualized in terms of two underlying bipolar dimensions—pleasure-displeasure and intensity of arousal. Significant advance in computer technology has enabled researchers to explore the cognitive structure of prototype facial expressions represented by not only still photographs but also computer-generated morphed facial expressions. Morphed facial expressions, in a sense, are complex and include diverse types of emotional information; therefore, discussing the structure of facial expression recognition appears to be extremely interesting and profitable for human nonverbal communication. First, I will briefly review earlier studies on facial expressions and major accounts of facial expression recognition. Second, I will discuss the internal structure of human facial expression recognition in detail as reported by some psychological experiments using morphing. Third, I will discuss the possibility of applying fractals, a concept of self-similarity, to facial expression recognition. Our experiment indicates that the structure of facial expression recognition definitely has a fractal aspect and a non-integer dimension of 1.18. The fact that the recognition system has fractal properties can perhaps be applied to not only psychology (nonverbal communication) but also various other domains of research.

INTRODUCTION

How can a person's emotional state be determined from his/her facial expressions? Since Darwin, several researchers have attempted to resolve this basic issue. Considering that facial emotional expressions are important in basic human communication (e.g., Ekman, 1984, 1993; Izard, 1977; Izard & Malatesta, 1987; Plutchik, 1980), exploring human facial expression recognition is essential.

From the 1910s to the 1920s, the main theme of facial expression recognition was whether people could simply recognize the emotional facial expressions of others. The experimental paradigm was the same as the recent one, i.e., that an experimenter presented a facial picture and a subject subsequently reported an emotion label. The response, however, was almost incorrect because the correct response required precise consistency between the emotion labels that an experimenter assumed and that reported by the subject (e.g., Langfeld, 1918; Ruckmick, 1921; Landis, 1924).

In the 1930s and 1940s, the low consistency rate was drastically improved. Woodworth (1938) subsequently attempted to construct his own scale by reanalyzing Feleky's experimental data (Feleky, 1914, 1922). This resulted in the finding that an emotion label did not correspond to a single emotion, i.e., happiness corresponding to happiness, but to a few similar emotions, i.e., happiness, love, and mirth corresponding to happiness. On the basis of studies which suggested that some facial expressions are more similar than others, Woodworth (1938) suggested a linear scale relating human emotional expressions.

In order to verify the reanalysis performed by Woodworth, Schlosberg (1941) conducted an experiment to test Woodworth's linear scale using Frois-Wittmann's (1930) facial pictures comprising 72 images. On the basis of the results of the experiment, Schlosberg confirmed Woodworth's hypothesis that a category could exist for each emotional expression; however, adjacent categories could overlap to some extent. Moreover, with regard to the color spectrum, Schlosberg (1941) proposed that emotional facial expressions could possibly be represented on a circular scale. During the 1950s, as an extension of Schlosberg's circular scale, Schlosberg (1952) also proposed that the circular scale consists of two orthogonal axes—Pleasant-Unpleasant and Attention-Rejection. Schlosberg's circular scale was later reconfirmed by several studies on facial expressions (e.g., Abelson & Sermat, 1962; Davitz, 1969; Engen, Levy, & Schlosberg, 1958; Levy & Schlosberg, 1960; Osgood, 1966; Royal & Hays, 1959; Triandis & Lambert, 1958) and has greatly influenced recent researches on facial expression, particularly those that advocated a dimensional account of facial expression recognition.

As briefly reviewed above, earlier scientific researches on facial expressions initiated by the pioneers were very important for future researchers to develop more elaborate experimental paradigm and theoretical framework. In other words, they greatly influenced several aspects of future researches on facial expressions. Concerning researches on the basic cognitive structure of facial expression recognition, which is one of the most important aspects of human communication, two major accounts have been asserted—a categorical account and a dimensional account. A categorical account that is one of the most prominent theories of facial expression recognition will be discussed in the following section.

CATEGORICAL ACCOUNT OF FACIAL EXPRESSION RECOGNITION

Several researchers favor the categorical account, which is based on Darwin's theory of evolution. Their assertion is that emotions are adaptations to problems encountered during evolution (e.g., Ekman, 1984; Izard, 1977; Johnson-Laird & Oatley, 1992; MacLean, 1993; Plutchik, 1984; Tooby & Cosmides, 1990). The researchers of facial expression recognition, who support the categorical account, generally suggest that facial expressions related to emotions are mutually independent and consist of a particular number of discrete categories of emotions such as Happiness, Sadness, Anger, etc. They assume that the system of facial expression recognition is discrete and the condition of the system changes at intervals as in the case of frame-by-frame cartoons. In addition, they consider that all facial expressions, including ambiguous facial expressions, fall into a particular emotion category. For example, Plutchik (1984) proposed eight emotions such as fear, anger, joy, sadness, acceptance, disgust, expectancy, and surprise as basic emotions, and MacLean (1993) proposed desire, anger, fear, dejection, joy, and affection. Although researchers differ on the precise number of basic emotions, most of them who support the categorical account commonly include five discrete emotions of happiness, sadness, anger, disgust, and fear as basic emotions (e.g., Ekman, 1984; Izard, 1977; Johnson-Laird & Oatley, 1992; Plutchik, 1980; Tomkins, 1962, 1963). On the basis of the results of several studies, Ekman and his colleagues concluded that basic facial expressions of emotion should be universally recognized (Ekman, 1972; Ekman & Friesen, 1971, 1975; Ekman, Friesen, & Ellsworth, 1982; Ekman, Friesen, O'Sullivan, Chan, Diacoyanni-Tarlatzis, Heider, Krause, LeCompte, Pitcairn, Ricci-Bitti, Scherer, Tomita, & Tzavaras, 1987; Izard, 1977; Ekman, 1994; Izard, 1994, Russell, 1994), and Ekman et al. (1982) proposed that the six emotions of Happiness, Sadness, Anger, Fear, Disgust, and Surprise were basic facial expressions. The researchers quoted earlier, however, proposed a particular number of emotions as the basic emotions, although Ortony and Turner (1990) noted great disagreement on what constitutes a "basic emotion," and thus, in the numbers of basic emotions (between 2 and 18). Oatley and Johnson-Laird (1996) also suggested that the precise number of basic emotions is not very important. The important point is that the supporters of the categorical account need to assert the discreteness of the system for recognizing facial expressions.

DIMENSIONAL ACCOUNT OF FACIAL EXPRESSION RECOGNITION

Several researchers who support the dimensional account for the structure of emotion agree that judgments of facial expressions of emotions can be described in terms of a small number of cognitive dimensions (e.g., Engen & Levy, 1956; Engen, Levy, & Schlosberg, 1957, 1958; Levy & Schlosberg, 1960; Neufield, 1975, 1976; Osgood, 1966; Schlosberg, 1941, 1952, 1954; Shepard, 1962a, 1962b; Triandis & Lambert, 1958). In their view, all faces can be represented in an n-dimensional psychological phase space such as Euclidean space, and the changes of recognition would be represented as continuous trajectory in space. Schlosberg (1941) hypothesized that emotion categories were neither mutually independent nor discrete but continuous. This view was supported by experiments through finding a continuum of emotion. For instance, Abelson and Sermat (1962) found a two-dimensional psychological space by multidimensional scaling (MDS). Furthermore, some researchers Royal and Hays, (1959; Shepard, 1962a, 1962b; Cliff & Young, 1968) found the structure very similar to that developed by Abelson and Sermat (1962), which could easily be interpreted in terms of dimensional account. These dimension models typically include the orthogonal dimensions of valence (Pleasant-Unpleasant) and perceived arousal or activation and are shown to have universal aspects of facial expressions of emotion in various cultures (e.g., Osgood, May, & Miron, 1975; Russell, 1991).

As compared to the original model, a more recent and complete model of emotion recognition is a two-dimensional model, the two dimensions being valence and arousal or activation (Feldman, 1995; Lang, Bradley, & Cuthbert, 1990; Reisenzein, 1994; Russell, 1980, 1989; also see Larsen & Diener, 1992; Thayer, 1989; Watson & Tellegen, 1985, for a different interpretation of the two dimensions). According to the two-dimensional model, emotion concepts vary in a continuous semantic space. Russell's circumplex model (1980), in particular, was prominent and he proposed that emotion concepts were arranged around a circumplex with varying coordinates of pleasure and arousal in the orthogonal and continuous bipolar field. Moreover, these dimensions are remarkably replicable and provide strong evidence for their existence across various cultures (e.g., Russell, 1983; Russell, Lewicka, & Niit, 1989).

RUSSELL'S CIRCUMPLEX MODEL AND A DIMENSIONAL MODEL

As stated above, Russell (1980) proposed a circumplex model of emotion concept. Russell and Bullock (1985, 1986) applied the two-dimensional model to the recognition of facial expressions and reported that recognition is represented in the same two dimensions consisting of pleasure-displeasure and intensity of arousal (Figure 1). This can be defined as a psychological space and derived by applying MDS to similarity ratings. MDS refers to a set of procedures used to depict spatial proximities between phenomena and to detect the hidden structure underlying complex cognitive constructs (Kruskal & Wish, 1978). One possible application of this scaling is in representing facial expressions of emotion, and a number of stimulus sets have been studied using a wide range of procedures to collect the data as well as a variety of MDS techniques (Bimler & Kirkland, 1997).

A frequently used model of facial expression recognition treats internal representations of faces as locations in a multidimensional psychological space. As discussed in the previous section, this space has proved to be a useful heuristic for understanding the recognition of facial expression with dimensions of pleasure-displeasure and intensity of arousal as the major dimensions (e.g., Schlosberg, 1952, 1954; Royal & Hays, 1959; Abelson & Sermat, 1962; Shepard, 1962a, b; Osgood, 1966; Russell & Bullock, 1985, 1986). The first dimension of pleasure-displeasure, however, has been frequently reported to be the only dimension in some cultures (Russell, 1983). Although studies were conducted on subjects of German (Gehm & Scherer, 1988), Swedish (Lundberg & Devine, 1975), Hebrew (Fillenbaum & Rapaport, 1971), Japanese (Yoshida, Kinase, Kurokawa, & Yashiro, 1970), and Ifalukian origin (Lutz, 1982), and they all yielded the pleasure-displeasure dimension; only Lundberg and Devine's research on Swedes produced a dimension that was interpretable as the intensity of arousal. Furthermore, some researches on brain damage have reported interesting findings about the two-dimensional structure. Calder, Young, Rowland, Perrett, Hodges, and Etcoff (1996) found that the extremes of the pleasure-displeasure dimension were judged correctly by two patients with bilateral amygdala damage, even though injury to this area is believed to impair the recognition of facial expressions (Adolphs, Tranel, Damasio, & Damasio, 1994).

The second dimension of intensity of arousal appears to be less strongly supported than the first dimension of pleasure. Katsikitis (1997) argued that this dimension was not clearly identified. Further, Katsikitis (1997) also generated a two-dimensional psychological space using MDS and claimed that the second dimension should be upper-face/lower-face dominance rather than intensity of arousal. Another meaningful interpretation of the psychological space was proposed by Tellegen and his associates (Zevon & Tellegen, 1982; Watson, Clark, & Tellegen, 1984, 1988; Tellegen, Watson, & Clark, 1999). They assumed the dimensions of Positive Affect and Negative Affect, which yielded a structure similar to a circumplex model and might be considered as a rotational version of the model.

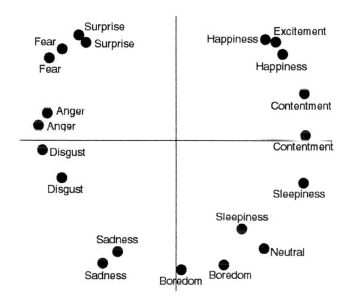

Figure 1. A two-dimensional psychological space derived by adults (Russell & Bullock, 1985).

A MORPHING TECHNIQUE AND RELATED RESEARCHES

Several studies mentioned above used prototype faces as stimuli. However, computer technology of the 1990s enabled researches to artificially generate many types of faces, including mixtures of a human and an animal. Similarly, various facial expressions can be generated by morphing between two faces (Figure 2). Using morphed facial images, detailed relationships of facial expressions in a psychological space have been examined (Takehara & Suzuki, 1997). Morphed faces represented expressions between adjacent prototype faces on the perimeter of a circumplex in an order defined by the morphing proportions. This result was obtained in the case of morphs between all possible pairs of six basic emotions of Happiness, Sadness, Anger, Fear, Disgust, and Surprise (Takehara & Suzuki, unpublished).

Figure 2. An example of morphing between a dog and a cat. Interestingly, the middle image appears to be both a dog and a cat.

Criticizing the use of morphing technology, some researchers state that images and sequences created by a computer do not occur in nature. Furthermore, some also claim that facial images generated artificially are "degraded"—the greater the degradation, the less discernable the emotion. Although morphed faces definitely do not exist in nature and it is indeed difficult to prepare spontaneous and mixed faces, morphing technology has the following advantages: (a) more objective and standardized images can be generated, (b) it has strictly equivalent physical increments, and (c) morphed faces are very similar to those in daily life. In fact, throughout the past decade, morphing has been used as an experimental technique in face research (e.g., Etcoff & Magee, 1992; Beale & Keil, 1995; Calder, Young, Perrett, Etcoff, & Rowland, 1996; Takehara & Suzuki, 1997, 2001a, unpublished; Young, Rowland, Calder, Etcoff, Seth, & Perrett, 1997; Busey, 1998; Lewis & Johnston, 1998, 1999; Tanaka, Giles, Kremen, & Simon, 1998; Blanz, O'Toole, Vetter, & Wild, 2000; Calder, Rowland, Young, Nimmo-Smith, Keane, & Perrett, 2000; Hancock, 2000). By means of a morphing procedure, researchers may be able to generate continua of facial stimuli in which emotional intensity is linearly varied.

INTERNAL STRUCTURE OF FACIAL EXPRESSION RECOGNITION (A STUDY BY TAKEHARA AND SUZUKI [2001B])

As reviewed above, several studies have indicated that recognition of facial expression is geometrically represented in terms of two underlying bipolar dimensions—pleasure-displeasure and the intensity of arousal. A psychological space defined by these two dimensions has been found under particular conditions using prototype faces; however, the question arises whether this two-dimensional psychological space is also an accurate representation for faces with lower emotional intensity. To test this, Takehara and Suzuki (2001b) focused on the internal structure of an affective circumplex and tried to clarify the structure in detail. Takehara and Suzuki's experiment (2001b) will now be analyzed in detail.

Their research used systematic experimental conditions so that ratings could be obtained from four different intensities of faces, i.e., 100% (as the prototype face), 75%, 50%, and 25% emotional intensities of facial expressions expressed as percentages of the prototype faces. Russell and Fehr (1987) stated, "the emotion space is a geometric metaphor for the internal scale on which any facial expression is judged" and "to judge the meaning of a particular facial expression is to place that expression within the emotion space." Accordingly, the recognition of facial expression in terms of dimensional account must meet two geometric conditions: (a) prototype faces are represented in a circumplex model, which has two dimensions; here, assumed to be pleasure-displeasure and intensity of arousal and (b) morphed faces represent expressions between the morphed prototype faces and their locations in the circumplex model correspond to the morphing proportions. If qualitatively similar representations are obtained for each of the four intensity conditions, the multidimensional psychological space could be considered more robust. Thus, the purpose of their study was to investigate whether a similar underlying structure in the recognition of facial expression can be found for each of the four different emotional intensity conditions. In order to test the above prediction, following the suggestion of Russell and Bullock (1986), multiple correlations were used in addition to the visual inspection from the representation by MDS.

They adopted four experimental conditions: (a) 100% expression (i.e., prototype expression), (b) 75% of prototype expression, (c) 50% of prototype expression, and (d) 25% of prototype expression. There were 29 participants for the 100% expression condition, 30 for 75%, 35 for 50%, and 34 for the 25% condition. Thus, a total of 128 undergraduate students from a University volunteered as participants for a one-credit psychology course. All had normal or corrected-to-normal vision.

Concerning facial images as stimuli, they selected the six basic prototype faces of Happiness, Sadness, Anger, Fear, Disgust, and Surprise and one Neutral from the Ekman and Friesen's face sets (Face JJ), Pictures of facial affect (1976), because the facial stimuli needed to be standardized and controlled for lighting, angle, orientation, and quality. Subsequently, to generate faces with 75%, 50%, and 25% intensities of expression, they morphed the Neutral face and each prototype face using the morphing software (Morpher for WindowsTM). In morphing, 200 feature points were selected for each prototype expression as anchor points similar to Takehara and Suzuki (1997). Thus, six prototypes were generated for each intensity of expression. The schematic representation of the four intensities is shown in Figure 3. Next, for each intensity, all possible pairs of the six basic facial images were morphed in the proportions of 75:25, 50:50, and 25:75, creating 51 faces (6 prototype parent faces and 45 morphed faces) for each of the four conditions. Since the collection of ratings of all 51 images was deemed necessary, the numbers of faces were limited in consideration of the fatigue and concentration variation of the participants.

An identical procedure was used for each of the four conditions. The 51 faces generated were displayed individually in a random order on a 14.1- inch LCD computer screen (240 × 320 pixels). The viewing distance between the participant and the monitor was approximately 50 cm. Data were collected using a Compaq personal computer (Deskpro; Pentium II Processor 350 MHz) with a two-button mouse and by rating software made with an Borland C++ compiler (Borland C++ Builder Version 4). Participants were asked to rate each facial image on a 6-point Likert-type scale with anchors of 1: "not at all" and 6: "very much so" on each item of the six basic emotions of Happiness, Sadness, Anger, Fear, Disgust, and Surprise by clicking the mouse. By single-clicking the "Next Image" button on the window, a neutral geographic pattern image was presented for two seconds, followed by the next facial image. No feedback was given. Two practice trials were performed prior to the rating. In each condition, the ratings on the 6-point scale were evaluated to MDS. The ratings were used to calculate a matrix of dissimilarities among all facial expressions, and MDS was used to find coordinates of all facial images in the Euclidean space for each of the four conditions. The ALSCAL procedure from the Statistical Package for the Social Science (SPSS) was used.

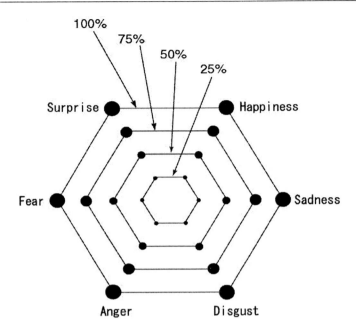

Figure 3. Schematic representation of the perimeter of the emotion circumplex used in their experiment. The emotions are not equidistant. Black circles indicate the prototype facial expressions, and the sizes of the circles correspond to the emotional intensities. For example, the sizes of the circles for 50% intensity are half of those for 100%.

To visualize the assumed two-dimensional psychological space framework, the relative positions of faces within the psychological space need to be specified. This can be accomplished with MDS, which derives a spatial representation of the stimuli from psychological data, such as ratings of perceived similarity (Shepard, 1980). MDS provides a geometric representation by placing the facial images judged as being more similar closer together, and those faces judged as being more dissimilar farther apart. As a result, two solutions were extracted from the MDS analysis. The two-dimensional solution for 100% condition is shown in Figure 4. A plot of the stress values, i.e., badness-of-fit, by the number of the dimensions for the MDS solution indicated a clear elbow at the two-dimensional solution, indicating the suitability of the solution.

The overall similarity across the conditions is clear, with the exception of some positions in the 25% condition and a small rotational difference. Rather than being a major problem, this rotational difference is irrelevant because we are free to rotate the axes in MDS. Except for the representation of the 25% condition, the six prototypes were positioned in a roughly circular order, similar to the arrangement in Figure 3. Moreover, almost all of the morphs across conditions were positioned between their parent prototypes in the location corresponding to the morphing proportion. For example, in the 100% condition, $H_{50}Su_{50}$ was positioned between the prototypes of Happiness and Surprise, and $H_{25}Su_{75}$ was positioned between the prototype Surprise and the morph $H_{50}Su_{50}$. The other morphs, even in the 25% condition, were positioned similarly. For the 25% condition, the prototype Fear was positioned near Disgust in the third quadrant, indicating that the perimeter of the circumplex might not be circular, and Fear and Disgust were clearly intermixed. In addition, the representations in the 25% condition were positioned near the origin in a large cluster rather than fragmented as in the other conditions. In relation to the interpretation of the axes, for each of the four conditions, the horizontal axis indicates pleasure-displeasure and the vertical axis indicates the intensity of arousal.

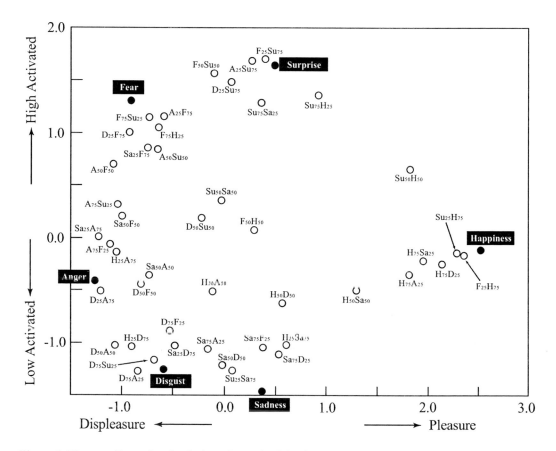

Figure 4. The two-dimensional solutions for each of the four conditions by MDS. Black circles indicate prototypes with the names of the emotion category. All morphed images are identified by their first letter or the first and second letters with white circles: Happiness = H, Sadness = Sa, Anger = A, Fear = F, Disgust = D, Surprise = Su. Synthesis or combination is identified by a hyphen and each number indicates the proportion of morphing. For instance, $H_{75}Su_{25}$ indicates that the facial image has 75% Happiness and 25% Surprise.

Although visual inspection indicated a clear similarity and identical interpretation of dimensions across conditions, this qualitative impression is insufficient to draw strong conclusions. Multiple correlations were used to assess the similarity quantitatively (Russell & Bullock, 1985, 1986). A quantitative test of the apparent convergence is given in Table 1. Given the rotational differences among solutions, Table 1 shows multiple correlations between a specified single dimension and each two-dimensional solution. For instance, the first dimension extracted from the 75% condition had a multiple correlation of 0.96 with the two-dimensional solution of the 100% condition. The value of 0.96 can be interpreted as the correlation of the first dimension from the 75% condition with one dimension from the 100% condition created by rotating the space. The critical issue is whether the dimensions found exactly correspond to the two dimensions. On the basis of the proposition strongly supported by the multiple correlations, it can be observed that this is true.

Table 1. Multiple Correlations between Two-Dimensional and Single Dimensions

Two-dimensional solution	Single Dimension			
	100%	75%	50%	25%
	First dimension			
100%		0.96	0.90	0.88
75%	0.96		0.96	0.93
50%	0.93	0.95		0.94
25%	0.89	0.87	0.94	
	Second dimension			
100%		0.98	0.95	0.56
75%	0.98		0.96	0.57
50%	0.92	0.97		0.74
25%	0.54	0.66	0.73	

Note: All the given multiple correlations are significant at the 0.001 level. The percentage the intensities of expressions.

In reiteration, I emphasize that several studies have examined whether recognition of prototypical facial expressions is represented in a two-dimensional psychological space (e.g., Abelson & Sermat, 1962; Osgood, 1966; Zevon & Tellegen, 1982; Watson, et al., 1984, 1988; Russell & Bullock, 1985, 1986; Adolphs, et al., 1994; Katsikitis, 1997; Takehara & Suzuki, 1997, 2001a; Tellegen, et al., 1999). A few researchers have found that the horizontal axis indicated pleasure-displeasure and the vertical axis indicated the intensities of arousal; however, others have interpreted the two axes differently. Although there have been a number of studies on prototypical expressions, Takehara & Suzuki's study (2001b) are the first to demonstrate that facial expressions with reduced intensities can be represented in a two-dimensional psychological space. Similar to the previous studies mentioned above, this study found the same two axes of pleasure-displeasure and intensities of arousal, and interestingly, morphed faces were consistently located between their parent prototypes in the order which corresponded to the morphing proportions in all the four conditions. It is noteworthy that the pattern found in their study, even in the condition of 25% intensity of expression, corresponds with the pattern found by Takehara and Suzuki (1997, 2001a).

The retention of the representation in the two-dimensional psychological space across four different intensities of expression indicates that people can recognize the emotional meaning from the physical features in all faces, including morphed faces, as suggested by Russell and Bullock (1986). On the other hand, several recently published studies on the categorical perception of faces have focused on facial expressions (e.g., Etcoff & Magee, 1992; Calder, Young, Perrett, Etcoff, & Rowland, 1996; Granato, Bruyer, & Révillon, 1996; de Gelder, Teunisse, & Benson, 1997; Young, et al., 1997; Bruyer & Granato, 1999; Calder, et al., 2000). The hallmark of evidence of categorical perception is better discrimination across the boundaries of categories than within categories (Harnad, 1987; Young, et al., 1997). From the results of this study, however, some locations of morphed faces appear to contradict this categorical perception effect. For example, while the morphed face $A_{50}F_{50}$ in the 100% condition is located near the prototype face for Fear, the face in the 75% condition is located near Anger. Further, while the morphed face $Su_{50}Sa_{50}$ is located near Surprise in the 100% condition, the face in 75% is not. Similarly, while the morphed face $A_{50}F_{50}$ in the 100% condition is located near the prototype face for Fear, the same face reported by Takehara and Suzuki (1997) was located at the midpoint between their prototypes. These results are in contrast with those expected for categorical account.

LIMITATION OF AN EXISTING DIMENSIONAL ACCOUNT AND A NEW THEORY

Although the results of Takehara & Suzuki's study (2001b) show the robustness of the two-dimensional representation of recognition of facial expression, the positions of the prototype and morphed faces remain questionable. If the psychological space was homogeneous, one would expect that the changes in the representative trajectory running from one prototype to another around a circumplex would be smooth and linear. For example, geometric relationships between the prototype faces would be mapped in the continuous space (see Figure 5). With respect to the morphed faces, $A_{50}F_{50}$, for example, should be located at the midpoint between Anger and Fear. Instead, this face was located near Fear in the 100% condition but near Anger in the other conditions. Moreover, all trajectories of continua running from one prototype face to another were not linear, instead they fluctuated. What is this fluctuation? It appears that this type of fluctuation may mask the possible fractality of the shape.

In the next section, I will introduce a concept of fractals that has never been mentioned in the area of psychological researches.

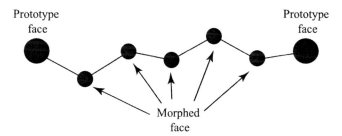

Figure 5. Schematic representation of a trajectory in a continuum running from one prototype to another depicted in the previous studies. The change is fluctuating rather than continuous.

WHAT IS FRACTAL?

In the discipline of geometry, namely, complex geometry, patterns and scaling have been shown to represent the common aspects of several processes occurring in an unusually diverse range of fields including physics, mathematics, biology, chemistry, economics, and even human behavior. The complex nature of various phenomena and objects is clarified in the underlying complicated geometry that, in most of the cases, can be described in terms of a non-integer dimension called a fractal dimension.

Fractals that are characterized by the fractal dimension and self-similarity are a concern of new geometry, in which the object is to describe a great variety of natural structures that have irregularities of various sizes. Assuming that Figure 6 is a picture of a coastline, if the length of the coastline was measured with a kilometer-long ruler, you could measure a certain distance as 16 km. On the other hand, if a foot-long ruler was used for the measurement, the length of the coastline would be greater than that measured by kilometer-long rulers. In other words, if shorter rulers were used for measurement, the length of the coastline would be greater, and with larger rulers, the length would be smaller, depending on the unit of measurement. This interesting phenomenon is due to the fact that the coastline is actually jagged. Ultimately, if you measured with infinitesimally shorter rulers, the coastline would be infinitely longer. This is one of the most important aspects of fractals.

Figure 6. A picture of a coastline at a certain scale

Moreover, the basic property of fractals is the notion of self-similarity. The concept of self-similarity is easy to explain using the Koch curve (Figure 7). The method of drawing the Koch curve is as follows: (a) draw a straight line segment, (b) divide the line segment into three equal pieces, (c) make four equal segments from the three equal pieces and remove the middle one, (d) follow this procedure for all the four segments, (e) perform the procedure many times (see Figure 8). Note that the Koch curve consists of several equilateral patterns. As a matter of fact, we can delve deeper into the Koch curve and discover further copies of the Koch curve. This is the concept of self-similarity.

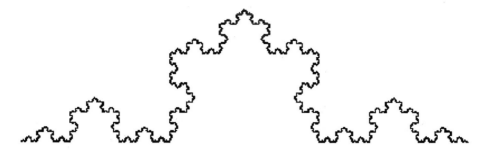

Figure 7. A Koch curve. This object has a fractal property, a self-similarity.

Here, a concept of dimension is considered. Generally, we may suppose that a line has dimension 1, a plane dimension 2, and a cube dimension 3. Is it true? If you broke a line segment into three self-similar pieces, each had the same length, and each of which could be magnified by a factor of 3 to yield the original segment. In the same manner, you are able to break a line segment into 10 self-similar pieces, each with magnification factor 10. Generally, for a line segment, you are able to break a line segment into N self-similar pieces, each with a magnification factor N. In case of a square, if you decomposed it into four self-similar sub-squares, the magnification factor would be 2. Similarly, one can break it into nine self-similar pieces with a magnification factor 3. Similar to the case of a square, you are also able to break a cube into eight self-similar sub-cubes, each with a magnification factor of 2. That is, a square can be broken into N^2 self-similar copies of itself, each of which must be magnified by a factor of N to yield the original shape, and a cube can be broken into N^3 self-similar copies of itself each of which is magnified by a factor of N. It may be determined that dimensions such as 1, 2, 3, etc. are basically the exponents of the number of self-similar pieces with magnification factor N.

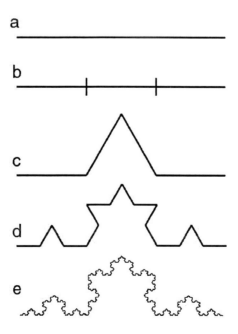

Figure 8. How to draw a Koch curve.

What is the dimension of the Koch curve on the basis of the logic? Note that we simply use logarithms to calculate the dimension. Specifically, the dimension D is calculated as follows,

$$D = \log_a b \tag{1}$$

where a is the magnification factor and b is the number of self-similar pieces. Hence, the dimension D of the Koch curve is as given below,

$$D = \log_3 4 \approx 1.26. \tag{2}$$

This non-integer dimension is the fractal dimension. In addition, the fractal dimension is also represented by an absolute value of a constant slope in a "log-log-plot." Dimension of 1.26, however, might be difficult for us to understand because it is not an integer dimension. Generally, the characterization of the fractal dimension is known to be used as a measure to describe a kind of complexity of an object. A dimension between 1 and 2, for example, means that the object is more complex than a line but simpler than a plane.

Until recently, various shapes or surfaces in nature have been explained as fractal in terms of their self-similarity (Avnir & Farin, 1984; Mandelbrot, 1967, 1982; Mandelbrot, Passoja, & Paullay, 1984; Morse, Lawton, Dodson, & Williamson, 1985). For example, it has been reported that the feeding behavioral pattern of Drosophila melanogaster (Shimada, Minesaki, & Hara, 1995) and the diving duration of whales (West, 1990) both showed a temporal fractal. In human physiology, the brain wave is proved to have a fractal dimension (Shinagawa, Kawano, Matsuda, Seno, & Koito, 1991); moreover, the heart rate spectrum also shows a fractal (Hughson, Maillet, Dureau, Yamamoto, & Gharib, 1995; Togo & Yamamoto, 2001; Yamamoto & Hughson, 1993; Yamamoto, Fortrat, & Hughson, 1995). However, to my best knowledge, I have not observed any studies that discussed fractals in relation to the complex world of human recognition. It is natural to assume that the human recognition system has a fractal structure, because behavior or a physiological response, which we can explain as fractal, can be modified by the recognition system. The complex shape in the representation of facial images in the two-dimensional space might be influenced by fractals. I will introduce Takehara, Ochiai, & Suzuki's research (2002) in the next section.

FRACTALS IN FACIAL EXPRESSION RECOGNITION (A STUDY BY TAKEHARA ET AL. [2002])

Although the structure of emotional facial expression recognition has been represented in the two-dimensional space, it was interesting to note that facial images formed a roughly circular structure. In other words, these experiments showed a slightly different distribution of facial images. In addition, results from Takehara and Suzuki's papers (1997, 2001b) showed complex and jagged arrangements between two prototype faces on a circumplex rather than a smooth and continuous distribution. Why did they obtain such complex and fluctuated representations? Takehara et al. (2002) considered that this kind of fluctuation may mask the possible fractality of the shape.

The purpose of their study, therefore, was to examine the possibility of a fractal structure underlying the facial expression recognition that is one of the most important parts of the human recognition system. If the representation of the perimeter of a circumplex is fluctuated by a fractal, it would have no characteristic length scale and it must, therefore, have a non-integer fractal dimension of D between 1.0 and 2.0.

Considering that eight facial expressions of Happiness, Calmness, Sleepiness, Sadness, Anger, Fear, Surprise, and Excitement were typical prototypes, they designed the perimeter of a circumplex varying clockwise as shown in Figure 9. To prepare different scales, the following four experimental conditions were set: (i) thirty-two-divided, (ii) forty-divided, (iii) forty-eight-divided, and (iv) sixty-four-divided conditions.

Figure 9. Schematic representation of eight prototype emotional facial expressions on Russell's circumplex.

All the participants of each of the four experimental conditions were undergraduate students, 23 for condition (i), 19 for (ii), 31 for (iii), and 28 for (iv). They volunteered to be research participants to get a credit for a psychology course. All had normal or corrected-to-normal vision.

On the basis of the arrangement illustrated in Figure 9, morphed facial images were generated between all adjacent prototype face pairs positioned on the perimeter in each of the four different scales using a morphing software (Morpher for Windows^{TM}). In condition (i), each interval between adjacent prototypes was divided into four segments and three morphed facial images were generated. In total, 32 facial images (8 prototypes and 24 morphs) were generated around a circumplex for condition (i). Similar to this condition, morphed facial images were generated for the other three conditions: 40 facial images (8 prototypes and 32 morphs) for condition (ii), 48 facial images (8 prototypes and 40 morphs) for (iii), and 64 facial images (8 prototypes and 56 morphs) for (iv).

For each of the four experimental conditions, participants were asked to rate all the facial images on a 6-point Likert-type scale (from "not at all" to "very much so") regarding each item of the eight prototype emotions of Happiness, Calmness, Sleepiness, Sadness, Anger, Fear, Surprise, and Excitement. In rating, facial stimuli were presented individually in a random order on a 14.1-inch LCD with 240 × 320 pixels. The distance between a participant and a display was approximately 50 cm. Data were collected using a Compaq personal computer (Deskpro; Pentium II Processor 350 MHz) with a two-button mouse and by a rating software made by a Borland C++ compiler (Borland C++ Builder Version 4). No feedback was provided.

Similar to the study by Takehara & Suzuki (2001b), in order to visualize the assumed two-dimensional psychological space framework, they needed to specify the relative positions of facial images within the psychological space. For each of the four experimental conditions, rating data were used to calculate a matrix of dissimilarities among eight facial emotion categories, which was then subjected to MDS to find coordinates of all facial images in two-dimensional space. For the two-dimensional configuration, all RSQ values, which are a measure of the proportion of the variance in the data accounted for by the MDS solution, were sufficiently high: 0.978 for condition (i), 0.971 for (ii), 0.976 for (iii), and 0.977 for (iv). Similar to the results of many previous studies, the positions of the prototypes fell in a roughly circular order and were rated in the same order under all conditions (Katsikitis, 1997; Russell & Bullock, 1985, 1986; Takehara & Suzuki, 1997, 2001a, b), and all morphs were plotted between their parent prototypes corresponding to their morphing proportions. The resultant configuration in condition (ii) is shown in Figure 10. Generally, each configuration may appear to form a circle, but it is noticed that the perimeter is complex and somewhat jagged rather than smooth. The distance of the perimeter of a circumplex is defined here as the total distance, which is the sum of the distances between adjacent facial images.

If the distance of the perimeter was exactly the same for the four conditions despite the different scales, it would not have fractal properties, thus suggesting that the perimeter has a fixed and characteristic length scale like a complete circle or a rectangle. On the contrary, if it were revealed that as the scale was made smaller, the distance of the perimeter tended to increase steadily without bounds, fractal dimension would be obtained, thus indicating that the perimeter had no characteristic length scale and it fluctuated by a fractal dimension. To test this, they calculated the length of the perimeter for each of the four experimental conditions using the coordinates in two dimensions.

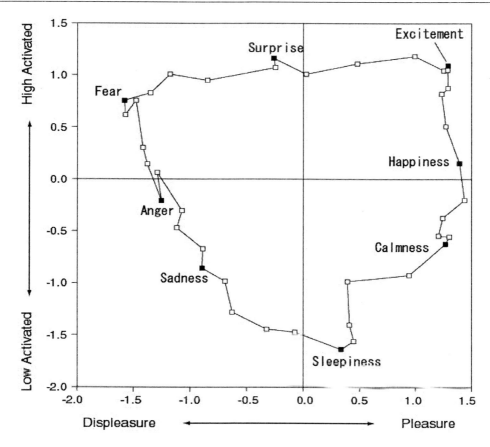

Figure 10. Configuration of prototype and morphed facial images in the two-dimensional psychological space. This example illustrates a resultant configuration of condition (ii). Black rectangles indicate the prototypes, while white rectangles indicate the morphs. Adjacent faces are tied with a straight line. All morphs are arranged between their prototypes, but the perimeter of a circumplex appears to be complex and jagged rather than smooth. The other conditions showed the same tendency.

As explained in the previous section, fractal dimension D can be calculated by an equation (1). Generally, a fractal dimension D is calculated from various relationships between a property P and the resolution r of the general form,

$$P = kr^{f(D)} \qquad (3)$$

where k is the prefactor for the power law and the exponent $f(D)$ is a simple function of D. The slope of the resulting line on the log-log-plot shown in Figure 11 was estimated by regression analysis. Subsequently, a fractal dimension of 1.18 was derived with an RSQ value of 0.998, indicating that a circumplex did not have a characteristic length scale. The fact that D is a fraction, 1.18 is highly impressive because the perimeter of the emotion circumplex in the psychological space has *not* been considered to have a fractional dimension nor has an integer dimension (two- or three-dimension) been major in psychology; furthermore, neither has a fractional dimension itself been conceptualized in the domain of human recognition.

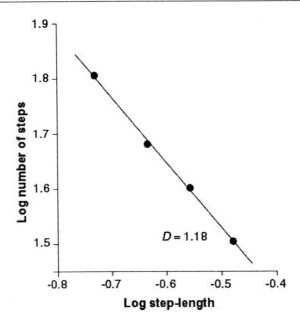

Figure 11. Linear regression of log distance of the perimeter on log step-length. The slope of the straight line gives -D, from which we determine a fractal dimension D = 1.18. RSQ value is 0.998.

Several studies have suggested that the representation of the structure of emotional facial expression recognition was a circumplex (e.g., Adolphs, Tranel, Damasio, & Damasio, 1995; Katsikitis, 1997; Russell & Bullock, 1985, 1986; Takehara & Suzuki, 1997, 2001b); however, no study has stated that the perimeter was complex and jagged rather than smooth. Focusing on the subtle fluctuation around the perimeter of a circumplex, Takehara et al. (2002) examined whether the emotion circumplex had a fractal structure in four different scales. The perimeter of a circumplex represented in the two-dimensional psychological space showed a fractal structure, indicating that human facial expression recognition, in some manner, had fractal properties and that the two-dimensional space itself was not homogeneous. Why is the perimeter of a circumplex fluctuated? Let me discuss the possible reasons.

In relation to the complex fluctuation of the perimeter around a circumplex, can we say that the fluctuation occurs in a random manner? The answer is negative, because if the wiggled perimeter was due to the randomness, the log-log-plot in Figure 11 could not be linear. The log-log-plot in their study showed a linear relation. It was, therefore, suggested that the fluctuated perimeter was not due to the randomness but due to a fractal. The perimeter, however, appeared to be irregularly jagged; the fractal regularity was hidden in the structure.

One reasonable interpretation for the fluctuated perimeter is that it may enhance the recognition efficiency for complex facial expressions that have various emotional components. For example, consider one continuum around the perimeter running from Happiness to Excitement. These two emotion categories occupy a similar region in the two-dimensional space. In addition, the morphs generated by interpolation of these two prototypes are complex facial expressions, which have at least more than two emotional components—Happiness and Excitement. The fact that the trajectory of the continuum was not linear but fractal might indicate the enhancement of the recognition efficiency for complex and subtle facial expressions through some fluctuations.

CONCLUSION

In this chapter, I have mainly addressed cognitive structure of human emotional facial expression recognition, which is one of the most important aspects for human communication, particularly because I have mentioned the structure in terms of a dimensional account. Few people who support the categorical account may refute my opinion; however, this is not the main issue. We have to note that new researches will bring forward new evidence and new methods.

The main topic of this chapter was the dimensional account of the structure of facial expression recognition, internal structure of the cognitive process, and application to the complex system. With concepts such as emotion, anger, disgust, etc., lacking a clear consensual definition, I believe that many readers of this chapter may realize the important aspects of a dimensional account and are also convinced that the application of research data to the complex system is very valuable. I hope that this chapter provides a useful opportunity for the renewal of the various basic questions that initiated this field of study.

What is the best approach for future research? As a first step, we need to test the fractal property inherent in the structure of human facial expression recognition in various situations. Accumulation of further data will lead us to new findings, because the fact that the recognition system has fractal properties can perhaps be applied to not only psychology but also other domains of research dealing with recognition, for example, clinical psychology, developmental psychology, artificial intelligence, human communication, brain research, and recognition engineering. In the near future, I hope that theoretical and empirical verifications will be carried out in an interdisciplinary manner since the topic of fractals has important implications to many disciplines.

ACKNOWLEDGMENTS

This work was partially supported by the Ministry of Education, Science, Sports and Culture, Grant-in-Aid for Young Scientists (B), 16700249, 2004. I am grateful to Masakazu Fujimiya for granting permission to use morphing photographs.

REFERENCES

Abelson, R. P., & Sermat, V. (1962). Multidimensional scaling of facial expression. *Journal of Experimental Psychology, 63*, 546-554.

Adolphs, R., Tranel, D., Damasio, H., & Damasio, A. R. (1994). Impaired recognition of emotion in facial expressions following bilateral damage to the human amygdala. *Nature, 372*, 669-672.

Adolphs, R., Tranel, D., Damasio, H., & Damasio, A. (1995). Fear and the human amygdala. *Journal of Neuroscience, 15*, 5879-5891.

Avnir, D., & Farin, D. (1984). Molecular fractal surfaces. *Nature, 308*, 261-263.

Beale, J. M., & Keil, F. C. (1995). Categorical effects in the perception of faces. *Cognition, 57*, 217-239.

Bimler, D., & Kirkland, J. (1997). Multidimensional scaling of hierarchical sorting data applied to facial expressions. *Scandinavian Journal of Psychology, 38*, 349-357.

Blanz, V., O'Toole, A. J., Vetter, T., & Wild, H. A. (2000). On the other side of the mean: the perception of dissimilarity in human faces. *Perception, 29*, 885-891.

Bruyer, R., & Granato, P. (1999). Categorical effects in the perception of facial expressions: MARIE—a simple and discriminating clinical tool. *European Review of Applied Psychology, 49*, 3–10.

Busey, T. A. (1998). Physical and psychological representations of faces: evidence from morphing. *Psychological Science, 9*, 476-483.

Calder, A. J., Rowland, D., Young, A. W., Nimmo-Smith, I., Keane, J., & Perrett, D. I. (2000). Caricaturing facial expressions. *Cognition, 76*, 105-146.

Calder, A. J., Young, A. W., Perrett, D. I., Etcoff, N. L., & Rowland, D. (1996). Categorical perception of morphed facial expressions. *Visual Cognition, 3*, 81-117.

Calder, A. J., Young, A. W., Rowland, D., Perrett, D. I., Hodges, J. R., & Etcoff, N. L. (1996). Facial emotion recognition after bilateral amygdala damage: differentially severe impairment of fear. *Cognitive Neuropsychology, 13*, 699-745.

Cliff, N., & Young, F. W. (1968). On the relation between unidimensional judgments and multidimensional scaling. *Organizational Behavior and Human Performance, 3*, 269-285.

Darwin, C. (1872). *Facial expression of emotion in man and animals.* London: John Murray.

Davitz, J. R. (1969). *The language of emotions.* New York: McGraw-Hill.

de Gelder, B., Teunisse, J. P., & Benson, P. J. (1997). Categorical perception of facial expressions: categories and their internal structure. *Cognition and Emotion, 11*, 1-23.

Ekman, P. (1972). Universals and cultural differences in facial expressions of emotion. In J. Cole (Ed.), *Nebraska symposium on motivation,* 1971. Vol. 19. Lincoln, Nebraska: University of Nebraska Press. Pp. 207-283.

Ekman, P. (1984). Expression and the nature of emotion. In K. R. Scherer & P. Ekman (Eds.), *Approaches to emotion* (Pp. 319-343). Hillsdale, New Jersey: Erlbaum.

Ekman, P. (1993). Facial expression and emotion. *American Psychologist, 48*, 384-392.

Ekman, P. (1994). Strong evidence for universals in facial expressions: A reply to Russell's mistaken critique. *Psychological Bulletin, 115*, 268-287.

Ekman, P. & Friesen, W. V. (1971). Constants across culture in the face and emotion. *Journal of Personality and Social Psychology, 17*, 124-129.

Ekman, P. & Friesen, W. V. (1975). *Unmasking the face.* Englewood Cliffs, New Jersey: Prentice-Hall.

Ekman, P., Friesen, W. V., & Ellsworth, P. (1982). *Emotion in the human face. (2nd ed.)* Cambridge, Massachusetts: Cambridge University Press.

Ekman, P., Friesen, W. V., O'Sullivan, M., Chan, A., Diacoyanni-Tarlatzis, I., Heider, K., Krause, R., LeCompte, W. A., Pitcairn, T., Ricci-Bitti, P. E., Scherer, K., Tomita, M., & Tzavaras, A. (1987). Universals and cultural differences in the judgments of facial expressions of emotion. *Journal of Personality and Social Psychology, 53*, 712-717.

Engen, T., & Levy, N. (1956). Constant-sum judgments of facial expressions. *Journal of Experimental Psychology, 51*, 396-398.

Engen, T., Levy, N., & Schlosberg, H. (1957). A new series of facial expressions. *American Psychologist, 12*, 264-266.

Engen, T., Levy, N., & Schlosberg, H. (1958). The dimensional analysis of a new series of facial expressions. *Journal of Experimental Psychology, 55,* 454-458.

Etcoff, N. L., & Magee, J. J. (1992). Categorical perception of facial expressions. *Cognition, 44,* 227-240.

Feldman, L. A. (1995). Valence focus and arousal focus: Individual differences in the structure of affective experience. *Journal of Personality and Social Psychology, 69,* 153-166.

Feleky, A. M. (1914). The expression of the emotions. *Psychological Review, 21,* 33-41.

Feleky, A. M. (1922). *Feeling and emotions.* New York: Pioneer Press.

Fillenbaum, S., & Rapaport, A. (1971). *Structures in the subjective lexicon.* New York: Academic Press.

Frois-Wittmann, J. (1930). The judgment of facial expression. *Journal of Experimental Psychology, 13,* 113-151.

Gehm, T. L., & Scherer, K. R. (1988). Factors determining the dimensions of subjunctive emotional space. In K. R. Scherer (Ed.), *Facets of emotion: recent research* (Pp. 99-113). Hillsdale, New Jersey: Erlbaum.

Granato, P., Bruyer, R., & Révillon, J. J. (1996). Etude objective de la perception du sourire et de la tristesse par la méthode d'analyse de recherche de l'intégration des émotions "MARIE". *Annales Médico-Psychologiques, 154,* 1–9.

Hancock, P. J. B. (2000). Evolving faces from principal components. *Behavior Research Methods, Instruments, & Computers, 32,* 327-333

Harnad, S. (1987). *Categorical perception.* Cambridge, United Kingdom: Cambridge University Press.

Hughson, R.L., Maillet, A., Dureau, G., Yamamoto, Y., & Gharib, C. (1995). Harmonic and fractal blood pressure variability in heart transplant patients. *Hypertension, 25,* 643-650.

Izard, C. E. (1977). *Human emotions.* New York: Plenum Press.

Izard, C. E. (1994). Innate and universal facial expressions: Evidence from developmental and cross-cultural research. *Psychological Bulletin, 115,* 288-299.

Izard, C. E., & Malatesta, C. Z. (1987). Perspective on emotional development 1: Differential emotions theory of early emotional development. In J. D. Osofsky (Ed.), *Handbook of infant development* (Pp. 494-554). New York: Wiley-Interscience.

Johnson-Laird, P. N., & Oatley, K. (1992). Basic emotions, rationality, and folk theory. *Cognition and Emotion, 6,* 201-223.

Katsikitis, M. (1997). The classification of facial expressions of emotion: a multidimensional-scaling approach. *Perception, 26,* 613-626.

Kruskal, J. B., & Wish, M. (1978). *Multidimensional scaling.* Newbury Park, California: Sage.

Landis, C. (1924). Studies of emotional reactions: I. A preliminary study of facial expression. *Journal of Experimental Psychology, 7,* 325-341.

Lang, P. J., Bradley, M. M., & Cuthbert, B. N. (1990). Emotion, attention and the startle reflex. *Psychological Review, 97,* 377-395.

Langfeld, H. S. (1918). Judgments of facial expression and suggestion. *Psychological Review, 25,* 488-494.

Larsen, R. J., & Diener, E. (1992). Promises and problems with the circumplex model of emotion. In M. S. Clark (Ed.), *Emotion. Vol. 13. Review of Personality and social psychology* (pp. 25-59). Newbury Park, California: Sage.

Levy, N., & Schlosberg, H. (1960). Woodworth scale values of the Lightfoot pictures of facial expression. *Journal of Experimental Psychology, 60*, 121-125.

Lewis, M. B., & Johnston, R. A. (1998). Understanding caricatures of faces. *Quarterly Journal of Experimental Psychology: Human Experimental Psychology, 51A*, 321-346.

Lewis, M. B., & Johnston, R. A. (1999). Are caricatures special? Evidence of peak shift in face recognition. *European Journal of Cognitive Psychology, 11*, 105-117.

Lundberg, U., & Devine, B. (1975). Negative similarities. *Educational and Psychological Measurement, 35*, 797-807.

Lutz, C. (1982). The domain of emotion words on Ifaluk. *American Ethnologist, 9*, 113-128.

MacLean, P. D. (1993). Cerebral evolution of emotion. In M. Lewis & J. M. Haviland (Eds.), *Handbook of emotions* (pp. 67-83). New York: Guilford Press.

Mandelbrot, B. B. (1967). How long is the coast of Britain? Statistical self-similarity and fractional dimension. *Science, 156*, 636-638.

Mandelbrot, B. B. (1982). *The fractal geometry of nature.* New York: Freeman.

Mandelbrot, B. B., Passoja, D. E., & Paullay, A. J. (1984). Fractal character of fracture surfaces of metals. *Nature, 308*, 721-722.

Morse, D. R., Lawton, J. H., Dodson, M. M., & Williamson, M. H. (1985). Fractal dimension of vegetation and the distribution of arthropod body length. Nature, 314, 731-733.

Neufield, R. W. J. (1975). A multidimensional scaling analysis of schizophrenics' and normals' perception of verbal similarity. *Journal of Abnormal Psychology, 84*, 498-507.

Neufield, R. W. J. (1976). Simultaneous processing of multiple stimulus dimensions among paranoid and non-paranoid schizophrenics. *Multivariate Behavioral Research, 11*, 425-441.

Oatley, K., & Johnson-Laird, P. N. (1996). The communicative theory of emotions: Empirical tests, mental models, and implications for social interaction. In L. L. Martin & A. Tesser (Eds.), *Striving and feeling: Interactions among goals, affect, and self-regulation* (pp. 363-393). Mahwah, New Jersey: Erlbaum.

Ortony, A., & Turner, T. J. (1990). What's basic about basic emotions? *Psychological Review, 97*, 315-331.

Osgood, C. E. (1966). Dimensionality of the semantic space for communication via facial expressions. *Scandinavian Journal of Psychology, 7*, 1-30.

Osgood, C. E., May, W. H., & Miron, M. S. (1975). *Cross-cultural universals of affective meaning.* Urbana, Illinois: University of Illinois Press.

Plutchik, R. (1980). *Emotion: A psychoevolutionary synthesis.* New York: Harper & Row.

Plutchik, R. (1984). A psychoevolutionary theory of emotions. *Social Science Information, 21*, 529-553.

Reisenzein, R. (1994). Pleasure-arousal theory and the intensity of emotions. *Journal of Personality and Social Psychology, 67*, 525-539.

Royal, D. C., & Hays, W. L. (1959). Empirical dimensions of emotional behavior. *Acta Psychologica, 15*, 419.

Ruckmick, C. A. (1921). A preliminary study of the emotions. *Psychological Monographs, 30*, 30-35.

Russell, J. A. (1980). A circumplex model of affect. *Journal of Personality and Social Psychology, 39*, 1161-1178.

Russell, J. A. (1983). Pancultural aspects of the human conceptual organization of emotions. *Journal of Personality and Social Psychology, 45*, 1281-1288.

Russell, J. A. (1989). Measures of emotion. In R. Plutchik & H. Kellerman (Eds.), *The measurement of emotions. Emotion: Theory, research, and experience* (Vol. 4, pp. 83-111). Toronto: Academic Press.

Russell, J. A. (1991). Culture and the categorization of emotions. *Psychological Bulletin, 110,* 426-450.

Russell, J. A. (1994). Is there universal recognition of emotion from facial expression? A review of the cross-cultural studies. *Psychological Bulletin, 115,* 102-141.

Russell, J. A., & Bullock, M. (1985). Multidimensional scaling of emotional facial expressions: similarity from preschoolers to adults. *Journal of Personality and Social Psychology, 48,* 1290-1298.

Russell, J. A., & Bullock, M. (1986). On the dimensions preschoolers use to interpret facial expressions of emotion. *Developmental Psychology, 22,* 97-102.

Russell, J. A., & Fehr, B. (1987). Relativity in the perception of emotion in facial expressions. *Journal of Experimental Psychology: General, 116,* 223-237.

Russell, J. A., Lewicka, M., & Niit, T. (1989). A cross-cultural study of the circumplex model of affect. *Journal of Personality and Social Psychology, 57,* 848-856.

Schlosberg, H. (1941). A scale for the judgment of facial expressions. *Journal of Experimental Psychology, 29,* 497-510.

Schlosberg, H. (1952). The description of facial expressions in terms of two dimensions. *Journal of Experimental Psychology, 44,* 229-237.

Schlosberg, H. (1954). Three dimensions of emotion. *Psychological Review, 61,* 81-88.

Shepard, R. N. (1962a). The analysis of proximities: multidimensional scaling with an unknown distance function. Part I. *Psychometrika, 27,* 125-139.

Shepard, R. N. (1962b). The analysis of proximities: multidimensional scaling with an unknown distance function. Part II. *Psychometrika, 27,* 219-246.

Shepard, R. N. (1980). Multidimensional scaling, tree-fitting, and clustering. *Science, 210,* 390-398.

Shimada, I., Minesaki, Y., & Hara, H. (1995). Temporal fractal in the feeding behavior of Drosophila melanogaster. *Journal of Ethology, 13,* 153-158.

Shinagawa, Y., Kawano, K., Matsuda, H., Seno, H., & Koito, H. (1991). Fractal dimensionality of brain wave. *Forma, 6,* 205-214.

Takehara, T., & Suzuki, N. (1997). Morphed images of basic emotional expressions: Ratings on Russell's bipolar field. *Perceptual and Motor Skills, 85,* 1003-1010.

Takehara, T., & Suzuki, N. (2000, February). Coexistence of categorical and dimensional models for the underlying structure of facial expression recognition. Unpublished manuscript, Doshisha University.

Takehara, T., & Suzuki, N. (2001a). Differential processes of emotion space over time. *North American Journal of Psychology, 3,* 217-228.

Takehara, T., & Suzuki, N. (2001b). Robustness of the two-dimensional structure of recognition of facial expression: Evidence under different intensities of emotionality. *Perceptual and Motor Skills, 93,* 739-753.

Takehara, T., Ochiai, F., & Suzuki, N. (2002). Fractals in emotional facial expression recognition. *Fractals, 10,* 47-52.

Tanaka, J., Giles, M., Kremen, S., & Simon, V. (1998). Mapping attractor fields in face space: the atypicality bias in face recognition. *Cognition, 68,* 199-220.

Tellegen, A., Watson, D., & Clark, L. A. (1999). On the dimensional and hierarchical structure of affect. *Psychological Science, 10*, 297-303.

Thayer, R. E. (1989). The *biopsychology of mood and arousal*. New York: Oxford University Press.

Togo, F., & Yamamoto, Y. (2001). Decreased fractal component of human heart rate variability during non-REM sleep. *American Journal of Physiology, Heart and Circulatory Physiology, 280*, H17-H21.

Tomkins, S. S. (1962). *Affect, imagery, consciousness: Vol. 1. The positive affects*. New York: Springer Verlag.

Tomkins, S. S. (1963). *Affect, imagery, consciousness: Vol. 2. The negative affects*. New York: Springer Verlag.

Tooby, J., & Cosmides, L. (1990). The past explains the present. Emotional adaptations and the structure of ancestral environments. *Ethology and Sociobiology, 11*, 375-424.

Triandis, H. C., & Lambert, W. W. (1958). A restatement and test of Schlosberg's theory of emotion with two kinds of subjects from Greece. *Journal of Abnormal and Social Psychology, 56*, 321-328.

Watson, D., & Tellegen, A. (1985). Toward a consensual structure of mood. *Psychological Bulletin, 98*, 219-235.

Watson, D., Clark, L. A., & Tellegen, A. (1984). Cross-cultural convergence in the structure of mood: a Japanese replication and a comparison with U.S. findings. *Journal of Personality and Social Psychology, 47*, 127-144.

Watson, D., Clark, L. A., & Tellegen, A. (1988). Development and validation of brief measures of Positive and Negative Affect: the PANAS scales. *Journal of Personality and Social Psychology, 54*, 1063-1070.

West, B. J. (1990). *Fractal physiology and chaos in medicine*. Singapore: World Scientific.

Woodworth, R. S. (1938). *Experimental psychology*. New York: Henry Holt.

Yamamoto, Y., & Hughson, R. L. (1993). Extracting fractal components from time series. *Physica, D68*, 250-264.

Yamamoto, Y., Fortrat, J. O., & Hughson, R. L. (1995). On the fractal nature of heart rate variability in humans: Effects of respiratory sinus arrhythmia. *American Journal of Physiology, 269*, H480-H486.

Yoshida, M., Kinase, R., Kurokawa, J., & Yashiro, S. (1970). Multidimensional scaling of emotion. *Japanese Psychological Research, 12*, 45-61.

Young, A. W., Rowland, D., Calder, A. J., Etcoff, N. L., Seth, A., & Perrett, D. I. (1997). Facial expression megamix: tests of dimensional and category accounts of emotion recognition. *Cognition, 63*, 271-313.

Zevon, M. A., & Tellegen, A. (1982). The structure of mood change: an idiographic/nomothetic analysis. *Journal of Personality and Social Psychology, 43*, 111-122.

In: Focus on Nonverbal Communication Research
Editor: Finley R. Lewis, pp. 89-100

ISBN 1-59454-790-4
© 2007 Nova Science Publishers, Inc.

Chapter 4

CARDIOVASULAR RESPONSES OF LAUGHTER

Tommy Boone

Professor and Chair, Department of Exercise Physiology
The College of St. Scholastica, Duluth, MN, USA

"Given a thimbleful of facts, we rush to make generalizations as large as a tub."

—G. Allport

ABSTRACT

Laughter is universal among humans. As an important part of life, few disagree with the statement: "Laughter is the best medicine." Even fewer would say laughter has no influence on the immune system, blood pressure, or cardiac output, which raises several questions: "What are the physiological responses during and following laughter?" Is laughter exercise and, if so, what are the health implications? Perhaps, the truth is somewhere in between the "best medicine" and the "promotion" of laughter as a business. The science of laughter is in its infancy. Hence, what is the physiology of laughter? What are the health benefits, given the interest in laughter as an alternative therapy? This chapter examines the cardiovascular responses to laughter. Cardiac output was measured during laughter to understand the role of the central (cardiac output) and peripheral (arterial-venous O_2 difference) components of oxygen consumption (VO_2) and its relation to energy expended. College subjects participated by sitting in a comfortable chair for 5 minutes, followed by viewing a videotape of a well-known comedian for 5 minutes, which was followed by sitting for 5 minutes. A repeated-measures ANOVA was used to analyze the data. During laughter, there were significant increases in stroke volume and cardiac output and significant decreases in arterial-venous O_2 difference and systemic vascular resistance. Following laughter, there was a significant decrease in oxygen consumption. More scientific research about laughter is needed to understand the healthcare implications. In the meantime, laughter is an important nonverbal communicative skill. It is fun to laugh, and it seems to decrease tension. People appear to feel good when they laugh, and maybe that is enough because it is pleasurable.

Everyday communication is an integrated approach of giving and receiving verbal and nonverbal messages. The interplay of the messages conveys meaning and, on occasion, contradictory meanings [1]. When people are face-to-face, their eyes interact along with selected verbal behavior [2]. Communication is therefore linked to verbal and nonverbal behaviors. In addition to words, facial expressions are especially important in conveying different kinds of meanings [3]. Gesturing with the hands while speaking is a recognized function of communication. Similarly, raising eyebrows, raising an index finger, and/or changing eye contact are all important nonverbal forms of communicating. Also, smiles, playfulness, touch, and laughter are thought to communicate a wide range of messages with different meanings [4]. Laughter, in particular, as a nonverbal communication, is a vital part of interpersonal communication.

Although not all laughter-inducing circumstances (like relief from tension or laughter from tickling) are humorous, the discussion of laughter in this chapter is viewed as that which generally results from humor [5]. It should be obvious that not all humor elicits laughter [6]. As a powerful and important component of life, few would disagree with the statement: "Laughter is the best medicine." However, is laughter actually a very powerful medicine? That is, like medicine, does it cure high stress, dissolve anger, and improve brain functioning? Mental health professionals believe that laughter has a positive effect on the immune system, endorphin levels, and blood pressure [7]. If so, what are the statistically demonstrated physiological responses during and following laughter? Does laughter actually boost endorphins? Intriguing as it sounds, does laughter increase the expenditure of energy? Does it attenuate stress-related hormones, increase the number of natural killer cells, or activate T cells and B cells?

Making sense of the physiological effects of laughter is not difficult, but appreciating that research has not proven the healthcare benefits of laughter is another matter. In other words, while there is considerable belief in the positive effects of laughter, there is still much to be learned about laughter. The fact that there are video and audiocassettes, books, journals, workshops, organizations, and conferences devoted to the physical and mental health benefits of laughter does not prove that it is so. Part of the problem is that there are too many unsubstantiated and distorted claims that cannot be ignored. Speculation and belief are not science, and perception is not empirical support for the claims that associate with laughter. Hence, the belief that laughter can help a person cope with pain may be more a cliché than a fact. This kind of thinking may well be driven by comments by Norman Cousin that were taken out of context [8, p. 39].

Much of what is known about health and wellness depends on the quality of the research, especially the analysis of scientific findings. Most people know the value of good research. Those who do not are likely to translate the data into advice or even therapy when it is inappropriate to do so. It is a safe bet that the benefits of laughter are still too complex to understand how and whether laugher establishes or even restores a positive psycho-physiologic environment throughout the body. Until more research is done, it is better to think about laughter as having the potential for favorable health benefits than believing that there is an absolute connection between the two. The impact on the body may be coincidental. Hence, as an example, whether it raises, lowers, or has no effect on blood pressure remains to be seen. Understanding the benefits of laughter begins first with understanding the physiology of laughter.

Most agree on the need for regular exercise, good nutrition, and avoidance of excessive habits like alcohol and caffeine. Most also agree that participation in a well-rounded wellness program is beneficial. Is it equally appropriate to conclude that taking time out at the workplace to laugh is important for health reasons? Some caregivers believe that this is the case. Perhaps life's issues and problems can be handled best when there is more time to laugh with colleagues and friends. However, for those who believe in evidence-based medicine and the importance of scientific thinking, there simply is not the research to support the assumed pleasures and wonders of laughing. This does not mean that learning new and different coping strategies, striving to maintain balance and harmony in work and at home, and communicating in nonverbal ways (such as laughing) singly or collective may not be beneficial [9].

The science of laughter is in its infancy. Unlike the knowledge gained from decades of comprehensive scientific studies about regular exercise, the assumptions about laughter are for the most part poorly researched. There is very little scientific support from the existing studies to state with a sense of sureness that laughter decreases the likelihood of disease and all other kinds of healthcare problems. In fact, at the present time, the list of unanswered questions and unsolved issues seems endless. A cheerful mood that may follow laughter is not evidence of statistically significant physiological changes in the response to the outburst of laughter. Other nonverbal styles of communicating, especially smiling or other facial changes during laughter, and even increasing the intensity of laughter may bear no relationship to a correct communication or a person's state of health. Moreover, given the context of a single laughing act of even 7 seconds, which is at the extreme duration of a laughing response, is it no wonder that many cardiovascular changes are not fully accounted for and await scientific analysis?

Hence, the belief that laughter creates positive physiological responses similar to the assumed responses to other types of nonverbal communication is interesting. Why should a laugh influence the body the same way as a smile or a touch? The physiological response to either is likely to be significantly different from laughter. If touch, for example, were to increase metabolism through enhanced central nervous system activity, why should laughter do the same? In other words, are different communicative styles distinctively more physical or emotional than others? Does a smile increase metabolism? Does laughter increase or decrease heart rate and, if so, what are the implications? If the brain is intimately involved in laughter, does that make laughing a psycho-physiological event?

At this point, one might ask the following questions: "What is the physiology of laughter?" "What are the health benefits?" The answer to the first question is based on a limited number of research studies. With regard to the second question, there is considerable interest in laughter as an alternative therapy. This is not new thinking. Alternative options for dealing with life's issues and concerns are increasingly popular. Caregivers seem convinced of the positive effects of laughter. It doesn't require any special equipment and many believe that laughter is the best medicine for a healthy mind-body balance. It has no ill side effects. It does not cost anything, and it is said to be an excellent way to release anti-depressant mood chemicals. However, the majority of the findings come from newsletters, magazines, presentations, and non-scientific articles written by humor professionals [10, 11]. This means one thing, the research is weak, premature, and exaggerated [12]. The research has several recognizable flaws, including but not limited to: (a) small sample size; (b) no randomized design; (c) no control group; (d) low statistical power; and (e) no standardized baseline measurements. Until the quality of the research improves, critical thinking caregivers should discuss and/or apply the physiology of laughter with caution.

As an example, the belief that laughter increases the release of endorphins is not supported by scientific research [6]. In fact, two studies found no significant change during laughter [13, 14]. More rigorous research is needed before firm conclusions can be drawn about possible health benefits of laughter [15]. Yet, in spite of the sparse and weak research designs, caregivers continue to advocate the use of laughter to improve the health of their clients. Similarly, it is reported that laughter decreases tension and anxiety [16] and, therefore, may contribute to a feeling of well-being [17]. As a result, the health benefits of laughter have gained widespread attention as an antidote for stress [18]. It is said to increase immunoglobulin A (IgA), which is believed to protect against upper respiratory infections [19]. Other studies have reported that laughter helps antibodies destroy defective or infected cells [20] and increases the number and activity of natural killer cells and T cells [21]. The evidence that laughter and health are inextricably intertwined [22] has encouraged caregivers to advocate the use of laughter to improve the health of their clients. This raises the concern that before laughter becomes recognized as a serious therapeutic coping mechanism (such as progressive muscle relaxation, imagery, and therapeutic massage), more must be known about the cardiovascular responses to laughter. Also, the analysis should go beyond the link between laughter and heart rate (HR) and/or systolic blood pressure (SBP) to understand its healing properties.

A comprehensive, scientific analysis of the cardiovascular responses of laughter is rare [23]. Laughter may relieve tension and help cope with painful feelings [24], but there is essentially no evidence that laughter affects cardiac output (Q). If tension is relieved by laughter, oxygen consumption (VO_2) should decrease. Since oxygen consumption is highly correlated with cardiac output, it should decrease. To know whether this is the case, the measurement of cardiac output [i.e., the product of heart rate (HR) and stroke volume (SV)] and the difference in the oxygen content of arterial and mixed venous blood (i.e., arterial-venous oxygen difference, a-vO_2 diff) is imperative. A change in any of these should help clarify the link between laughter and oxygen consumption, given that it is the product of cardiac output (the "central" component of VO_2) and arterial-venous oxygen difference (the "peripheral" component).

Boone and colleagues [23] determined the cardiovascular responses of laughter, using an ABA research design (Control #1, Treatment, and Control #2; each 5 minutes in duration). Eight college-age subjects (4 female and 4 male) volunteered to participate in the study. The subjects provided written consent. The Human Subjects Review Committee of The College of St. Scholastica approved the experimental protocol. The subjects' mean (±SD) age, body mass, and height were 22 ±.5 yr, 63 ±8 kg, and 165 ±1.2 cm, respectively for the female volunteers, and 23 ±2 yr, 88 ±9 kg, and 177 ±1.4 cm, respectively for the male volunteers. Prior to the videotape presentation, the subjects rested for 5 minutes while sitting in a comfortable chair positioned directly in front of a television (Control #1). During the 5-minute Treatment period, the subjects viewed a previously selected part of the laughter videotape that consisted of humorous age-appropriate jokes by Robin Williams (a Home Box Office presentation entitled, "The Evening of the Met"). After the treatment, the subjects remained in the chair for the final 5 minutes of data collection (Control #2).

Oxygen consumption data were averaged across the 5 minutes of Control #1 to establish the subjects' baseline measures, across the 5 minutes of viewing the videotape, and across the 5 minutes of Control #2 using a Medical Graphics CPX/D metabolic analyzer (Medical Graphics Corporation, St. Paul, MN). The CPX/D flow device for measuring volume is a bi-directional differential pressure preVent Pneumotach with a range of ±18 L/sec and an accuracy of $\pm3\%$ or 50 mL, whichever is greater. The O_2 analyzer has a range of 0 - 100%, response time (10 - 90%) <80 msec, and an accuracy of $\pm0.03\%$. The CO_2 analyzer has a range of 0 - 10%, response time (10 - 90%) <130 msec, and an accuracy of $\pm0.05\%$. All metabolic assessments were made in a temperature-controlled laboratory.

Cardiac output (Q) was determined during minute 5 of each 5-minute period using the indirect CO_2 rebreathing technique [25]. Published results derived from the breath-by-breath gas analyzers demonstrate that the cardiac output measurement is reproducible [26] and valid [27]. The CO_2 analyzer and the CO_2 rebreathing method are widely used for the determination of cardiac output [28]. Arterial CO_2 (PaCO$_2$) was derived from the end-tidal pulmonary CO_2 (PETCO$_2$). Mixed venous pulmonary CO_2 (PvCO$_2$) was derived from the CO_2 rebreathing (bag) procedure [29]. Arterial CO_2 and mixed venous contents were calculated from arterial CO_2 and PvCO$_2$ respectively, using the standard oxygenated CO_2 dissociative curve [30]. The metabolic analyzer displayed the CO_2 signal graphically to ensure the PvCO$_2$ equilibrium. Stroke volume was estimated by dividing cardiac output by heart rate. Arterial-venous oxygen difference (a-vO$_2$ diff, mL/100 mL) was calculated by dividing oxygen consumption by cardiac output [31].

Heart rate (HR) was monitored during the last 10 seconds of each minute of data collection in each period, using the Physio-Control LIFEPACK 9 defibrillator/monitor (Physio-Control Corporation, Redmond, WA). The device is used to routinely monitor heart rate in medical settings using a 3-lead wire configuration. The heart rate data were averaged across the 5 minutes of each period. Systolic and diastolic blood pressure measurements were determined by auscultation of the left brachial artery using a standard mercury sphygmomanometer during minute 5 of each period. Systolic blood pressure (SBP) was determined as the point of appearance of Korotkoff sounds, while the point of disappearance was the diastolic pressure. Mean arterial pressure (MAP) was calculated by adding one-third of the pulse pressure (the difference between SBP and DBP) to the diastolic pressure [32]. Systemic vascular resistance (SVR) was calculated by dividing mean arterial pressure by cardiac output [31]. Arterial-venous oxygen difference was calculated by dividing oxygen consumption by cardiac output [33].

Although oxygen consumption was not affected by laughter (.28 to .27 L/min, p > .05), several components of the VO$_2$ equation [VO$_2$ = Q x a-vO$_2$ diff] were significantly changed. Stroke volume increased during laughter (75 to 88 ml, p = .04), which was physiologically responsible for the increase in cardiac output (4.99 to 6.13 L/min, p = .02). The increase in stroke volume and cardiac output during laughter was accompanied by relaxing the smooth muscle walls of the arterioles, resulting in the decrease (19 to 16 mmHg/L/min, p = .02) in systematic vascular resistance (SVR). The peripheral extraction of oxygen (a-vO$_2$ diff) was statistically decreased (5.74 to 4.58 mL/100 mL, p = .01). Hence, with the increase in cardiac output, the VO$_2$ equation was balanced and total body oxygen consumption remained constant.

Contrary to the increase in heart rate reported by Averill [34] and McGhee [19], the subjects' heart rate was statistically unchanged during laughter (69 to 73 beats/min, p = .24). This is an interesting departure from the assumption that heart rate increases with laughter. In actuality, there are simply too few scientific studies on laughter to know for certain the influence of laughter on heart rate. Also, there are essentially no studies that have analyzed the role of age, gender, and culture on the physiology of laughter. This point is demonstrated in the blood pressure responses to laughter. Most caregivers believe that blood pressure is increased with laughter, and then decreases following laughter. However, Boone and colleagues [23] found the opposite in both situations. Blood pressure was unchanged during laughter versus the control period, and it was unchanged following laughter. Laughter did not affect the subjects' blood pressure, which disagrees with a report [35] that found an increase in blood pressure during laughter.

The decrease in the subjects' systemic vascular resistance (SVR) during laughter is consistent with the unchanged mean blood pressure response (90 to 92 mmHg, p = .28). That is, since laughter increased the subjects' cardiac output with a decrease in afterload (SVR), the adjustment in the latter kept the mean arterial pressure unchanged. Had the subjects' laughter resulted in a vigorous contraction of the muscles of the upper limbs and/or the smooth muscles of the arterioles, the increase in arterial pressure would very likely have been associated with an increase in afterload. This would have increased the pressure that the ventricles would develop to eject blood into the arterial system. As a result, the work of the heart would have increased with a corresponding increase in myocardial oxygen consumption (MVO_2).

The caloric cost of the laughter period (5 kcal x .27 L/min = 1.35 kcal/min) was the same as the prelaughter baseline measurement (5 kcal x .28 L/min = 1.4 kcal/min). This finding indicates that laughter is not exercise! Contrary to what some advocates of laughter therapy think, the benefits of aerobic exercise cannot be realized by laughing. To illustrate this point, an exercise intensity of 120 beats/min or 60% of maximum heart rate (assuming 200 bpm at maximum) is usually the lowest exercise heart rate intensity used to realize a cardiovascular benefit from exercise training [36]. If the submaximal exercise oxygen consumption is in the range of 1.5 L/min, the caloric cost per minute of exercise would be 7.5 kcal (1.5 x 5 kcal) or better than 5 times (.28 L/min x 5 kcal) the energy expended per minute during one minute of laughter. There simply is no way that laughter, regardless of the number of laughs per minute (even after 10 minutes of laughter) can equal the intensity of energy expended during exercise. For example, 10 minutes of laughter at .28 L/min times 5 kcal equals 14 kcal of energy expended versus 10 minutes of exercise at 60% heart rate intensity, which equals 75 kcal (1.5 L/min x 5 kcal/L of O_2 consumed x 10 minutes = 75 kcal).

During the period following laughter, oxygen consumption was significantly decreased (.27 to .24 L/min). However, it could be argued that the decrease has little physiological or clinical value because the central (Q, 6.13 vs. 5.90 L/min, p > .05) and peripheral (a-vO_2 diff, 4.58 vs. 4.11 mL/ 100 mL, p > .05) components of oxygen consumption were unchanged. Similarly, the post-laughter heart rate (73 vs. 71 beats/min, p > .05), systolic blood pressure (124 vs. 120 mmHg, p > .05, and systemic vascular resistance (16 vs. 16 mmHg/L/min, p > .05) responses were not influenced by the laughter period. One might have expected that following the laughter period, the subjects' physiological responses would have decreased. Such a response would be consistent with a post-laughter relaxing effect. However, it is clear that this did not happen in this study. When the post-laughter cardiovascular responses are compared to the baseline measurements (Control #1) prior to the laughter period (Treatment), oxygen consumption was significantly decreased (.28 to .24 L/min). However, this finding may also have little practical value in terms of energy expenditure (1.4 vs. 1.2 kcal/min or 7 vs. 6 kcals for each 5-minute period, Control vs. Treatment, respectively).

In general, the data indicate that the Treatment period (laughter) versus the Control #1 period resulted in cardiovascular changes in stroke volume, cardiac output, arterial-venous O_2 difference, and systemic vascular resistance. The increase in ventricular contractility was offset by the decrease in systemic vascular resistance, which kept blood pressure from increasing. The decrease in tissue extraction (a-vO_2 diff) offset the increase in cardiac output, thus oxygen consumption was unchanged. Following the laughter period (Control #2), the subjects' responses remain essentially the same as during the laughter period. This indicates that the effects of laughter continued for at least 5 minutes following laughter and that the effects are similar to the same cardiovascular responses during the laughter period versus Control #1.

The problem faced by the caregiver is the interpretation of the physiology of laughter in relation to a response pattern that is believed to be healthy. Obviously, the physiology of laughter per se must be validated in terms of health benefits in clinical practice. Numerous key questions concerning laughter, health, and recovery from illness remain unanswered. For example, given that oxygen consumption was significantly decreased following laughter when compared to before laughter, what is the health implication, if any? Given that stroke volume was significantly increased following laughter versus before laughter, is the increased work of the heart consistent with a positive health benefit? Also, given that systemic vascular resistance was significantly decreased following laughter versus before laughter, is laughter therefore beneficial for hypertensive patients? Likewise, what is the explanation for the observation that laughter or humorous anecdotes release tension and promote better health? To what extent is the observation biased? Answers to these question may begin with the physiology of laughter, but they certainly are not limited to physiological analyses. An important question is, which laughter-induced cardiovascular response in combination with psychological responses are the right prescription for better health and/or recovery from illness?

A limitation of the study by Boone and colleagues [23] is the small sample size. Also, another limitation is the subjectivity of a videotape of laughter. What may be humorous to one subject may not be humorous to another. For this reason, the repeated measures design was used because it is more sensitive than an independent-groups design to differences in dependent variables between the three conditions (Control, Treatment, and Control). Because the same subjects served in all conditions, they were identical in every other respect. This reduced between-subject variability, thus improved the chances of detecting any effects caused by the independent variable (the humorous videotape). Another limitation of the study that should be noted is that the subjects were required to watch the videotape with a rubber mouthpiece and plastic nose clip. Although the subjects indicated that the equipment did not keep them from laughing along with the videotape, the equipment had to make it harder to laugh. The subjects were familiar with the laboratory setting and the cardiovascular measurement techniques. Laughter was evident with each subject tested, although specific documentation as to how long each subject laughed, how often and/or the intensity of the laughter was not part of the data collection process. After data collection, the subjects generally expressed that the laughter had contributed to a positive feeling. However, before laughter is used to inform healthcare practice and policy, the data and findings must be independently observed and verified [37] from a larger sample.

This does not mean that knowledge and work experiences derived primarily through one's healthcare practice are not useful [38]. On the contrary, this kind of information has the potential for becoming more formal knowledge derived from research and scholarship. As such knowledge becomes debated and verified through scientific scrutiny and public view, it may become part of the quantitative evidence-based research data that supports laughter as a nonverbal "health-benefiting" communicative skill [39]. But, to be fair, research evidence does not always provide answers with absolute certainty and may change as new research is published. All research evidence should be viewed as provisional [40]. What is known today about laughter may change considerably in 10 or 15 years. This is important in light of the following unpublished research from the Graduate Exercise Physiology Laboratory of The College of St. Scholastica. The findings [41] have not been peer-reviewed. The research design consisted of a Control period followed by a Treatment period. The same metabolic equipment was used (along with standard data gathering procedures) as was previously outlined in the 2000 issue of *Applied Nursing Research* [23]. Ten college-age subjects (8 female and 2 male) volunteered to participate in this study. The subjects' mean (±SD) age, body mass, and height were 21 ±1 yr, 73 ±6 kg, and 169 ±1.2 cm, respectively. They were instructed to refrain from eating, drinking caffeine, and exercising for 2 hours before testing. Prior to the videotape presentation, the subjects rested for 10 minutes while sitting in a comfortable chair positioned directly in front of a television (Control period). During the next 15 minutes, the Treatment period, the subjects viewed two age-appropriate tapes. The first was the "dentist" sketch from "Bill Cosby: Himself" and the second was the "dinner table" scene from the movie, "The Nutty Professor."

Contrary to the first study in which the laughter period was 5 minutes in duration, 15 minutes of laughter resulted in a significant increase in oxygen consumption. Statistically speaking, the subjects expended more energy during the laughter period (1.2 metabolic equivalents, METs vs. baseline, 1 MET). However, it is important to point out that the difference, even across 25 minutes is still small and has little to no practical value. By rearrangement of the Fick equation (VO_2 = Q x a-vO_2 diff), it is clear that the increase in oxygen consumption (VO_2) during laughter resulted from the subjects' central adjustment in cardiac output (5.2 to 7.3 L/min, p = .012). This finding agrees with the earlier work by Boone and colleagues [23]. The increase in heart rate (from 76 to 86 beats/min, p = .0007) was responsible for the increase in cardiac output, which is consistent with the reports by Averill [34] and McGhee [19] but disagrees with the Boone et al. paper [23]. The increase in cardiac output occurred even though the stroke volume was not statistically increased (68 to 84 ml, p = .06) during laughter, which disagrees with stroke volume response of Boone et al. [23]. Systemic vascular resistance was significantly decreased (from 17.5 to 13 mmHg/L/min, p = .03) during laughter [43], which agrees with Boone et al. [23].

The heart's need for oxygen (MVO_2) correlates (r = 0.88) with the product of heart rate and systolic blood pressure (double product). The 15 minutes of laughter resulted in a significant increase in double product (95 to 114, p = .0001) due to the increase in heart rate and systolic blood pressure (125 to 133 mmHg, p = .0001). Hence, using the regression equation: [MVO_2 = 0.14 (HR x SBP x 10^{-2}) -6.3], it can be estimated that myocardial oxygen consumption increased 17% during laughter. The subjects' peripheral extraction of the delivered oxygen (arterial-venous oxygen difference) was unchanged during laughter (i.e., 4.1 mL/100 mL during the Control and 3.7 mL/100 mL during the Treatment, p = .43). With the increase in cardiac output, the VO_2 equation was unbalanced in favor of an increase in energy expended as a function of increased work of the heart and not an increase in tissue extraction. This conclusion is warranted since cardiac output was increased without an increase in arterial-venous O_2 difference.

The blood pressure data agree with the work by Fry and Savin [35]. They documented an increase in blood pressure during laughter. Again, since systolic blood pressure (SBP) reflects the work of the heart, laughter increased the heart's need for oxygen. This relationship is also expressed in the formula: [SBP = Q x SVR]. Either cardiac output increased more so than the decrease in systemic vascular resistance or the resistance in the arterioles failed to decrease sufficiently to offset the central response. It is likely that the flow of blood from the arteries into the capillaries was hindered by the occasional movement of the smaller muscle mass of the upper body with the laughter response, thus elevating both systolic blood pressure by 6% and mean arterial pressure (MAP) by 4% (91 to 95 mmHg, p = .001).

Systemic vascular resistance during laughter was decreased, but the percent change was small (26%) compared to the decrease in vascular resistance during exercise. For example, an exercise cardiac output of 15 L/min with a mean arterial pressure of 100 mmHg equals a systemic vascular resistance of 6.67 mmHg/L/min or a decrease of 67% from an average beginning (or resting vs. exercise) SVR of 20 mmHg/L/min. This indicates that the 13 mmHg/L/min during laughter is not a typical decrease in afterload since resistance to blood flow usually decreases to 5 or 7 mmHg/L/min during exercise. Thus, once again, the benefits of aerobic exercise cannot be realized during laughter since a high afterload (resistance in the vascular system) would tend to keep cardiac output low [44].

The subjects' mean heart rate of 86 beats/min during laughter approximates 45% of the subjects' anticipated training intensity. Future studies should be designed with longer laughter periods in order to address whether there is an independent effect of abrupt and sustained laughter on heart rate and other physiological responses. Although the results of this unpublished study are limited by the small number of subjects studied, they are important for two reasons. First, they represent a basic but comprehensive cardiovascular analysis of laughter. Second, they help to define, physiologically speaking, what laughter is not. In regards to its frequent association to exercise, perhaps, a longer laughter period may result in a higher expenditure of energy and a higher heart rate response. Additionally, while this study did not evaluate the subjects' physiological responses after the 15 minutes of laughter, it is possible that the effects of the longer laughter period may have additional benefit to the physiology of the mind-body connection.

Healthcare professionals interested in the physiology of laughter should plan comprehensive cardiovascular studies that allow for a better understanding of laughter as well as the validation of its use in healthcare. Many key questions concerning laughter, health, and recovery from illness remain unanswered. For example, what is the physiological explanation for the belief that laughter releases tension and promotes better health? Again, the answer to this question is likely to require an understanding of the physiology of laughter. But, since much about laughter is unknown, the science of laughter will encompass the study of many different aspects of the mind-body complex. Determining which laughter-induced cardiovascular response is the right prescription to better health and/or recovery from illness will not be easy. Again, there is an obvious paucity of data regarding these effects and/or the interaction of mind-body factors. Additional research is warranted.

On the other hand, laughter, as a nonverbal communicative skill, may help deal with stressful times in life and may help build positive relationships at home and at work [45]. Whether the "atmosphere of general goodwill" helps to reverse the classic stress response remains to be determined. Similarly, whether the sound of laughter helps to foster relaxation and protect the heart remains to be determined. Or, stated somewhat differently, if laughter does decrease serum cortisol [13], it still remains to be determined if the decrease strengthens the immune system [46]. It also remains to be determined whether the assumed healthcare role of laughter as a healing therapy works across gender lines, ethnicity lines, and age demographics. In other words, laughter may be contagious but it is not an understood science.

At the present time, there is no clear-cut majority of evidence-based research to support laughter as a prescriptive method of alternative treatment to mind-body issues and concerns. This raises very important questions regarding health benefits. In particular, the desire of healthcare professionals to catapult laughter to the level of other alternative healthcare treatments may have violated the "first rule of holes, that is, when you're in one, stop digging." This does not mean that laughter is not important or an essential part of life. Laughter is an important nonverbal communicative skill. It is fun to laugh. Laughter appears to reduce tension. People appear to feel good when they laugh, and maybe that is enough because it is pleasurable [47]. Perhaps equally important, laughter can be used to cheer up someone else's life. For many people, communication in any form is important.

REFERENCES

[1]   Bugental, D.E., Kaswan, J.W., and Love, L.R. (1970). Perceptions of contradictory meanings conveyed by verbal and nonverbal channels. *Journal of Personality and Social Psychology*. 16, 647-655.

[2]   Cegala, D., Sydel, S., and Alexander, A. (1979). An investigation of eye gaze and its relation to selected verbal behavior. *Human Communication Research*. 5, 99-108.

[3]   Mehrabian, A. and Ferris, S.R. (1967). Inference of attitudes from nonverbal communication in two channels. *Journal of Consulting Psychology*. 31, 248-252.

[4]   Grammer, K. (1990). Stranger meet: laughter and nonverbal signs of interest in opposite-sex encounters. *Journal of Nonverbal Behavior*. 14,4, 209-235.

[5]   Howe, N.E. (2002). The origin of humor. *Medical Hypotheses*. 59,3, 252-254.

[6]   Mahony, D.L. (2000). Is laughter the best medicine or any medicine at all? *Eye on Psi chi*. 4,3, 18-21.

[7]   Sowell, C. (1996). Is laughter the best medicine? Quest. 3,4 [Online]. *http://www.mdausa.org/publications/Quest/q34laughter.html*

[8]   Cousins, N. (1979). Anatomy *of an illness as perceived by the patient: reflections on healing and regeneration.*. New York, NY: Norton.

[9]   Hertzler, J. (1970*). Laughter, a socio-scientific analysis*. New York, NY: Exposition Press.

[10]   Basmajian, J.V. (1998). The elixir of laughter in rehabilitation. *Archives of Physical Medicine and Rehabilitation*. 79,12, 1597.

[11] Sultanoff, S.M. (1999). Examining the research on humor: being cautious about our conclusions. *Therapeutic Humor*. 13,3, 3.

[12] Berk, R. (2004). Research critiques incite words of mass destruction. The Humor Connection. Association for Applied and Therapeutic Humor. [Online]. *http://aath.org/art_berkr01.html*.

[13] Berk, L.S., Tan, S.A., Fry, W.F., Napier, B.J., Lee, J.W., Hubbard, R.W., Lewis, J.B., and Eby, W.C. (1989). Neuroendocrine and stress hormone changes during mirthful laughter. *American Journal of Medical Sciences*. 298, 390-396.

[14] Yoshino, S., Fujimori, J., and Kohda, M. (1996). Effects of mirthful laughter on neuroendocrine and immune systems in patients with rheumatoid arthritis. *Journal of Rheumatology*. 23, 793-794.

[15] Martin, R.A. (2001). Humor, laughter, and physical health: methodological issues and research findings. *Psychological Bulletin*. 127, 4, 504-519.

[16] Goodman, J. (1983). How to get more mileage out of your life: making sense of humor, and then serving it. In P.E. McGhee and J.H. Goldstein (Eds.), *Handbook of Humor Research*. Vol. 11 (pp. 1-22). New York: Springer-Veriag.

[17] Buffum, M.D. and Brod, M. (1998). Humor and well-being in spouse caregivers of patients with Alzheimer's disease. *Applied Nursing Research*. 11, 12-18.

[18] Wooten, P. (1994). *Heart, Humor and Healing*. Mt. Shasta: Communeakey.

[19] McGhee, P. (1996). *Health, Healing, and the Amuse System*. Dubuque, IA: Kendall/Hunt.

[20] Berk, L.S. and Tan, S.A. (1995). A positive emotion, the eustres of mirthful laughter modulates the immune system lymphokine interferon-gamma. *Psychoneuroim munology Research Society Annual Meetings* (abstract supplement), A1.

[21] Nevo, O., Keinan, G., and Teshimousky-Ardit, M. (1993). Humor and pain tolerance. International *Journal of Humor Research*. 6, 71.

[22] Parse, R.R. (1994). Laughing and health: a study using Parse's research method. Nursing *Science Quarterly*. 7, 55-63.

[23] Boone, T., Hansen, S., and Erlandson, A. (2000). Cardiovascular responses to laugher: a pilot project. *Applied Nursing Research*. 13,4, 204-208.

[24] Rowell, L.B. (1993). *Human Cardiovascular Control*. New York: Oxford University Press.

[25] Kirby, T.E. (1985). The CO_2 rebreathing technique for determination of cardiac output: Part I. *Journal of Cardiac Rehabilitation,* 5, 97-101.

[26] Boone, T., Redondo, D., and Cortes, C. (1990). Reproducibility of the CO_2 rebreathing method to estimate cardiac output at rest and during exercise. Abstract. *Southeast Chapter of the American College of Sports Medicine*, February 1-3.

[27] Beekman, R.H., Katch, V., Marks, D., and Rocchini, A.P. (1984). Validity of CO_2-rebreathing cardiac output during rest and exercise in young adults. *Medicine & Science in Sports & Exercise*, 16, 306-310.

[28] Hopman, M.T., Osesburg, B., and Binkhorst, R.A. (1994). Cardiac output determined by the CO_2 rebreathing method during arm exercise. *Clinical Physiology*, 14, 37-46.

[29] Defares, J. (1958). Determination of $PvCO_2$ from the exponential CO_2 rise during rebreathing. *Journal of Applied Physiology*, 13, 159-164.

[30] Ferguson, R.J., Faulkner, J.A., Julius, S., and Conaway, J. (1968). Comparison of cardiac output determined by CO_2 rebreathing and dye-dilution methods. *Journal of Applied Physiology*, 25, 450-454.

[31] Robergs, R.A. and Roberts, S.O. (1997). *Exercise physiology*. St. Louis: Mosby.

[32] Fox, S.I. (1996). *Human physiology*. Chicago: Wm. C. Brown.

[33] Foss, M.L. and Keteyian, S.J. (1998*). Fox's physiological basis for exercise and sport*. New York: McGraw-Hill.

[34] Averill, J.R. (1969). Automatic response patterns during sadness and mirth. *Psychophysiology*. 5, 399-414.

[35] Fry. W.R. and Savin, M. (1982). Mirthful laughter and blood pressure. Paper presented at the *Third International Conference on Humor*. Washington, DC.

[36] Costill, D.L. and Wilmore, J.H. (1994). Physiology of Sport and Exercise. Illinois: *Human Kinetics*.

[37] Davies, H.T.O., Nutley, S., and Smith, P. (2000). Introducing evidence-based policy and practice in public services. In *What Works? Evidence-Based Policy and Practice in Public Services*. (Davies, H.T.O., Nutley, S., and Smith, P.C., eds) The Policy Press, Bristol, pp. 1-11.

[38] Eraut, M. (2000). Non-formal learning and tacit knowledge in professional work. *British Journal of Educational Psychology*. 70, 113-136.

[39] Rycroft-Malone, J., Seers, K., Titchen, A., Harvey, G., Kitson, A., and McCormack, B. (2004). What counts as evidence in evidence-based practice? *Journal of Advanced Nursing*. 47(1), 81-90.

[40] Upshur, R.E.G. (2001). The status of qualitative research as evidence. In *The Nature of Qualitative Evidence* (Morse, J.M., Swanson, J.M., and Kuzel, A.J., eds) Sage, Thousand Oaks, CA, pp. 5-26.

[41] Boone, T., Riley, P., Gordon, C.. Burkard, E., and McNeal, B. (2004). Physiological responses during laughter. Unpublished paper from the *Graduate Exercise Physiology Laboratory of The College of St. Scholastica*, Duluth, MN.

[42] McArdle, W.A., Katch, F.I., and Katch, V.L. (1996). *Exercise physiology: energy, nutrition, and human performance*. Baltimore, MD: Williams & Wilkins.

[43] Rowell, L.B. (1993). *Human cardiovascular control*. New York: Oxford University Press.

[44] Costill, D.L. & Wilmore, J.H. (1994). Physiology of sport and exercise. Illinois: *Human Kinetics*.

[45] Riley, J.B. (2004). Taking life lightly: humor, the great alternative. In Invitation to Holistic Health: A Guide to Living a Balanced Life (Eliopoulos, C.). Boston: *American Holistic Nurses Association*, pp. 251-264.

[46] Wooten, P. (1997). The physiology of humor. *Electric Perspectives*. 22, 72.

[47] Bickel, B. and Jantz, S. (2001). *Simple matters: almost everything you need to know about life, relationships, and knowing God*. Uhrichsville, OH: Promise Press.

In: Focus on Nonverbal Communication Research
Editor: Finley R. Lewis, pp. 101-124

ISBN 1-59454-790-4

Chapter 5

AGING AND THE USE OF ELECTRONIC SPEECH GENERATING DEVICES IN THE HOSPITAL SETTING

Mary Beth Happ,[1] Tricia Roesch,[1,4] Sarah H. Kagan,[1] Kathryn L. Garrett [2] and Nedra Farkas [3]*

[1]School of Nursing, University of Pittsburgh, Pittsburgh, PA, USA
[2]Rangos School of Health Sciences, Duquesne University, Pittsburgh, PA, USA
[3]School of Nursing, Pennsylvania State University, Altoona, PA, USA
[4]University of Maryland Medical Center, Baltimore, MD, USA

ABSTRACT

Electronic speech generating devices (SGDs) offer a vehicle for communicating with family and caregivers to hospitalized patients who lose the ability to speak during critical illness or following surgery. However, there is little empiric evidence regarding the abilities and preferences of nonspeaking, hospitalized older adults with regard to SGD use. This chapter presents a secondary analysis of data from two small pilot studies to explore the communication ability, frequency, content, method, SGD use, quality of SGD communication, and barriers to communication with SGDs among seriously ill hospitalized older adults. Both studies used a mixed methods, complementary design involving qualitative and quantitative data obtained by direct observation, survey, interview, and clinical record review. This analysis focused on the subsample of adult participants who were over 55 years of age. Eight patients, 66.4±8.5 years with 12.5±1.4 years of education and moderately severe illness (APACHE III= 39.2±14.5), had SGDs in their hospital rooms in the medical intensive care unit (n=4) or the otolaryngology surgical unit (n=4), for 1 to 13 (5.7±6.2) days. In total, 46 topics were recorded and categorized for the 32 observed communication events in this older adult sample. The greatest number of messages were about physical care and comfort. Seven (21.8%) of the observed communication events involved SGDs for message construction. SGDs were

---
* *Corresponding Author:* Dr. Mary Beth Happ, 311 Victoria Building, 3500 Victoria Street, School of Nursing, University of Pittsburgh, Pittsburgh, PA 15261; Email: mhapp@pitt.edu; Phone: 412-624-2070

used by patients more often than other nonvocal communication methods to initiate communication and to construct messages about sentiments, emotions, home and family. Ease of Communication scores (ECS) showed improvement after use of the SGDs (23.3±9.7) when compared with pre-intervention scores (31.0±13.8) for older adults where lower scores indicate less difficulty with communication. This chapter includes descriptive observations of communication interactions involving SGDs and poignant quotations from patients, family members and clinicians about SGD use. In conclusion, SGDs can be used by nonspeaking seriously ill older adults for message building and as components of a comprehensive augmentative and assistive communication plan. The successful use of SGDs by acutely and critically ill older adults despite sedation and narcotic analgesia and in the absence of formalized education or feature matching is impressive. However, further research and development activities should be directed toward adapting SGDs for use by older adults and instructing communication partners on cueing and assistance strategies.

INTRODUCTION

Electronic speech-generating devices (SGDs) can offer hospitalized patients who lose the ability to speak during critical illness or following surgery a vehicle for communicating with family and caregivers. [1] Clinicians, speech-language pathologists, or family members can program relevant messages onto a variety of commercially available SGDs so that nonspeaking patients can communicate wants and needs, social closeness, or informative questions or answers in a timely manner. [2] SGD use is not universal practice in the intensive care unit (ICU), however, clinical reports of SGD use with nonspeaking, ICU patients suggest the potential for SGD use to have positive effects on patient affect, motivation, and ability to have needs met. [3-5]

Benefits and barriers to SGD use have recently been documented for the general population of ICU patients. [1, 6] To date, however, issues related to SGD use with the elderly nonspeaking ICU population have received minimal attention. Incidence of SGD use with older adults who are intubated and nonspeaking is unknown, although it is suspected that many clinicians assume that older patients are unable or unwilling to use electronic SGDs during hospitalization for acute or critical illness. Certainly, the cognitive effort required to learn and successfully use a new technology during serious illness is an important consideration, especially for older adults who may have underlying cognitive impairment and are more likely to experience delirium and/or short-term memory loss during critical illness. However, little empirical evidence documents the abilities and preferences of nonspeaking, hospitalized older adults with regard to SGD use. This chapter presents a secondary analysis of data on older patients from two small pilot studies that explored the use of SGDs with seriously ill hospitalized adults.

BACKGROUND

Communication is a complex process involving the sensory, linguistic, cognitive, and neuromotor systems of both the sender and receiver of each message. The amount of shared context, the participants' motivation to interact socially, and their respective social roles and/or familiarity with the communication partner also influence the success of any communication interaction. Whether the sender's intended message results in an identical interpretation in the mind of the receiver is also determined by the participants' abilities to communicate vocally, verbally, by gesture, or through other nonverbal means. [7, 8] Environmental distracters, interruptions, or negative attitudes toward the other participant are among some of the external barriers that can also degrade the quality, success, and intelligibility of a communicated message. The condition of nonspeakingness (for either the sender or receiver of the message) further confounds the communication process, and in fact becomes a formidable barrier to communication in the critical care environment for individuals of all ages.

The aging process can also significantly interfere with an individual's ability to send and receive messages during both unaided (natural) or aided (i.e., augmented with an SGD) communication interactions. [7, 9, 10] Deterioration of sensory skills is experienced by the majority of elders; the course of onset may be insidious and gradual or very sudden. For example, presbyopia (the inability to focus on nearby objects), cataract formation (a disease in which the lens of the eye becomes opaque), sensitivity to glare and light flicker, altered color perception, and altered depth perception are visual changes common in the older adult years. [11, 12] Any of these visual changes may alter the non-speaking older patient's ability to read written cues or instructions, spell using an alphabet board, or view the electronic display screen on an SGD. In an optical simulation study, older adults demonstrated a tendency to confuse colors, inaccurately perceive depth, and experience difficulty reading electronic displays. [13]

Alterations in hearing can reduce the older patient's ability to receive auditory messages, including questions, explanations, and instructions from staff in the ICU environment. Presbycusis, the hearing loss most commonly associated with aging, is manifested by a reduced sensitivity to higher frequency sounds, decreased ability to discriminate between consonants, and general reduction in ability to attend to and comprehend spoken messages. [12] In addition, the noisy and chaotic critical care environment and use of invasive technologies such as mechanical ventilation may interfere with the older adult's interpretation of and response to auditory input. Kline and Scialfa [14] reported that speech is more difficult for the elderly to hear when a person speaks rapidly and when external interference is present, such as machinery, alarms, or background conversation. Bergman [15] found that there was a marked reduction in elders' ability to understand overlapping words, reverberated speech, or interrupted speech. These results reasonably suggest that some elders' ability to comprehend synthesized speech generated by SGDs may also be limited by their diminished hearing acuity and speech discrimination skills.

Two types of electronic speech output options are currently incorporated into commercially-available SGDs. Simple SGDs with limited message capacity often produce spoken messages via digitized speech technology, a more realistic-sounding alternative to synthesized speech. (See Figure 1). Synthesized speech sounds more robotic because sounds are individually programmed into the device. Digitized speech typically is used to represent whole messages on an SGD; synthesized speech is necessary when a communicator wishes to spell their messages or use a complex device with a large vocabulary capacity (See Figure 2). Draeger and Reichle [16] studied the comprehensibility of synthesized speech with older adult subjects when the listener's attention was divided. The results indicated that synthesized speech discourse can be adequately comprehended by older adults in a focused attention condition. However, under conditions of distraction, older adults comprehended significantly less information when presented via synthesized speech versus natural speech. This reduction in comprehension of synthesized speech may affect older adult communication partners as well as patients who utilize SGDs to communicate within the noisy and distracting ICU environment. Although the presence of the visual message display on an SGD may enhance spoken messages produced via synthesized speech, little data are currently available on the functional ability of elders to comprehend either visually-supplemented synthesized speech or digitized speech output from SGDs in a complex medical setting.

Figure 1. MessageMate™ (WordsPlus, Inc., Lancaster, CA).

Figure 2. DynaMyte™ (DynaVox Systems, Inc., Pittsburgh PA).

The changing dynamic of message transmission and response during aging may also contribute to communication barriers. Nussbaum and colleagues [12] reported that elderly individuals required increased time to encode and decode spoken messages produced by communication partners with normal speech abilities as compared to younger counterparts. In addition, older adults may be slower in planning what to say and then retrieving the sounds/letters, words and sentence structure to produce the message. These subtle changes in linguistic processing skills may be manifested by hesitations, false starts, and repetitions when attempting to communicate via natural speech. [12] Similar delays in processing may be evident for older adults who use SGDs. They may need more time to answer a question by retrieving a stored message from an SGD or to encode (i.e., spell, retrieve and sequence individual words or phrases) a novel comment or request.

Communicators who use SGDs also need to have adequate perceptual-motor coordination to successfully access messages from the SGD display, even if they are simply touching each message space with their fingers to activate the voice output. However, sedating medications, muscle weakness, pain, and fatigue can produce psychomotor delays among seriously ill, hospitalized patients. Moreover, perceptual-motor adaptability, as tested by eye-hand coordination, declines with age. [17] Therefore, a greater degree of psychomotor retardation may be experienced by seriously ill older adults during SGD use. This may also contribute to message transmission errors when elderly patients attempt to select and sequence individual letters or whole messages from an AAC display.

Older adults often experience cognitive changes as a result of aging that can degrade the communication process. [18] In the area of memory, the ability to recognize something familiar can be relatively preserved, but recall appears to be more difficult. For example, older adults often complain that they can recognize a familiar name that is spoken aloud but cannot retrieve the name upon demand. Although world knowledge, declarative (i.e., factual) memory, and semantic memory can actually increase with age, memory processes that rely upon fast and accurate processing of brief information doses (e.g., short term verbal or visual memory, long term memory under conditions of alternating or interrupted attention) often declines. [19] Elders complain of increased difficulty with multi-tasking, or the ability to alternate between two tasks. Procedural memory (i.e., the memory for how to do things) is relatively preserved, even in the early stages of dementia. [20] However, learning new procedures appears to occur at a slower rate than in young adults, and recall of those procedures is less accurate. Accuracy of problem solving is reduced for novel situations, and in early dementia, dissipates for even familiar problems such as what to do with one's dirty laundry. In short, cognitive processes such as attention, concentration, memory, and problem-solving can all be affected by the normal aging process. AAC strategies typically require additional cognitive effort from the elder because they are novel and require multiple operational steps. It is therefore incumbent upon the clinician to match AAC strategies to the cognitive capabilities of the older communicator, and to also provide the instruction and support they need to communicate effectively with electronic devices.

Social factors may also impact the communication of elders who are hospitalized or healthy. Ryan [7] suggested that older adults often experience a phenomenon they term, *the communication predicament of aging*, a self-repeating cycle of reduced expectancies for elders, (even when elders actually have communication competence), followed by their withdrawal from communication situations in which these negative expectations occur. Ryan [7], Kemper [21] and others also noted that communication partners often accommodate their communication (e.g., by exaggerating their articulation, simplifying messages, or reducing the frequency of communication) in response to perceptions of reduced competence that may, in fact, be unfounded. The net result is that older adults may gradually be excluded or voluntarily withdraw from communication exchanges as the momentum of this cycle builds. Onset of physical or psychological disabilities, such as those experienced by patients in the acute medical environment, may compound the effects of this cycle unless specific interventions to improve communication competence, such as SGDs, are introduced.

A recent Scottish study [6] to develop and test a computer-based SGD for use with alert, intubated ICU patients included a significant proportion (57.9%) of patients over 60 years of age, however, the researchers did not specifically address the communication abilities, SGD use, or user satisfaction of the older participants. In summary, despite data on the sensory and social implications of aging on communication, little evidence is available regarding the use of SGDs by hospitalized older adults who are experiencing serious and/or life threatening illness.

By combining data from two pilot studies that investigated the effects of introducing SGDs to intubated patients who were over 18 years of age, we explored the ability of temporarily nonspeaking, hospitalized *older* adults to use electronic SGDs. The studies used nearly identical research methods, which have been described elsewhere [1, 22, 23], with two different inpatient populations: medical ICU and otolaryngology surgical unit. This analysis of the data aimed to describe the:

1. *Patient characteristics* (illness severity, neuromotor ability)
2. *Communication frequency and content*
3. *SGD usage patterns* (message categories, frequency, assistance required)
4. *SGD communication quality* (ease, satisfaction)
5. *Barriers* to SGD use

with eight temporarily nonspeaking, hospitalized older adults.

STUDY METHOD

Design

The original studies employed a complementary design combining qualitative and quantitative techniques for more complete description of the use and communication with SGDs. [24] The parent study data set included a total of 89 communication event observations for 21 hospitalized, nonspeaking adults. This secondary analysis focused on data from the eight adult participants who were over 55 years of age.

Procedure

Detailed descriptions of procedures and SGD equipment used in these pilot studies are available in published literature. [1, 23] Two SGDs were used in this study: (1) A battery powered, small message capacity, multilevel recorder with digitized speech output, the MessageMate[TM] (WordsPlus, Inc., Lancaster, California), and (2) A large message capacity, dynamic display device with synthesized speech, the DynaMyte[TM] (Dynavox Systems, Inc., Pittsburgh, PA). Three older adult patients received the MessageMate[TM] and five received the DynaMyte[TM]. Patients were instructed on the use of the SGD by the researchers (MBH, TR) in 20-minute sessions at the bedside; additional reinforcement was provided as needed throughout the study period. The devices were configured with standard messages based on the literature on communication needs of intubated, hospitalized patients, [3, 25-27] however, patients were assisted to customize messages and display configurations after they reviewed the original setup. Standard messages common to all cases included pain, shortness of breath, request for suctioning, help, hot/cold, home, family, anxiety and/or worry. Study participants were followed until extubation or hospital discharge, whichever occurred first. Investigators (MBH, TR) carried pagers, rotating "on call" to solve problems or answer questions about the device.

Instruments

Patient Characteristics

Demographic and clinical data were obtained by chart review, patient report, and family report. *Acute Physiology and Chronic Health Evaluation* (APACHE III), a well accepted and widely used illness severity measure, [28, 29] was used to measured severity of illness on the day of study enrollment. The *Therapeutic Index of Severity Score* (TISS) [30] is a well-tested, quantification of 76 therapeutic interventions that was employed to measure technologic intensity at time of entry into the study. [31] Glasgow Coma Scale (GCS) was applied as a gross measure of cognition at study entry and at each observation timepoint, with appropriate modifications to verbal score for intubated patients. [32] Full verbal score points were awarded on the GCS if the study patient was able to consistently communicate (yes/no, or writing, or gesture) via nonvocal methods. Interrater reliability for the APACHE III, TISS, and GCS was maintained at > 0.90 by testing a randomly selected 10% sample of case data using item agreement tallies. [1]

Outcome Measures

To assess changes in patient perception of communication difficulty, with and without the SGD, participants completed the *Ease of Communication Scale* (ECS) developed and revised by Menzel, [33] before introduction of the SGD (pre-treatment) and after the SGD had been utilized (post-treatment). The researcher read the 10 item, Likert-type statements about perceived communication difficulty to patients who referred to a card with response selections (0 = not hard at all, 1 = a little hard, 2 = somewhat hard, 3 = quite hard, 4=extremely hard) printed in a large (38-point) font. Possible ECS scores range from 0-40, with higher scores indicating greater difficulty with communication. The original 6-item ECS showed good internal validity (alpha = .88). [33] Internal consistency for the revised ECS was established with the first eleven MICU study patients at alpha= 0.93. [1]

A primary investigator (MBH or TR) observed study participants for at least 20 minutes each day and described their communication interactions with nurses, other clinicians, and/or family members. Characteristics of observed communication interactions between the patient and communication partner, such as initiation of communication, position of device, methods of communication, message content, frequency of SGD use, and assistance required by the communication partner, were documented on the investigator-developed *Observation of Communication Event Record*. [1] Distinctly different communication interactions with different partners (e.g., family visitor and nurse) during a single 20-minute observation period were counted as separate communication events. If possible, patients, clinicians, and family members were asked about their experience with the device, including validation of message content heard by observers, after each observation. Clinical records were also reviewed for documentation of nonvocal communication method, content, and SGD use. Observational interviews and clinical record review were documented in descriptive field notes. The *Communication Methods Checklist*, [33] a summation of communication methods by report (from patient, family, nurse) and direct observation while the patient is unable to speak, was also reviewed and updated daily. In all, thirty-nine (39) observations were conducted on this sub-sample of 8 older adults.

Post-observation interviews were conducted with 6 older adult patients, 2 family members, and 4 clinicians (3 nurses and 1 respiratory therapist) involved in the care of these older adult patients to determine satisfaction with the device, barriers to SGD use, and common messages from the perspective of the study participants and their communication partners. The SGDs were used during the interview to question participants about each screen and message option. Interviews were audiotaped whenever possible, transcribed verbatim, reviewed for accuracy and corrected by the interviewer.

Setting/Sample

The studies were sequentially conducted in a (1) medical ICU and (2) an otolaryngology surgical unit in an urban, tertiary care hospital. Patients 18 years of age or older were eligible to participate if they had respiratory tract intubation, consistently followed verbal commands, and were able to complete an Initial Cognitive-Linguistic Screen. [34] In total, 25 patients met study criteria and were invited to participate, 4 declined participation resulting in an 84% recruitment rate. All of those who declined to participate were older adults. The final sample included 21 patients with 8 (38%) participants over 55 years of age. This analysis focused on these eight older adult participants.

Data Analysis

Codes were developed from qualitative field notes and the *Observation of Communication Event Record* for the following variables: communication method(s), number of communication partners, role of communication partner, position of partner, patient, and device, initiator of message, message validation, message content, sedation/analgesia use, and physical restraint, and barriers to SGD use. These code values were entered onto an Excel spreadsheet, and tabulated. Quantitative data were analyzed using descriptive statistics (mean, SD, frequency) and pattern identification via data matrices. [35]

The following categories of SGD usage was developed from the observation data, patient, family, and nurse reports and documentation in the clinical record after the first eleven MICU patients [1] and subsequently applied to all cases: (1) little to no use, (2) occasional use with cueing, (3) some independent use, and (4) dominant form of communication. Two independent raters categorized SGD usage by reviewing data files for each study participant according to these categories. Because cognitive and motor abilities can fluctuate quickly and dramatically in the seriously ill patients, we categorized patient device use according to their "best use." Discrepancies were resolved by consensus agreement following review of the data and category definitions.

RESULTS

Patient Characteristics

The older adult participants, 5 men and 3 women, aged 66.4, ±8.5 years, were equally distributed between the medical intensive care unit and the otolaryngology surgical unit. All participants had completed high school and one was educated at the master's level; half reported previous experience with computers or touch screen computer technology (e.g., automatic teller machines). Most (n=7) participants were Caucasian. Other sample characteristics are described in Table 2. All of these older adult patients reported using some corrective lenses for vision, however, corrective lenses were unavailable in hospital for 2 of the participants. One participant reported impaired hearing and was without the use of hearing aids, and one participant had impaired hearing but used a hearing aid in hospital.

Table 1. SGD Set Up [1]

Features Used	MessageMate™	DynaMyte™
Number of icons/messages on display	36	6-12/page
Spell?	NO	YES
Number of words in output message	1-7	1-10
Direct Select (point)	YES	YES
Auditory Scan/Switch	NO	NO
Visual Scan/Switch	NO	NO
Battery Power	YES	NO*
Dimensions (inches)	11.75 x 4 x 1.25	8 x 7 x 2
Weight (pounds)	1.66	3.20

* Although equipped with a 6-7 hour rechargeable battery, the device was connected to battery charger and power source continuously for this study.

Note: Permission requested from Elsevier, Inc. to reprint this table with modification from Happ et al (2004). Electronic voice-output communication aids for temporarily nonspeaking patients in a medical intensive care unit: a feasibility study. *Heart & Lung - The Journal of Acute and Critical Care,* 33 (2): 94.

Narcotic analgesia, anxiolytics, or other sedating medications were administered within 6 hours in 12 (37.5%) of the communication observations. Two of these observations included the use of both narcotic analgesics and sedation. Physical restraint use was rare (twice in all observations). Only one patient, who experienced upper extremity weakness and difficulty in positioning and reaching the device due to morbid obesity and possible critical care myopathy, was unable to successfully complete the motor screening tasks. An extension wand was constructed for this patient, after which he could successfully activate the SGD display screen.

Communication Frequency and Content

Actual patient communication events were observed and documented on structured Communication Observation Records and expanded field notes in 82% (n=32) of the 39 observations involving older adults. In this analysis, communication content was categorized into 7 topical categories based on the literature on communication with nonspeaking hospitalized patients and previous research. [3, 25-27] A single communication event may have involved several back and forth exchanges between the patient and communication partner about more than one topic. In total, 46 topics were recorded and categorized for the 32 observed communication events.

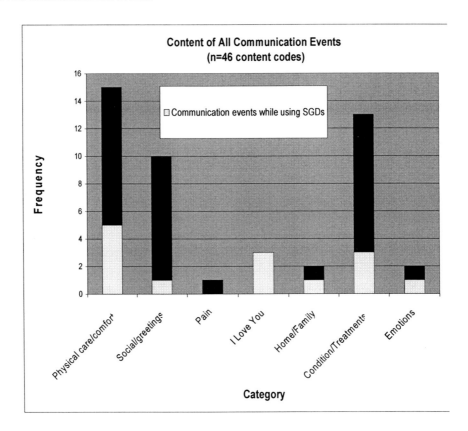

Figure 3. Communication Content

Figure 3 depicts the communication content of all communication events including those constructed with SGDs. The largest number of messages was about physical care and comfort. This category included requests for mouth care, suctioning, bedpan, and complaints of thirst. In some instances, patients used SGDs to initiate physical care requests as a summons to the nurse who was outside of the room.

Hearing a voiced request was unusual for MICU nurses who were accustomed to silent patients. As one nurse described with amusement and some surprise, "[The patient] used it to get my attention...I was standing in the hall and heard *bedpan*!" When the nurse entered the room, the elderly patient repeated his request by again selecting the same "bedpan" message on the SGD.

SGDs were not always successful in summoning the nurse and, indeed, are not intended to be a nurse call system. In fact, as a safety precaution, patients were reminded to use the nurse call light to summon the nurse. For example, an 82 year-old woman who was recovering from laryngectomy surgery began coughing and pushed the "I need suctioning!" message. The nurse did not hear the SGD voice output, and the patient continued to cough but did not replay the message or activate the nurse call light. The researcher intervened by summoning the nurse and instructing the patient to use the nurse call light.

In addition to physical care or comfort requests, patients used SGDs to ask questions about their treatment or condition, to express love and emotions, and to ask about home and family as illustrated in the following field note observation of Jim, a 72 year-old gentleman who was intubated and unable to speak in the MICU for 11 days before receiving a DynaMyte^{TM}.

> Jim was immediately encouraged by his visitors to use the SGD to speak with them. Jim's cousin, a petite woman with short dark hair, stood on a footstool on the right side of his bed leaning over the device to view the message selection while his friend, Bill, stood on the opposite side of the bed reading the message selections out loud Jeopardy-style. Jim's first selection was from the "Questions" menu: "When will the breathing tube come out?" His visitors responded immediately by explaining ventilator weaning and the use of the tracheostomy tube. They told Jim that he was not on the machine all of the time, that it was an improvement, and asked "Isn't it (tracheostomy) better, more comfortable than having the tube in your mouth?" Jim shrugged his large shoulders and lifted his hands, palms upward, in an "I don't know?" gesture. Then, the visitors redirected the patient back to the device. Jim chose from the "About me" menu: "I'm thirsty." Then, from the main screen, he selected, "I love you!" His visitors both responded affirmatively, enthusiastically, "We love you, Jim. We're here for you. Your Christmas gifts are still waiting at home."

Another MICU patient, 57 year-old Manny, reported using the SGD keyboard primarily with his family to communicate a variety of messages, such as requests for the newspaper, a drink, and the following list:

> It's cold in here.
> Can you turn the lights out?
> That machine is beeping.
> I dropped something on the floor. I can't pick it up.

We also observed two interactions between clinicians and seriously ill, nonspeaking older adults that involved decision making about life sustaining treatment and discharge. The SGDs were rejected by clinicians and patients in these instances as illustrated in the following field note:

The physician enters the patient's room wearing a fresh pair of latex isolation gloves. He is a tall man with brown hair and a gentle demeanor. He is unhurried, solemn, respectful as he talks with this elderly patient. The physician greets the patient and moves to the left side of his bed, pushing the DynaMyte™ out of the way, as he helps to reposition the slumping gray-haired man to a more erect sitting position in the bed.

Physician (to patient): "We need to talk about the results of your CT scan. The cancer is back in your lung and also in your spine. I've talked to your wife and your relatives. We're going to need to make some decisions."

The patient indicates via gesture that he wants the endotracheal tube out.
The physician begins to explain the option of a tracheostomy "hole in the throat" which he says would be performed surgically at the bedside.

Physician: "It would be my recommendation. It can help us to take care of you in case you don't do well without the ventilator."
The patient nods "yes" in understanding.

Physician: "You don't have to make decisions now. I want you to know that we will continue to support you and keep you comfortable. (brief pause) If your heart stops beating, do you want us to do everything we can? Usually in cases like yours, that is not helpful."
Patient nods.

The physician then asked the patient if he wanted to write.
The patient indicated "no" then he reached up to touch the endotracheal tube.
The physician reminded the patient that his hands are not tied down.

Patient (using gestures and mouthing words): "I want the tube out now."
Physician: "We can wait and give you some time."
Patient (mouthing words): "I don't have time."

Later, the nurse told me that the patient indicated by making a duck quacking gesture with his hand – hand open and closed, thumb to middle finger - that he wants to talk.

After the endotracheal tube was removed, the patient talked with his wife and together, they decided to forego further life sustaining treatment. The physician offered the following opinion, "[The patient] doesn't like to use [the SGD]. I tried to get him to use it to express his wishes. I think he finds it tedious. We hit him with a lot [of information]. He really wanted to talk…I do think [the SGD] is useful…with nurses for little things…but this was profound."

SGD Usage

Seven (21.9%) of the 32 observed communication events involved the use of SGDs. Messages were constructed by accessing pre-stored phrases, spelling, or combining SGD output with other natural communication methods such as gesture (n=5), mouthing words (n=4), writing (n=3), and head nods (n=4). Patients, family members, and nurses reported additional SGD use that was not directly observed by the researchers. Assistance from the communication partner, such as device positioning, cueing, and/or message validation, was required in 4 of the 7 communication interactions involving SGDs. The following field note observation of nurse-patient communication illustrates a combination of communication methods (head nods, gesture and SGD) and communication partner assistance (cueing and questioning) during message co-construction with a seriously ill older adult.

> The patient's nurse call light is alarming and the nurse enters the room.
> Nurse (to patient): What do you need?
> Patient: (gesturing with his left arm).
> Nurse: Can you spell it out for me here? (pointing to the DynaMyte™ keyboard) Just give me the first letter.
> Patient: (spelling) H-E-L-P
> Nurse: Help what?
> Patient: (spelling) M-E
> Nurse: Help me what?
> - The nurse then began a series of yes/no questions. -
> Nurse: Do you want turned?
> Patient: No
> Nurse: Do you want your head up?
> Patient (nods): Yes.

Communication exchanges that involved SGD use were most often initiated by patients (see Figure 4). None of the older adults used the SGD as the dominant method of communication, however, most patients used the SGD independently (n=3) or with cueing (n=3). Visual inspection of the usage data showed a trend toward greater usage for patients who used the DynaMyte™ (see Table 2). By comparison, the older adult subsample achieved occasional SGD use with cueing and some independent SGD use in greater proportions than the younger cohort (45.5 ± 4.87 years old; range = 20-52) of 13 patients (See Figure 5). Both patients who did not have visual corrective lenses available were able to achieve relatively high usage rates (i.e., some independent use) on the DynaMyte™. Usage categories did not appear to be associated with illness severity (i.e., APACHE III scores) as shown by scatterplot in Figure 6.

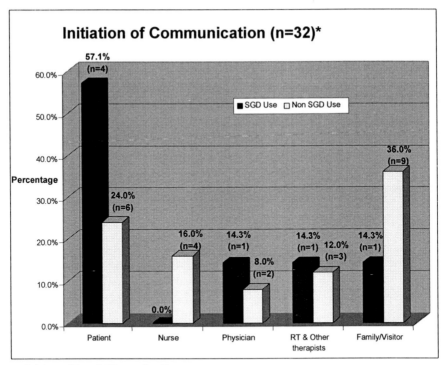

*Unknown initiator, Non-SGD use (n=1)

Figure 4: Initiation of Communication with and without SGDs

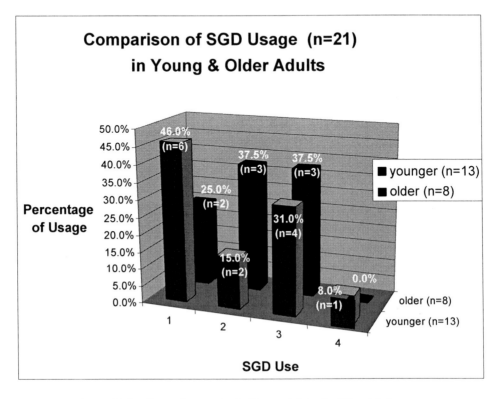

Figure 5. Comparison of SGD Usage Categories in Young Adults & Older Adults

Table 2. Sample Characteristics

Case	Age	Diagnosis	Days With SGD	Days Intubated (nonspeaking) Prior to SGD	APACHE III	TISS Score	ECS Pre Score	ECS Post Score	SGD Usage Category	Airway	Sedation And/or Analgesia	Prior Computer or ATM Use	Legible Writer
1#	72	Sepsis	11	11	51	42	40	27	1	Trach	Y	Y	N
2*	61	Pneumonia Lung Cancer	5	6	54	29	40	N/A	3	ETT	Y	N	N
3	57	Respiratory Failure	2	8	47	32	39	23	2	ETT	Y	Y	N
4*	58	Respiratory Failure	1	0.5	16	25	8	7	3	ETT	N	N	Y
5	82	Supraglottic Laryngectomy	13	0	53	27	N/A	36	2	Trach	Y	N	Y
6	63	Total Laryngectomy	3	1	40	35	N/A	N/A	3	Trach	Y	Y	Y
7	66	Total Laryngectomy	7	0	25	20	N/A	27	1	Trach	Y	N	Y
8	72	Total Laryngectomy	4	0	28	23	28	20	2	Trach	N	Y	Y
Mean	66.38		5.75	3.31	39.25	29.13	31.00	23.33	2.13				
SD	8.50		4.30	4.38	14.52	7.08	13.82	9.65	0.84				

Airway Type: ETT= Endotracheal tube, Trach = tracheostomy

ECS (*Ease of Communication Score*): possible score 0-40 (40=highest difficulty)

SGD Usage Category: 1=Little or no independent use, 2=Occasional use with cueing, 3=Some consistent independent use, 4=AC device as dominant from of communication

N/A = data not available in hospital.

* Eyeglasses not available in hospital.

Unable to complete motor screening tasks due to upper extremity muscle weakness and morbid obesity limiting reaching movement.

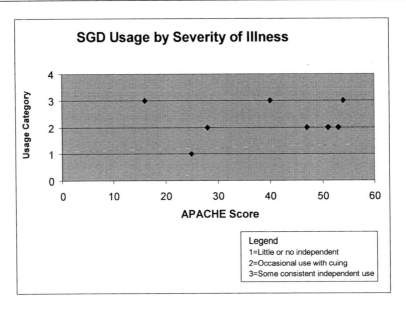

Figure 6. Scatterplot Comparing Device Usage with Severity of Illness (n=8 older adults)

Communication Quality

Communication Ease

Ease of Communication scores (ECS) showed improvement after use of the SGDs (23.3±9.7) when compared with pre-intervention scores (31.0±13.8) for older adults where lower scores indicate less difficulty with communication. Because ECS data were not completed at both (pre- and post-intervention) time points for all of the older adults in the study, the four elderly patients with complete data at both time points were compared (see Figure 7). Results for these individuals showed within-subject improvement for all cases.

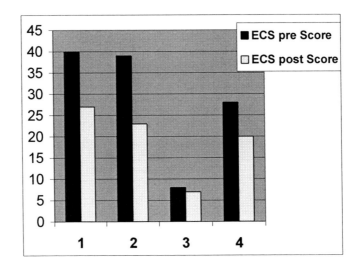

Figure 7. Ease of Communication Within Case Comparison (n=4)

Satisfaction with SGDs

Most family members responded positively, even enthusiastically, to the devices and made comments such as "I think this is great" or "it's a good idea." One family member of an older adult with a lengthy ICU stay said,

> [The patient] has communicated more in the first few minutes here (with the SGD) than in all the time in the ICU. Before, he tried to write but wasn't really able to and would get so frustrated. He worked really hard and made an 'F' on the paper and we just couldn't figure out what he was trying to say. Then he pointed to his stomach and we realized that he was saying "food." So, he was hungry.

Older adult patients acknowledged that the SGDs required some "getting used to" and offered the following modest praise and criticisms:

> It worked pretty good. You could talk with it...It (message selections) pretty much covered everything.
> It was frustrating at first and then it got easier. The letters didn't always come up. I have to punch them two or three times... It saved me a lot in trying to explain things to somebody... I think they could use or make a small laptop for cheaper. It *is* compact but I think you could get something better for less money...It's a good idea but needs improvement.
> Half of the time it didn't have what I want to say...You have to get used to it.

A 66 year-old post-operative head and neck cancer patient complained that the voice and message selections were impersonal. A 73 year-old woman who was unable to speak after laryngectomy surgery suggested that the MessageMate™ needed backlighting to be seen at night and would have preferred to hold the device on her lap or arm rather than have it mounted on a swivel arm.

Barriers to Communication with SGDs

Poor device positioning, deterioration or fluctuation in patient condition (e.g., medical instability, decreasing motor and/or cognitive function), device malfunction, staff time constraints, staff lack of familiarity with the device, and device complexity (multi-level message screens) were the primary barriers to VOCA use among older adult patients.

Devices were found out of reach for older patients in approximately one-third (n=11) of the communication observations. The wife of a 61 year-old man with metastatic lung cancer told us that the device "wasn't close enough for him to use...it was too far away." She recalled pulling the device closer to him when she visited and asking if he wanted to use it. The patient immediately pressed the heart icon "button" and the machine's voice said, "I love you." This communication between husband and wife occurred three days before the patient died.

Fatigue or weakness was identified as a barrier in 7 (21.9%) communication observations and three of the older adult patients complained of upper extremity weakness as a barrier to using the device. These were due in large part to their primary disease conditions rather than age. For example, a MICU patient experienced a complication of advanced lung cancer, called superior vena cava syndrome, that left him without feeling or movement in his right, dominant arm. A 57 year-old man with chronic obstructive lung disease had difficulty using the keyboard function on the DynaMyte[TM]. He reported that "the letters didn't always come up" (appear on the screen) when he tapped them with his finger. After watching him accessing the keyboard, we realized that digital clubbing of his fingertips and upper extremity weakness made touch screen selection difficult and inaccurate. Other examples of primary disease states impeding SGD use include: a morbidly obese 72 year-old MICU patient with profound upper extremity weakness who was unable to fully extend his arms to reach the device and a 66 year-old post operative head and neck cancer patient who experienced a severe headache for 6 of the 7 days in which he had the SGD available.

Study Limitations

The two parent studies used small, purposefully selected samples of MICU and post-operative head and neck cancer patients. Selection criteria (performance of Cognitive-Linguistic Screening Tasks) excluded the most seriously ill, agitated, or confused patients and nurses were reluctant to recommend study participation for depressed patients. The small number of observed communication events using the SGDs (DynaMyte[TM] and MessageMate[TM]) precluded comparisons between two devices. Further, a speech-language pathologist was not used to match device features to patient abilities. Nevertheless, the observers documented that all of the patients in this study demonstrated the capability to use these SGDs. Only one elderly patient (Case 3), who sustained a neurocognitive complication on the fourth post-operative day, lost the ability to use the systems as designed.

Finally, the observational data are limited by the high noise levels, room configurations, and multiple simultaneous interactions indigenous to the acute and critical care settings. Patient, family, and clinician reports indicated slightly greater use than we were able to directly observe. Therefore, these data present a conservative assessment of patient communication in general, and SGD use in particular.

CONCLUSION

Communication technology and aging is a topic that is gaining in popularity and relevance as communication technologies improve and proliferate and as greater numbers of Americans enter older adulthood. [36] Communicating with older adult patients in acute and critical care settings continues to be challenging for clinicians and researchers, especially when older patients are unable to speak. [37] Speech generating device (SGD) designs for elderly patients may require changes in touch sensitivity, screen size, lighting, or contrast, and voice output volume, quality, and pace.

Patient Characteristics

Hospitalized older adult patients ranging in age from 57–82 years of age and with low-to-moderately high illness severity were able to use the SGDs to varying degrees. The patients in this study had relatively high levels of education and cognitive function and half had some prior familiarity with touch screen computer technology.

SGD Usage Patterns and Message Content

The success of a SGD-based AAC intervention in a hospital setting is dependent on many factors, including the availability of AAC technology, patient capabilities, device complexity, and partner familiarity and training. [38-40] Additionally, fluctuations in hospitalized older adults' cognitive, motor, and medical status clearly influence ability to effectively utilize SGD systems. Despite these potential challenges, 6 out of 8 (75%) patients in this study were able to use SGDs with minimal assistance and instruction despite serious illness, poor positioning, sedation, narcotic analgesia, and no "feature match." Moreover, nonspeaking hospitalized older adults fared as well as or better than their younger counterparts in SGD usage (Figure 5), potentially refuting assumptions that older adults may be less able to use SGDs. It is not surprising that patients did not use the devices exclusively to communicate with others. This is consistent with findings from a recent pilot test of a new SGD, *ICU-Talk*, developed by a Scottish multidisciplinary team specifically for use in the ICU. [6] Moreover, a portion of patient communication in the ICU, especially for frequent and predictable needs, can be accomplished by facial, hand, or body gestures. [41]

Importantly, elderly patients in this study initiated over half of the observed communication interactions involving SGDs. This differs from previous studies of nurse-patient communication in which nurses were more often the initiators of communication. [42-46] SGDs may afford seriously ill elderly patients more control or equity in communication interactions. [1] In this study, expressions of sentiments (e.g., "I love you") and physical comfort requests, were the most frequently observed messages constructed wholly or partially with SGDs. These messages were most often initiated by the patient who then directed them to family members. SGDs were also used by older adults to express feelings (e.g., worry, fear) and to ask questions about their condition and treatment (e.g., "when will the breathing tube come out?"). Importantly, sentiment, emotions, and questions about home and family were expressed more often through the use of SGDs in these observations.

The lack of observed SGD-assisted communications initiated by nurses (0%) does not mean that nurses were not involved in SGD-assisted communication interactions. On the contrary, nurses were observed cueing patients to use the SGDs in message construction in several instances. Insufficient staff education and training in use of SGDs and greater use of yes/no questions and anticipatory communications by nurses may have limited nurse-initiated SGD-assisted communications. Family members were the most frequently observed communication partner (Figure 4) and patients reported using SGDs most often with families. If seriously ill patients need to construct more complex messages with family members than with nurses as suggested by Menzel [33], SGDs may facilitate construction and delivery of those messages.

Communication Quality

Ease

Although half of this sub-sample were unable to complete the revised ECS at both time points, data from the four patients with pre and post-intervention ECS scores showed notable reductions in perceived difficulty with communication after using the SGD.

Satisfaction with SGDs

Based on feedback from patients, family members, and nurses, satisfaction with the SGDs was mixed – enthusiasm tempered with suggestions for improvement. The need for better alternative and assistive communication strategies was recognized by all who were involved in communicating with these seriously ill nonspeaking older adults, and most users viewed the electronic SGD as a helpful communication tool. However, some improvements in design, positioning, and instruction are indicated.

Barriers to SGD Use

The barriers to SGD use identified in our studies are similar to reasons for AAC intervention failure in the ICU previously described by Dowden and colleagues. [34] Our findings are also consistent with the Scottish study in which nurses reported that a large screen device and related positioning arms were cumbersome, primarily due to weight (8 kg). [6] The Scottish team noted better results with a smaller device mounted on bed siderails. [6]

Older adults are particularly vulnerable to the affects of serious illness and hospitalization on short-term memory, [26, 27, 47, 48] therefore, AAC device formats should be easily recognizable, instructions may need to be repeated and reviewed frequently, and communication partners (nurses, family members, therapists) must be instructed in appropriate cueing techniques with seriously ill elderly patients. In clinical and research settings, patient understanding and ability to use SGDs should be tested regularly with changes in functional ability documented and necessary adjustments made to the AAC plan of care. Similarly, regular assessment of psychomotor task performance is indicated by the observation of profound psychomotor retardation in patients receiving sedatives and narcotics. [1] This observation also suggests that busy clinicians who are unable or unwilling to wait for a seriously ill elderly patient to complete slow message generation may underestimate the patient's communication abilities. [1, 25]

Based on our experience in these two pilot studies, the following SGD features are suggested as optimal for hospitalized older patients: [1 (p.100)]

(1) easily programmable,
(2) long battery life (>24 hours),
(3) 2 – 3 basic message display formats that can be individualized and saved like a word-processing file,
(4) few speaker holes or crevasses for cleaning,
(5) able to withstand nonabrasive, antibacterial cleaner,
(6) light weight,

(7) large, backlit display screen ($\geq$ 8x11),

(8) high quality speech.

In summary, SGDs can be used by nonspeaking seriously ill older adults for message building and as components of a comprehensive augmentative and assistive communication plan. Refusals for study participation were received disproportionately from older adults indicating that older adults may be less willing to use electronic augmentative and assistive communication devices. Further research and development activities should be directed toward adapting SGDs for use by older adults, instructing communication partners on cueing and assistance strategies, and measuring differences in time for older adults to use SGDs to construct novel messages or to respond to the communications of others. This study is noteworthy in demonstrating successful use of SGDs by acutely and critically ill older adults despite sedation and narcotic analgesia and in the absence of formalized education or feature matching. These results show promise for the development and use of communication interventions that incorporate SGDs and other augmentative and alternative communication techniques to improve communication with hospitalized older adults who are unable to speak.

ACKNOWLEDGEMENTS

This chapter is based on a paper presented at the 2002 Gerontological Society of America Annual Meetings in Boston, MA. Our thanks to Elizabeth Holmes, MSN, and Monica Helinski, BSN for assistance with data collection and management and to Dana DiVirgilio Thomas for assistance in manuscript preparation. Ms. Roesch was a graduate student research assistant at the University of Pittsburgh at the time this study was conducted.

FUNDING

American Association of Critical Care Nurses/Sigma Theta Tau Critical Care Research Grant; Oncology Nursing Society Foundation/Orthobiotech Research Grant

In kind equipment loans provided by AbleNet, Inc., DynaVox Systems, Inc. and WordsPlus, Inc.

REFERENCES

[1]   Happ MB, Roesch TK, Garrett K. Electronic voice-output communication aids for temporarily nonspeaking patients in a medical intensive care unit: a feasibility study. *Heart & Lung: Journal of Acute & Critical Care.* 2004;33(2):92-101.

[2]   Light J. Interaction involving individuals using augmentative and alternative communication systems: state of the art and future directions. *AAC.* 1988;4(2):66-82.

[3]   Costello JM. AAC Intervention in the intensive care unit: The Children's Hospital Boston Model. *AAC.* 2000;16:137-153.

[4]   Dowden P, Beukelman D, Lossing C. Serving nonspeaking patients in acute care settings: Intervention outcomes. *AAC.* 1986(2):38-44.

[5]   Fried-Oken M, Howard, J.M., Stewart, S.R. Feedback on AAC intervention from adults who are temporarily unable to speak. *Augmentative and Alternative Communication.* 1991;7:43-50.

[6]   Etchels MC, MacAulay F, Judson A, Ashraf S, Ricketts IW, Walter A, Alm N, Warden A, Gordon B, Brodie J, Shearer AJ. ICU-Talk: the development of a computerized communication aid for patients in ICU. *Care of Crit Ill.* 2003;19(1):4-9.

[7]   Ryan EB, Giles H, Bartolucci G, Henwood K. Psycholinguistic and social psychological components of communication by and with the elderly. *Language & Communication.* 1986;6(1/2):1-24.

[8]   Lindblom B. On the communication process: speaker-listener interaction and the development of speech. *AAC.* 1990;6:220-230.

[9]   Wahl H, Tesch-Romer C. Aging, sensory loss, and social functioning. In: Charness N, Parks DC, Sabel BA., ed. *Communication, Technology, and Aging.* New York, NY: Springer Publishing Company; 2001:108-126.

[10] Garrett K, Yorkston K. Assistive technology for elders with cognitive and language disabilities. In: Lubinski R, Higginbotham J., ed. *Communication technologies for the elderly: vision, hearing and speech.* San Diego, CA: Singular Publishing Group, Inc.; 1997:203-234.

[11] Kline DW, & Scialfa, CT. Sensory and Perceptual Functioning: Basic Research and Human Factors Implications. In: Fisk AD, & Rogers, W.A., ed. *Handbook of human factors and the older adult.* San Diego, CA: Academic Press; 1997:419.

[12] Nussbaum JF, Pecchioni, L.L, Robinson, J.D., Thompson, T.L. Communication and Aging: Pragmatic and Theoretical Considerations. *Communication and Aging.* 2nd ed. Mahwah, NJ: Lawrence Erlbaum Associates; 2000.

[13] Ishihara K, Ishihara S, Nagamachi M, Hiramatsu S, Osaki H. Age-related decline in color perception and difficulties with daily activities-measurement, questionnaire, optical and computer-graphics simulation studies. *Int J Ind Ergonomics.* 2001;28:153-163.

[14] Kline DW, & Scialfa, CT. Visual and Auditory Aging. In: Birren JA, & Schaie, K.W., ed. *Handbook of the psychology of aging.* 4th ed. San Diego, CA: Academic Press; 1996.

[15] Bergman M. Hearing and aging. *Audiology.* 1971;10:164-171.

[16] Drager KD, Reichle JE. Effects of discourse context on the intelligibility of synthesized speech for young adult and older adult listeners: applications for AAC. *Journal of Speech, Language, & Hearing Research.* 2001;44(5):1052-1057.

[17] Guan J, Wade MG. The effect of aging on adaptive eye-hand coordination. *Journals of Gerontology Series B-Psychological Sciences & Social Sciences.* 2000;55(3):P151-162.

[18] Charness N. Aging and communication: human factors issues. In: Charness N, Parks DC, Sabel BA., ed. *Communication, Technology, and Aging: Opportunities and challenges for the future.* New York, NY: Springer Publishing Company; 2001:30-46.

[19] Bayles KA, Kaszniak, AQ. *Communication and cognition in normal aging and dimentia.* Austin, TX: Pro-Ed; 1987.

[20] Bayles K. Alzheimer's disease symptoms: prevalence and order of appearance. *J Appl Geriatr.* 1991;10:419-430.

[21] Kemper S. Over-accommodations and under-accommodations to aging. In: Charness N, Parks DC, Sabel BA., ed. *Communication, Technology, and Aging: Opportunities and challenges for the future.* New York, NY: Springer Publishing Company; 2001.

[22] Happ MB, Roesch T, Kagan SH. Communication needs, methods, and perceived voice quality head and neck surgery: a literature review. *Cancer Nursing.* 2004;27(1):1-9.

[23] Happ MB, Roesch T, Kagan SH. (2005). Patient communication following head and neck cancer surgery: A pilot study using electronic speech generating devices. *Oncology Nursing Forum,*32 (6):1179-1187.

[24] Morgan DL. Practical strategies for combining qualitative and quantitative methods: applications to health research. *Qual Health Res.* 1998;8(3):362-376.

[25] Happ MB, Tuite P, Dobbin K, DiVirgilio-Thomas D, Kitutu J. Communication ability, method, and content among nonspeaking nonsurviving patients treated with mechanical ventilation in the intensive care unit. *American Journal of Critical Care.* 2004;13(3):210-218.

[26] Fowler SB. Impaired verbal communication during short-term oral intubation. *Nursing Diagnosis.* 1997;8(3):93-98.

[27] Robillard AB. Communication problems in the intensive care unit. *Qual Soc.* 1994;17(4):383-395.

[28] Knaus WA, Wagner DP, Draper EA, et.al. The APACHE III prognostic system: Risk prediction of hospital motrality for critically ill hospitalized adults. *Chest.* 1991;100:1619-1636.

[29] Wagner DP, Knaus WA, Harrell FE, Zimmerman JE, Watts C. Daily prognostic estimates for critically ill adults in intensive care units: results from a prospective, multicenter, inception cohort analysis. *Crit Care Med.* 1994;22(9):1359-1372.

[30] Cullen DJ, Civetta JM, Briggs BA, Ferrara LC. Therapeutic intervention scoring system: a method for quantitative comparison of patient care. *Crit Care Med.* 1974;2(2):57-60.

[31] Keene AR, Cullen DJ. Therapeutic Intervention Scoring System: update 1983. *Crit Care Med.* 1983;11(1):1-3.

[32] Teasdale G, Jennett, B. *The Glasgow Coma Scale.* Vol 2: Lancet; 1974.

[33] Menzel LK. Factors related to the emotional responses of intubated patients to being unable to speak. *Heart Lung.* 1998;27(4):245-252.

[34] Dowden P, Beukelman D, Lossing C. Serving nonspeaking patients in acute care settings: Intervention outcomes. *AAC.* 1986b(2):38-44.

[35] Miles MB, and A.M. Huberman. *Qualitative Data Analysis: An expanded sourcebook.* 2nd ed. Thousand Oaks: Sage Publishing; 1994.

[36] Charness N, Parks, Denise C., Sabel, Bernhard, A, ed. *Communication, Technology and Aging: Opportunites and Challenges for the Future.* New York: Springer Publishing; 2001.

[37] Hodes RJ, Ory MG, Pruzan MR. Communicating with older patients: a challenge for researchers and clinicians. *Journal of the American Geriatrics Society.* 1995;43(10):1167-1168.

[38] Beukelman DR, Mirenda, P. *Augmentative and alternative communication.* 2nd ed. Baltimore, MD: Paul Brookes Publishing Co; 1998.

[39] Garrett K, Kimelman M. Cognitive-linguistic considerations in the application of alternative communication strategies for aphasia. In: Beukelman D, Yorkston K,

Reichle J., ed. *Augmentative Communication for Adults with Neurogenic and Neuromuscular Disabilities*. Baltimore, MD: Paul H. Brookes Publishing Company; 2000.

[40]   McNaughton D, Light J. Teaching facilitators to support the communication skills of an adult with severe cognitive disabilities: a case study. *AAC*. 1989;5:35-41.

[41]   Connolly M. *Temporarily nonvocal trauma patients and their gestures: A descriptive study* [doctoral dissertation]. Chicago, IL, Rush University; 1992.

[42]   Ashworth P. *Care to Communicate*. London: Whitefriars Press; 1980.

[43]   Baker C, Melby V. An investigation into the attitudes and practices of intensive care nurses towards verbal communication with unconscious patients. *J Clin Nurs*. 1996;5(3):185-192.

[44]   Leathart AJ. Communication and socialisation (1): An exploratory study and explanation for nurse-patient communication in an ITU. *Intensive Crit Care Nurs*. 1994;10(2):93-104.

[45]   Sayler J, Stuart BJ. Nurse-patient interaction in the intensive care unit. *Heart Lung*. 1985;14(1):20-24.

[46]   Hall DS. Interactions between nurses and patients on ventilators. *Am J Crit Care*. 1996;5(4):293-297.

[47]   Jones C, Griffiths RD, Humphris G. Disturbed memory and amnesia related to intensive care. *Memory*. 2000;8(2):79-94.

[48]   Russel S. An exploratory study of patients' perceptions, memories, and experiences of an intensive care unit. *J Adv Nurs*. 1999;29:783-791.

In: Focus on Nonverbal Communication Research   ISBN 1-59454-790-4
Editor: Finley R. Lewis, pp. 125-147   © 2007 Nova Science Publishers, Inc.

Chapter 6

ASSESSING THE END-OF-LIFE-CARE EDUCATIONAL NEEDS OF ELDERLY DEAF PERSONS: LESSONS ON LANGUAGE AND CULTURE FOR RESEARCHERS AND HEALTH PRACTITIONERS

Barbara Allen[1], *, Nancy Meyers[2],*
John Sullivan[3] and Melissa Sullivan[3],†
[1] Carleton College, USA
[2] Deaf End-of-Life Care Education Project, DEAF-MADC
(Minnesota Association of Deaf Citizens), USA
[3] University of Minnesota, MN, USA

ABSTRACT

This chapter reports on a community-based participatory research (CBPR) strategy for collecting health related data from a linguistic minority in the United States: self-identified members of Deaf community. The literature available on deaf and hard of hearing persons' health and healthcare status suggests that these individuals rarely participate in surveys of citizens' well-being. Recent work assessing "health literacy" among hearing adults shows that obstacles to gaining healthcare information, including limited proficiency in English, impede healthcare knowledge, utilization, and costs, as well as health itself. Culturally identified Deaf individuals often view researchers from the "hearing world" with suspicion. Using CBPR and ASL-GLOSS (an American Sign Language—ASL—linguistics method) trained Deaf interviewers asked 130 Deaf senior citizens who depend on a signed language for communication about cultural practices and linguistic barriers to healthcare, focusing on end-of-life care information.[1] Interviews

---

* Contact Information: Barbara Allen ballen@carleton.edu, Department of Political Science, Carleton College, Northfield, MN 55407; 507-646-4117; fax 507-646-5615
† (now deceased)

were videotaped, while a centrally located monitor received direct feeds from five enclosed interview booths allowed the research team to make adjustments to ensure consistency among interviewers during the study. A mirror placed behind the respondents enabled interviewer and respondent to be captured on the same videotape. The closed-ended questions of the half-hour interviews were coded on-site by the Deaf interviewers for statistical analysis. A team of Deaf interviewers reviewed the tapes to check the reliability of the initial coding and assign categories and codes to open-ended questions. A focus group comprised of expert Deaf interviewers, community leaders, and hearing researchers reviewed and interpreted the findings. The survey instrument and method revealed important findings concerning deaf senior citizens' perceptions about their end-of-life care needs, enabling the development of appropriate educational materials and information dissemination strategies. The research team concluded that the conceptual, sociocultural, and linguistic challenges of culturally identified deaf and hard of hearing persons can be addressed using CBPR strategies and ASL-GLOSS linguistic methods. These innovations in survey design and method can have a significant impact on collecting valid and reliable data from this underrepresented population. Moreover, the research experience speaks to the broader concern of health literacy among members of the Deaf community.

INTRODUCTION: THE LESSONS INSPIRING COMMUNITY-BASED PARTICIPATORY RESEARCH

In 1999, eight Deaf and two hearing Minnesotans established the leadership team of *The End-of-Life Care Education Project of the Minnesota Deaf Community* (the Project).[‡] The team's aims included training Deaf hospice volunteers and producing linguistic and culturally appropriate end-of-life care educational materials for Deaf people and their families. The tremendous response of healthcare professionals and Deaf families to the Project's activities underscored not only this population's need for access to information and services, but also the educational needs of professionals charged with providing services for this community. Several experiences in hospice care settings revealed barriers to communication: Project-trained volunteers encountered Carl, whose brain injury made his signing legible to only those whose first language was American Sign Language (ASL); the volunteers also met Clara, a ninety-year-old woman who was the only Deaf resident at her care facility, cutting her off from all social intercourse. In Carl's case, communication barriers brought humiliation until Deaf volunteers explained to caregivers that his small gestures were in fact the ASL sign for "toilet" (Allen et al. 2002). In Clara's case, Deaf volunteers were able to show that Clara's lack of communication was not a manifestation of dementia, but an artifact of the linguistic isolation of a lucid elderly adult, with limited English literacy skills and a cultural reluctance to confide in a hearing person (a hospice chaplain).

[‡] We use the lowercase *deaf* when referring to the audiological condition of not hearing, and the uppercase *Deaf* when referring to a particular group of Deaf people residing in the United States and Canada who share a culture, use sign language as their primary means of communication among themselves, and hold a set of beliefs about themselves and their connection to the larger society (Padden and Humphreys 1988).

Anecdotal reports suggested other significant obstacles to healthcare and information, including, for example, caregivers who relied on a Deaf patient's hearing family members for interpreting, not realizing that their patient might withhold important information about symptoms, rather than risk embarrassment (see also Committee on Disabilities of the Group for the Advancement of Psychiatry 1997) or a family member who may be reluctant to pass on difficult news. Differences within the deaf population—age of on-set of deafness, residential school experience versus mainstreaming and a variety of communication preferences—further indicated the complexity of addressing the informational and care needs of the Deaf community. As Project team members considered the formal assessment of Deaf senior citizens' needs for health and end-of-life care information, it seemed clear that to generate reliable, valid, and useful knowledge, members of the community could benefit greatly by collaborating with and using the expertise of academics, in this case social scientists. Members of the Deaf community initiated the collaboration, making it all the more critical that Deaf people be involved in all aspects of the study—from constructing linguistically and culturally appropriate questions to interpreting results.

COMMUNITY-BASED PARTICIPATORY RESEARCH

Community-based participatory research (CBPR) begins by acknowledging the community as an aspect of collective and individual identity (Israel 2000; Israel, Parker, and Becker 1998). Indeed, in response to our question in Figure 1, our study found that a majority of Deaf seniors (65%) see themselves as "Deaf" first and as members of the United States polity second.

The next question is about how you identify yourself, or what you call yourself. **WHICH YOU WANT IDENTIFY YOURSELF? WHICH FIRST DEAF, SECOND AMERICAN. FIRST AMERICAN, SECOND DEAF, WHICH?**

		N	% Responding
1.	Deaf American	80	65.0
2.	American who is deaf	36	30
3.	"R" sees no difference	6	5
Total		125	100.0

Figure 1: Primary Identity

Other principles of CBPR include: building on the organizational strengths, relationships, social structure, and other resources of the community/culture; collaborating as partners in all phases of research (iterative processes of design, data collection, and analysis); and creating opportunities for co-learning and empowerment in the interpretation and dissemination of results.

Community-based research (CBR) has revealed important cultural differences related to healthcare, a first step in increasing the relevance of research, identifying intervention strategies and adopting "best practices" within studied communities. By adding *participation* to the CBR philosophy, researchers in diverse communities have not only furthered these aims, but also enhanced trust and mutual respect among community members, researchers, and health professionals. CBPR has been shown to empower community members, enabling them to redirect their resources toward educational and action programs designed to promote well-being in their community (CDC 1997; Hall 1992; Schulz, et al. 1998).

In sum, CBPR partnerships join participants with diverse skills, knowledge, and expertise to address complex problems (Butterfoss, Goodman, and Wandersman 1987; Hall 1992; Himmelman 1992). Our experience suggests that CBPR played a vital role in collecting and interpreting data as well as in disseminating educational materials based on study findings. The sustained commitment of the researchers and Deaf community members in implementing "best practices" has produced subsidiary partnerships among Project team members, local institutions of higher education, Deaf (and hearing) hospice volunteers and practitioners, healthcare providers, and Deaf individuals and their families (see also Israel, Schurman, and Hugentobler 1992).

HEALTHCARE RESEARCH AND THE DEAF COMMUNITY

Nearly 23 million people (9.35% of the population) in the United States are categorized as having a hearing loss; approximately 4.8 million of these individuals cannot hear or understand speech (Adams, Hendershot, and Marano 1999, Table 62, p. 93; Barnett 1999; Harmer 1999, Tamaskar et al. 2000). For those who are pre-lingually deaf and many others for whom deafness resulted from disease or injury at an early age, signed language is the primary mode of communication. Following Spanish, American Sign Language (ASL) is the second most commonly used minority (non-English) language in the United States (Barnett 1999); researchers estimate that at least two million Americans use ASL for everyday communication (Zieziula 1998). Although ASL represents the first language of a sizable number of Americans, there is no national database on deaf and hard of hearing (D/HOH) persons and little reliable data on the demographics, morbidity, or mortality of the deaf population or the ASL language group. For example, a recent examination of data sources of potential value for assessing the health and healthcare status of D/HOH on Medicare raised serious doubts about the reliability of the Medicare Current Beneficiary Survey (MCBS); 20% of people reporting a hearing loss in 1998 report normal hearing in 1999 and only 47% of people identified as deaf on the MCBS in 1998 also indicated that they remained deaf a year later (Delmarva Foundation and Gallaudet Research Institute 2002). The National Health Interview Survey (NHIS) records numbers of "hearing impaired" persons (Adams, Hendershot, and Marano 1999), but the survey does not distinguish the members of the distinct linguistic group—users of signed language—who were the focus of the present study.

The Deaf community is a unique languaculture (Agar 1994) whose members share a common language and history and participate in the formal societal structure of this distinct group (Becker 1980; Cohen 1995; Lane 1996; Lane 1993; Padden and Humphries 1988; Parasnis 1996; Sacks 1994). Research on this population's health and healthcare status remains extremely limited (Barnett 2002) and findings on medical care resource-use patterns are inconsistent (Delmarva Foundation and Gallaudet Research Institute 2002). Two results are remarkably uniform across all studies: 1) language differences raise a significant obstacle to the adequate care of Deaf individuals and 2) this population must be aggressively sought out and included in the national research agenda to improve the quality of healthcare for culturally diverse populations.

Differences in language and culture between the majority hearing population and Deaf people influence the healthcare provider-patient/client relationship (Barnett 2002b; Barnett 1999; Dipietro 1981; Ebert and Heckerling 1995; Harmer 1999; Lotke 1995; MacKinney et al. 1995; Shelp 1997; Solow 1981); may impede diagnostic and other aspects of healthcare provision for this linguistic minority (Harmer 2002; Iverson 2000; MacKinney et al. 1995; Steinberg, Sullivan, and Loew 1998; Zazove et al. 1993); and may significantly limit the Deaf individual's information on prevention and treatment of serious medical conditions (Baker-Duncan et al. 1997; Ebert and Heckerling 1995; Harmer 1999; Joseph 1995; Lass et al. 1978; Tamaskar et al. 2000; Woodroffe et al. 1998; Zazove 1997; Zazove and Doukas 1994; Zazove et al. 1993). In the context of end-of-life care, language and cultural differences have an impact on the quality of end-of-life care and decision-making as well as bereavement counseling for dying persons who are Deaf, their family members, or Deaf persons who grieve the loss of family members, whether they are hearing or Deaf (Hines 2002; Zieziula 1998). The growing understanding of health literacy also presents additional concerns for all cultural and linguistic minority populations— including members of the Deaf community. (Nielson-Bohlman, Panzer and Kindig 2004.) The combined forces of a vastly different language, the relative isolation of the community with undefined geographic boundaries, as well as cultural differences and limited health literacy present significant challenges in creating a data base of reliable, valid research (Barnett 1999; Li et al. 2001).

Telephone surveys, while relatively inexpensive, under-represent this population (Barnett and Franks 1999) and, for reasons discussed at greater length below, self-administered (written) English questionnaires most likely will be unreliable. Yet, the costs of interpreted interviews, translation, and transcription to written English for the purpose of data analysis can be significant. Sampling also presents a research challenge, given the difficulties in identifying the portion of the population classified as D/HOH and the lack of registries for users of ASL, one indicator of affinity for the Deaf community. In many populations, the use of fortuitous samples (e.g. drawn from the membership of social organizations or responding to study advertisements) is generally acknowledged to introduce the potential for bias. Deaf clubs in towns and cities as well as national organizations draw from a highly networked population bound by residential school ties, highly subscribed local and national Deaf media, and annual national social and sports event gatherings (Becker 1980; Lane 1996; Lucas, Bayley, and Valli 2001; Padden and Humphries 1988; Parasnis 1996; Sacks 1994). Researcher biases—which can occur in instrument design, data collection, and the interpretation of findings—may present an even more significant challenge than sampling bias for those who attempt to study this relatively closed community. A history of mistrust of hearing health professionals and academics compound the difficulties of research within this non-English language community (Barnett 2002b; Lane 1993; Li et al. 2001; Padden and Humphries 1988).

Beyond our experiences which led to the adoption of CBPR as a general research strategy, the reports of other researchers indicate three additional lessons for studies of Deaf individuals: 1) An interview protocol administered in person by a trained interviewer is preferable to a self-administered written survey or telephone interview; 2) Interviews should be conducted in the first language of the respondent (most often a signed language); 3) The benefits of fortuitous samples may mitigate the potential problems of bias. Further review of the literature on signed languages and Deaf culture suggests other factors affecting the researcher's ability to collect reliable data about Deaf people who use ASL as their primary mode of communication.

SIGNED LANGUAGE AND DEAF CULTURE

In addition to the many anticipated challenges posed by language differences in cross-cultural studies, the linguistics of ASL raises several unique issues for researchers (Allen et al. 2002; Barnett 2002a; Barnett 2002b; Zazove 1997). ASL is a visual language whose signs are not adequately represented in written form (Baker-Shenk and Cokely 1991; Valli and Lucas 2002). The structure and grammatical characteristics of ASL are independent of English (Liddell 1980); *American* Sign Language designates the name of a language used by Deaf persons in North America, not (as is commonly believed) the signed equivalent of English. ASL provides no immediate or general access to the English language or any other spoken language.

The acquisition of English or another spoken language is extremely difficult for people who cannot hear (Hansen 2002). For most pre-lingually (and, depending on the individual's age of onset of hearing loss, many post-lingually) Deaf persons, English remains a second language (Caprici et al 2002; Liddell 1980; Lotke 1995; Moores 1997); average English reading levels for Deaf Americans have hovered around the fourth-grade equivalent for several decades (Holt, Traxler, and Allen 1997; Livingston 1997). As a result, the use of written English language questionnaires and other written modes of English-based communication between Deaf and hearing individuals are potentially unreliable. Questions phrased at the fourth-grade reading level may fail to reflect adequately the cognitive sophistication and depth of experience of Deaf respondents and question translation may be inconsistent across ASL interpreters. More significantly, important differences in the language, including the lack of homonyms, non-equivalence of metaphor, simile, and idiom, and the representation of some parts of speech (e.g. pronouns) by spatial references rather than signs (Baker-Shenk and Cokely 1991), may give ambiguous meaning to *validated* English-language measures. For example, anecdotal evidence reveals the depth of such problems in the contemporary example of the misinterpretation of the multiple meanings of the English term "positive," which leads Deaf individuals to understand their HIV+ status as a beneficent sign of health (See also Barnett 2002a).

Inconsistent interpretation of English constructs only increases the potential for data collected in English to be invalid or unreliable. Written questionnaires or ASL interpreted English-questionnaires that have been pre-tested on a Deaf sample may be adequate for the cost-effective measurement of some constructs (e.g. self-reported health habits such as smoking and alcohol use, number of visits to the doctor annually, and demographic data) (Lass et al. 1978; Tamaskar et al. 2000; Zazove et al. 1993), but a more complete picture of Deaf persons' experiences, beliefs, attitudes, and behaviors related to healthcare and end-of-life care may well necessitate multi-method approaches consisting of qualitative indicators and quantitative measures utilizing ASL (MacKinney et al. 1995; Witte and Kuzel 2000) and, for some constructs, Deaf interviewers and focus group facilitators (Allen et al 2002).

The unique language, values, and history of Deaf culture imply not only that construct validity, but also the accurate interpretation and acceptance of findings may depend on the continuing participation of members of the Deaf community in all research agendas. Unlike other minority languacultures, the Deaf community is often pathologically defined, an issue that continues to provoke distrust of medical professionals among individuals who define themselves as members of a distinct cultural minority (Lane 1993; Padden and Humphries 1988). In contrast to individuals who become deaf or hard-of-hearing later in life, many pre-lingual deaf individuals do not express their Deaf identity as a deficiency or the condition of deafness as a loss or lack. Rather, they present Deaf identity as one of the myriad distinct possibilities for the human being and, indeed, no data suggest that the lives of Deaf persons are less fulfilling than those of other (hearing) communities (Barnett 2002a; Barnett 2002b; Committee on Disabilities of the Group for the Advancement of Psychiatry 1997; Sacks 1994; Zazove 1997). Our study confirmed these findings and provided additional information about the residential school experience, socialization, and barriers that continue to impede access to adequate health information.

Most Deaf seniors in our sample created lifelong bonds with their residential school cohorts maintaining friendships that transcend geographic separation. In contrast, they shared a common language with neither their hearing parents nor, in most cases, their hearing siblings (Allen et al. 2002; Lane 1993; Padden and Humphries 1988). Ninety-five percent (a statistic that has remained remarkably consistent) of all deaf children are born to hearing parents many of whom do not learn ASL. Our sample population reflected this general finding (see Figure 2). Deaf culture, thus, differs in how it is transferred among its members. Unlike other cultures, the language, norms, and values of Deaf culture are transferred from peer to peer ("horizontally") instead of intergenerationally ("vertically") from parent to child (Barnett 2002a; Becker 1980; Committee on Disabilities of the Group for the Advancement of Psychiatry 1997; Parasnis 1996; Sacks 1994). Whether it is Deaf children with hearing parents or Deaf parents with hearing children, horizontal transference of culture presents significant issues for end-of-life caregivers and practitioners, including who is defined as "family."

Did you attend a residential school for Deaf children?
FINISH WENT DEAF INSTITUTION?

Were Your Parents Hearing?
YOUR PARENTS HEARING?

			N	% Responding
4.	Attended Residential School	Yes	113	91.1
		No	11	8.9
	Total		124	100.0
5.	Both parents hearing	Yes	117	94.4
		No	7	5.6
	Total		124	100.0

Figure 2: Residential School Attendance and Parents' Hearing Status

As Figure 2 shows, a preponderance of our sample population lived in residential schools, some up to 14 years. Most students returned home to their family of origin only at holidays severely limiting opportunities to participate in many family rites and rituals, including those related to death. Indeed, these respondents' views of "family" inclined to friends who shared the formative experience of Deaf residential school culture, rather than the biological tie generally understood by the majority culture as the basis of kinship (Allen et al. 2002; Becker 1980). The residential school experience influenced not only patterns of socialization, but also changed the individual's understanding and orientation to healthcare practices and information. Separation from the family of origin limited this population's access and understanding of such basic information as family medical history—indeed, anecdotal evidence indicates that in many cases, linguistic barriers prevented these Deaf seniors from knowing their own medical history (Allen et al. 2002; Barnett 1999; Clark 1995). As other studies have shown, children may not learn the causes of their illnesses when they do not share the language of their adult caregivers. Examination of residential health education curricula and preventive care instructions given by parents (or teachers) who do not use ASL also suggests that information may be limited to behavioral commands, without reference to the rationale for a given action (e.g. "brush your teeth," omitting the reason, "so you don't get cavities") (Clark 1995).

In addition to the language and cultural differences that distinguish this languaculture from other diverse populations is the lack of exposure to "incidental information"—news passively received by overhearing conversations, radio or television in the course of mundane activity. Lack of access to this kind of information, which plays a significant role in a person's ability to gather and analyze new concepts and ideas, generally is not accessible to Deaf persons, placing them at an even greater disadvantage when compared with their hearing counterparts. These factors—the lack of a common language and, in most cases, the cumulative experiences shared across generations with the family of origin as well as the inaccessibility of incidental information—have a profound affect on a Deaf persons' store of background knowledge. The existence of a sign for "background knowledge" illustrates the degree to which this reality is recognized within the broader Deaf community. The understanding of this concept (confirmed by the existence of a sign) stands in stark contrast to the lack of a sign for "hospice" or "advanced directive"—concepts not understood prior to the development of workshop materials and videotapes resulting from our research. The lack of background knowledge and access to information created a system of peer learning to fill information gaps, generating extensive networks that may amplify as well as correct misinformation (Becker 1980). Our findings suggested two related results: 1) gaps in background knowledge must be addressed before concepts relevant to end-of-life care can be made wholly intelligible and 2) the Deaf communication network is a highly evolved, sophisticated medium into which new information may be introduced (Allen et al. 2002).

Finally, the visual quality of ASL makes face-to-face communication essential, further encouraging the extensive relational networks at the core of the culture. Not only practical information, but also the literature and history of this culture are conveyed primarily in settings that allow for face-to-face interactions. Technological changes, including telecommunication devices (TTY/TDD) and e-mail, have enhanced rather than supplanted the cultural value of these networks. For all of these reasons, the norms of this "relational culture" must play an important role in the design of end-of-life care research. We believe that by addressing the unique characteristics of this population through a CBPR strategy, we have developed prototype research instruments that will allow other researchers to discover reliable and valid knowledge about the Deaf community in the healthcare setting.

Hearing individuals may not immediately grasp the profound difference between acquiring a spoken language by hearing the language and relying wholly on learning a language in its written form. ASL is acquired naturally; concrete experiences and abstract concepts are transmitted with the immediacy of a spoken language (Capirci et al. 2000; Lucas, Bayley, and Valli, 2001; and Washabaugh, Woodward, and DeSantis 1980). Nevertheless, the task of composing a grammatically correct English sentence without the benefit of modeling by hearing conventional usage requires additional skills that must be painstakingly acquired (Gallaudet Research Institute 1996; Gray 1956; Hansen 2002; and Holt, Traxler, and Allen 1997). Depending solely on English for communication with Deaf individuals invariably increases the probability of misunderstanding and stress.[§] Deaf elderly patients are not cognitively impaired, nor do they have limited life experience or suffer from an inability to communicate all the subtleties of emotion and ideas about their experience—in their own language. They will, however, like most of us, have difficulty communicating the full range of experiences very well in a second language. In that the Deaf individual may need to attain English proficiency to function in the hearing world, that hearing world has an ethical obligation to address barriers to communication in the healthcare setting.

Implications of Signed Language for Health Research and Care

A brief summary of some of the key elements of the language will illustrate the depth of the issues Deaf people, researchers, and healthcare professionals may encounter when communicating with one another. ASL, in summary, is a nonlinear language using space, facial expressions, and hand and body movements, fully exploiting the capacities of vision, spatial relations, and visual-kinetic memory for storing and processing concurrent layers of information (Lane, Hoffmeister, and Bahn. 1996, 91). Facial expressions, "non-manuals," convey meaning. They include adverbs and information about sentence structure and organization. Linguists have identified over 250 grammatically governed facial expressions in ASL. Yet, while these signifiers may be described, they involve subtle movements of face, tongue, eyes, eyebrows, lips, and mouth, and cannot be represented as written symbols.

ASL also displays grammatical elements such as the actors and objects of actions spatially. By pointing to a space(s) in front of the signer's body, the signer is able to use spatial arrangements to carry complex meanings that would require a lengthy text or explanation, if the same information were to be conveyed in a spoken or written language. The location of the sign relative to the body also carries information and can change the meaning of the sentence—including signs for "past," "present," and "future." An individual communicating her/his "pain" would perform that sign in the location where the pain occurs. Locating the sign by the temple for example, would indicate the individual has a headache.

---

[2] The Project conducted three focus groups in which participants viewed three closed-caption videotapes about end-of-life care. Participants unanimously agreed that the English language usage was an obstacle to their learning about healthcare information.

Whether it is for purposes of conducting survey research or assessing pain, a very basic understanding of the linguistics of ASL can be instructive and increase one's appreciation for why some research with this population has produced unreliable data. A brief example illustrates the linguistic rule that signifies and distinguishes interrogative from declarative statements. "Yes/No" questions must be marked by raised eyebrows; "Wh-questions" (what, where, when, why, and how) must be indicated with eyebrows down. To ask the question, "do you have any pain?" with eyebrows down is not only grammatically incorrect it may make some communication confusing. A recent study of the neurological controls of facial expressions of Deaf signers confirms two distinct functions of facial expressions — affective and linguistic (Corina, Bellugi, Reilly, 1999). Now consider the "Faces Pain Rating Scale," (Figure 3) a visual scale that often is used to help healthcare providers assess a patient's level and type of pain (Herr 2002; Herr 1998; Herr and Garland 2001; Herr, Mobily, Richardson, and Spratt 1997; and Wong and Baker 1988). The intent of the Faces Pain Rating is affective (Herr 1998) and in ASL has no linguistic association with pain. Rather, the linguistic function of the facials illustrated in Figure 3 are co-occurring facials used with the signs for happy, glad, surprise, depressed, sad, and cry (Costello 1994).

Wong-Baker FACES Pain Rating Scale

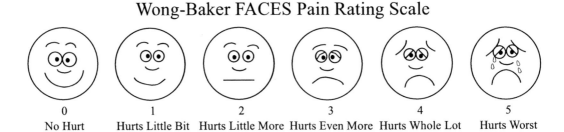

0	1	2	3	4	5
No Hurt	Hurts Little Bit	Hurts Little More	Hurts Even More	Hurts Whole Lot	Hurts Worst

Figure 3.

Numeric Pain Rating Scales (NRS), another popular pain assessment tool, rank orders pain numerically along a horizontal continuum that is typically graded as an interval measure ranging from zero to five, arrayed from left to right according to English language reading conventions. [**] This spatial orientation has no meaning in ASL, where such ordering bears no connection to gradations of measurement, but often carries other meanings that convey depth and detail in the essentially non-linear narrative form of the language. We will address similar difficulties with Likert scales later in this chapter.

Mindful of the centrality of facials to ASL, we asked a few Deaf adults to tell us their opinion about probable results in using the Faces Pain Rating Scale (FPRS) with members of the ASL linguistic community. The results of this informal survey suggested that Deaf people, particularly individuals who are more vulnerable or with low reading literacy, might find the facials confusing. When symbolic faces are used in print to convey sentiments, they carry another set of meanings. Since humor and teasing cannot be communicated and understood by voice, Deaf people often use words [(smile) or (haha)] parenthetically in the

[**] These scales are among the pain assessment tools made available to palliative care providers on many websites, including *Partners Against Pain* as cited, http://www.partnersagainstpain.com, accessed 5/10/02 and the American Medical Directors Association, http://www.amda.com/clinical/chronicpain/pain-face.html, accessed 5/15/02. Although neither organization recommends the use of this scale in groups other than those intended by Wong and Baker (1988), it has increasingly been accepted for use with adults under palliative care.

body of their TTY or e-mail messages and have adopted a series of keystroke conventions to convey specific affects. In fact, in one edition of a widely circulated national Deaf newspaper, *Silent News,* the entire back page was devoted to the keystrokes used to make a variety of "smiley faces." This range of "faces" seems to have found a place within the culture unrelated to any associations with the somatic conditions of pain.

Difficulties in communication pose similar difficulties in collecting data and disseminating information within the Deaf community. Our goal of obtaining a representative national sample required that the vast majority of the Deaf seniors be able to comprehend and answer our questions accurately. The only way to achieve this goal was to administer surveys in ASL—*in their own language*—thereby allowing our Deaf respondents to communicate the subtleties of emotion and ideas about their experience. Beyond the question of language proficiency lie other issues, including cultural differences, which language holds in the deep recesses of interpretation and meaning.

Cross-cultural study may intensify problems typically encountered in social science research, including well-known tendencies toward response bias and similar concerns. Social scientists find that respondents often try to accommodate the researcher, giving what the respondent perceives as the popular, appropriate, or desired answer to a question. In cross-cultural research this particular bias is increased, especially if respondents are of a minority culture or language group—or simply perceive themselves to differ from the enculturated assumptions displayed by the researcher, research instrument, or research methodology. Using the first language of the respondent is a necessary to gather accurate information about respondents' preferences, attitudes, and behaviors in cross-cultural research, but linguistic translation is only the first step toward effective cross-cultural communication.

Health Literacy and Deaf Culture

The National Library of Medicine defines health literacy as: "the degree to which individuals have the capacity to obtain, process, and understand basic health information and services needed to make appropriate health decisions" (Nielsen-Bohlman, Panzer and Kindig 2004, 4). Characteristics of the individual as well as his or her culture, society, and immediate community influence the capacity for health literacy. Proficiency in reading, writing, and numeracy are among the skills enabling greater health literacy; as important, according to many educators, are listening and speaking as well as the broader cultural framework which invest data with meaning and link new information with conceptual knowledge. As one review of the literature on health literacy has concluded, "current assessment tools and research findings cannot differentiate among (a) reading ability, (b) lack of background knowledge..., (c) lack of familiarity with language..., or (d) cultural differences in approaches to health and healthcare" (Nielsen-Bohlman, Panzer and Kindig 2004, 6). The studies of health literacy reviewed, which focus on the hearing population of the United States, show that the obstacles and consequent limitations in basic knowledge most often confront older adults and individuals of any age with limited education or limited English language proficiency. The vast majority of seniors in our sample relied on ASL or another signed language for communication; almost three quarters of the sample said it was "very important" for them to receive healthcare information in their language (see Figure 4). Our study corroborates other research on the limited English reading proficiency of many Deaf adults, suggesting that what may be said of barriers impeding the dissemination of healthcare information among non-English *speakers* and readers, will be compounded by deafness.

Deaf people have different preferences for communication.
What is your preference? ASL, Signed Exact English, Lipreading, Finger-spelling, Voice, something else?

DEAF PEOPLE HAVE PREFERENCES COMMUNICATION, DIFFERENT, DIFFERENT, DIFFERENT. YOUR PREFERENCE, WHAT?

		N	% Responding
6.	ASL	97	77.6
7.	Signed English	10	8.0
8.	Lip Reading	3	2.4
9.	Finger-spelling	3	2.4
10.	Voice	0	0.0
11.	Other/combination	12	8.9
	Total	125	100.0

How important is it for you to get health information in the language you prefer?
YOU PICK____(repeat response) NOW TELL-ME (TO) GET HEALTH INFORMATION, HOW IMPORTANT USE? HOW?

		N	% Responding
1.	Very Important	89	71.2
2.	Important	28	22.4
3.	Somewhat Important	6	4.8
4.	Not very important	2	1.6
5.	Not at all Important	0	0.0
	Total	125	100.0

Figure 4: Language Preference

Although a causal relationship between health literacy and health remains to be established, studies finding an association between limited health literacy to poor health appear to be increasing (Nielsen-Bohlman, Panzer and Kindig 2004, 81). The consequences of limited health literacy, while difficult to establish, embrace ethical as well as economic dimensions of health policy (Allen et al 2002; Nielsen-Bohlman, Panzer and Kindig 2004; Giloth et al 2004). Econometric measures predict higher inpatient spending and emergency care costs for individuals with limited health literacy, controlling for health status (Nielsen-Bohlman, Panzer and Kindig 2004).

Health literacy, like literacy broadly conceived, is often context specific, and must, furthermore, be understood as the result of a continuous evolution of experience and social learning. The activities of the Project team in the Deaf community suggested that linguistically and culturally appropriate research instruments were the first step in designing educational materials to improve access to knowledge about end-of-life care concerns and decisions for Deaf adults and their families.

Signed Language and Community-Based Participatory Research

In addition to technical and ethical concerns about language and facility with English, we were also aware of cultural differences that influence our findings as well as the care and education of the Deaf elderly. Language and culture are necessarily connected, as anthropologists have shown (Agar 1994, 60). The "Deaf experience" of our sample population was profoundly influenced by the residential school experience and subsequent outcomes that is central to aspects of Deaf culture.

One such outcome of the residential school was noted in anthropologist Gaylene Becker's 1976 pioneering study of Deaf seniors. Becker found that her respondents developed a peer learning process as "a formalized mechanism for coping with the information vacuum" (Becker 1980, 66-67). Peer learning is unlikely to address the individual's lack of family medical history, however, and it may not be a reliable source of public information, including news about health issues. As Becker also notes, information reliability is desirable, but difficult to maintain. As she explains, when stories are incomplete, people speculate; in any community, when the data do not add up, people bring as much coherence to the matter as they can, but rumor and misinterpretation often abound. On going access to information is crucial to correcting misperceptions and, more importantly, preventing the amplification of errors in peer learning networks. Such earlier research findings played an important role in our efforts to assess the needs of the Deaf elderly for end-of-life care information.

To summarize this overview of research as it relates to our study, we conclude that self-administered English language questionnaires will be less effective in collecting reliable data than interviews conducted by Deaf interviewers in ASL. Furthermore, available research suggests that translations of English language questionnaires by non-native ASL users are likely to be ineffective in capturing the subtleties of cultural differences between members of the Deaf community and hearing ASL interpreters. Finally, existing research suggests that members of the Deaf community must be an integral part of all phases of research if we hope to collect and interpret data reliably.

THE STUDY

Overview

On September 12–14, 2001, 130 Deaf senior citizens attending the Deaf Seniors of America (DSA) conference participated in 30-minute interviews about their experiences and issues related to end-of-life care. The probability sample was drawn from the DSA list of 1000 registered conference participants. Invitations that included a form for scheduling an interview during the conference were mailed to the participants. Potential participants were contacted by fax, TTY, or email (according to their preference) to remind them of their appointments. These invitations, which were added to the general DSA conference mailing, confused some conference attendees, generating multiple contacts with the randomly selected group and their peers. News of the study spread quickly throughout the national networks of the Deaf community and we soon had a significant number of "volunteers" who contacted us, hoping to be interviewed. Subsequent volunteer recruitment proved vital to the project when the events of 11 September made it impossible for about half of the probability sample to attend the conference. Individuals participating in the interviews represented 33 states and all regions of the United States. Initial statistical analysis of the data show no significant differences related to our study's objectives between the probability sample and the volunteers. Key demographic information was collected from a self-administered English language questionnaire prior to the interviews. Answers to these questions were validated throughout the depth-interviews conducted in ASL by the fourteen Deaf interviewers, who we had recruited and trained in two, three-hour sessions where they learned research protocol and interviewing techniques. In addition to the majority of respondents who used ASL as their primary means of communication (97 respondents, 80 percent of the sample) about a fifth of the randomly selected respondents indicated their preference to have the study administered another signed language when they returned their study registration cards. The final respondent pool included twenty-eight individuals who requested that their interview be administered in Conceptually Accurate Signed English (CASE), the Rochester method (emphasizing finger spelling), or the Oral method, which incorporates speech and speech reading (Solow 1981). Members of the interview team accommodated these requests as well as the needs of one deaf/blind individual who had been randomly selected for the sample.

Interviews ranged from 30–40 minutes and covered nine topics: 1) English reading and media use; 2) information dissemination; 3) obstacles to receiving information; 4) experiences with healthcare, especially communicating with a doctor; 5) end-of-life care and hospice; 6) decision making; 7) death and Deaf culture; 8) the Deaf community; and 9) Deaf self-identification. Interviewers coded responses to closed-ended questions during the interviews. The one hundred twenty-eight interviews were recorded digitally and on VHS (two respondents declined to be videotaped) in five enclosed interview areas set up in a meeting room at the conference hotel. A video monitor, placed in the center of the room received direct feeds from each of the cameras that recorded activity in the interview booths. This technology allowed us to switch among booths to monitor interviews and identify and address problems.

A long mirror placed next to the respondent allowed the camera to capture both the interviewer signing questions and the respondent signing an answer (Figure 5). This set-up enabled us to capture questions and answers as a check on consistency, interviewers' use of discretionary probing questions, and problems or concerns with question wording in order to confirm interviewer reliability. Recording the responses of Deaf seniors also reflected our method for accommodating the requirements of a visual language, enabling members of the Deaf community to participate fully in subsequent aspects of data analysis. Interviewers also coded responses to the questions during the interviews providing data for preliminary analysis. A complete review of the data required a detailed content analysis of the videotaped interviews, based on content categories generated in focus group discussions held with members of the Deaf community who are uniquely qualified to interpret the respondents' narrative explanation of their answers to our questionnaire.

Figure 5: Interviewer Set-up

Using CBPR to Develop the Questionnaire

From their experience with patients like Carl and Clara, mentioned earlier, The Minnesota Deaf End-of-Life Care Project team learned that they needed more information about the population they serve: How could the Deaf elderly best gain access to end-of-life care educational materials? What did the Deaf elderly know about this topic? What did they believe they needed to know? The Project team engaged two hearing social scientists to discuss the principles of CBPR and collaborate with members of the Deaf community to design a questionnaire and undertake the study.

Using standard survey research techniques, the principal investigators designed an English language interview schedule using validated measures of constructs when such questions were available. Leaders in the Deaf community (selected because of their years of experience in the Deaf community, participation in Deaf organizations, or their occupational expertise) discussed and revised the interview schedule in individual consultations and focus group settings. These sessions helped identify oppressive or intimidating questions, confusing question wording, and questions that reflected "English" cultural assumptions that were inappropriate to the Deaf cultural experience.

Some changes were surprising; for example, standard media use items failed to give reliable responses and even the apparently straightforward question: *How much do you understand when you read the newspaper?* overestimated reading comprehension. One of our Deaf consultants explained that we must first ask which sections of the newspaper the respondent had read (headlines, sports, news stories, etc.), otherwise we might measure only that the respondent understood some proportion of the comics or the headlines. After more than a dozen iterations of critique and revision, two pre-lingually Deaf University professors were trained in interviewing techniques and the survey tool was pre-tested on a small sample of Deaf seniors.

Following further revision of the instrument, one of the interviewers was selected to sign the questions and create a practice videotape. At this stage of the instrument design phase, the researchers became aware of the wide latitude interviewers might have in interpreting, translating, and signing the English questions. Concerns with interviewer reliability (signing the questions consistently) were first addressed by use of the model videotape. A lead Deaf interviewer met with the other thirteen interviewers to describe how to use the model tape as a guide in preparing for administering the interview schedule. The interviewers included linguists, teachers of ASL at the elementary, secondary and post-secondary level, Deaf ministers, and other professionals for whom ASL was their native language.

During the interviewer training sessions, these individuals also functioned as a focus group to determine question wording after the research team explained the intent and objective of each question. In these discussions it became clear that the linguistics of ASL would have a tremendous impact on all levels of our research. Even with agreement on question wording, disagreements about the specific signs that best represented the intended meaning of the question and the inflection to be used in distinguishing the intervals enumerated on the Likert scales remained. Scientifically reliable responses required the interviewers to reproduce the scalar intervals consistently; the content validity of the intervals, thus, depended entirely on the consistent presentation of the non-manual adverbial markers of ASL. Despite initial skepticism about the reliability of these "facials," the investigators observed and accepted that their place in the linguistic structure of the language are no different than English grammar rules that govern the use of adverbs and adjectives. Decisions about the use of particular signs were made by the now-expert interviewers through consensus (a cultural preference for decision-making). Nevertheless, the significant differences between spoken and written languages and a visual, manual, and spatial language raised doubts about the effectiveness of the training video in ensuring reliability. The lessons we learned in translating our English-language questionnaire into ASL hold broader implications for communication in signed languages in research—and in healthcare settings.

GLOSS—Successful Interview Training and Reliable Data

Although we believed we had faithfully recorded in English the back-translation of our experts' final decisions in ASL, in truth, we had failed. The interviewers worried that the translations represented on the training video were open to alternative interpretations and, indeed, they often failed to render the English into a consistent set of signs. Our next step, also unsuccessful, was to engage the assistance of a bi-lingual (but culturally Deaf) senior citizen to write simple English sentences in ASL word order omitting the parts of speech that do not exist in ASL. Although we were moving in the right direction, our interviewer team found our representation of the ultimately unintelligible, if perhaps amusing. Our interviewer focus groups reminded us that there is no written form of ASL, suggesting that we use ASL-GLOSS to represent ASL equivalents of English. The representation of English in GLOSS required advanced linguistics skills available to only a few of our Deaf consultants or interviewers. ASL was not recognized as a legitimate language until the late 1960's, making it unlikely that many deaf people would have learned such a skill or, in many cases, even the rudiments of ASL grammar and syntax. One of our younger, more recently educated interviewers had the GLOSS skills we needed. Ultimately, GLOSS, the unique ASL linguistic method for translating and transcribing the cognitive equivalent of an English word or phrase, allowed for the reconstruction of the interview schedule in a uniquely "Deaf" final form.[††]

GLOSS is defined as English word or words used to represent a particular ASL sign in its most common meaning. GLOSS is not a written form of ASL, rather it represents common English equivalents of ASL signifiers (Valli and Lucas 2002). Although post-secondary schools, (e.g. Gallaudet University) teach this linguistic method and GLOSS has recently been introduced in primary grades as an aid to English language writing instruction (Mozzer-Mather 1990), "translating" from English to GLOSS is an advanced skill. Our team was fortunate to have a Deaf member with this advanced skill. Deaf interviewers with advanced degrees in ASL and linguistics understood the role that GLOSS could play in addressing the challenges that the investigators faced. Though most Deaf people do not have the linguistic skills to change English to GLOSS they had no difficulty reading GLOSS and signing it as written. GLOSS, in its complete form, represents all aspects of ASL (facial expressions, indexing or referring to a person or object spatially and body or role shifting.) Different use of any of these ASL grammatical markers can completely change the meaning and intent of a sentence. A signer, using the exact signs for TODAY RAIN, PICNIC CANCEL can change the meaning of this sentence by adding the co-occurring facial, "eyebrows up." With no facial, the sentence reads, "It's raining today, and the picnic is cancelled." With eyebrows up, the meaning changes to "If it is raining today, the picnic is cancelled." (Corina, Bellugi, Reilly 1999.) The Deaf interviewers however, felt that because of their intense participation in interpreting the meaning and intent of the questions, reading GLOSSED sentences written in bold, uppercase English would be sufficient—it was not necessary to diagram co-occurring facial expression and manual signs grammatically. The GLOSS method proved to be the methodological discovery—a breakthrough resulting from the collaborative research approach—that addressed the threats to the study's reliability and validity by ensuring that the questions would be asked consistently in every interview.

Adaptation of Likert Scales

Likert scales are traditionally used to assess degrees of agreement or importance, as in "Do you strongly agree, agree, disagree, or disagree strongly" with this [given] statement. As we observed in our discussion of pain analogue instruments, scalar representations ranging from left to right may not work effectively with ASL users, who more typically arrange degrees of measurement vertically and, in general, convey myriad meanings through a complex array of spatial orderings. Following the advice of a Deaf psychologist with whom we consulted, we changed the traditional horizontal scale to a vertical scale to accommodate ASL spatial reference points and non-linear attribute of ASL. Simply put, our consultant said, "everyone knows 'up' and everyone knows 'down.'" ASL also has its own numbering system. This does not mean that English numbers are not understood, it does however require that potentially serious ill Deaf patients "translate" a scale with numerals 1–5 below a line and facials above a line into a meaningful way to communicate their level of pain.

[††] GLOSS represents the common English equivalent of an ASL signifier, or sign. For example, in the English question, "Should ASL interpreters be available for on-call emergency use?" the concept "on-call" was rendered in GLOSS as GO-GO-GO, meaning essentially, always ready to go or continually ready.

We encountered other problems in the conceptual response set for Likert scales, including the function of negation in ASL, especially the prohibited use of double negatives. Much like the English use of a rhetorical question—"You wouldn't want some ice cream, would you?"—as an affirmation, narrative conventions in ASL include the rhetorical use of negation to signal a speaker's desire for confirmation or agreement: an insidious source of bias to the unwary researcher. In ASL, double negation results in a nonsensical loop of "cancelled" meanings, compounding the problem of interpretation. For our research, ASL convention required us to recast scale categories so that, for example, "Not very important" became *IMPORTANT LITTLE* and "Somewhat important" became *SO-SO*. After reading the ASL question, the interviewer prompted respondents using 8 ½" x 11" cards showing numbered scalar categories, a device suggested by one of the interviewers that greatly facilitated the speed and ease of interviewing. The scalar categories appeared in GLOSS on one side of the card and English on the other side, giving the interviewer flexibility in accommodating literacy skills of Deaf interviewees.

Questionnaire Layout

Our twenty-two page survey went through fourteen complete revisions, including changes to the layout that improved the visual accessibility of the instrument. Interviewers had 30 minutes in which to ask 64 questions and code responses. To facilitate the administration of the questionnaire by people who rely solely on visual cues, we formatted the entire survey in two columns and color-coded features. (See Figure 6.)

Topic # 3 – Questions about Obstacles in Getting Information	
I will ask you questions about obstacles/frustrations in getting health information	
⇒ Deaf people have different preferences for communication. What is your preference? 12. DEAF PEOPLE HAVE PREFERENCE COMMUNICATION, DIFFERENT, DIFFERENT, DIFFERENT. YOUR PREFERENCE, WHAT? *(sign list in right column ⇒)*	ASL Signed English Lip reading Fingerspelling Other
⇒ How important is it for you to get **health information** in the way you prefer? 12. YOU PICK _____ *(repeat response above)* NOW YOU-TELL-TO-ME UNDERSTAND HEALTH INFORMATION, HOW IMPORTANT USE? HOW IMPORTANT? *(sign list in right column ⇒)*	1. Very important 2. Important 3. Somewhat important 4. Not very important 5. Not at all important 1. VERY IMPORTANT 2. IMPORTANT 3. IMPORTANT SO-SO 4. IMPORTANT LITTLE 5. NOT IMPORTANT

Figure 6: Questionnaire Format

The topics of each of the nine section of the questionnaire were represented in green. The English version of the question (black) was followed by the GLOSSED version in bold uppercase. Short instructions to guide the interviewers were in red while the scalar representations appearing in the second column were in blue. The Likert scales appeared in written English followed by a GLOSSED version of the scale. The interviewer focus groups and instrument pretests confirmed the importance of the visually oriented, color-coded layout of the questionnaire presented in English and ASL GLOSS. Ultimately, every aspect of the survey instrument was designed to accommodate the demands of a visual, manual language. From the color coding and page layout, to adaptations of the Likert scales and the use of ASL-GLOSS, our questionnaire reflected the collaboration of hearing researchers and members of this distinct linguistic minority.

CONCLUSION

This chapter highlights a cross-cultural research strategy for research in the Deaf community, suggesting how full participation of Deaf citizens as experts in their culture enable a research process designed to overcome cultural barriers to research and, potentially, health knowledge. Using CPBR, we were able to engage the Deaf community's expertise to design a questionnaire and interview format that has allowed us to collect reliable valid information about Deaf seniors' end-of-life care knowledge, attitudes, preferences, desires, and experiences. Our study confirms that language and cultural differences matter, whether researchers are gathering data or care providers are disseminating healthcare information. Ninety-two percent of our respondents told us that they learn best when information is presented in a visual format and that complex information is most easily understood in a signed language; about ninety-four percent indicated that it was important that they receive health-related information in their preferred language. Deaf individuals who cannot access general information in their language cannot fully participate in meaningful conversations in the public arena. Lack of access to health-related information raises issues of ethics and economics in healthcare policy and practice.

Our experience with CBPR confirms that the participation of members of the Deaf community enabled us to identify ethical dilemmas posed by linguistic and cultural differences as well as the impact the lack of background knowledge has on an individual's health literacy. The ethical issues implied by our results continue to emerge as we work with members of the Deaf community in focus groups designed to help us interpret our data. Thus far, it seems clear that a combination of visual media and ASL is the best way to convey healthcare information to the Deaf community. Our research experience suggests that Deaf people must be a part of the team charged with designing and presenting such instructional media. In this case, doing *with* rather than doing *for* a community is much more than a slogan. Collaboration may be the only approach that can bring members of the Deaf community the information they need to make informed, thoughtful decisions about their care; collaboration in developing intervention activities and strategies for practitioners who provide services for this unique languaculture may, likewise, be imperative. Finally, we note that "culture" and social learning are both on-going activities in all human communities. Communities and individuals are shaped by their experiences. The activities involved in community based *participatory* research uniquely respond to the shared learning across cultures that enhance health literacy, resulting, in the present study in widely disseminated educational materials about end-of-life care decisions.

REFERENCES

Adams, P.F., G.E. Hendershot, and M.A. Marano. 1999. Current Estimates from the National Health Interview Survey 1996. National Center for Health Statistics. Vital Health Stat 10 (2000). Hyattsville (MD): U.S. Department of Health and Human Services Publication (PHS) 99-1528.

Agar, M. 1994. Understanding the Culture of Conversation. New York: William Morrow.

Allen, B., N. Meyers, J.L. Sullivan, and M. Sullivan. 2002. "Sign Language and End-of-Life Care: Research in the Deaf Community." Healthcare Ethics Committee Forum: An Interprofessional Journal on HealthCare Institutions' Ethical and Legal Issues 14 (3):197–208.

Baker-Duncan, N., J. Dancer, B. Gentry, P. Highly, and B. Gibson. 1997. "Deaf Adolescents' Knowledge of AIDS." American Annals of the Deaf 142 (5): 368–372.

Baker-Shenk, C. and D. Cokely. 1991. American Sign Language: A Teacher's Resource Text on Grammar and Culture. Washington: Gallaudet University Press.

Barnett, S. 2002a. "Cross-cultural Communication with Patients Who Use American Sign Language." Family Medicine 34 (5): 376–82.

Barnett, S. 2002b. "Communication with Deaf and Hard-of-Hearing People: A Guide for Medical Education." Academic Medicine 77 (7): 694–700.

Barnett, S. 1999. "Clinical and Cultural Issues in Caring for Deaf People." Family Medicine 31 (1):17–22.

Barnett, S. and P. Franks. 1999. "Telephone Ownership and Deaf People: Implications for Telephone Surveys." American Journal of Public Health 89 (11): 1754–1756.

Becker, G. 1980. Growing Old in Silence. Berkeley: University of California Press.

Breivik, E., A. Gudmundur, and E. Skovlund. 2000. "A Comparison of Pain Rating Scales by Sampling From Clinical Trial Data." The Clinical Journal of Pain 16: 22–28.

Butterfoss, F.D., R.M. Goodman, and A. Wandersman. 1993. "Community Coalitions for Prevention and Health Promotion." Health Education Research 8: 315–330.

Capirci, O et al. 2002. "Gesture and the Nature of Language in Infancy: The Role of Gesture as a Transitional Device En Route to Two-Word Speech." In The Study of Signed Languages, eds. D.F. Armstrong, M.A. Karchmer, and J.V. Van Cleve. Washington, DC: Gallaudet University Press, 213–246.

Center for Disease Control and Prevention (CDC) and Agency for Toxic Substances and Disease Registry. 1997. Principles of Community Engagement. Atlanta: CDC Public Health Practice Program.

Clark, J.K. 1995. "Health Education Curricula in Residential Schools for the Deaf." American Annals of the Deaf 140 (5): 410–414.

Cohen, L.H. 1995. Train Go Sorry: Inside a Deaf World. New York: Vintage.

Committee on Disabilities of the Group for the Advancement of Psychiatry. 1997. "Issues to Consider in Deaf and Hard-of-Hearing Patients." American Family Physician 56 (8): 2057–2064.

Corina, David P., Bellugi, Ursula, Reilly, Judy. 1999. "Neuropsychological Studies of Linguistic and Affective Facial Expression in Deaf Signers." Language and Speech 42 (2-3): 307–331.

Costello, E. ed. 1994. American Sign Language Dictionary. New York: Random House.

Delmarva Foundation for Medical Care, Inc. and Gallaudet Research Institute. 2002. Identification of Performance Standards for the Deaf and Hard of Hearing: Report on the Analysis of Data Sources for Assessing the Health Status of Deaf and Hard of Hearing People. Washington: Gallaudet University Press.

DiPietro, L.J., C.H. Knight and J.S. Sams. 1981. "Health Care Delivery for Deaf Patients: the Provider's Role," American Annals of the Deaf. 126(2):106–112.

Ebert, D.A., and P.S. Heckerling. 1995. "Communication with Deaf Patients: Knowledge, Beliefs, and Practices of Physicians." Journal of the American Medical Association 273 (3): 227–9.

Gallaudet Research Institute. 1996. Stanford Achievement Test, 9th Edition, Form S, Norms Booklet for Deaf and Hard-of-Hearing Students. Washington, DC: Gallaudet University.

Giloth, B., T. Perlman, H. Margellos, L. Miller, T. Hedding, and D. DeGutis. 2004. "Designing More Effective Health Promotion Programs for Prelingually Deaf Populations." Presented at the American Public Health Association: Public Health and the Environment Conference, Washington D.C.

Gray, W.S. 1956. The Teaching of Reading and Writing: An International Survey. Chicago: Scott Foresman & Co.

Hall, B. L. 1992. "From Margins to Center? The development and purpose of Participatory Research" American Sociologist 23: 15-28.

Hansen, B. 2002. "Bilingualism and the Impact of Sign Language Research on Deaf Education." In The Study of Signed Languages, eds. D.F. Armstrong, M.A. Karchmer, and J.V. Van Cleve. Washington, DC: Gallaudet University Press, 172–189.

Harmer, L.M. 1999. "Health Care Delivery and Deaf People: Practice, Problems, and Recommendations for Change." Journal of Deaf Studies and Deaf Education 4 (2): 73–110.

Herr, K. 1998. "Evaluation of the Faces Pain Scale for Use with the Elderly," The Clinical Journal of Pain 14: 29–38.

Herr, K. and L. Garland. 2001. "Assessment and Measurement of Pain in Older Adults." Clinics in Geriatric Medicine 17 (3): 457-478.

Herr, K. as reported at http://www.nursing.uiowa.edu/research/news/elderpain, accessed 5/10/02.

Herr, K. P. Mobily, G. Richardson, and K. Spratt. 1997. "Pain Intensity Assessment: Use of Experimental Pain to Compare Psychometric Properties and Usability of Selected Scales in Adults and Older Populations." Presented at Annual Conference of the Pain Society, New Orleans.

Himmelman, A.T. 1992. Communities Working Collaboratively for a Change. Minneapolis: Humphrey Institute of Public Affairs, University of Minnesota.

Hines, S.K. 2002. "The Unique Bereavement Counseling Needs of the Deaf and Hard of Hearing." The Thanatology Newsletter 8 (1): 6–9.

Holt, J.A., C.B. Traxler, and T.E. Allen. 1997. Interpreting the Scores: A User's Guide to the 9th Edition Stanford Achievement Test for Educators of Deaf and Hard-of-Hearing Students. Gallaudet Research Institute Technical Report 97–1. Washington, DC: Gallaudet University.

Israel, B.A. 2000. "Community-Based Participatory Research: Principles, Rationale and Policy Recommendations." Address, National Institute of Environmental Health Services, Division of Extramural Research and Training Meeting on Successful Models of Community-Based Participatory Research, Washington, DC.

Israel, B.A., E.A. Parker and A.B. Becker. 1998. "Review of community-based research: Assessing partnership approaches to improve public health." Annual Review of Public Health 19: 173–202.

Israel, B.A., S.J. Schurman and M.K. Hugentobler. 1992. "Conducting Action Research: Relationships between Organization Members and Researchers." Journal of Applied Behavioral Science 28: 74–101.

Iverson, L. 2000. "Long-Term Care for Deaf Elders: Exploring Residential Options." Geriatric Care Management Journal 10 (4): 7–16.

Joseph, J.M. 1995. "Sexual Knowledge, Behavior, and Sources of Information Among Deaf and Hard or Hearing College Students." American Annals of the Deaf 140 (4): 338–344.

Lane, H., R. Hoffmeister, and B. Bahn. 1996. A Journey into the Deaf-World. San Diego, CA; 1996.

Lane, H. 1993. The Mask of Benevolence: Disabling the Deaf Community. New York: Vintage.

Lass, L.G., R.R. Franklin, W.E. Bertrand, and J. Baker. 1978. "Health Knowledge, Attitudes, and Practices of the Deaf Population in Greater New Orleans—A Pilot Study." American Annals of the Deaf 123 (5): 960–967.

Li, R.M., P. McCardle, R.L. Clark, K. Kinsella, and D. Berch. 2001. Diverse Voices—The Inclusion of Language-Minority Populations in National Studies: Challenges and Opportunities. Bethesda: National Institute on Aging.

Liddell, S.K. 1980. American Sign Language Syntax. The Hague, Netherlands: Mouton Press.

Liddell, S.K. 2002. "Modality Effects and Conflicting Agendas." In The Study of Signed Languages, eds. D.F. Armstrong, M.A. Karchmer, and J.V. Van Cleve. Washington, DC: Gallaudet University Press, 53–81.

Livingston, S. 1997. Rethinking the Education of Deaf Students. Portsmouth (NH): Elsevier.

Lotke, M. 1995. "She Won't Look at Me." Annals of Internal Medicine 123 (1): 54–7.

Lucas, C., R. Bayley, and C. Valli. 2001. Sociolinguistic Variation in ASL. Vol. 7 of Sociolinguistics in Deaf Communities. Washington, DC: Gallaudet University Press.

MacKinney, T.G., D. Walters, G.L. Bird, and A.B. Nattinger. 1995. "Improvements in Preventive Care and Communication for Deaf Patients: Results of a Novel Primary Health Care Program." Journal of General Internal Medicine 10 (3): 133–137.

Moores, D.F. 1997. "Psycholinguistics and Deafness." American Annals of the Deaf 142 (3): 80–88.

Mozzer-Mather, S. 1990. "A Strategy to Improve Deaf Students' Writing Through the Use of Glosses of Signed Narratives." Gallaudet Research Institute working paper 90–4. Washington: Gallaudet University Press.

Nielsen-Bohlman, L., A.M. Danzer and D.A. Kindig, eds. 2004. Health Literacy: A Prescription to End Confusion. Washington, D.C.: National Academies Press.

Padden, C. and T. Humphries. 1988. Deaf in America, Voice from a Culture. Cambridge, MA: Harvard University Press.

Parasnis, Ila. ed. 1996. Cultural and Language Diversity and the Deaf Experience. New York: Cambridge University Press.

Sacks, O. 1994. Seeing Voices: A Journey Into the World of the Deaf. New York: Harper Collins.

Schulz, A.J., B.A. Israel, S.M. Selig, I.S. Bayer, and C.B. Griffin. 1998. "Development and Implementation of Principles for Community-Based Research in Public Health." In Research Strategies for Community Practice. ed. R.H. Macnair. New York: Haworth Press. 83–110.

Shelp, S.G. 1997. "Your Patient is deaf, Now what?" Registered Nurse. 60(2):33–37.

Solow, S.N. 1981. Sign Language Interpreting: A Basic Resource Book. Silver Springs: National Association of the Deaf.

Steinberg, A.G., V.J. Sullivan, and R.C. Loew. 1998. "Cultural and Linguistic Barriers to Mental Health Service Access: The Deaf Consumer's Perspective." American Journal of Psychiatry 155 (7): 982–984.

Tamaskar, P., T. Malia, C. Stern, D. Gorenflo, H. Meador, and P. Zazove. 2000. "Preventive Attitudes and Beliefs of Deaf and Hard-of-Hearing Individuals." Archives of Family Medicine 9 (6): 518–525.

Valli, C., and C. Lucas. 2002. Linguistics of American Sign Language. 3rd ed. Washington: Gallaudet University Press.

Washabaugh, W., J.C. Woodward, and S. DeSantis. 1980. Providence Island Sign: A context-dependent language. Washington, DC: Gallaudet University Press.

Witte, T.N. and A.J. Kuzel. 2000. "Elderly Deaf Patients' Health Care Experiences." Journal of the American Board of Family Practice 13 (1): 17–22.

Wong, D.L. and C.M. Baker. 1988. "Pain in Children: A Comparison of Assessment Scales," Pediatric Nursing 14 (1): 9–17.

Woodroffe, T., D.W. Gorenflow, H.E. Mador, and P. Zazove. 1998. "Knowledge and Attitudes about AIDS among Deaf and Hard of Hearing Persons." AIDS CARE 10 (3): 377–386.

Zazove, P. 1997. "Understanding Deaf and Hard of Hearing Patients." American Family Physician 56 (8): 1953–1954.

Zazove, P. and D.J. Doukas. 1994. "The Silent Health Care Crisis: Ethical Reflections of Health Care for Deaf and Hard-of-Hearing Persons" Family Medicine 26 (6): 387–90.

Zazove, P., L. C. Niemann, D.W. Gorenflo, C. Carmack, D. Mehr, J.C. Coyne, and T. Antonucci. 1993. "The Health Status and Health Care Utilization of Deaf and Hard-of-Hearing Persons." Archives of Family Medicine 2 (4): 745–752.

Zieziula F. 1998. "The World of the Deaf Community." In Living with Grief, eds. K. Doka and J. Davidson. Levitown, PA: Bruner/Mazel Publishers, 181–198.

In: Focus on Nonverbal Communication Research
Editor: Finley R. Lewis, pp. 149-160

ISBN 1-59454-790-4
© 2007 Nova Science Publishers, Inc.

Chapter 7

UNHEARD EMOTIONS AND UNSEEN DEPRESSION: IMPROVING CAREGIVER AWARENESS OF DEMENTIA PATIENTS' AFFECTS

Carol Magai[1], Kyle Arnold[1], David Gomberg[1] and Carl I. Cohen[2]
[1] Long Island University, USA
[2]SUNY Health Science Center, USA

ABSTRACT

Among late-state dementia patients, depression and behavioral problems are both prevalent and highly difficult to treat. This paper offers a review of the literature in this area, interpreting findings in the light of dynamic systems theory and interpersonal process. It is argued that the cognitive disturbances present in late-stage dementia severely impair patients' ability to express emotions verbally, particularly depressed affect, though, as recent research has shown, non-verbal markers are patently in evidence. Caregivers have a great deal of difficulty accurately understanding and responding to dementia patients' emotions. If consistently misunderstood, dementia patients may try to communicate affects by increasing the intensity of their emotional behaviors. These are typically interpreted by caregivers as "behavioral problems," rather than emotional communications and caregivers tend to respond by becoming frustrated and critical. Patients then may feel more misunderstood and their behavioral disturbances may escalate. This vicious circle, it is argued, can be broken by educating caregivers about affect in late-stage dementia. An educative program developed by the authors is described.

A handful of particularly intractable neuropsychiatric symptoms are commonly found among nursing home residents with late-stage dementia. These may include apathy, agitation, explosive emotional reactions, and depressive symptoms. Some of these symptoms partly relate to the cognitive deficits characteristic of dementia, which impair patients' capacity to regulate and verbalize emotions. Evidence has accumulated, however, that such symptoms are also linked to a particular kind of interpersonal disjunction that tends to develop between dementia patient and caregiver. The available data indicate that because late-stage dementia patients are typically unable to verbalize their affective states, caregivers find it difficult to recognize and respond appropriately to these states. We believe that this sets a vicious cycle in motion, in which patients' desperate attempts at nonverbal communication and caregivers' uncomprehending and exasperated responses to these communications reciprocally exacerbate each other. Patients may struggle desperately to convey their emotional states by increasingly dramatic behavioral expressions of frustration, sadness and rage, while caregivers in turn become progressively more intolerant of behaviors they interpret as irrational and uncooperative. In this conceptualization, the symptoms described are not located exclusively within the patient, but rather are seen as emergent properties of the interpersonal system encompassing dementia sufferer and caregiver.

The affective and behavioral problems we view as characteristic of this relational disturbance are remarkably pervasive in nursing homes. Teresi, Abrams, Holmes, Ramirez, and Eimick (2002), who examined prevalence of depression in 319 nursing home residents, reported that 14.4% of their sample fit the diagnosis of major depressive disorder, 16.8% had minor depression, and 44.2% evinced significant depressive symptomatology. Among those nursing home residents with dementia, in a study of three nursing homes in New York City, our group (Cohen, Hyland, and Magai, 1998) found prevalence rates of depression (major and minor) of 19% and 33% among Black and White patients, respectively. Research by Bartels and colleagues (2003) indicated that dementia with mixed agitation and depression is present in more than a third of those suffering from complicated dementia, and is linked to multiple psychiatric and medical needs and the utilization of high-cost health services. Wagner and colleagues (1995), studying a nationwide sample of patients with severe cognitive deficits, reported that 49% displayed signs of suspiciousness, 48% seemed anxious or worried, 37% appeared sad or depressed, and 22% had crying spells. Ninety percent of this sample exhibited 10 or more behavior problems, and 37% had over 20. These findings correspond to evidence of similarly widespread strain experienced by caregivers of dementia patients, 50% of whom report psychological distress (Margallo, Reichelt, Hayes, Lee, Fossey, O'Brien, and Ballard, 2001). Many of the behavioral problems linked with dementia, including agitation, depression, aggressivity, resistance, and nonresponsiveness, have been shown to elicit feelings of frustration, anxiety, and helplessness in nurses (Norberg & Asplund, 1990; Akerland & Norberg, 1990; Hallberg & Norberg, 1996). These feelings contribute to burnout and job turnover in nursing home staff (Astroem, Norberg, Nilsson & Winblad, 1987; Duquette, Kerouac, & Beaudet, 1994; Harris, 1989; Melchior, Phillipsen, Sandhu, & Abu-Saad, 1996; Wallis, 1987, Almberg, Grafstroem, Krichbaum, Kathleen, Winblad, 2000), which in some circumstances is 100% for nurses' aides and nearly 30% for registered nurses and licensed practical nurses (Stanley, 1986). Patients' disruptive behaviors add to the already exhausting working environment nursing home staff must tolerate, an environment that usually includes long hours, low pay, and an overwhelming workload. According to a recent study conducted by the Nursing Home Community Coalition of New York State, nursing home staff are stretched so thin that individual patients usually receive less than 4.1 hours of direct care daily (Perez-Pena, 2003).

In the following paper, a review of relevant literature is presented and interpreted in the light of a relational systems approach (Magai & Nusbaum, 1996). Evidence is presented in support of the interpretation that the cognitive and expressive impairments characteristic of late stage dementia interfere with the dementia sufferer's ability to verbalize his or her emotional states and make them known to others. Consequently, it is argued, caregivers of dementia patients may draw the mistaken conclusion that these patients' affective lives are themselves somehow impoverished, a conclusion that the work of the present authors (Magai, Cohen, Gomberg, Malatesta, & Culver, 1996) and others has demonstrated to be highly questionable. Evidence is presented to support the thesis that the disjunction between dementia patients' actual emotions and caregivers' perception of those emotions can contribute to a variety of clinical problems, an outstanding example being the under-diagnosis of depression in dementia patients. An intervention developed by the authors (Magai, Cohen, & Gomberg, 2000) designed to improve caregiver-patient communication is then outlined. Finally, recommendations for treatment are discussed.

AFFECT IN DEMENTIA

Although it is clear that the relational problem we describe has multiple determinants, one important contributing factor appears to be the widespread myth that dementia patients experience blunted affectivity. To be sure, many faculties deteriorate as Alzheimer's disease progresses. During the degenerative course of the disease, Alzheimer's patients undergo progressive developmental regression, sometimes called "reverse ontogeny:" Memory loss is usually the first sign of encroaching dementia; later in the disease, functional abilities associated with instrumental activities of daily living are lost to the disease process; this is followed by loss of bladder and bowel control, and finally loss of language. Late stage patients (GDS stages 6 and 7) demonstrate the mental equivalence and functional abilities of 1 to 2 year old infants, that is, the sensorimotor stage of mental and social development (Magai, Auer, Reisberg, Sclan, & Cohen, 1992). Pre-linguistic, sensorimotor infants are skilled communicators, as they must rely on expressive behavior to signal their wants, needs, fears, likes and dislikes (Malatesta & Haviland, 1982; Malatesta, Culver, Tesman, & Shepard, 1989; Malatesta, 1985). Until the advent of language, they are entirely dependent on their nonverbal signaling system and the responsivity of caregivers for the satisfaction of their needs. This same dependence on non-verbal communication, we would argue, obtains in the case of late stage dementia patients who have lost most or all of their ability to speak coherently. Adding to these difficulties, dementia disrupts the sufferer's cognitive ability to accurately recognize and respond to the emotional expressions of others (Fernandez-Duque & Black, 2005; Lavenua & Pasquiera, 2005; Shimokawa, Yatomi, Anamizu, Torri, Isono, Sugai, & Kohno, 2001). These factors tend to give caregivers the mistaken impression that patients' affectivity itself has diminished.

To the contrary, research over the past few years has provided substantial evidence that even middle- and late-stage dementia sufferers are capable of a wide range of affective expressions. Lawton, Van Haitsma, and Klapper (1996), studied emotion expression in older demented and non-demented adults using a behavioral coding system--the Philadelphia Geriatric Center Affect Rating Scale--and direct observation. They found that all basic emotions were present to some degree in the dementia patients, and all but anger were evident in the nondemented residents. Pleasure, interest, and contentment ratings were greater in cumulative duration among the nondemented versus demented residents, while anxiety ratings were lower. There was no difference between the two groups on sadness. Two studies by the present authors (Magai, Cohen, Gomberg, Malatesta, & Culver, 1996; Magai, Kennedy & Cohen, 1997) also indicated that late stage patients retain the ability to experience and express a range of emotions. In the first study Magai et al. (1996) coded facial expressions of emotion in dementia patients (GDS stages 5-7) using a behavioral coding scheme and direct observation during a family visit. Facial expressions were coded on a second-to-second basis by research assistants trained in Izard's (1979) Maximally Discriminative Facial Movement Coding System (MAX). Expressions of interest, anger, contempt, sadness, joy, disgust, and fear were coded. Although disgust and fear were too infrequent for parametric analysis, the latter were almost exclusively observed in Stage 7 patients. Recognizable facial expressions of emotion were observed at each of the cognitive stages, including the most severely impaired, end-stage patients, although there were changes with advancing intellectual impairment. Moreover, the contexts in which these emotional expressions occurred indicated that they had specific instrumental relationships to patients' goals and concerns.   The verbal and cognitive impairments caused by dementia nevertheless place significant constraints on how patients can express emotions. When the dementia patient communicates an affect, she may attempt to do so using nonverbal behavioral and vocal expressions. These nonverbal expressions are often magnified and may even be inappropriate. Research on depressed affect in dementia provides a telling example. Evidence suggests that when states of depression occur in the context of communication impairments, they are likely to result in aggressive and disruptive behaviors. Talerico, Evans, and Strumpf (2002) in a study of 405 nursing home residents, found that communication deficits were connected with all types of aggression, and depression was specifically related to physical aggression. Investigating depression in vocally disruptive nursing home residents, Dwyer and Byrne (2001) observed that vocally disruptive patients scored significantly higher than controls on two measures of depression. Accordingly, these authors suggested that depressed affect may be one determinant of disruptive vocalizations. This is especially striking in light of evidence that nursing home staff have remarkable difficulty recognizing depressed affect in cognitively disturbed patients. In a study of concordance rates between self-reported depression and staff-reported depression among dementia patients, Owens, Webber, and Lindeman (1996) found that when staff attempted to assess depression in patients with moderate cognitive impairment, they could clearly distinguish between patients who reported many depressive symptoms and those who reported only a few. When evaluating severely cognitively impaired patients, by contrast, staff were unable to distinguish between mild and severe depression. In another study, Teresi, Abrams, Holmes, Ramirez, Shapiro, and Eimicke (2002) found that social workers tend to under-recognize depression in cognitively impaired nursing home residents. Additionally, there is a well-known trend in physicians toward under-diagnosis and under-treatment of depression in dementia patients. Research by Evers, Samuels, Lantz, Khan, Brickman, and Marin (2002) confirmed that this trend remains prominent. Overall, it has been estimated that only one-third to one-half of dementia patients with a major depressive disorder, and half of those with less severe depressive symptoms, are being properly identified (Brad, Esser, Tyriver & Striepling, 2000). These data suggest that in patients with severe cognitive deficits, depressed affect tends to be both elusive to observers and contributory to behavioral problems.

We have interpreted the above findings in light of the fact that in late stage dementia subcortical areas of the brain, often associated with affect, remain relatively intact compared to cortical regions. Consequently, in the absence of verbal facility, late stage patients may rely on nonverbal affective communication. When their own affective cues are ignored or misunderstood, dementia patients may be compelled to use more dramatic means of nonverbal expression to convey their mental states to caregivers. These attempts at communication, if persistently misunderstood, can develop into disruptive behaviors and vocalizations. This implies that it is particularly important for caregivers to be attuned to dementia patients' nonverbal affective cues if they are to respond adequately to patients' needs and wishes, and prevent behavioral problems from arising (Cohen-Mansfield & Mintzer, 2005).

THE EFFECTS OF CAREGIVER-PATIENT RELATIONSHIPS ON PATIENT SYMPTOMATOLOGY AND BEHAVIOR

Malattunement between caregiver and dementia patient has been shown to be associated with a variety of relational and symptomatic difficulties. In a recent review of the literature on social support and symptomatology in dementia patients, Flannery (2002) concluded that disrupted social supports can have profoundly invidious effects on patients' longevity, subjective sense of well-being, and health outcome. Orrell, Butler, and Bebbington (2000) likewise discovered that dementia patients who lack social support tend to have higher mortality rates than those with strong support networks. Hollinger and Pearson (2000) found that patients who perceived nurses as unempathic tended to report significantly more severe depressive symptomatology.

In addition, a particular pathogenic relational pattern known as "expressed emotion" (EE) has also been demonstrated to be closely related to patient symptomatology. "Expressed emotion" refers to a type of relationship in which criticism, hostility, and emotional overinvolvement are prominent. Vitaliano, Young, Romano, and Magana-Amato (1993) found that high EE in family caregivers of dementia sufferers was predictive of increases in patients' problem behaviors over a year, despite the restriction of range of such behaviors. These authors reasoned that the predictive power of EE can be accounted for if it is assumed that there are strong feedback loops over time between caregiver EE and disruptive patient behaviors. Cognitive and functional behaviors, in contrast, were not affected by EE. Vitaliano et al. (1993) speculated that negative behaviors in dementia patients may be more readily influenced by caregiver affect than functional or cognitive ability because of these patients' sensitivity to interpersonal dynamics.

It has also been found that criticism of mentally ill inpatients by staff is tied to patient aggressivity, attention-seeking behavior, and underactivity (Moore, Ball, & Kuipers, 1992). More specifically, the severity of dementia patients' behavioral problems has been shown by Edberg, Nordmark, and Hallberg (1995) to correlate significantly with the relative harshness of nurses' tones of voice. Fearon, Donaldson, Burns, and Tarrier (1998), furthermore, found that low intimacy in the dementia patient-caregiver relationship was closely related to high

EE. In a more recent study, Spruytte, Van-Audenhove, Lammertyn, and Storms (2002) established that high EE in caregivers could be predicted both by dementia patients' behavioral disturbances and caregivers' perceptions of these disturbances.

Caregivers, likewise, often suffer from deleterious effects of relational problems with patients. According to a study by Argimon, Limon, Vila, and Cabezas (2004), female caregivers of dementia patients experience a considerably lower quality of life then other women. Townsend and Franks (1995) found significant correlations between conflict in the caregiver-patient relationship and higher stress, more depression, and lower feelings of efficacy in caregivers. Bledin and colleagues (1990) discovered that female caregivers with a more critical attitude towards patients tended to report more strain and distress than less critical peers. Supporting this finding, a study by Vitaliano, et. al. (1993) showed that the more critical caregivers were, the more they displayed depression and low life satisfaction. More recent research by Shaw, Patterson, Semple, Dimsdale, Ziegler, and Grant (2003) found that caregiver hostility was associated with dementia patients' problem behaviors and functional deficits. These findings are consistent with the interpretation that dementia symptomatology tends to cause caregiver strain and stress, consequently eliciting hostility.

These data indicate that the quality of caregiver-patient interactions is firmly connected with the affective and behavioral symptomatology of dementia patients (Cohen-Mansfield & Mintzer, 2005). When confronted with behavior that is difficult to understand and manage, caregivers seem to become frustrated and hostile. Patients react to this hostility with increases in symptomatology. This line of thinking suggests that interventions targeting the caregiver-patient relationship—the dynamic systems component (Magai & Nusbaum, 1996)--could comprise a fruitful component of the treatment of dementia, possibly leading to a diminution of patients' behavioral and affective symptomatology.

IDENTIFYING DEPRESSED MOOD IN LATE-STAGE DEMENTIA

As noted above, clinicians and caregivers have difficulty recognizing depression in the later stages of dementia when verbal abilities decline. The data on the effectiveness of antidepressants in late-stage dementia are mixed (Magai, Kennedy, Cohen, & Gomberg, 2000), in part because problems in identifying depression make outcome assessment tenuous. Traditional scales such as the Cornell Scale for Depression in Dementia (Alexopoulos et al., 1988) rely to some extent on the ability of persons to report ideational disturbances such as suicidal thoughts, pessimism, self-blame, and delusions. Several clinical scales such as the Gestalt Depression Scale (Greenwald et al., 1991) and the Depressive Signs Scale (DSS; Katona & Aldridge, 1985) were developed for persons with late stage dementia. The former is a 5-item measurement that relies on observational assessment and the latter is 8-item scale based on observation and informant reports of behavioral changes. However, some of the items included in the DSS may reflect cognitive deficits rather than affective elements. In a recent paper, Greenberg et al. (2004) concluded that none of the existing depression scales are adequate for identifying depression in dementia patients. In our own work (Magai, Kennedy, Cohen, & Gomberg, 2000), we have used patterned facial behaviors, indexed by certain well-defined facial configurations such as "horse-shoe mouth" (frown), oblique brows, and "knit-brow." The knit-brow expression is thought to indicate distress in the "pre-cry" infant face.

Importantly, in a study comparing the effects of sertraline and placebo in the treatment of probable depression in late-stage dementia, although both groups showed improvement, decrease in the "knit brow" expression was the one indicator that distinguished sertraline from the placebo group (p<.10) on 8-week follow-up. This finding suggested that facial expressions may be more robust markers for assessing dysphoria in late-stage dementia, a suggestion that contributed to our work on a clinical intervention described below.

TREATING THE CAREGIVER-PATIENT RELATIONSHIP

Although a variety of treatments for affective and behavioral problems in dementia patients have been implemented (Carpenter, Ruckdeschel, Ruckdeschel, & Van-Haitsma, 2003; Panzer & Sheridan, 2000; Tune, 1998) few focus on the relationship between caregiver and patient. Reviewing the extant literature in this area, Finnema, Droees, Ribbe, and Tilburg (2000) reported that attempts to educate caregivers to be attuned to the emotions of late-stage dementia patients have thus far shown promising results.

In an effort to further develop such interventions, the authors designed an emotion-oriented training program aimed at improving caregivers' ability to empathize and communicate with dementia patients (described in detail in Magai, Cohen, & Gomberg, 2000; manual available from the authors on request). This two-week long program comprised ten hour long lecture/experiential sessions designed to train caregivers in the identification and validation of patients' non-verbal signals of emotion. Material covered during the sessions included both invariant and culture-bound features of ten basic emotions. Facial, vocal, and bodily cues differentiating emotion, selective perception of emotion, deleterious effects of particular modes of emotion communication on patients, and personal emotional triggers were discussed. Also, participants practiced with a variety of media to improve their abilities to recognize emotion cues, and received emotion validation skills training.

To study the efficacy of this training program, we recruited 91 mid-to-late stage dementia patients and their caregivers, who were randomly assigned to three groups. One third of the caregivers (treatment group) participated in the emotion- focused training program described above. One third (control group) received an equal number of training sessions emphasizing cognitive and behavioral features of dementia. The last third (control group) was wait-listed. All training sessions were conducted by a clinical psychologist who was not informed of the purpose of the study. Before the initial training sessions, patient mood was assessed by the Maximally Discriminative Facial Movement Coding System (Izard, 1979) affect coding system during a face-to-face interview. Two measures of behavioral disturbance, the Cohen-Mansfield Agitation Inventory (Cohen-Mansfield, et al., 1989) and the Cornell Scale for Depression in Dementia (Alexopoulos et al., 1988) were also administered to patients, and caregivers were asked to complete a measure of psychological distress, the Brief Symptom Inventory (Derogatis & Spencer, 1982). Following the completion of all training sessions, these measures were again administered four times at three-week intervals. It was hypothesized that the training would result in decreased problem behaviors in residents and improved morale and well being in caregivers. In testing these hypotheses, analyses used repeated measures ANOVAs with the treatment group as the independent variable, time of measurement as the repeated measure, and baseline scores and race as co-variates.

Positive affect in patients in the treatment group rose sharply during the first six weeks of the study, while the affect of patients in both control groups remained unchanged. Caregivers in all three groups reported improved psychological states. Despite this improvement, positive affect in treatment-group patients began to recede after the first six weeks of the study, and after twelve weeks no affective difference could be discerned between treatment and control groups. No change in patients' behavioral symptomatology was apparent. Thus, a two-week, ten-session program had a dramatic impact on patient well-being for six weeks, but this impact faded without refresher sessions. This finding implies that a short course of in-service training has the potential to contribute to substantial improvements in caregivers' attunement to patients' nonverbal affect expressions. Yet, it also indicates that this program is not by itself sufficient to maintain these improvements without refresher sessions.

CONCLUSION

The verbal and cognitive impairments present in dementia sufferers make it difficult for these patients to convey their affective states to caregivers verbally, though non-verbal markers are patently in evidence. However, it is clear that caregivers must be able to comprehend dementia patients' affective states if they are to respond appropriately. Both the authors' work (Magai, Cohen, & Gomberg, 2000) and that of Finnema and colleagues (2000), accordingly, emphasize educating caregivers about modes of emotional expression in dementia. In light of our findings, we believe that educative programs should be supplemented with regular refresher courses, to avoid the drop-off in positive treatment effects that occur after six weeks.

REFERENCES

[1] Akerland, B. & Norberg, A. (1990). Powerlessness in terminal care of demented patients: An exploratory study. *Omega, 21,* 15-19.
[2] Alexopoulos, G. S., Abrams, R. C., Young, R.C., & Shamoian, C.A. (1988).Cornell scale for depression in dementia. *Biological Psychiatry*, 23, 271-284.
[3] Almberg, B., Grafstroem, M., Krichbaum, K., & Winblad, B. (2000). The interplay of institution and family caregiving: Relations between patient hassles, nursing home hassles and caregivers' burnout. *International Journal of Geriatric Psychiatry, 15,* 10, 931-939.
[4] Argimon, J., Limon, E., Vila, J., & Cabazes, C. (2004). Health-related quality of life in carers of patients with dementia. *Family Practice, 21,* 454-457.
[5] Astroem, S., Norberg, A., Nilsson, M., & Windblad, B. (1987). Tedium among personnel working with geriatric patients. *Scandinavian Journal of Caring Science, 1,* 125-132.
[6] Bartels, S., Horn, S., Smout, R., Dums, A., Flaherty, E., Jones, J., Monane, M., Taler, G., & Voss, A. (2003). Agitation and depression in frail nursing home elderly patients with dementia. *American Journal of Geriatric Psychiatry, 11,* 231-238.

[7] Bledin, K., MacCarthy, B., Kuipers, L., & Woods, R. (1990). Daughters of people with dementia. *British Journal of Psychiatry, 157,* 221-227.

[8] Brad, A., Esser, W., Tyriver, C., Striepling, A. (2000). The behavioral assessment of depression for people with dementia. *American Journal of Alzheimer's Disease, 15,* 303-307.

[9] Carpenter, B., Ruckdeschel, K., Ruckdeschel, H., & Van Haitsma, K. (2003). R-E-M psychotherapy: A manualized approach for long-term care residents with depression and dementia. *Clinical Gerontologist, 25,* 25-49.

[10] Cohen, C.I., Hyland, K. & Kimly, D. (in press). The utility of mandatory depression screening of dementia patients in nursing homes. *American Journal of Psychiatry.*

[11] Cohen , C.I., Hyland K, & Magai, C. (1998). Interracial and intraracial differences in neuropsychiatric symptoms, sociodemography, and treatment among nursing home patients with dementia. *The Gerontologist,* 38, 353-361.

[12] Cohen-Mansfield, J., Marx, M.S., & Rosenthal, A.S. (1989). A description of agitation in a nursing home. *Journal of Gerontology 44,* 77-86.

[13] Cohen-Mansfield, J., & Mintzer, J. (2005). Time for change: The role of nonpharmacological interventions in treating behavior problems in nursing home residents with dementia. *Alzheimer Disease & Associated Disorders. 19,* 37-40

[14] Dcrogatis, L. R., & Spencer, M. S. (1982). *The Brief Symptom Inventory: administration, scoring and procedures Manual-I.* Baltimore: Johns Hopkins University School of Medicine, Clinical Psychometrics Unit.

[15] Duquette, A., Kerouac, S., Bandhu, B., & Beaudet, L. (1994). Factors related to nursing burnout: A review of empirical knowledge. *Issues in Mental Health Nursing, 15,* 337-358.

[16] Dwyer, M. & Byrne, G. (2001). Disruptive vocalization and depression in older nursing home residents. *International Psychogeriatrics, 12,* 463-471.

[17] Edberg, A., Nordmark, A., & Hallberg, I. (1995). Initiating and terminating verbal interaction between nurses and severely demented patients regarded as vocally disruptive. *Journal of Psychiatric and Mental Health Nursing, 2,* 159-167.

[18] Evers, M., Samuels, S., Lantz, M., Khan, K., Brickman, A. & Marin, D. (2002). The prevalence, diagnosis and treatment of depression in dementia patients in chronic care facilities in the last six months of life. *International Journal of Geriatric Psychiatry, 17,* 464-472.

[19] Fearon, M., Donaldson, C., Burns, A., & Tarrier, N. (1998). Intimacy as a determinant of expressed emotion in carers of people with Alzheimer's disease. *Psychological Medicine, 28,* 1085-1090.

[20] Fernandez-Duque, D &, Black S. (2005). Impaired recognition of negative facial emotions in patients with frontotemporal dementia. *Neuropsychologia, 43,* 1673-87.

[21] Finnema, E., Droees, R., Ribble, M., & Tilburg, W. (2000). The effects of emotion-oriented approaches in the care for persons suffering from dementia. *International Journal of Geriatric Psychiatry, 15,*141-161.

[22] Flannery, R. (2002). Disrupted caring attachments: Implications for long-term care. *American Journal of Alzheimer's and Other Dementias, 17,* 227-231.

[23] Greenberg, L., Lantz, M., Likourezos, A., Burack, O., Chichin, E., & Carter, J. (2004). Screening for depression in nursing home palliative care patients. *Journal of Geriatric Psychiatry and Neurology, 17,* 212-218.

[24] Greenwald B., Kramer-Ginsberg E., Kremen N.J., et al (May, 1991). Depression complicating dementia. Paper presented at the 144th Annual Meeting of the American Psychiatric Association, New Orleans, LA, Hallberg & Norberg, (1996). Nurses' experiences of strain and their reactions in the care of severely demented patients. *International Journal of Geriatric Psychiatry, 10,*757-766.

[25] Harris, R. (1989) Reviewing nursing stress according to a proposed coping-adaption framework. *Advances in Nursing Science, 11,* 12-28.

[26] Hollinger, S. & Pearson, J. (2000). The relationship between staff empathy and depressive symptoms in nursing home residents. *Aging and Mental Health, 4,* 56-65.

[27] Izard, C. (1979). The maximally discriminative facial movement coding system (MAX). Newark: University of Delaware, Instructional Resources Center.

[28] Katona C.L.E., & Aldridge C.R.(1985). The dexamethosone suppression test and depressive signs in dementia. Journal of Affective Disorders 8, 83-89.

[29] Lawton, M.P., Van Haitsma, K., & Klapper, J. (1996). Observed affect in nursing home residents with Alzheimer's disease. *Journal of Gerontology, 51,* 3-14.

[30] Lavenue, I. & Pasquiera, F. (2005). Perception of emotion on faces in frontotemporal dementia and Alzheimer's disease: A longitudinal study. *Dementia and Geriatric Cognitive Disorders, 19,* 37-41

[31] Magai, C., Auer, S., Reisberg, S., Sclan, S. & Cohen, C. (1992). The assessment of sensorimotor and social intelligence in late stage Alzheimer's disease. Paper presented at the Gerontological Society of America, Washington, D.C.

[32] Magai, C., Cohen, C.I., & Gomberg, D. (2000). Impact of training dementia in sensitivity to nonverbal emotion signals. *International Psychogeriatrics, 14,* 25-38.

[33] Magai, C., Kennedy, G., Cohen, C.I.., & Gomberg, D. (2000). A controlled clinical trial of sertraline in the treatment of depression in nursing home patients with late-stage Alzheimer's disease. *American Journal of Geriatric Psychiatry, 8,* 66-74.

[34] Magai, C., Cohen, C.I.., Gomberg, D., Malatesta, C., & Culver, C. (1996). Emotion expression in late stage dementia. *International Psychogeriatrics, 8,* 383-396.

[35] Magai, C. & Nusbaum, B. (1996). Personality change in adulthood: Dynamic systems, emotions, and the transformed self. In C. Magai & S. McFadden (Eds.), *Handbook of Emotion, Adult Development and Aging,* pp. 403-420. San Diego: Academic.

[36] Malatesta, C.Z. (1985). The developmental course of emotion expression in the human infant. In G. Zivin (Ed.), Expressive development: Biological and environmental interactions. NY: Academic Press.

[37] Malatesta, C.Z., Culver, C., Tesman, J., & Shepard, B. (1989). The development of emotion expression during the first two years of life. Monographs of the Society for Research on Child Development, Vol. 54, Nos. 1 & 2,pp. 1-104. Chicago: University of Chicago Press.

[38] Malatesta, C.Z. & Haviland, J.M. (1982). Learning display rules: The socialization of emotion expression in infancy. Child Development, 53, 991-1003.

[39] Margallo, L., Reichelt, K., Hayes, P., Lee, L., Fossey, J., O'Brien, J., & Ballard,C. (2001). Longitudinal comparisons of depression, coping, and turnover among NHS and private sector staff caring for people with dementia. *British Medical Journal, 322,* 769-770.

[40] Melchoir, M., Phillipsen, H., & Abu-saad, H. (1996). The effectiveness of primary nursing on burnout among psychiatric nurses in long-stay settings. *Journal of Advanced Nursing, 24*, 694-702.

[41] Moore, E., Ball, R., & Kuipers, L., (1992). Expressed emotion in staff working with the long-term mentally ill. *British Journal of Psychiatry, 161*, 803-808.

[42] Norberg, A. & Asplund, K. (1990). Caregivers' experience of caring for severely demented patients. *Western Journal of Nursing Research, 12*, 75-84.

[43] Orrell, M., Butler, R., & Bebbington, P. (2000). Social factors and the outcome of dementia. *International Journal of Geriatric Psychiatry, 15*, 515-520.

[44] Owens, D., Webber, P., & Lindeman, D. (1996). Dementia and depression: Concordance rates between dementia patients' self report of mood and nursing staff observers ratings of patients' mood. *Clinical Gerontologist, 17*, 21-41.

[45] Panzer, K. & Sheridan, L. (2000). Effects of animal-assisted therapy on depression and morale among nursing home residents. Unpublished dissertation, Rutgers University.

[46] Perez-Pena, R. (2003, June 8). Nursing home workers vent frustrations. *The New York Times*, 47.

[47] Shaw, W., Patterson, T., Semple, S., Dimsdale, J., Ziegler, M., & Grant, I. (2003). Emotional expressiveness, hostility and blood pressure in a longitudinal cohort of Alzheimer caregivers. *Journal of Psychosomatic Research, 54*, 293-302.

[48] Shimokawa, A., Yatomo, N., Anamizu, S., Torii, S., Isono, H., Sugai, Y., & Kohno, M. (2001). Influence of deteriorating ability of emotional comprehension on interpersonal behavior in Alzheimer-type dementia. *Brain and Cognition, 47*, 423-433.

[49] Spitz, R. (1945). Hospitalism. *The Psychoanalytic Study of the Child*, 1, 53-72.

[50] Spruytte, N., Van Audenhove, C., Lammertyn, F., & Storms, G. (2002). The quality of the caregiving relationship in informal care for older adults with dementia and chronic psychiatric patients. *Psychology and Psychotherapy, 75*, 295-311.

[51] Stanley, A. (1986). Ethical considerations and morale in nursing homes: Implications for research. In M. S. Harper & B. D. Lebowitz (Eds), *Mental illness and nursing homes: Agenda for research*. DHHS Publications, Rockville, Md.

[52] Talerico, K., Evans, L., & Strumpf, N. (2002). Mental health correlates of aggression in nursing home residents with dementia. *Gerontologist, 42*, 169-177.

[53] Teresi, J., Abrams, R., Holmes, D., Ramirez, M., & Eimicke, J. (2002). Prevalence of depression and depression recognition in nursing homes. *Social Psychiatry and Psychiatric Epidemology, 36*, 613-620.

[54] Teresi, J., Abrams, R., Holmes, D. Ramirez, M., Shapiro, C., & Eimicke, J. (2002). Influence of cognitive impairment, gender, and African-American status on psychiatric ratings and staff recognition of depression. *American Journal of Geriatric Psychiatry, 10*, 506-514.

[55] Townsend, A. & Franks, M. (1995). Binding ties: Closeness and conflict in adult children's caregiving relationships. *Psychology and Aging, 10*, 343-351.

[56] Tune, L. (1998). Treatments for dementia. In P. Nathan & J. Gorman (Eds.) *A guide to treatments that work*. London: Oxford University Press.

[57] Vitaliano, P. P., Young, H. M., Romano, R. J., & Magana-Amato, A. (1993). Does expressed emotion in spouses predict subsequent problems among care recipients with Alzheimer's disease? *Journal of Gerontology, 48*, 202-209.

[58] Wagner, A., Teri, L., & Orr-Rainey, N. (1995). Behavior problems of residents with dementia in special care units. *Alzheimer Disease and Associated Disorders, 9,* 121-127.
[59] Wallis, D. (1987). Satisfaction, stress, and performance. *Work and Stress, 1,* 113-128.

In: Focus on Nonverbal Communication Research
Editor: Finley R. Lewis, pp. 161-197

ISBN 1-59454-790-4
© 2007 Nova Science Publishers, Inc.

Chapter 8

PERCEPTUO-MOTOR INTERACTIONS: INTERINDIVIDUAL DIFFERENCES IN MULTIMODAL INTEGRATION

Philippe Boulinguez, Frédéric Sarès,
Abdelrhani Benraiss and Joëlle Rouhana
Laboratoire Performance Motricité & Cognition,
MSHS, Université de Poitiers, France

ABSTRACT

Communication between subject and his close environment is a continuous and necessary condition for the organization and control of goal-directed actions. This includes the processing of various exteroceptive (visual, auditory, etc...) and interoceptive (proprioception, motor commands, etc...) information, in other words, the involvement of both internal and external communication. The continuous processing of multimodal and interdependent information, the so-called sensory or sensorimotor integration, is the basic mechanism for humans both to perceive themselves, their close environment and to interact with it. In this chapter, we argue these perceptuo-motor interactions are highly flexible (adaptation of integrative mechanisms to contextual conditions) and variable (differences in integrative mechanisms across subjects).

CROSS-MODAL SENSORY INTEGRATION AND SENSORIMOTOR COORDINATE TRANSFORMATIONS

Coding the position of a visual object in space with regard to the observer's actual position seems to be a simple processing. In fact, this requires multiple sensory signals to be combined together by the central nervous system (CNS). To interpret the position of the object on the retina, the visual system also needs to receive information about the position of the eye in the orbit and the position of the head with regard to the trunk. This is for example given, among other signals, by extraocular and neck muscles proprioception (see Jeannerod, 1988 for review). This simplest example of sensory integration shows that coherent perception, even when building a unimodal representation, needs cross-modal interactions. Obviously, most of the *perceptuo-motor* interactions of our daily life are based on multimodal representations elaborated thanks to more complex sensorimotor integration mechanisms.

The problem of sensorimotor integration may be viewed as a series of transformations between different frames of reference used to code internal and external information. It is often considered that two main classes of representations of space are used: egocentric and allocentric (in the first one, objects are encoded with reference to the body and in the second one objects are encoded with reference to fixed extrapersonal space properties). In fact, numerous spatial coordinate systems could be used by the central nervous system to build perception and organize goal-directed actions (eye, head, hand, trunk, gravity... object location, objects relative positions...), and it is possible to determine experimentally the frame of reference in which a particular behavior is expressed (Soechting, Tong & Flanders, 1996). Obviously, the complexity of the neural computations leading to a coherent perception and/or control of movement depends on how many information is encoded and how it is encoded at any structural level. For each part of this chapter, we propose a short review of how the brain encodes and processes these multiple representations used for perceptuo-motor interactions.

SENSORIMOTOR INTEGRATION: WHAT CAN WE LEARN FROM HIGHLY SKILLED INDIVIDUALS?

Sensorimotor integration cannot always be directly observed. It is generally inferred from behavioral observations aiming at explaining inter-individual differences. Accordingly, two main means were privileged to construct sensory integration theories: the developmental and especially the neuropsychological approaches (see for example Bundy, Lane & Murray, 2002). In both, relation between changes in behavior and the evolution of the neural correlates of sensorimotor integration can be made. The basic principle is to compare performances of brain injured patients (or children across the lifespan) to normal adult subjects. However, strokes studies in humans are often biased because they generally affect large parts of the brain, leading to strong confusions in the literature (see for example Karnath, Ferber & Himmelbach, 2001 and Graziano, 2001a, for discussion on the role of the parietal lobe in hemispatial neglect and/or sensorimotor integration). In addition, characterizing the reference population is a significant but often ignored difficulty related to interindividual variability.

This problem of variability is crucial because theories of plurimodal sensory integration suggest that different mechanisms (operating for example in specific reference frames) could either be at work to perform the same process. In other words, if basic sensory functions can be clearly identified, the higher order recoding mechanisms of multisensory integration are difficult to understand probably because it is not normalized across individuals.

In this chapter, we argue that interindividual differences in perceptuo-motor interactions and integration processes are related to expertise and subjects skill level. Because perceptuo-motor processes involved in movement control are optimized with intensive practice, expert athletes in some sports have extremely high visuomanual skill levels. The interest of studying such particular subjects is obvious. In normal subjects, some functionalities of the human sensorimotor system are not observable. They are simply not developed and just remain a functional potential. Accordingly, studying expert athletes is not interesting only for finding the determinants of high perceptual and motor skills, it also gives the opportunity to provide new insights into sensorimotor integration theories.

In this chapter, we will especially focus on *visuo-manual aiming and sensory dominance*, *integration of gravity* among other sensorimotor information, and relation between *sensory dominance and perceptuo-motor interference* to illustrate this main general idea. For each section, we propose a short review of the literature and illustrate some aspects of the theory by more detailed experimental evidence. This includes some current original data from our laboratory showing how expertise can modulate perceptuo-motor processes.

VISUO-MANUAL AIMING AND SENSORY DOMINANCE

Standard Theory

Vision uses an eye-centered frame of reference because of the topographic organization of the retina. More generally, each other sensory modality (audition, proprioception…) uses specific coding according to its natural frame of reference. Similarly, at system output, each module encodes information in its own specific frame of reference (saccadic eye movement, reaching…). The standard theory considers that, somewhere between, a single function is responsible for mapping and translation from the sensory to the motor modules. The best candidate structure responsible for this integration was many times described as the posterior parietal lobe (e.g., Andersen, Snyder, Bradley & Xing, 1997). However, many contradicting and conflicting results in behavioral and neurophysiological data prevent from considering sensorimotor integration as a simple convergence and translation mechanism acting within a single and linear process in a single brain area (e.g., Desmurget, Pelisson, Rossetti & Prablanc, 1998; Pouget & Snyder, 2000; Pouget, Deneve & Duhamel, 2002). Sensorimotor integration is not a simple mathematical operation of summation or mean of afferent/efferent information with specific weight, and is not a single, linear, intermediate and independent perceptual process.

Neural Basis of Sensorimotor Integration for Visuomanual Aiming

Sensory channels provide redundant information about the same objects. When planning goal-directed hand movements, hand position is mainly coded by vision, proprioception and the motor commands themselves. Typically, in order to build a motor plan, that is a set of motor commands before movement initiation, the CNS has to solve 3 kinds of problems using these various afferent and efferent signals: *i)* target localization, *ii)* definition of the initial state of the motor apparatus and *iii)* hand trajectory formation (see Desmurget et al., 1998 for review). Finally, after movement has been initiated on the basis of the initial motor plan, it is continuously monitored during execution. The CNS has then to solve a fourth problem: *iv)* estimate the current state of the limb with reference to the target goal and correct the movement if necessary (see Desmurget & Grafton, 2000 for review). Neural bases of visually guided reaching reveal that many different frames of reference can be used by the CNS to integrate all sensorimotor information (especially body-, eye-, hand-centered coordinates), and that these various redundant representations can in turn be integrated to form a relevant coding for the output module (see Graziano, 2001b for review).

i) Classically, the problem of *target localization* is viewed as a series of transformations from target position information in an eye-centered to a head-centered and ultimately to a trunk-centered frame of reference. Retinal signals are combined with eye position signals given by extra-ocular proprioception but even more by efferent oculomotor signals (see section *iv* for more details about forward models). They are also combined with head position signals arising from proprioceptive and vestibular inputs. These interactions between retinal and extra-retinal information have been observed at different levels. Target internal representation can be elaborated both at a single cell level and a population level. Integration by single units means that single cells code target position in one or any other reference frame irrespective of any other information (e.g., Duhamel, Bremmer, BenHamed & Graf, 1997). Coding of target position at a population level is based on statistical combination of various elementary information. Such coding is distributed across large neuronal populations (Brotchie, Andersen, Snyder & Goodman, 1995). It is however still unclear if single cell coding results from population coding activity (and vice- versa) or if these two kinds of representations can be, partly at least, independent each other.

Although the parietal integration function is largely accepted, modulations and interactions between retinal and extra-retinal signals are observed all along the dorsal visuomotor cortical stream (from V1 to premotor cortex), as well as in subcortical structures (note the crucial role the superior colliculus plays in visuospatial coding, both for attention and eye movements). In other words, many different brain structures belonging to the visuo-motor channel are involved in integrating information for visual target localization (Desmurget et al., 1998 for review).

ii) The possibility to make accurate arm movements requires a spatial representation of both hand and target in the same egocentric frame of reference prior movement planning (Jeannerod, 1991). Firstly, the CNS needs to elaborate a representation of the *initial state of the motor apparatus*. Obviously, arm proprioception is mainly involved in this process (e.g., Ghez, Gordon & Ghilardi, 1995). However, since Prablanc, Echallier, Jeannerod, & Komilis (1979), it is well known that a close coupling between visual and proprioceptive signals is required for an optimization of hand localization in normal subjects. This was especially evidenced in studies introducing perceptual conflicts during sensory encoding of the initial state of the motor apparatus, biasing either vision or proprioception (e.g., Rossetti, Desmurget & Prablanc, 1995). The static position of the arm prior to movement initiation is represented both in the parietal cortex (Lacquaniti, Guigon, Bianchi, Ferreina & Caminiti, 1995) and in the premotor cortex of the monkey brain by means of a convergence of visual and proprioceptive cues onto the same neurons (Graziano, 1999, Graziano & Ghandi, 2000). These representations could be either centered on the body (e.g., Lacquaniti et al., 1995) or on the eye (Batista, Buneo, Snyder & Andersen, 1999).

iii) Hand trajectory formation relies on two main conceptual operations. First, movement must initially be planned, that is, a desired trajectory must be elaborated on the basis of target position and the current state of the motor apparatus. Second, movement must be programmed, that is, a set of coordinated muscle commands must be elaborated to execute the desired trajectory. We refer here to the classical conception distinguishing the neuronal activity associated on the one hand with the vectorial coding of visually guided arm movements and on the other hand with the pattern of muscle activity required to achieve those movements (e.g., Crutcher & Alexander, 1990). Note that these two operations are conceptual rather than real hierarchical computational steps. Indeed, the degree of overlap is extensive both from spatial (movement and muscle coding are observed both in frontal "motor" and parietal "spatial" areas) and temporal (these activities are quite simultaneous) points of view. Accordingly, these operations are likely to be processed in a parallel fashion (Alexander & Crutcher, 1990; Burnod et al., 1999; Calvert & Thesen, 2004).

How the CNS encodes movement as a displacement of the effector along a given trajectory is still a matter of debate (see task space vs. joint space hypotheses clearly synthesized by Desmurget and colleagues, 1998). However, whatever the theoretical framework, the central problem is the linkage between initial and desired hand location information. Obviously, this operation clearly involves all transformations given by the other processes previously described, leading *in fine* to a vectorial coding of hand displacement related to the estimation of the initial hand position (Vindras, Desmurget, Prablanc & Viviani, 1998). In other words, the movement planning key process would rather use various redundant representations that are themselves integrated to form a relevant coding for motor programming (Graziano, 2001b). This is sometimes described as calibrating various spatial and motor maps related to extra personal space. However, there is no clear agreement in the literature concerning which reference frame provides the relevant coding for movement planning. behavioral studies rather suggest that the reference frame used to plan reaching movements can vary according to the task constraints (e.g., Andersen et al., 1997). These theoretical problems are solved in a very seductive way using a neural network simulation developed on the basis of these neurophysiological observations (see Burnod et al., 1999, for description of a neurophysiology based model of the parieto-frontal network involved in the coding of reaching). Matching different sources of signals in order to operate sensorimotor transformation would rely on the gradual distribution of these different types of reach-related signals. These so-called gradients (visual to somatic, sensory to motor and position to direction) are coherent simulations of the functional anatomical cortico-cortical recurrent connections observed between parietal and frontal cortices that align distributed sensory and motor representations (e.g., Caminiti, Ferraina & Johnson, 1996). These functional overlaps, where reach-related neurons tuning to multiple signals coexist, define "combinatorial domains". This model is fundamentally opposed to the notion of functional specialization of segregated reach-related area for processing each step of movement planning in specific frames of reference. This allows to explain the flexibility of coding and the great variability often observed according to contextual or interindividual effects.

Finally, the motor plan must be transformed onto a coordinated sequence of muscular events. The problem can be viewed as the last step for coordinates transformations (i.e., in the muscles space). Here again, we argue against an old classical view considering this process as the final sequentially organized module of visuo-motor interactions. Enough evidence was provided since Crutcher & Alexander (1990) to consider that muscle pattern related activity largely overlaps with directional coding in motor structures. The elaboration of the appropriate motor commands that generate muscle synergies can rather be interpreted as a progressive combination of derived information about target and hand location thanks to a continuous matching of different sources of signals within multiple coding processes given by recurrent connections (Burnod et al., 1999). In other words, motor maps are integrated in the framework as well as other sources of information and the old dichotomy between perceptual and motor functionally segregated processes must be definitely refuted. Nevertheless, the supplementary information needed to be integrated and matched with others at this level is related to the physical and physiological properties of the effector. Such information is provided by some internal models of the body. Namely, inverse models constitute a representation of the dynamical (inertial, biomechanical...) properties of the effector (eye, arm...) that allow to elaborate motor commands that match the desired trajectory (Kawato, 1999).

iv) During movement execution, the CNS has to solve a fourth integrative problem: to estimate the current state of the limb with reference to the target goal and to correct the movement if necessary. This problem was largely discussed in the literature as feedback control strategies (as opposed to motor programs exclusively elaborated before movement initiation, e.g., Keele, 1968). Most often, these models suggest that feedback loops would rely exclusively on sensory information. More precisely, reafferent visual and proprioceptive information about both the target goal and the limb should be integrated by the CNS to detect and correct spatial motor errors. It is nowadays obvious that these sensory feedback loops have a marginal role in online corrections, especially because of the sensory delays necessary to process reafferences (longer than the earliest movement modifications observed) and because of contradictory deafferentation studies (see Desmurget & Grafton, 2000 for review). Online control can be implemented only if the instantaneous location of the hand can be integrated together with the current state of the motor command with no delay. To this aim, the CNS mainly uses internal models as sources of information for the coding of hand position (and more extensively of kinematic properties of goal-directed movements). Namely, forward models predict the behavior of the motor system when a motor command is elaborated (Desmurget & Grafton, 2000). This allows the CNS to estimate the future state of limb on the basis of the command itself. Theoretically, hand position can be estimated at any time during voluntary movement without peripheral information. Practically, this efferent information is likely to be integrated with other afferent sources but is the faster and the most useful one (even if it generally remains difficult to estimate the respective contribution of each modality in the sense of position because both proprioception and efferent information are quite difficult to dissociate experimentally in normal subjects). A complementary argument is provided by the sensory suppression effect: Voluntary actions produce suppression of neural activity in sensory areas. Recent computational models of motor control have linked this effect to motor prediction: an efferent signal from motor areas may cancel the sensory reafferences predicted as a consequence of movement (Blakemore, Wolpert & Frith, 1998; Haggard & Whitford, 2004).

The Posterior Parietal Cortex and the Cerebellum play a critical role in sensorimotor integration for computation of dynamic motor errors (Desmurget & Grafton, 2000; Schweighofer, Arbib & Kawato, 1998). Note that the PPC could also be involved in the formation of the internal representation of instantaneous hand location (the forward model, Desmurget et al., 1999). Finally, the Supplementary motor area (SMA) may be the key-structure for sensory suppression during movement execution providing the efferent signal which is used by other brain areas to modulate somatosensory activity (Haggard & Whitford, 2004).

The Concept of Dominance and the Coding of Arm Position in Highly Skilled Individuals

In psychological studies, the concept of dominance is often used to describe the fact that, among all sensory information, one is solely or mainly used by the process under scrutiny. This is opposed to the classical redundancy situation in non dominant subjects where all sensory inputs are considered as equivalently informative and can be collapsed and used as a kind of averaged information. These concepts are largely issued from the standard psychological theory considering sensory integration as a single sequential "between" module responsible for elaborating a unified perception and translating information from the sensory to the motor modules.

Obviously, this concept of dominance does not fit with the models of sensorimotor integration evoked in this chapter, where transformations are neither sequential nor hierarchical and linear (i.e., output coordinates cannot be obtained through a simple sum or averaging of the input coordinates). In neural networks models, the intermediate layers of units are responsible for the non linear combinations between each input/output layers. Sensorimotor integration can either be viewed in these layers as a progressive match of retinal, gaze, arm, muscle, etc... signals suitable for moving the hand toward the target (Burnod et al., 1999), or as statistical inferences (Deneve & Pouget, 2004). In these models, variability was largely assessed according to contextual changes (constraints or noise). Intra-individual variability and the effects of task constraints on sensorimotor integration (when multisensory cues come with different degrees of reliability according to the context) has been described as being related to the modification of the relative weighting of each sensory modality. For instance, auditory cues are sometimes more reliable than visual cues to localize objects (e.g., in darkness or unstructured visual environments). Similarly, visual and proprioceptive cues can be used with various relative influences in visuo-manual aiming according to the process under scrutiny (e.g., Desmurget et al., 1998; Sober & Sabes, 2003). However, the variability was only investigated across contextual conditions and the concept of dominance (considered as the variability of the relative weighting of the input layers in the neural networks across subjects) was not evoked in these models. In fact, inter-individual variability regarding dominance has poorly been investigated, either in psychological or neurophysiological and neural networks models, at least for the understanding of sensorimotor integration.

We now propose some experimental evidence showing that interindividual differences in basic sensorimotor functions can rely on integrative mechanisms variability. The experiment presented here (Boulinguez, Toussaint, Abed-Meraim & Collignon, 2001b, with permission) focused on sensory dominance in arm position coding. More precisely, since the elaboration of a representation of the initial state of the motor apparatus by the SNC is supposed to involve both proprioception (e.g., Ghez et al., 1995) and vision (e.g., Prablanc et al., 1979; Rossetti et al., 1995) in normal subjects, we asked if the relative weighting of these afferences could vary according to subjects' skill level.

Nineteen control subjects were selected on the basis of a weak practice of visuomanual skills in any sport or professional domains, estimated by questionnaire. They were compared to 10 international fencers presenting high visuomanual skill derived from the optimization required and developed with practice of the perceptuo-motor processes involved in movement control (Boulinguez, 1999). The task consisted in encoding various arm positions while introducing perceptual conflicts thanks to prismatic deviation, and repositioning the arm without any more perceptual conflict. On the encoding phase, the subject was blindfolded while his index finger was positioned on a target after passive, random and complex displacement (in order to avoid the use of efference copy -forward model- and kinaesthetic cues). Then, vision remained available, and the subject was instructed to see and memorize the position of his finger, while prismatic glasses deviated the visual field 30° to the right, inducing visuoproprioceptive discordance. Finally, the blindfolded subject's hand was passively repositioned at the starting position. Immediately at the end of the encoding phase, the retention phase began without wearing prisms. For each target, in darkness the subject was asked to position his index finger precisely on the memorized location.

Results are presented in Figure 1. Skilled fencers showed much reduced directional errors for the retention phase (+ 0.61 cm), whereas controls showed larger directional errors (+ 6.03 cm equivalent to 12° on the right) corresponding to the direction of the resultant deviation induced by the prisms during the encoding phase. The difference between the deviation induced by the prisms (30° on the right) and the mean directional error (12° on the right) suggests that non expert subjects used both visual and proprioceptive signals for the encoding of hand position. Conversely, the negligible mean constant error of skilled fencers suggests that they used only proprioceptive stataesthetic signals for the encoding of hand position. In other words, it is clear that the relative weighting of the afferent inputs in the integrative networks can vary extensively across subjects. More precisely, sensorimotor integration processes coding static hand position could vary with the amount of perceptuo-motor skill in the way of a progressive independence from visual inputs, i.e., a proprioceptive dominance.

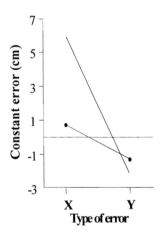

Figure 1. Mean X-Y error for hand position coding after prismatic exposure for normal (white dots) and highly skilled (black dots) individuals (reproduced from Boulinguez et al., 2001b, with permission).

Performance in Movement Control According to Eye-hand Coordination

Eye-hand coordination is a key function in movement control. The question of which kind of afferent, oculomotor, internal, etc... information is used to detect and to correct the ongoing motor error has been the centre of many controversies during a long time. We have seen in this chapter that many different codes were shown to be potentially used by the SNC during visuomotor transformations. We argue here that sensorimotor integration during movement execution can also be subject to interindividual differences in eye-hand behavioral patterns and the use of eye related signals. We propose to reanalyze some data previously published (Boulinguez, Blouin & Nougier, 2001a).

In this paper, we used a classical double-step procedure (pointing toward a target that could be displaced during the movement) to test the integration of retinal, gaze and oculomotor signals in defining and amending current motor errors. In some conditions, we introduced a temporal gap between the offset of the first target to reach and the onset of the second one. Compared with the classical condition where both events were synchronized (simulating a target "jump"), this situation induced a shorter corrective saccadic reaction time to the second target but a longer time to correct hand movement and to reach the second target (movement time -MT-). This gap effect for eye movement is known to be due to the release of the inhibition of the superior colliculus on the ocular motoneurons (thanks to the removal of the fixation point) that helps keeping the eyes stationary on a visual target during pointing movements (e.g., Neggers & Bekkering 2000). However, because shorter corrective eye movements toward the second target did not benefit to hand movement corrections, we concluded that the current target position was better encoded when gaze direction signals were combined with retinal inputs of both the initially foveated target and the new peripheral retinal target. In the Gap condition, when this integration is not possible, hand corrections would rather be based on information derived from the corrective saccade-related signals.

Reanalysing these data aims at differentiating subjects' performance according to the eye-hand coordination involved in both conditions. The group revealed an important variability regarding performance (as measured by MT) in the control condition (no gap). Thus, we have segregated it in two sub-groups *a posteriori* according to subjects' performance (high and low groups, 5 subjects each). Figure 2 shows how these two groups behaved in both conditions (gap and no gap) regarding corrective saccadic reaction times (CSL), time to second target fixation (FT2), hand trajectory correction latency (TCL) and movement time (MT).

Statistically, the high and low groups are not different in the control condition regarding CSL. In other words, the time for the eye to react to the double step does not have a key-role in correcting movement trajectory. This is confirmed by the fact that hand movement is always corrected earlier in the high group than in the low group while no difference is observed between groups regarding the time needed to react and to acquire the second target with the eye. Interestingly, in the gap condition, two main observations can be made: i) hand trajectory corrections are linked to oculomotor reactions, and simultaneously ii) the high and low groups do differentiate neither for performance (MT) nor eye-hand coordination pattern (note that the low group shows the same pattern in the gap and no gap conditions). In other words, when task constraints force subjects to use oculomotor signals for defining the new target goal and correcting hand path, the most skilled subjects are behaving like the less skilled participants always do.

We assume sensorimotor integration in eye-hand coordination is subject to interindividual differences related to skill level. More precisely, the retinal error (when encoding the second target position through gaze direction signals combined with retinal inputs from both the initially foveated target and the new peripheral retinal target) seems to be more reliable than the oculomotor signals only for the most skilled individuals.

In conclusion, we have seen in this section that contextual and interindividual variabilities have a key-role in sensorimotor integration. Neuromimetic networks propose interesting models, biologically plausible and based on neuroanatomical evidence, that strongly suggest this central phenomenon relies on adaptation and learning. It is likely to be due to the relative weighting of information sources and to connections reinforcement in matching units of the integration network. Behavioral consequences can be seen through the elicitation of various dominance effects especially modulated by expertise. These effects are supposed to depend on the relative reliability of each cue according to the context. However, this last point merits to be further debated, since other parameters (like for instance afference latency) can be responsible for the privileged use of one source of information among others.

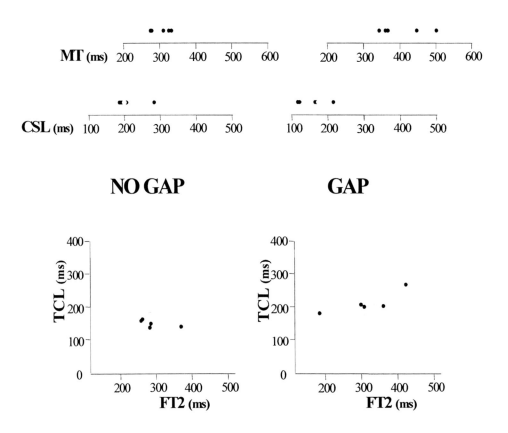

Figure 2. Eye-hand coordination patterns in a double-step reaching task (pointing toward a "jumping" target) according to target presentation conditions (NO GAP vs GAP) and subjects performance (as revealed by MT in the NO GAP control condition: faster subjects -black dots- and slower subjects -white dots- were defined *a posteriori*). In the NO GAP condition, hand correction delays did not depend on corrective oculomotor signals for the faster subjects (no correlation between hand trajectory correction latency -TCL- and time to second target fixation -FT2- or corrective saccadic reaction times -CSL-). Conversely, when task constraints force subjects to use oculomotor signals for defining the new target goal and correcting hand path (GAP condition), the most skilled subjects are behaving like the less skilled participants always do, as revealed by the relation between TCL and FT2. This shows subjects do not always use the same signals to control rapid movements. This variability is both contextual and interindividual. (adapted from Boulinguez et al., 2001a).

THE SPECIAL ROLE OF GRAVITY IN SENSORIMOTOR INTEGRATION

It is generally accepted that when we move in the environment, the CNS uses sensory inputs to construct and update stable representations of body/environment relationships. Such representations provide spatial orientation necessary to maintain a continuous communication between external and internal information. Gravity has a key role in elaborating these representations. The main purpose of this second part of the chapter is to review psychophysical and behavioral studies reporting how gravity, a special and omnipresent stable reference, is integrated within perceptuo-motor transformations. Indeed, Gravity must obviously be taken into account to maintain equilibrium, but also to perceive the body and the environment as well as to control any motor action (Paillard, 1991). As a consequence, integration of gravity is likely to have a key role in interindividual variability of perceptuo-motor skill. However, gravity has not been taken into account in the works on sensorimotor integration derived from the models described in the previous section. In this section, we will try to integrate data issued from different theoretical and methodological origins in the same conceptual framework.

This part is divided into three sub-sections. The first aims at reconciling theoretical divergent concepts sometimes observed in the literature according to studies dealing or not with gravity. The second part broadly presents how the CNS solves the specific problems of integrating gravito-inertial cues to perceive visual movement, to assess vertical direction, body orientation, and to control posture and movement. Third, we show how the concept of dominance and interindividual variability (related to skill level) in gravity integration applies specifically to posture control, and how some studies strongly suggest that they could also be extended to the control of motor actions. Finally, we propose to have a brief look at motion sickness as an illustration of interindividual variability of the vegetative consequences of gravity integration.

Integration of Gravity in Standard and Current Theories

For years, the classical literature has introduced a strong dichotomy between sensorimotor and cognitive levels of representation, suggesting that perception and motor control were separately and independently processed. That is one of the reasons why psychological models dealing with interindividual variability were restricted to perceptual representations. These representations are thought to rely on various frames of reference. In line with this assumption, between subjects' variability may rely on the "choice" of a specific frame of reference or a privileged cue to meet the constraints associated with a particular situation. This choice would be possible thanks to the perceptive systems' "vicariousness" (Ohlmann, 1990). Such a concept, which introduces a kind of contingence in the perceptive phenomenon, is inspired by Reuchlin (1978)'s differential psychology. It has considerably fed our knowledge and understanding of intra- and inter-individual variability. However today, the scientific community shares the opinion that, likely, sensorimotor and cognitive levels of representation would not be so segregated.

If the recent Bayesian or neural models (see previous section) provide a new conception of sensorimotor integration based on biological and neuro-anatomical data, they still are limited to few sensory modalities (e.g. vision and audition, vision and proprioception, etc). They obviously do not take into account the whole sensory cues that are supposed to be integrated. Accordingly, integration of gravity has not been tackled yet by these models. However, Mergner & Rosemeier (1998) proposed a model of sensory integration both for perception and motor action. According to this model, the representation of body in space is built on the basis of two representations. The first one - the representation of the support in space - is built from sensory information involved in a "down channelling". The second one - the body on support - is built on the first one from sensory information involved in an "up channelling". The combination of these two representations provides the representation of body-on-support-in-space. It is important to notice that, one more time, this model differs from the old classical conception of sensory integration based on the simple and sequential addition of sensory inputs. Indeed, it takes into account the scattered location of the different sensors upon the body. Moreover, this model is not linear since the different sensory inputs are integrated at different stages depending on the intermediate frame of reference they are elaborating. Then, these intermediate representations (such as head-in-space, head-on-trunk, body-on-support) can be specifically solicited through the two channelings. These intermediate representations may fit together like "Matryoshka dolls" do (Mergner, 2002), the in-space representations being the "most peripheral doll". These theoretical conceptions are compatible with the Bayesian and neural models of multimodal integration.

According to these recent models, the old dichotomy between egocentric or allocentric frames of reference may vanish. Indeed, the frame of reference used in a specific task may be built through the integration of both egocentric and allocentric cues (more particularly, those related to the gravity) and vary extensively according to the task requirements (e.g. Ghafouri, Archambault, Adamovich & Feldman, 2002). Here again, behavioral correlates of these theoretical conceptions are in accordance with the models' predictions.

Sensorimotor Integration of Gravity

We will illustrate in this paragraph how gravity is taken into account at each stage of internal/external communication between subject and his environment, from the most basic visual processes to the most complex mechanisms of movement control.

Visual Movement Perception

A large number of studies shows that gravity is implicitly taken into account to estimate spatial and temporal properties of visual motion. For instance, when catching a falling ball, we need to estimate the time to contact (TTC) in order to accurately synchronize our movement with the ball trajectory. According to ecological psychology models, our brain may only need visual information - the visual flow generated by the movement of the ball image upon the retina - to assess TTC. The optical variable "tau" provided by the inverse of the dilatation rate of the retinal image of the object (Lee, 1980), is a first order estimation of TTC and is then only accurate for constant velocity motion. And yet, when a ball is falling, it accelerates under the action of gravity. Internal models theory considers that the brain has stored up knowledge about the physical environmental laws. So when catching a ball, the brain may use a second-order internal model of gravity to accurately predict the ball path and TTC. These two opposite theories predict different behavior in microgravity, since the ball keeps its initial speed in weightlessness. If the brain were to use a first order estimation of TTC directly from the visual flow, no behavioral difference would be observed. Results of recent microgravity experiments (McIntyre, Zago, Berthoz & Lacquaniti, 2001) strongly suggest that the brain may estimate TTC with an internal model of gravity rather than on the simple basis of the visual flow. Thus, this example reveals the CNS may be able to integrate representations of environmental physical laws early in perception to make accurate predictions on temporal but also spatial aspects of visual motion processing.

Gravito-inertial and Vertical Cues

Gravity-imposed verticality is a key element of spatial orientation. Perception of verticality and horizontality are privileged processes compared with the perception of other tilted orientations (Luyat, Gentaz, Corte & Guerraz, 2001). For instance, in darkness, normal subjects are able to set a visual rod to the vertical with an accuracy of 1° (Mann, Berthelot-Berry & Dauterive, 1949). This task reflects a complex mechanism of sensory integration. Indeed, the orientation of the rod image upon the retina must be compared to the internal representation of gravity. This representation is a multimodal construction involving not only exocentric but also egocentric cues. Although vestibular apparatus is considered as the privileged detector of gravity, graviceptors such as blood vessels and/or kidney also constitute a relevant source of information about the direction of the forces acting on the body (Mittelstaedt, 1995). Since somesthetic sensors constitute an interface between body and support, they provide cues (in particular from the plantar sole) that are integrated with the latters. Obviously, visual cues are also integrated. These cues are especially important not only because gravity determines the orientation of the visual environment but also because the orientation of a visual frame of reference can reciprocally influence the perception of gravity (Witkin & Asch, 1948b). Since all these sensors are located in different parts of the body, the integration of information they provide cannot be linear, as we mentioned in the previous sub-section. Accordingly, proprioception and efferent copy are also likely to play an important role in taking into account the specific location of these sensors.

Influence of Body or Head Tilt

Broadly, mechanisms of integration are more accessible when sensory modalities are incongruent. Integration processes may obey to common global rules, since perception of verticality is generally influenced in the same way across subjects by the sensory context (cues availability according to the amount of stimulation). For example, in the dark, head or body tilt is known to modify the perception of verticality as a function of the postural inclination magnitude (for a review, see Howard, 1986). For body-roll tilts up to 60°, the vertical is perceived as tilted in the opposite direction to body tilt (the Müller- or E-effect). Conversely for body-roll tilts beyond 60°, the vertical is perceived as tilted in the same direction as body tilt (the Aubert- or A-effect). The interpretation of these two effects still remains obscure since it reflects complex mechanisms of sensory integration depending on the availability of the dynamic factors determining how body tilt angle is reached (Udo de Haes & Schöne, 1970; van Beuzekom & van Gisbergen, 2000). Today, we can assert that A- and E- have not a vestibular origin as it was previously believed (e.g. Schöne, 1964), since patients with bilateral labyrinthectomy also express the A- and E-effects (Miller, Fregly &

Graybiel, 1968). The A-effect may rather be due to an egocentric parameter that influences the perception of verticality: the idiotropic vector, i.e. the internal representation of the longitudinal body axis (Mittelstaedt, 1983). This idiotropic vector may be elaborated by means of somatosensory cues since deafferented patient expressed an E-effect for large body tilt (Yardley, 1990a). This somatosensory origin may explain why results are more controversial when the tilt is restricted to the head (*E-effect*: Witkin & Asch, 1948a; Wade, 1968; *A-effect*: Dichgans, Diener & Brandt, 1974; Parker, Poston & Gulledge, 1983; *no effect*: Merker & Held, 1981; DiLorenzo & Rock, 1982) since, during head tilt information is given by neck proprioceptive but not somatosensory cues. All these data give an account of the complexity of multisensory integration in the perception of verticality and its contextual variability.

Influence of Visual Origin

The orientation of visual objects and surfaces generally remains stable and aligned with gravity to meet the balance requirements. Thus, visual cues play a key role in the elaboration of the internal representation of gravity. Accordingly, judgments of verticality are influenced by the manipulation of peripheral visual information. For instance, the manipulation of static visual peripheral information by tilting a visual frame of reference (optostatic stimulation) leads to deviations of the subjective visual vertical in the direction of frame tilt (Witkin & Asch, 1948b). Such a frame effect may result from the illusory sensation of body tilt induced by the frame tilt and increases with the frame angular size (Ebenholtz & Benzschawel, 1977). In addition, perception of verticality is also modified when dynamic visual information is manipulated. For example, in front of a rotating visual background (optokinetic stimulation), the subjective visual vertical is deviated in the direction of the visual background rotation (Dichgans, Held, Young & Brandt, 1972). Such a phenomenon may be linked to the illusory sensation of self motion called "vection". The vestibular nuclei may be strongly implicated in this vection phenomenon (Dichgans & Brandt, 1972). More recently, Brandt, Bartenstein, Janek & Dieterich (1998) specified that vection could result more precisely from an inhibition of the parieto-insular vestibular cortex caused by the moving visual scene. Such inhibitions may have the functional role of neutralizing the vestibular cues generated by involuntary head movements.

Coupling Visual stimuli With Head Tilt

Information related to head tilt visual background interact within the mechanisms of sensory integration to elaborate the internal representation of gravity. Indeed, when optostatic or optokinetic stimulation is coupled with an ipsilateral head tilt, the effects on the perception of verticality have been found to be larger than those observed with head or visual stimulation alone (Dichgans et al. 1974; Parker et al. 1983; DiLorenzo & Rock, 1982; Goodenough, Cox, Sigman & Strawderman, 1985; Zoccoloti, Antonucci, Goodenough, Pizzamiglio & Spinelli, 1992). In the particular case of head roll during optostatic stimulation, deviations of the subjective vertical may result both from frame and head effects (Poquin et al., 1995; Guerraz, Poquin & Ohlmann, 1998). Not surprisingly, this combination would take place in a non-linear manner (Mars, Vercher & Blouin, 2004).

Concerning head tilt during optokinetic stimulation, the interpretation of the results appears more complex. Indeed, it has been reported that deviations of the subjective vertical were always shifted in the direction of the visual background rotation (Dichgans et al., 1974;

Merker & Held, 1981; Parker et al., 1983; Guerraz et al., 1998). Moreover, the effect increased when the head was tilted contra-laterally with respect to optokinetic stimulation direction. The understanding of this latter effect is still under theoretical debate and is currently explored in our laboratory. Some data suggest such an effect could be linked to the special role integration of ocular torsion could play.

Influence of Ocular Torsion

We showed that the internal representation of gravity direction results from multisensory integration of various egocentric and allocentric cues. As previously mentioned, other sensorimotor cues (efferent copy and limb proprioception) are also integrated, allowing the switch from one frame of reference to another. For instance, the coordinate transformation from an eye-centered to a head-centered frame of reference (or vice-versa) necessitates the accurate coding of the position of the eye in the orbit (see previous section). However, the third degree of freedom (ocular torsion; that is the rotation of the eye about the line of sight) is generally occulted since it is implicitly controlled. And yet, specific stimulations such as head tilt (Diamond & Markham, 1983), optostatic or optokinetic stimuli (Crone, 1975) are known to trigger ocular torsion. Currently, we still do not know precisely if this eye rotation is fully taken into account in the sensorimotor transformation between coordinate systems. Several studies strongly suggest it is not the case since the ocular torsion modifies the perception of visual orientation (Cheung & Howard, 1991; Curthoys & Wade, 1995; Wade & Curthoys, 1997). The visual object is indeed perceived as tilted in the direction opposite to that of eye torsion, increasing the E-effect. Such data make even more complex the interpretation of the mechanisms of sensorimotor integration involved in the perception of gravity.

Some researchers have tried to determine the role of ocular torsion in the perception of verticality when head tilt is combined to optokinetic stimulation (e.g. Finke & Held, 1978), but no clear element was provided in favour of a specific role of this eye movement.

Body Orientation

The perception of body orientation in space is also relevant for spatial orientation (Clark & Graybiel, 1962). However, it is not clear whether the same neural mechanisms serve both the perception of verticality and the perception of body orientation since, from a theoretical point of view, one should be deduced from the other. However, several recent studies suggest that perception of body orientation seems to rely on processes that differ from those involved in the perception of verticality. For instance, some studies found no correlation between the perception of body orientation and the perception of earth-centered reference (e.g. Mast & Jarchow, 1996). Perception of postural vertical may rely mostly on somatosensory rather than on vestibular and optokinetic cues (Bisdorff, Wolsley, Anastasopoulos, Bronstein & Gresty, 1996). Indeed, patients with unilateral vestibular lesion perceive the orientation of their body as accurately as normal subjects but show difficulties to assess the verticality, (Anastasopoulos, Haslwanter, Bronstein, Fetter & Dichgans, 1997). Thus perception of body orientation may rely on egocentric but not on geocentric references, contrary to the perception of verticality which requires both.

Through the last two sub-sections, we showed that the perception of orientation (with the special role of verticality perception) is a result of complex and variable multisensory integration processes. In the next two sub-sections, we will present some data showing how gravity is taken into account in the control of posture and motor action by means of the supplementary integration of motor cues and internal models.

Control of Posture

Posture is based on the orientation of the body and parts of the body with respect to gravity (Mittelstaedt, 1998) and ensures two main functions (Massion, 1994; Massion, 1997). On the one hand, it acts against gravity by maintaining muscle tone and body balance. On the other hand, it constitutes a stabilised egocentric reference *per se* to serve perceptive and motor ends. Thus, the CNS may use an internal representation of gravity as reference to regulate posture i.e. to maintain body equilibrium despite movement. The "servomechanism" may then detect any difference between body orientation and gravity through the mechanisms of sensorimotor integration.

In order to control posture, the CNS integrates various inputs, such as peripheral visual (Amblard & Carblanc, 1978), vestibular (Bronstein, 1988; Clément & Lestienne, 1988), somesthetic cues (Kavounoudias, Roll & Roll, 1998; Jeka & Lackner, 1994) or graviceptors (Mittelstaedt, 1995). Obviously, the "proprioceptive chain" from extra-ocular muscles to ankle muscles also plays an important role in controlling posture (Nashner & Wolfson, 1974; Roll & Roll, 1988; Kennedy & Inglis, 2001). The copy of the motor command responsible for eye closure may also be integrated since sways magnitude with closed eyes is smaller than with opened eyes in the dark (Litvinenkova & Baron, 1968).

In normal condition, all these inputs provide congruent information and seem to be redundant. Beyond this apparent redundancy, all these sensory inputs present some complementarities since they do not operate amongst the same frequency range. For instance, the visual system detects slower frequencies than the vestibular system. In addition, it has been shown that, during postural control, detection of body sways mainly relies on ankle proprioception and on vision, the threshold of the vestibular system being higher than those of the two other systems (Fitzpatrick & McCloskey, 1994). These results confirm that the vestibular system is a motor responses "trigger" rather than a slow accelerations "detector". Thus, this difference in perceptive threshold and specific bandwidth may play an important role in the variability observed in the control of posture. There again, contextual variability is observed in sensorimotor integration. Then, the relative weighting of sensory cues in postural control appears to be directly linked to the variability of their reliability according to the conditions of stimulation.

Control of Movements

In the previous section, we showed that in order to carry out goal-directed movement, it was necessary to i) localize target, ii) localize effector's initial position, and iii) program and regulate the movement. Now we will see that gravity is taken into account in each one of these stages.

Internal models of physical properties of limbs are especially used under the action of environmental forces (See Vercher, Sarès, Blouin, Bourdin & Gauthier, 2003 for a review). For instance in the dark, subjects in a lying position commit more pointing errors than in an upright position since, in the former condition, gravity acts differently as usually (Smetanin & Popov, 1997). These errors may be related both to a mislocalization of the target and to the inability to take gravity-derived information into account to program motor action (Smetanin & Popov, 1998). Another argument in favour of taking into account of gravity in the control of movements is based on the fact that stimulations influencing perception of gravity also influence the accuracy of arm movement control. For instance, it has been shown that head roll induced arm deviations (Berger et al., 1998; Guerraz, Blouin & Vercher, 2003; Sarès et al., submitted). Such head tilt-induced effects on arm control may be due to the integration of neck proprioception cues (Guerraz et al., 2003; Sarès et al., submitted). In addition, such results cannot be explained by simple reflex such as tonic neck or tonic vestibular reflexes because, during head tilt, these two tonic reflexes are known to cancel each other (Roberts, 1973). These effects may rather be due to a mislocalization of the target-goal of the movement since vestibular (Bresciani et al., 2002) and neck (Biguer, Donaldson, Hein & Jeannerod, 1988) information is involved in the estimation of target position.

Visual background manipulations suggest goal-directed movements are elaborated on the basis of sensorimotor transformations that combine both egocentric and exocentric parameters. For instance, facing a tilted visual environment induced an illusory perception of hand tilt (Bock, 1997) as well as azimuth pointing errors in the direction of the frame tilt (Sarès et al., submitted). This latter effect suggests that subjects use neither a pure egocentric frame of reference nor in a pure allocentric frame of reference. These observations are in accordance with predictions of basic neural network models of sensorimotor integration (e.g., Burnod et al., 1999). Indeed, gravity related cues are likely to be gradually and non linearly matched with other sensory and motor signals (as somatosensory, motor and visual cues do for reaching thanks to functional overlaps of the "combinatorial domains"). Accordingly, this hypothesis suggests gravity is not represented in a segregated process acting in one specific frame of reference. Here again, this conceptual framework would allow to explain the flexibility of coding and the great variability often observed according to contextual or interindividual effects when processing spatial and body orientation.

The Concept of Dominance for Perception, Posture, and Movement Control

Field Dependency

In the previous sub-sections, we showed that gravity could be integrated at many different levels and with a great contextual variability. Some people can present a kind of visual dominance in the perception of verticality since, in front of a tilted frame, they tend to perceive the vertical as aligned with the frame margin (Witkin, 1950). Such a visual field dependency is generally observed in women and children (Nyborg, 1980). However, despite few studies are provided by the literature, a high level of sport practice requiring the privileged and reinforced use of visual spatial references would favor the development of field dependency. Conversely, the use of egocentric or gravito-inertial references does not favor the development of field dependency. For instance, professional male dancers or experts in acrobatic sports were found to be less field dependent than untrained male subjects or racquet sport experts (Golomer, Crémieux, Dupui, Isableu & Ohlmann, 1999; Guillot & Collet, 2004). By contrast, young adults with a high level of practice in climbing or judo were found to be more field dependent than sedentary people (Crémieux, Isableu & Ohlmann, 1995). More generally, field dependency seems very flexible according to subjects' experience. If static visual cues involved in orientation processes lead to strong individual differences when manipulated, dynamic visual cues rather involved in stabilization processes lead to smaller interindividual differences.

Dominance in Perception of Orientation

Several studies suggest that somatosensory cues are more informative than vestibular cues for perceiving postural orientation (Bisdorff et al., 1996; Anastasopoulos et al., 1997; Bringoux et al., 2002, Bringoux, Nougier, Barraud, Marin & Raphel, 2003). However the role and the efficiency of the graviceptors such as the vestibular apparatus in estimating postural orientation can be improved by specific training. We propose to detail some experimental data (Bringoux, Marin, Nougier, Barraud & Raphel, 2000; with permission) showing that expertise in gymnastic - an activity requiring a fine control of body orientation - modifies the processes leading to the perception of body orientation. A classical "sensorial suppression paradigm" was used in order to highlight the role of otolithic and somesthetic cues. Two interesting experiments were conducted in this study.

In the former, the authors assessed the otolith detection threshold in two groups of subject (5 expert gymnasts and 5 novices). Subjects were tilted in the sagittal plane in total darkness with an acceleration that remained below the semi-circular threshold (0.005 deg.s-2). They were instructed to verbally indicate when they perceived a tilt together with its direction. The task was performed in two conditions of body restriction: 1- subjects were strapped to the tiltable platform (somatosensory cues were available). 2- subjects were strapped in a body cast composed by envelops containing micro-marbles and related to a depressurization device (somatosensory cues were altered). Results of this experiment are presented in Figure 3A. Experts detected the tilt faster than novices. Moreover, threshold detection was higher in the body cast condition for novices but not for experts.

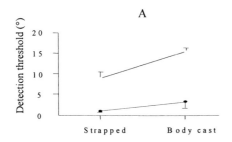 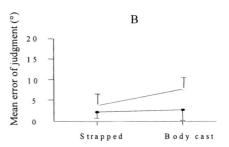

Figure 3. Mean angular thresholds for the perception of body tilt and standard deviation for the novice (white dots) and expert (black dots) groups (A). Mean subjective postural judgments and standard deviation for the novice (white dots) and expert (black dots) groups (B) (adapted from Bringoux et al., 2000, with permission).

The second experiment investigated the role of expertise in estimating postural vertical. Here again, two groups of subjects (6 expert gymnasts and 7 novices) were asked to verbally indicate when their longitudinal axis crossed the verticality in the pitch plane, as their body was rotated from a specific initial orientation (± 10, 20, 30°). The task was performed in the same two conditions of body restriction. Results showed that the two groups of subjects were rather accurate in the simple strap condition. However, whereas there was no effect of the body restriction condition in experts, novices committed more estimation errors in the body cast condition (Figure 3B).

Taken together, these two experiments indicate that the CNS shows an important variability in the determination of perception thresholds (peripheral adaptation) and the relative weighting of specific sensory cues in the elaboration of internal representations (central adaptation). Such variability across subjects for central adaptation may reflect the effects of extensive practice, as perfectly simulated by specific connections reinforcement through learning in neural networks models of sensorimotor integration (e.g., Burnod et al., 1999).

Dominance in the Control of Posture

Control of posture is strongly prone to contextual variability. For instance, some subjects rely on visual cues whereas others rather rely on non visual cues (Van Parys & Njiokiktjien, 1976). Similarly, some subjects seem to mainly use dynamical visual cues rather than static visual cues and vice-versa. This variability was assessed as well by sensory suppression paradigms (e.g., stroboscopic lighting, Crémieux & Mesure, 1994) as by sensory discordance paradigms (e.g., optostatic stimulation: Bles & van Raay, 1988; Zikmund & Balla, 1973; optokinetic stimulation: Dichgans et al., 1972; Lestienne, Berthoz, Mascot & Koitcheva, 1976). This variability is especially observed across lifespan: for example, children are particularly influenced by optokinetic stimulation (Lee & Aronson, 1974).

Interestingly, it appears that these various manifestations of variability and dominance effects could be linked each other. For instance, it has been shown that field dependent subjects standing in front of a tilted visual frame expressed a postural frame effect characterized by body reorientation in the direction of the frame tilt (Isableu, Ohlmann, Crémieux & Amblard, 1997). Such a postural frame effect was also observed for head posture (Sarès et al., 2002). Interestingly, the weight attributed to the frame seems to be greater when the gravitoinertial vector and the body longitudinal axis are dissociated. Therefore, it is likely that a close link exists between the field dependency in estimating the verticality and the preferential use of visual information to control posture. This is for example the case for vestibular schwannoma patients who show visual dependency both to control their posture (de Vries, Bles & Feenstra, 1985) and to perceive the verticality (Hafstrom, Fransson, Karlberg & Magnusson, 2004).

Another illustration of the variability and adaptability of sensorimotor integration processes is given by post-lesional or post-neurotomy plasticity. For instance, after labyrinthectomy, patients could reverse their sensory strategy (Lacour et al., 1997): Those who were visual dependent to control their posture switched for a non visual strategy and vice-versa.

If we have highlighted the link between the processes involved in spatial orientation and in sensorimotor control of posture (i.e. between subjective vertical and actual postural vertical), the possible link between perception of orientation and control of movements has not been tackled yet through interindividual differences. However, data and theory previously presented strongly suggest that it could be possible to discriminate various patterns of integration for orientation coding according to subjects' skill level for movement control.

Until yet, studies using expert/novice paradigms evolved in parallel with the evolution of sensorimotor integration models. In the future, these two kinds of studies must converge. Indeed, models derived from neurophysiological studies should serve as a strong theoretical support for studies dealing with interindividual variability. In return, models may be refined with regard to such experimental data and evolve through the taking into account of a larger number of cues.

Vegetative Consequences of Integration of Gravity: Motion Sickness

As reviewed in the previous section, sensorimotor integration is especially complex during motion. As the probability for perceptual conflicts increases as a function of the number of cues that must be integrated, it is obvious that integration processes involved in spatial orientation are responsible for motion sickness (MS). In other words, sensory stimulation induced by particular self displacements and moving environments can generate incoherent central interpretations leading to spatial disorientation and MS.

MS problem which is of public interest has not been solved yet. For instance, the development of tilted trains was slowed down because of MS occurrence in passengers (Fµrstberg, Andersson & Ledin, 1998; Neimer et al., 2001). Such problems also extend to sea sickness (since navies have opted for the development of smaller but less stable ships) and space sickness (since in space the inner ear is exposed to stimuli - G-loads or weightlessness - that strongly differ from that experienced on earth). All these examples suggest that measures to prevent motion sickness should attract scientists' interests even further. In the same time, MS is a privileged way to understand multisensory integration mechanisms since its effects are highly variable across individuals.

Sensory Origin of Motion Sickness

The vestibular apparatus seems to have a key role in MS triggering, since patients with bilateral vestibular lesions do not present any MS symptoms (Kennedy, Graybiel, McDonough & Beckwith, 1968). That may be the reason why making head movements in a MS-provocative environment enhances motion sickness (Lackner & Graybiel, 1986). Similarly, wearing a heavy helmet increases head inertia and enhance motion sickness (Lackner & DiZio, 1989). On the other hand, visual cues do not seem to be a determinant element of MS occurrence. Indeed, blind people also suffer from MS (Graybiel, 1970). However, MS can also be triggered by an optokinetic stimulation.

MS is classically interpreted in terms of sensory conflict (Reason & Brandt, 1975; Oman, 1982). Indeed, it generally occurs when "exproprioceptive" signals provided by the eyes, graviceptors (e.g. vestibular apparatus) and other proprioceptors are either in contradiction with one another or with those expected from the previous experience. More explicitly, MS emerges when the sensory inflow (vector representing the afferent sensory information) differs from the sensory expectations (vector representing the expected sensory information) (Oman, 1982). So, this conflict theory gives a key role to internal models (sensory predictions/expectations), but reaches its limits when sensory conflicts do not cause MS. It is for example the case for low frequency stimuli where visual and vestibular cues provide complementary information because of their different bandwidth. More recently, another conflict theory was proposed that makes MS interpretation more specifically related to processes involved in spatial orientation: the subjective vertical conflict. From this point of view, MS occurs in each situation where the perceived vertical (subjective vertical) differs from the experience-based expected vertical (Bles, Bos, de Graaf, Groen & Wertheim, 1998; Bles, Bos & Kruit, 2000). Such a concept is able to explain non-nauseogenic situations in which the sensory conflict theory predicted that MS would occur.

Interindividual Differences for Motion Sickness

Large interindividual differences exist with regards to MS. Thus, it is important to find reliable methods to estimate MS susceptibility. Behavioral elements may serve as reliable MS predictors. For instance, it is the case for postural stability since postural instability generally precedes MS (Riccio & Stoffregen, 1991; Stoffregen & Smart, 1998; Smart, Stoffregen & Bardy, 2002). It is also the case for the monitoring of ocular torsion (Diamond & Markham, 1991; Markham & Diamond, 1992) since ocular countertorsion is considered as a useful indicator of otolithic function (Diamond & Markham, 1983; Groen, Bos & de Graaf, 1999). Because ocular torsion is conjugated for the two eyes in normal subjects (Diamond & Markham, 1983), disconjugate eye torsion may indeed reveal anatomical or physiological asymmetries of the two utricles that are known to be responsible for MS. Such online diagnostic tools are interesting but i) are difficult to set up ii) do not prevent MS occurrence. And yet, it is still difficult to evaluate precisely MS susceptibility. Consequently, despite the fact it is trivial to assert there is a strong interindividual variability in MS susceptibility, it remains difficult to correlate integrative processes and symptoms.

However, it has been hypothesized that individual differences with regards to MS susceptibility result from the relative weighting of visual and vestibular cues. The more weighted visual information is, the higher MS susceptibility is. Conversely, the more weighted vestibular information is, the lower MS susceptibility is. For instance, navy crew suffering from chronic sea sickness presented an unusual degree of visual dependence for postural control (Bles, De Jong & Oosterveld, 1984). More recently, other studies tried to highlight the link between processes involved in spatial orientation and motion sickness, by assessing for instance the subjective vertical in MS resistant and susceptible subjects facing an optokinetic stimulation (Yardley, 1990b). Results showed that susceptible subjects (particularly susceptible women) made more perceptive error than resistant subjects. All these studies suggest that susceptibility to motion sickness may strongly be related to the individual differences observed in spatial orientation and to the underlying processes, as well as the way the relative weighting of sensory cues is done during integration. This is strengthened by the fact that exposure to rapid optokinetic stimulation could desensitize subjects to motion sickness (Hu, Stern & Koch, 1991).

Most studies suggest that perceptual and motor tasks involve sensory integration processes that share common internal representations. However, the key element of this second part of the chapter is that interindividual differences observed in spatial orientation are likely to be related to: i) a non-linear integration and ii) a long term adaptive mechanism of relative weighting of the whole sensorimotor signals. All these data highlight even further the complexity of sensorimotor integration mechanisms with regard to contextual variability. We conclude by suggesting the special case of gravity-related cues integration related in this section may provide an interesting support to refine models of multisensory integration.

SENSORY DOMINANCE AND PERCEPTUO-MOTOR INTERFERENCE

Interference in perceptuo-motor processes can be caused by numerous types of conflicts. They may originate from incongruence between multimodal information, afferent and efferent information or among motor processes. Anyway, this question of the large variety of interference observations is not central for the goal of this chapter. Here, we just aim at understanding various aspects of sensorimotor integration by means of evidencing the role of sensory dominance in a classical case of perceptuo-motor interference.

Integration of Multiple Cues for Concurrent Processes

In the first two sections, we have reviewed how the CNS encodes and deals with redundant (or apparently redundant) multimodal cues in order to control one motor action at a time. In other words, we focused on how various coding of the same information (e.g., target location by sound, haptic and visual cues; hand position coding by vision, proprioception and efference copy, etc.) are combined and differentially weighted according to processes, context or practice, thanks to recurrent connections in the neural networks. Here, we extend the problem to the integration of multiple cues coding different information involved in concurrent tasks. The effect of processing two tasks at the same time is known as the dual-task interference (see Pashler, 1998 for review). We think this interference effect is a privileged mean to assess sensorimotor integration because, first, multitask processing is a daily problem that faces the CNS, and second, it provides the opportunity to reach the limits of the human information processing system. We argue in this section that integrative mechanisms, sensory dominance and expertise also have a key role in this effect despite the fact it was many times described as being neither sensory nor perceptually based.

Perceptuo-motor Interference: The Standard Theory

One of the most important functions of the brain is to regulate the constant influx of stimuli competing for a share of information processing mechanisms. This ability is generally thought to involve attentional mechanisms, which help resolving this competition by biasing processing in favor of stimuli currently relevant for behavior at the expense of non-relevant stimuli (Kastner & Ungerleider, 2000). However, attentional modulation is limited, such that when attention must be allocated on two concurrent events (dual-task processing) there is often a processing cost, called interference. Such limitation is typically observed when subjects have to carry out two speeded simple tasks (reaction time -RT-), each requiring a response (R1 & R2) to separate individual stimuli (S1 & S2).

Psychological Model

As Telford (1931) first observed, the total processing duration required in the dual-task condition (RT1 + RT2) is always greater than the sum of the two RT when processed separately. This difference is called the "psychological refractory period" (PRP). However, the time required to carry out both tasks in the dual-task condition (the interval between S1 and R2) is often substantially less than the sum of the times required to complete each task separately. Taken together, these data indicate i) an interference cost, and ii) a partial overlap in some aspects of processing.

Since this pioneering work, the dual-task interference effect has been studied for several decades with different paradigms. Depending on the nature of stimuli and tasks, interference was found to be potentially observable for any process of perceptuo-motor communication. However, some of these effects evidenced in the literature are just the manifestation of attentional limitations within the same sensory modality. For example, it is obvious that identifying two complex visual objects located in two opposite parts of the visual field causes strong supplementary delays to process the task. However, at a perceptual step, restricted attentional capacity to concurrent attention and awareness was found to apply only at a modality specific level, but not between sensory modalities (Duncan, Martens & Ward, 1997). This particular perceptual limitation case apart (e.g., Jiang, 2004), interference is known to arise for decisional and response selection processes (for a review, see Pashler, 1998). All other sensory and motor mechanisms could be ruled out with a large degree of overlap, as we argued previously. In other words, processing two tasks at the same time would require the parallel involvement of all processes except the critical response selection step that would be carried out sequentially or at least with limited capacities between tasks.

Two interpretations of this interference effect acting on decisional processes are provided: The bottleneck model (Welford, 1952; Pashler & Johnston, 1989) and the capacity sharing model (Navon & Gopher, 1979; Tombu & Jolicoeur, 2002). The former refers to the concept that a central bottleneck is introduced in the information processing flow at the decisional step, leading to the strictly sequential operation of responses selection. The alternative interpretation rather suggests that the interference is due to the fact that decisional mechanisms have access to a limited pool of resources in order to be performed, and that sharing these resources reduces dramatically the efficiency of this operation.

Possible Interactions between Executive and Integrative Networks

However, in any case, the weakness of both psychological models is that the notion of resources is not clearly identified from a neurophysiological point of view and is not unequivocally supported by neuroanatomical data. Few works in neuroimagery are available in the literature, and they do not provide a clear understanding of dual task interference. Some have proposed the lateral prefrontal cortex as the key site of interference (Koechlin, Basso, Pietrini, Panzer & Grafman, 1999; Goldberg et al., 1998), whereas others did not (Bunge, Klingberg, Jacobsen & Gabrieli, 2000; Klingberg, 1998). In attempt to solve some methodological problems, Szameitat and colleagues (Szameitat, Schubert, Muller & von Cramon, 2002; Schubert & Szameitat, 2003) recently published a series of studies clarifying some inconsistencies previously observed in the literature. They found dual-task activations both in the prefrontal, temporal, parietal, and occipital cortices. In other words, processing concurrent tasks could generate distributed interference, overlapping extensively the ventral and dorsal streams involved in visuomanual and perceptual processing. However, specific activations were found to be more evident in the superior parietal and the lateral prefrontal cortices (Szameitat et al., 2002), and the special focus of the dual-task-related activation was supposed to be located more precisely in regions surrounding the left inferior frontal sulcus (Schubert & Szameitat, 2003).

On the one hand, the parietal cortex is known to be highly involved in sensorimotor integration mainly with the posterior, intermediate and anterior regions (see Burnod et al., 1999 for review). However, the superior parietal cortex could also have a special role in complex sensorimotor integration, as recently demonstrated for interhemispheric sensorimotor integration (Iacoboni & Zaidel, 2004). On the other hand, despite the fact that the lateral prefrontal cortex is not directly a key structure of the parieto-frontal network for visuomotor integration, functional connections with some of these frontal structures (especially the medial frontal cortex) were evidenced (see Ridderinkhof, Ullsperger, Crone & Nieuwenhuis, 2004 for review). In other words, regulatory frontal processes involved in dual-task interference are likely to have functional interactions with the neighbouring integrative structures. As a consequence, it seems more generally that integrative networks could have tight links with executive networks involved in the interference effect, both from neuroanatomical and functional points of view.

However, whatever the psychological model of interference, sensorimotor integration has a supplementary meaning in the dual-task condition compared with the description we have proposed in the first two sections: in the context of large capacity of sensorimotor processes illustrated by extensive overlapping, parallel processing and automatic sensorimotor combinations, it also involves the concept of priority for concurrent processing.

Sensory Dominance in Dual-task Interference

In the PRP paradigm, two overlapping tasks are carried out and subjects are asked to react as fast as possible for both of them. Most often, there is one primary and one secondary task, that is, the same stimulus is always presented first and the second one is presented with a variable delay (SOA). The standard perceptuo-motor interference theory (bottleneck model) predicts RT slowing in the second task. In other words, it assumes the cognitive priority is given to the first task, independently of the nature of sensory modalities used in each task. This prediction is reinforced by the fact that restricted attentional capacity to concurrent attention and awareness was found to apply only at a modality specific level but not between sensory modalities.

However, the concept of sensory dominance was never evoked within the framework of dual-task interference. We propose in this section that the concept of priority assigned to one of the two tasks of a dual-task paradigm (when it is not imposed by experimental conditions) may be linked to a kind of sensory priority. We assume this effect may be a special form of sensory dominance applying specifically to multitask processing. We present here some original experimental data actually in progress in our laboratory testing this hypothesis.

The study aims at investigating whether dual-task interference effects vary or not across subjects as a function of perceptual dominance (viewed as sensory priority when processing two concurrent tasks at the same time). The main originality of this experiment was to handle SOA in both directions, in other words, to present visually or auditory stimuli in a random order or simultaneously so that no priority was given beforehand to any of the two tasks. The motor tasks required to assess interference were obviously chosen for their similarity (key-pressing tasks using both hands) in order to put the emphasis exclusively on the relation between sensory modality and SOA.

Forty eight naive subjects (aged 18 to 21 years old) participated in the experiment. They all had normal or corrected-to-normal vision and normal auditory acuity. Subjects were sitting in a dark room, 30 cm in front of a computer screen, the eyes fixed on a central fixation target. Two squares (8 by 8 cm) were centered 16.2deg on each side of the central fixation dot. The visual task consisted in reacting as soon as possible to the appearance of a target (a white cross of 3.5deg of visual angle) in one of these two locations by pressing the left or right keys with the thumb and index fingers of one hand. The auditory task consisted in reacting as soon as possible to the presentation of a low or high tone by pressing the bottom or up keys with the thumb and index fingers of the other hand. Note that spatial compatibility was obvious for both tasks and that the hands used for each one were counterbalanced across subjects and conditions.

Three conditions of presentation were performed, including dual-task and control conditions: i) simple visual task (VT, 2 blocks of 36 trials each, only one of the two possible visual stimuli could appear with a randomized delay), ii) simple auditory task (AT, 4 blocks of 20 trials, same procedure), and iii) dual-task (DT, 2 blocks of 36 trials) where both visual and auditory stimuli were presented with variable SOA (-100 ms -the auditory stimulus preceded the visual one-, 0 ms -auditory and visual stimuli appeared simultaneously- and +100 ms -the visual stimulus preceded the auditory one-).

First of all, we ensured this dual-task provided interference as predicted by the above mentioned theories, by comparing simple tasks averaged RT (collapsed VT and AT) with dual-task RT. As expected, mean RT largely increased when processing two tasks concurrently compared with processing one task at a time (Figure 4). Individual analyses were performed to evaluate more specifically this dual-task interference. Individual normalyzed and vincentized dual-task RTs were submitted to a 2 Stimulus (V, A) x 3 SOA (-100ms, 0 ms, +100ms) ANOVA. This allowed categorizing subjects according to five attentional profiles:

- Absolute visual dominant group (AV): subjects responded systematically to the visual stimulus first then to the auditory one whatever SOA condition.
- Relative visual dominant group (RV): subjects responded to the visual stimulus first only for -100 and 0 ms SOA conditions.
- Non dominant group (ND): subjects' response order depended on stimuli presentation order. In other words, an effect of SOA but no effect of Stimulus was observed.
- Relative auditory dominant group (RA): subjects responded to the auditory stimulus first only for 0 and 100 ms SOA conditions.
- Absolute auditory dominant group (AA): subjects responded systematically to the auditory stimulus first then to the visual one whatever SOA condition.

According to the standard theory of perceptuo-motor interference, all subjects should be included in the ND group since stimuli temporal order is supposed to have the key role in the decisional cueing effect. Inadequately, the 48 subjects were distributed across all categories: 29.1% AV, 16.6% RV, 31.2% ND, 14.5% RA and 8.3% AA (Figure 5). Broadly, 68.5% of the population shows a pattern of dominance whereas only 31.2% do not give any priority to one or the other sensory modality. Among the dominant subjects, most of them (2/3) are visual.

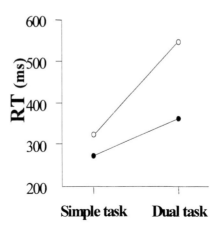

Figure 4. Mean reaction times as a function of the type of task (simple vs. dual) for normal (white dots) and expert (black dots) subjects. A significant interaction Group x Task (F(2,54)=18.7, p<0.01) especially reveals that interference is of greater extent in normal subjects.

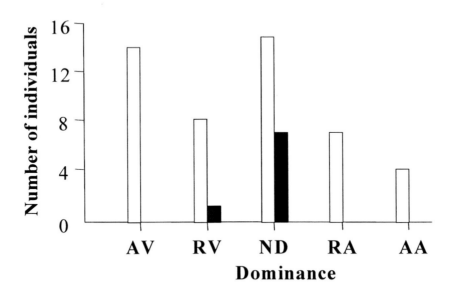

Figure 5. Representation of interindividual variability as regard to the distribution of normal (white dots) and expert (black dots) subjects in the 5 possible categories of perceptual dominance.

This result clearly suggests that multisensory integration in the case of non redundant stimuli also plays an important role in perceptuo-motor interference. Multisensory integration in this particular situation could be viewed as the weighting of sensory cues in the temporal domain. This effect could be explained by a kind of endogenous sensory-based mechanism acting on the temporal queuing supposed to affect decisional processes. However, we do not claim this effect is directly responsible for interference. We rather suggest this sensory-based priority is likely to influence the decisional cueing mechanism.

Interindividual Variability and the Effects of Expertise

The purpose of this section is to better understand the relationship between perceptuo-motor interference and the mechanisms underlying sensory dominances. To this aim, we hypothesize that, similarly to what was described in the previous sections, expertise may influence sensorimotor integration processes. Evidencing this interaction could help us understanding the origins of the interindividual variability observed in normal subjects, i.e., the flexibility and adaptability of the temporal integration of multisensory concurrent signals.

Nowadays, video-game has such an important place in entertainment that it has became a considerable industry, extending to the organization of international competitions where professional players regularly meet. These "experts" have obviously developed specific sensorimotor abilities depending on the game they play. Broadly, they are likely to have better attentional skills and a better visuomotor coordination than normal subjects. Studies including many experiments of Flanker compatibility effect, enumeration task, attentional blink and training showed that video-game players reveal enhanced visual attention capacities, both for spatial distribution and temporal resolution of attentional shifts (Riesenhuber, 2004). This improvement was evidenced after repetitive training, and it was suggested that practice may reduce interference in normal subjects (Green & Bavelier, 2003). The goal of this last experimental part is to test the relation between the evolution of the interference effect and the possible corollary evolution of sensory dominance.

The same experiment was done with a group of 8 professional video-game players experts in "Counter Strike", a game specifically based on auditory and visual speeded reactions. They were aged from 18 to 21 years old and all reported normal or corrected-to-normal vision and normal auditory acuity. The same methods were used to estimate interference and to categorize subjects' dominance.

We used a 2 Task (Simple, Dual) x 2 Group (novices, experts) ANOVA to test the interference effect. Figure 5 shows the significant interaction between these two factors. Experts clearly differentiate from novices since: i) basically, they are slightly but significantly faster for simple tasks, and above all ii) mean RT increases significantly less in dual-task, evidencing that interference is shorter in the formers.

This observation is in line with previous studies dealing with interference and expertise. However, the main interesting result is provided by our analysis of individual dominance profiles in video-gamers. Figure 5 shows how the 8 subjects are distributed among the 5 categories according to the distribution of the normal subjects' group. Very clearly, experts mainly belong to the ND category (7/8 subjects). In other words, becoming unconstrained by any sensory dominance for assigning priority in dual-task processing reduces interference. In most of the normal subjects, the lengthening of RT would be caused by the addition of a supplementary PRP when gating the non dominant cue even when this stimulus is presented first.

This experiment leads to two main conclusions. First, sensorimotor integration should also be considered in the temporal domain since the order simultaneous information can be used depends on their sensory nature. As evidenced in the first two sections, this special kind of integration is also subject to contextual and interindividual variability. Second, the effects of expertise on the ability to process several tasks at the same time clearly oppose to the effects of expertise generally observed when processing redundant information for a single task. More precisely, whereas sensory dominance often correlates with the level of expertise for reaching, body orientation perception, etc, independence from any dominance seems to characterize the efficiency in dual-task processing.

CONCLUSION

The central nervous system is able to use many different combinations for internal/external communication, both in encoding target locations or body positions, planning hand displacement or controlling posture, as well as dual-task processing, etc. The brain can select different combinations of sensory inputs on the basis of the computation in which the resulting estimate will be used. For example, coding the position of the arm for movement vector planning would rely mostly on visual input, whereas the estimate used to compute the joint-based motor command would rather rely on proprioceptive signals (Sober & Sabes, 2003). In this chapter's review and with the help of some original experimental data, we suggest that such various forms of dominance are especially modulated by perceptuo-motor expertise. We propose expertise can take various forms depending on the processes mainly involved in the task. This is illustrated by multiple examples of dominance patterns (proprioception, visual-field dependency, oculomotor signals, vestibular weighting, etc) or conversely by examples of non dominance patterns (concurrent processes) contrasting with normal subjects' behavior.

Facing this variability, sensorimotor integration should be viewed as a continuous dialogue between all sensory modalities, motor processes and internal models rather than a convergence of all information onto a supramodal function and area. Neuromimetic models (e.g., Burnod et al., 1999; Deneve & Pouget, 2004) propose such a theoretical framework. They are based on biological plausibility (simulating neuronal activity both at a single unit and a population levels), knowledge of neuroanatomical integrative networks (simulating brain functional architecture) and experimental data in animals and humans (simulating behavior). These models can predict efficiently most of the effects observed experimentally in numerous studies (context, constraints, variability, learning and adaptation, etc). We are convinced they should be considered more extensively in behavioral and psychological studies because they provide new convincing insights into sensorimotor integration theory. We claim they could put to an end some old controversies regarding this function and underpin our knowledge of perceptuo-motor skills.

REFERENCES

Alexander, G.E., & Crutcher, M.D. (1990) Neural representations of the target (goal) of visually guided arm movements in three motor areas of the monkey. *Journal of Neurophysiology, 64,* 164-178.

Amblard, B., & Carblanc, A. (1978) Role of foveal and peripheral information in maintaining postural equilibrium in man. *Agressologie, 19,* 21-22.

Anastasopoulos, D., Haslwanter, T., Bronstein, A.M., Fetter, M., & Dichgans, J. (1997) Dissociation between the perception of body verticality and the visual vertical in acute peripheral vestibular disorder in humans. *Neuroscience Letters, 233,* 151-153.

Andersen, R.A., Snyder, L.H., Bradley, D.C., & Xing, J. (1997) Multimodal representation of space in the posterior parietal cortex and its use in planning movements. *Annual Review of Neuroscience, 20,* 303-330.

Batista, A.P., Buneo, C.A., Snyder, L.H., & Andersen, R.A. (1999) Reach plans in eye-centered coordinates. *Science, 285,* 257-260.

Berger, M., Lechner-Steinleitner, S., Kozlovskaya, I., Holzmuller, G., Mechtcheriakov, S., Sokolov, A., & Gerstenbrand, F. (1998) The effect of head-to-trunk position on the direction of arm movements before, during, and after space flight. *Journal of Vestibular Research, 8,* 341-354.

Biguer, B., Donaldson, I., Hein, A., & Jeannerod, M. (1988) Neck muscle vibration modifies the representation of visual motion and direction in man. *Brain, 111,* 1405-1424.

Bisdorff, A.R., Wolsley, C.J., Anastasopoulos, D., Bronstein, A.M., & Gresty, M.A. (1996) The perception of body verticality (subjective postural vertical) in peripheral and central vestibular disorders. *Brain, 119,* 1523-1534.

Blakemore, S.J., Wolpert, D.M., & Frith, C.D. (1998) Central cancellation of self-produced tickle sensation. *Nature Neuroscience, 1,* 635-640.

Bles, W., & van Raay, J.L. (1988) Pre- an Postflight (D-1) postural control in tilting environments. *Advances in Oto-Rhino-Laryngology, 42,* 13-17.

Bles, W., Bos, J.E., & Kruit, H. (2000) Motion sickness. *Current Opinion in Neurology, 13,* 19-25.

Bles, W., Bos, J.E., de Graaf, B., Groen, E., & Wertheim, A.H. (1998) Motion sickness: only one provocative conflict? *Brain Research Bulletin, 47,* 481-487.

Bles, W., De Jong, H.A.A., & Oosterveld, W.J. (1984) Prediction of sea-sickness susceptibility. In: *Motion sickness: mechanisms, prediction, prevention and treatment.* Proceedings of the AGARD symposium, May 1984, Williamsburg, Va. Loughton, England. Pp. 27.1-27.5.

Bock, O. (1997) Effect of a tilted visual background on human sensory-motor coordination. *Experimental Brain Research, 115,* 507-512.

Boulinguez, P. (1999) Les avantages liés a la latéralité manuelle en escrime sont-ils l'expression d'asymétries cérébrales fonctionnelles? *Sportmedizin und Sporttraumatologie, 47,* 63-67.

Boulinguez P., Blouin J., & Nougier V. (2001a) The gap effect for eye and hand movements in double-step pointing. *Experimental Brain Research, 138,* 352-358.

Boulinguez, P., Toussaint, L., Abed-Meraim, B., & Collignon, F. (2001b) Nature of the perceptual encoding of hand positions according to subject's perceptuo-motor expertise. *Perceptual and Motor Skills, 93,* 24-30.

Brandt, T., Bartenstein, P., Janek, A., & Dieterich, M. (1998) Reciprocal inhibitory visual-vestibular interaction. Visual motion stimulation deactivates the parieto-insular vestibular cortex. *Brain, 121,* 1749-1758.

Bresciani, J.P., Blouin, J., Popov, K., Bourdin, C., Sarlegna, F., Vercher, J.L., & Gauthier, G.M. (2002) Galvanic vestibular stimulation in humans produces online arm movement deviations when reaching towards memorized visual targets. *Neuroscience Letters, 318,* 34-38.

Bringoux, L., Marin, L., Nougier, V., Barraud, P.A., & Raphel, C. (2000) Effects of gymnastics expertise on the perception of body orientation in the pitch dimension. *Journal of Vestibular Research, 10,* 251-258.

Bringoux, L., Nougier, V., Barraud, P.A., Marin, L., & Raphel, C. (2003) Contribution of somesthesic information to the perception of body orientation in the pitch dimension. *Quarterly Journal of Experimental Psychology, 56,* 909-923.

Bringoux, L., Schmerber, S., Nougier, V., Dumas, G., Barraud, P.A., & Raphel, C. (2002) Perception of slow pitch and roll body tilts in bilateral labyrinthine-defective subjects. *Neuropsychologia, 40,* 367-372.

Bronstein, A.M. (1988) Evidence for a vestibular input contributing to dynamic head stabilization in man. *Acta Oto-laryngologica, 105,* 1-6.

Brotchie, P.R., Andersen, R.A., Snyder, L.H., & Goodman, S.J. (1995) Head position signals used by parietal neurons to encode locations of visual stimuli. *Nature, 375,* 232-235.

Bundy, A.C., Lane, S.J., & Murray, E.A. (2002) Sensory integration: Theory and practice. Philadelphia: F. A. Davis.

Bunge, S. A., Klingberg, T., Jacobsen, R. B., & Gabrieli, J. D. E. (2000) A resource model of the neural basis of executive working memory. *Proceedings of the National Academy of Sciences, U.S.A., 97,* 3573-3578.

Burnod, Y., Baraduc, P., Battaglia-Mayer, A., Guigon, E., Koechlin, E., Ferraina, S., Lacquaniti, F., & Caminiti, R. (1999) Parieto-frontal coding of reaching: an integrated framework. *Experimental Brain Research, 129,* 325-346.

Calvert, G.A., & Thesen, T. (2004) Multisensory integration: methodological approaches and emerging principles in the human brain. *Journal of Physiology, 98,* 191-205.

Caminiti, R., Ferraina, S., & Johnson, P.B. (1996) The sources of visual information to the primate frontal lobe: a novel role for the superior parietal lobule. *Cerebral Cortex, 6,* 319-328.

Cheung, B.S., & Howard, I.P. (1991) Optokinetic torsion: dynamics and relation to circularvection. *Vision Research, 31,* 1327-1335.

Clark, B., & Graybiel, A. (1962) Perception of the postural vertical in normals and subjects with labyrinthine defects, *Journal of Experimental Psychology, 65,* 294-301.

Clément G., & Lestienne F. (1988) Adaptive modifications of postural attitude in conditions of weightlessness. *Experimental Brain Research, 72,* 381-389.

Crémieux, J., & Mesure, S. (1994) Differential sensitivity to static visual cues in the control of postural equilibrium in Man. *Perceptual and Motor Skills, 78,* 67-74.

Crémieux, J., Isableu, B., & Ohlmann, T. (1995) Contrôle postural et perception visuelle de la verticale: début d'approche. In P.M. Gagey & B. Weber (Eds.), *Entrée du systume postural fin*. Paris: Masson. Pp. 3-9.

Crone, R.A. (1975) Optically induced eye torsion. II. Optostatic and optokinetic cycloversion. *Albrecht Von Graefes Archiven Klinsche Experimental Ophthalmologie, 196*, 1-7.

Crutcher, M.D., & Alexander, G.E. (1990) Movement-related neuronal activity selectively coding either direction or muscle pattern in three motor areas of the monkey. *Journal of Neurophysiology, 64*, 151-163.

Curthoys, I.S., & Wade, S.W. (1995) Ocular torsion position and the perception of visual orientation. *Acta Oto-laryngologica. Supplement, 520*, 298-300.

de Vries, N., Bles, W., & Feenstra, L. (1985) Patients with an acoustic neurinoma examined with a tilted room. *Clinical Otolaryngology, 10*, 103-108.

Deneve, S., & Pouget, A. (2004) Bayesian multisensory integration and cross-modal spatial links. *Journal of Physiology, 98*, 249-258.

Desmurget, M., & Grafton, S. (2000) Forward modeling allows feedback control for fast reaching movements. *Trends in Cognitive Science, 4*, 423-431.

Desmurget, M., Epstein, C.M., Turner, R.S., Prablanc, C., Alexander, G.E., & Grafton, S.T. (1999) Role of the posterior parietal cortex in updating reaching movements to a visual target. *Nature Neuroscience, 2*, 563-567.

Desmurget, M., Pelisson, D., Rossetti, Y., & Prablanc, C. (1998) From eye to hand: planning goal-directed movements. *Neuroscience and Biobehavioral Reviews, 22*, 761-788

Diamond, S.G., & Markham, C.H. (1983) Ocular counterrolling as an indicator of vestibular otolith function, *Neurology, 33*, 1460-1469.

Diamond, S.G., & Markham, C.H. (1991) Prediction of space motion sickness susceptibility by disconjugate eye torsion in parabolic flight, *Aviation, Space, and Environmental Medicine, 62*, 201-205.

Dichgans, J., & Brandt, T. (1972) Visual-vestibular interaction and motion perception. *Bibliotheca ophthalmologica, 82*, 327-338.

Dichgans, J., Diener, H.C., & Brandt, T. (1974) Optokinetic-graviceptive interaction in different head positions. *Acta Oto-laryngologica, 78*, 213-221.

Dichgans, J., Held, R., Young, L.R., & Brandt, T. (1972) Moving visual scenes influence the apparent direction of gravity. *Science, 178*, 1217-1219.

DiLorenzo, J.R., & Rock, I. (1982) The rod and frame effect as a function of the righting of the frame. *Journal of Experimental Psychology: Human Perception & Performance, 8*, 536-546.

Duhamel, J.R., Bremmer, F., BenHamed, S., & Graf, W. (1997) Spatial invariance of visual receptive fields in parietal cortex neurons. *Nature, 389*, 845-848.

Duncan, J., Martens, S., & Ward, R. (1997) Restricted attentional capacity within but not between sensory modalities. *Nature, 387*, 808-810.

Ebenholtz, S.M., & Benzschawel, T.L. (1977) The rod and frame effect and induced head tilt as a function of observation distance. *Perception and Psychophysics, 22*, 491-496.

Finke, R.A., & Held, R. (1978) State reversals of optically induced tilt and torsional eye movements. *Perception and Psychophysics, 23*, 337-340.

Fitzpatrick, R., & McCloskey, D.I. (1994) Proprioceptive, visual and vestibular thresholds for the perception of sway during standing in humans. *Journal of Physiology, 478*, 173-186.

Fürstberg, J., Andersson, E., & Ledin, T. (1998) Influence of different conditions for tilt compensation on symptoms of motion sickness in tilting trains. *Brain Research Bulletin, 47*, 525-535.

Ghafouri, M., Archambault, P.S., Adamovich, S.V., & Feldman, A.G. (2002) Pointing movements may be produced in different frames of reference depending on the task demand. *Brain Research, 929,* 117-128

Ghez, C., Gordon, J., & Ghilardi, M.F. (1995) Impairments of reaching movements in patients without proprioception. II. Effects of visual information on accuracy. *Journal of Neurophysiology, 73,* 361-372.

Goldberg, T. E., Berman, K. F., Fleming, K., Ostrem, J., Van Horn, J., Esposito, G., Mattay, V. S., Gold, J. M., & Weinberger, D. R. (1998) Uncoupling cognitive workload and prefrontal cortical physiology: A PET rCBF study. *Neuroimage, 7,* 296-303.

Golomer, E., Crémieux, J., Dupui, P., Isableu, B., & Ohlmann, T. (1999) Visual contribution to self-induced body sway frequencies and visual perception of male professional dancers. *Neuroscience Letters, 267,* 189-192.

Goodenough, D.R., Cox, P.W., Sigman, E., & Strawderman, W.E. (1985) A cognitive style conception of the field-dependence dimension. *Current Psychology of Cognition, 5,* 687-705.

Graybiel, A. (1970) Susceptibility to acute motion sickness in blind persons. *Aerospace Medicine, 41,* 650-653.

Graziano, M.S. (1999) Where is my arm? The relative role of vision and proprioception in the neuronal representation of limb position. *Proceedings of the National Academy of Science of the United States of America, Neurobiology, 96,* 10418-10421.

Graziano, M.S. (2001a) Awareness of Space. *Nature, 411,* 93-94.

Graziano, M.S. (2001b) Is reaching eye-centered, body-centered, hand-centered, or a combination? *Reviews in Neurosciences, 12,* 175-185.

Graziano, MS & Gandhi, S. (2000) Location of the polysensory zone in the precentral gyrus of anesthetized monkeys. *Experimental Brain Research, 135,* 259-66

Green, C.S., & Bavelier, D. (2003) Action video game modifies visual selective attention. *Letters to Nature, 423,* 534- 537.

Groen, E., Bos, J.E., & de Graaf, B. (1999) Contribution of the otoliths to the human torsional vestibulo-ocular reflex. *Journal of Vestibular Research, 9,* 27-36.

Guerraz, M., Blouin, J., & Vercher, J.-L. (2003) From head orientation to hand control: evidence of both neck and vestibular involvement in hand drawing. *Experimental Brain Research, 150,* 40-49.

Guerraz, M., Poquin, D., & Ohlmann, T. (1998) The role of head-centric spatial reference with a static and kinetic visual disturbance. *Perception and Psychophysics, 60,* 287-295.

Guillot, A., & Collet, C. (2004) Field dependence-independence in complex motor skills. *Perceptual and Motor Skills, 98,* 575-583.

Hafstrom, A., Fransson, P.A., Karlberg, M., & Magnusson, M. (2004) Ipsilesional visual field dependency for patients with vestibular schwannoma. *Neuroreport, 15,* 2201-2204.

Haggard, P., & Whitford, B. (2004) Supplementary motor area provides an efferent signal for sensory suppression. *Cognitive Brain Research, 19,* 52-58.

Howard, I.P. (1986) The perception of posture, self motion, and the visual vertical. In K.R. Boff, L. Kaufman, & J.P. Thomas (Eds.), *Handbook of perception and human performance*. New York: Wiley & Sons. Pp.18.1-18.62.

Hu, S.Q., Stern, R.M., & Koch, K.L. (1991). Effects of pre-exposures to a rotating optokinetic drum on adaptation to motion sickness. *Aviation Space and Environmental Medicine, 62,* 53-56.

Iacoboni, M., & Zaidel, E. (2004) Interhemispheric visuo-motor integration in humans: the role of the superior parietal cortex. *Neuropsychologia, 42,* 419-425.

Isableu, B., Ohlmann, T., Crŭmieux, J., & Amblard, B. (1997) Selection of spatial frame of reference and postural control variability. *Experimental Brain Research, 114,* 584-589.

Jeannerod, M. (1988) *The neural and behavioral organization of goal-directed movements.* Oxford: Oxford University Press.

Jeannerod, M. (1991) The interaction of visual and proprioceptive cues in controlling reaching movements. In D.R. Humphrey & H. J. Freund (Eds.), *Motor Control: Concepts and issues.* New York: Wiley. Pp. 277-291.

Jeka, J.J., & Lackner, J.R. (1994) Fingertip contact influences human postural control. *Experimental Brain Research, 100,* 495-502.

Jiang, Y. (2004) Resolving dual-task interference: an fMRI study. *Neuroimage. 22,* 748-54.

Karnath, H.O., Ferber, S., & Himmelbach, M. (2001) Spatial awareness is a function of the temporal not the posterior parietal lobe. *Nature, 411,* 950-953.

Kastner, S., & Ungerleider, LG. (2000) Mechanisms of visual attention in the human cortex. *Annual Review of Neuroscience, 23,* 315-341.

Kavounoudias, A., Roll, R., & Roll, J.P. (1998) The plantar sole is a 'dynamometric map' for human balance control. *Neuroreport, 9,* 3247-3252.

Kawato, M. (1999) Internal models for motor control and trajectory planning. *Current Opinion in Neurobiology, 9,* 718-727.

Keele, S.W. (1968) Motor control in skilled motor performance. *Psychological Bulletin, 70,* 387-403.

Kennedy, P.M., & Inglis, J.T. (2001) Modulation of the soleus H-reflex in prone human subjects using galvanic vestibular stimulation. *Clinical Neurophysiology, 112,* 2159-2163.

Kennedy, R.S., Graybiel, A., McDonough, R.C., & Beckwith, F.D. (1968) Symptomatology under storm conditions in the North Atlantic in control subjects and in persons with bilateral labyrinthine defects. *Acta Oto-Laryngologica, 66,* 533-540.

Klingberg T. (1998) Concurrent performance of two working memory tasks: potential mechanisms of interference. *Cerebral Cortex, 8,* 593-601.

Koechlin, E., Basso, G., Pietrini, P., Panzer, S., & Grafman, J. (1999) The role of the anterior prefrontal cortex in human cognition. *Nature, 13,* 148- 151.

Lackner, J.R., & DiZio, P. (1989) Altered sensory-motor control of the head as an etiological factor in space motion sickness. *Perceptual and Motor Skills, 68,* 784-786.

Lackner, J.R., & Graybiel, A. (1986) Head movements in non-terrestrial force environments elicit motion sickness: implications for the etiology of space motion sickness. *Aviation Space and Environmental Medicine, 57,* 443-448.

Lacour, M., Barthélémy, J., Borel, L., Magnan, J., Xerri, C., Chays, A., & Ouaknine, M. (1997) Sensory strategies in human postural control before and after unilateral vestibular neurotomy. *Experimental Brain Research, 115,* 300-310.

Lacquaniti, F., Guigon, E., Bianchi, L., Ferraina, S., & Caminiti, R. (1995) Representing spatial information for limb movement: role of area 5 in the monkey. *Cerebral Cortex, 5,* 391-409.

Lee, D.N., & Aronson, E. (1974) Visual proprioceptive control of standing in human infants. *Perception and Psychophysics, 15*, 529-532.

Lee, D.N. (1980) Visuo-motor coordination in space-time. In G. Stelmach and I. Requin (Eds.), *Tutorials in Motor Behavior*, North Holland: Amsterdam. Pp. 281-293.

Lestienne, F., Berthoz, A., Mascot, J.C., & Koitcheva, V. (1976) Postural effects induced by a visual scene in linear movement. *Agressologie, 17*, 37-46.

Litvinenkova, V., & Baron, J.B. (1968) Variations of postural regulation as a fonction of visual and oculomotor information. *Comptes Rendus des Süances de la Sociütü de Biologie et de Ses Filiales, 162*, 1294-1299.

Luyat, M., Gentaz, E., Corte, T.R., & Guerraz, M. (2001) Reference frames and haptic perception of orientation: body and head tilt effects on the oblique effect. *Perception and Psychophysics, 63*, 541-554.

Mann, C.W., Berthelot-Berry, N.H., & Dauterive, H.J. (1949) The perception of verticality: I. Visual and non-labyrinthine cues. *Journal of Experimental Psychology, 39*, 538-547.

Markham, C.H., & Diamond, S.G. (1992) Further evidence to support disconjugate eye torsion as a predictor of space motion sickness. *Aviation, Space, and Environmental Medicine, 63*, 118-121.

Mars, F., Vercher, J.-L., & Blouin, J. (2004) Perception of the vertical with a head-mounted visual frame during head tilt. *Ergonomics, 47*, 1116-1130.

Massion, J. (1994) Postural control system. *Current Opinion In Neurobiology, 4*, 877-887.

Massion, J. (1997) *Cerveau et motricité*. Paris: Presse Universitaire de France.

Mast, F., & Jarchow, T. (1996) Perceived body position and the visual horizontal. *Brain Research Bulletin, 40*, 393-398.

McIntyre, J., Zago, M., Berthoz, A., & Lacquaniti, F. (2001) Does the brain model Newton's laws? *Nature Neuroscience, 4*, 693-694.

Mergner, T., & Rosemeier, T. (1998) Interaction of vestibular, somatosensory and visual signals for postural control and motion perception under terrestrial and microgravity conditions - a conceptual model. *Brain Research Reviews, 28*, 118-135.

Mergner, T. (2002) The Matryoshka Dolls principle in human dynamic behavior in space: A theory of linked references for multisensory perception and control of action. *Current Psychology of Cognition, 21*, 129-212.

Merker, B.H., & Held, R. (1981) Eye torsion and the apparent horizon under head tilt and visual field rotation. *Vision Research, 21*, 543-547.

Miller, E.F., Fregly, A.R., & Graybiel, A. (1968) Visual horizontal-perception in relation to otolith-function. *American Journal of Psychology, 81*, 488-496.

Mittelstaedt, H. (1983) A new solution to the problem of the subjective vertical. *Naturwissenschaften, 70*, 272-281.

Mittelstaedt, H. (1995) Evidence of somatic graviception from new and classical investigations. *Acta Oto-laryngologica. Supplement, 520*, 186-187.

Mittelstaedt, H. (1998) Origin and processing of postural information. *Neuroscience and Biobehavioral Reviews, 22*, 473-478.

Nashner, L.M., & Wolfson, P. (1974) Influence of head position and proprioceptive cues on short latency postural reflexes evoqued by galvanic stimulation of the human labyrinth. *Brain Research, 67*, 255-268.

Navon, D., & Gopher, D. (1979) On the economy of the human processing system. *Psychological Review, 89*, 214-255.

Neggers, S.F., & Bekkering, H (2000) Ocular gaze is anchored to the target of an ongoing pointing movements. *Journal of Neurophysiology, 83,* 639-651.

Neimer, J., Eskiizmirliler, S., Ventre-Dominey, J., Darlot, C., Luyat, M., Gresty, M.A., & Ohlmann, T. (2001) Trains with a view to sickness. *Current Biology, 11,* R549-R550.

Nyborg, H. (1980) Psychological differentiation in school children. Maturation, cognition, and personality development. *Psychological Reports Aarhus, 5.* Denmark: University of Aarhus.

Ohlmann, T. (1990) Les systèmes perceptifs spatiaux vicariants. In M. Reuchlin, J. Lautrey, C. Marendaz, & T. Ohlmann (Eds.), *Cognition: l'individuel et l'universel.* Paris: Presses Universitaires de France. Pp. 21-58.

Oman, C.M. (1982) A heuristic mathematical model for the dynamics of sensory conflict and motion sickness. *Acta Oto-Laryngologica. Supplement, 392,* 1-44.

Paillard, J. (1991) *Brain and space.* Oxford: Oxford University Press.

Parker, D.E., Poston, R.L., & Gulledge, W.L. (1983) Spatial orientation: visual-vestibular-somatic interaction. *Perception & Psychophysics, 33,* 139-146.

Pashler, H., & Johnston, J. (1989) Chronometric evidence for central postponement in temporally overlapping tasks. *The Quarterly Journal of Experimental Psychology, 41,* 19-45.

Pashler, H. (1998) *The Psychology of Attention.* Cambridge, M.A: MIT Press.

Poquin, D., Guerraz, M., Ohlmann, T., Marendaz, C., Brenet, F., & Raphel, C. (1995) Visual disturbance, head tilt and Aubert effect. *Current Psychology of Cognition, 14,* 231-253

Pouget, A., & Snyder, L. (2000) Computational approaches to sensorimotor transformations. *Nature Neuroscience, 3,* 1192-1198.

Pouget, A., Deneve, S., & Duhamel J.R. (2002) A computational perspective on the neural basis of multisensory spatial representations. *Nature Reviews Neuroscience, 3,* 741-747.

Prablanc, C., Echallier, J.E., Jeannerod, M., & Komilis E. (1979) Optimal response of eye and hand motor systems in pointing at a visual target. II. Static and dynamic visual cues in the control of hand movement. *Biological Cybernetics, 35,* 183-187.

Reason, J.T., & Brand, J.J. (1975) *Motion sickness.* London: Academic Press.

Reuchlin, M. (1978) Processus vicariants et différences interindividuelles. *Journal de Psychologie, 2,* 133-145.

Riccio, G.E., & Stoffregen, T.A. (1991) An ecological theory of motion sickness and postural instability. *Ecological Psychology, 3,* 195-240.

Ridderinkhof, K.R., Ullsperger, M., Crone, E.A., & Nieuwenhuis, S. (2004) The role of the medial frontal cortex in cognitive control. *Science, 306,* 443-447.

Riesenhuber, M. (2004) An action video game modifies visual processing. *Trends in Neurosciences, 2,* 72-74.

Roberts, T.D.M. (1973). Reflex balance. *Nature, 244,* 156-158.

Roll, J.P., & Roll, R. (1988) From eye to foot: a proprioceptive chain involved in postural control. In: B Amblard, A Berthoz, F Clarac (eds), *Posture and gait.* Elsevier: Amsterdam. Pp. 155-164.

Rossetti, Y., Desmurget, M., & Prablanc, C. (1995) Vectorial coding of movement: vision, proprioception, or both? *Journal of Neurophysiology, 74,* 457-463.

Sarès, F., Bourdin, C., Prieur, J.-M., Vercher, J.-L., Menu, J.-P., & Gauthier, G.M. (submitted), Effects of postural, visual, and gravitoinertial constraints on goal-directed arm movements.

Sarès, F., Prieur, J.-M., Bourdin, C., Gauthier, G.M., Blouin, J., & Vercher, J.-L. (2002). Peripheral visual information influences head posture during gravitoinertial changes. *Current Psychology of Cognition, 21*, 455-477.

Schµne, H. (1964) On the role of gravity in human spatial orientation. *Aerospatial Medicine, 35*, 764- 772.

Schubert, T., & Szameitat, A.J. (2003) Functional neuroanatomy of interference in overlapping dual tasks: an fMRI study. *Cognitive Brain Research, 17*, 733-746.

Schweighofer, N., Arbib, M.A., & Kawato, M. (1998) Role of the cerebellum in reaching movements in humans. I. Distributed inverse dynamics control. *European Journal of Neuroscience, 10*, 86-94.

Smart, L.J.Jr., Stoffregen, T.A., & Bardy, B.G. (2002) Visually induced motion sickness predicted by postural instability. *Human Factors, 44*, 451-65.

Smetanin, B.N., & Popov, K.E. (1997) Effect of body orientation with respect to gravity on directional accuracy of human pointing movements. *European Journal of Neuroscience, 9*, 7-11.

Smetanin, B.N., & Popov, K.E. (1998) Relations between the errors of targeted movements and inexactitude of visual perception of space. *Neurophysiology, 30*, 149-154.

Sober, S.J., & Sabes, P.N. (2003) Multisensory integration during motor planning. *Journal of Neuroscience, 23*, 6982-6992.

Soechting, J.F., Tong, D.C., & Flanders, M. (1996) Frames of reference in sensorimotor integration: Position sense of the arm and hand. In A. M. Wing, P. Haggard & J. R. Flanagan (Eds.), *Hand and Brain: The neurophysiology and psychology of hand movements.* San Diego, CA: Academic Press, Inc. Pp. 151-167.

Stoffregen, T.A., & Smart, L.J.Jr. (1998) Postural instability precedes motion sickness. *Brain Research Bulletin, 47*, 437-448.

Szameitat, A.J., Schubert, T., Muller, K., & von Cramon, D.Y. (2002) Local-ization of executive functions in dual-task performance with fMRI. *Journal of Cognitive Neuroscience, 14*, 1184-1199.

Telford, C. W. (1931) The refractory phase of voluntary and associative responses. *Journal of Experimental Psychology, 14*, 1-36.

Tombu, M., & Jolicoeur, P. (2002) All-or-none bottleneck versus capacity sharing accounts of the psychological refractory period phenomenon. *Psychological Research, 66*, 274-286.

Udo de Haes, H.A., & Schµne, H. (1970) Interaction between statolith organs and semicircular canals on apparent vertical and nystagmus. Investigations on the effectiveness of the statolith organs. *Acta Oto-Laryngologica, 69*, 25-31.

Van Beuzekom, A.D., & Van Gisbergen, J.A.M. (2000) Properties of the internal representation of gravity inferred from spatial-direction and body-tilt estimates. *Journal of Neurophysiology, 84*, 11-27.

Van Parys, J.A.P., Njiokiktjien, C. (1976) Romberg sign expressed in a quotient. *Agressologie, 17*, 95-100.

Vercher, J.-L., Sarès, F., Blouin, J., Bourdin, C., & Gauthier, G.M. (2003) Role of sensory information in updating internal models of the effector during arm tracking. *Progress in Brain Research, 142*, 203-222.

Vindras, P., Desmurget, M., Prablanc, C., & Viviani, P. (1998) Pointing errors reflect biases in the perception of the initial hand position. *Journal of Neurophysiology, 79*, 3290-3294.

Wade, N.J. (1968) Visual orientation during and after lateral head, body, and trunk tilt. *Perception & Psychophysics, 3*, 215-219.

Wade, S.W., & Curthoys, I.S. (1997) The effect of ocular torsional position on perception of the roll-tilt of visual stimuli. *Vision Research, 37*, 1071-1078.

Welford, A. T. (1952) The "psychological refractory period" and the timing of high speed performance: A review and a theory. *British Journal of Psychology, 43*, 2-19.

Witkin, H.A., & Asch, S.E. (1948a) Studies in space orientation: III. Perception of the upright in the absence of visual field. *Journal of Experimental Psychology, 38*, 603-614.

Witkin, H.A., & Asch, S.E. (1948b) Studies in space orientation: IV. Further experiments on perception of the upright with displaced visual fields. *Journal of Experimental Psychology: Human Perception and Performance, 38*, 762-782.

Witkin, H.A. (1950) Individual differences in ease of perception of embedded figures. *Journal of Personality, 19*, 1-15.

Yardley, L. (1990a) Contribution of somatosensory information to perception of the visual vertical with body tilt and rotation visual field. *Perception & Psychophysics, 48*, 131-134.

Yardley, L. (1990b) Motion sickness susceptibility and the utilisation of visual and otolithic information for orientation. *European Archives of Oto-Rhino-Laryngology, 247*, 300-304.

Zikmund, V., & Balla, J. (1973) The effect of directional optic stimuli on body gravity centre projection in standing man. *Agressologie, 14 Spec B*, 71-77.

Zoccolotti, P., Antonucci, G., Goodenough, D.R., Pizzamiglio, L., & Spinelli, D. (1992) The role of frame size on vertical and horizontal observers in the rod-and frame illusion. *Acta Psychologica, 79*, 171-187.

In: Focus on Nonverbal Communication Research
Editor: Finley R. Lewis, pp. 199-213
ISBN 1-59454-790-4
© 2007 Nova Science Publishers, Inc.

Chapter 9

EFFECTS OF EXPLANATION ON EMOTION ATTRIBUTION

Kumari Fernando and Jamin Halberstadt
University of Otago, Dunedin, New Zealand

ABSTRACT

People are motivated to talk about emotional events with other people (Rime, 1994) and in these verbal interactions they frequently refer explicitly to emotional states ("I thought he looked quite annoyed with me"; "She looked jealous"). But accurately decoding emotional states is difficult; emotional expressions are often complex blends of a number of emotions (Scherer & Tannenbaum, 1986), and language may not be the best medium in which to disambiguate them. Indeed Halberstadt and colleagues have recently shown that explaining the emotional states of others, rather than improving emotion perception, can paradoxically impair it by biasing emotion encoding in the direction of the explanation (Halberstadt & Niedenthal, 2001; Halberstadt, 2003; Halberstadt, 2005). In these studies participants who explained why a target was feeling sad (for example) remembered her face as expressing more sadness than it actually did.

The purpose of the present chapter is to explore the implications of this "explanation bias" for emotion attributions themselves. We will first review the work done by Halberstadt and colleagues and Halberstadt's (2003; 2005) argument that explanation effects are due to a shift in processing strategy associated with verbalization. Next, we propose that social situations can be understood as configural stimuli and as such should be vulnerable to the same biases as facial expressions. We then report preliminary data that show an explanation bias for emotion attributions of gender-congruent targets in an ambiguous emotional situation. Finally, we explore the implications of these results in particular, and the importance of configural and featural encoding in social situations more generally.

EFFECTS OF EXPLANATION
ON MEMORY FOR EMOTIONAL EXPRESSIONS

Halberstadt and colleagues have demonstrated that talking about the emotional state of others may disrupt memories for the emotions they expressed. In a typical experiment (see Halberstadt & Niedenthal, 2001), participants were shown an ambiguous emotional face (e.g., a face that is a constructed blend of both angry and sad emotions). Participants were then asked to explain why the person was feeling one of the blended emotions, or else were presented with an emotion label (e.g., "This person is sad") but were not asked to explain it. Later, in a surprise recognition test, participants were played a movie in which the face they saw earlier changed continuously from one of the blended emotions to the other, and they were asked to identify the facial expression that they had seen at encoding. Participants' encoding bias was defined as the difference (in movie frames) in memory for faces explained in terms of sadness and faces explained in terms of anger. Halberstadt and Niedenthal (2001) demonstrated that the faces participants recalled were biased in the direction of their explanation (see Figure 1). When participants explained why a target person was angry, they remembered seeing an angrier face than when they explained the same target in terms of sadness. Furthermore, the bias was significantly greater when participants explained the emotions than when participants were merely provided disambiguating labels, suggesting that the explanation process itself enhanced the use of emotion categories to encode the faces.

Halberstadt (2003) proposed a two-part process to explain these results, combining recent work on the effects of language on face processing with social cognitive theory about the primacy of social categorization. Schooler and his colleagues have demonstrated that language is an imprecise, and possibly inappropriate tool for representing certain kinds of stimuli. In a seminal study Schooler and Engstler-Schooler (1990) reported that experimental participants who verbally described the face of the perpetrator of a bank robbery were less accurate at recognizing his face in a line up. Subsequently this "verbal overshadowing" effect has been replicated with a variety of stimuli, including colors (Schooler & Engstler-Schooler, 1990), wines (Melcher & Schooler, 1995) and music (Houser, Fiore, & Schooler, 2003).

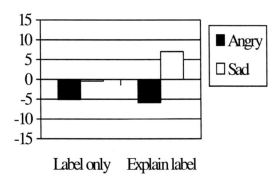

Figure 1. Recognition of ambiguous anger-sad target faces as a function of the emotion label provided with the face and whether the participant was asked to explain it . Negative and positive numbers indicate that the face was remembered as more angry and sad, respectively, than it really was. Data from Halberstadt and Niedenthal (2001).

One thing that verbally overshadowed stimuli appear to have in common is that they are processed "configurally" --as a whole that is not normally decomposed into meaningful parts (Halberstadt, 1996; Schooler, 2002). The configurality of faces in particular is demonstrated, for example, by the dramatic disruption of perception and recognition that results from face inversion, which in theory forces perceivers to rely on relatively ineffective feature-based processing (Valentine, 1988), and by the disproportionate effects of featural changes on overall face perception (e.g., Young, Hellawell, & Hay, 1987). Schooler (2002) has proposed that verbalization produces a "featural shift", possibly associated with brain hemispheric differences between verbal and nonverbal processing, such that verbalized faces are perceived and encoded in terms of their component features rather than the overall wholes those features compose. Indeed Halberstadt (2005) found that although memory for verbalized faces was impaired, memory for particular features of those faces was enhanced. Furthermore, manipulations that influence configural processing also moderate the verbal overshadowing effect. For example, Fallshore and Schooler (1995) reported that other-race faces (which are in theory processed more featurally than same-race faces; Rhodes, Brake, Taylor & Tan, 1989) are immune to interference by verbalization, while Halberstadt (2005) found that "featural" faces (which were inverted or had their features isolated with a mask) were less influenced by explanation than unaltered faces.

If verbalization indeed "decomposes" facial configurations into their component features, those features are likely to be organized quickly into more meaningful categories. Fiske and Neuburg (1990) argued that social information is primarily stored in categorical rather than piecemeal form. People attempt to fit new information (including new people that they encounter) into existing schemas, even when there is information to indicate that the schemas are inappropriate (Hastie & Kumar, 1979). People, that is, are motivated to see configurations, not features, and decomposed faces are therefore vulnerable to reintegration in terms of available emotion concepts. In the context of emotion explanations, the most available emotion concepts are contained in the explanations themselves. Thus verbal explanation provides both the mechanism of configural decomposition and the content with which to reintegrate emotional faces, thereby leading to biased encoding (Halberstadt, 2003).

Halberstadt (2005) recently provided evidence for the reintegration stage of this model, arguing that if reintegration has taken place then the target faces, but not particular features of the faces, should be influenced by explanation. As in Halberstadt & Niedenthal's (2001) original studies participants were asked to explain why anger-sad targets were feeling either anger or sadness, or else were presented with biasing labels without instructions to explain them. Later, they attempted to recognize either the target's face or the target's eyes (on her face). The emotion movies used in the recognition task were identical in the face and feature conditions. Explanation, however, only biased memory for the faces themselves.

Additional data argue against several alternatives to the configural decomposition account. One possibility, for example, is that explanation strengthens semantic memory for emotion labels. In this account, participants who were asked to construct an explanation of emotion may have been simply more likely to remember the disambiguating labels associated with the targets and to use them to reconstruct the face they saw at encoding. However Halberstadt and Niedenthal (2001) included a condition in which participants were asked to remember their emotion explanations for presentation to the experimenter later in the study. If explanation simply aids memory for the emotion label provided by the experimenter, then these participants, who would have been especially motivated to remember those labels, should have shown stronger memory bias for the faces. There was, however, no effect of timing of explanation; explanation had no more of an effect when it was (presumably) remembered than when it was presented to the experimenter earlier in the experiment. Even more telling, Halberstadt (2005) reported that, when directly queried, participants were no better than chance at remembering which emotion label accompanied which face. Together these data are inconsistent with the hypothesis that explanation merely enhances label memory without affecting configurality.

Another possibility is that verbalization does impair configural processing of faces, but only because language cannot adequately represent configural information, rather than via a global processing shift toward featural processing. The implication of this account is that if participants could find words to capture the configural relationships they see in faces then verbalization would not impair, and might even improve, face memory. Indeed, Melcher and Schooler (1996) proposed such an account in a study in which verbalization impaired wine memory only for those participants with moderate expertise in wine tasting. According to the researchers, experts and novices were not impaired because, for them, their perceptual and verbal expertise were congruent: experts could discriminate many wines and had precise language to describe their experiences, whereas novices had neither the ability nor the language to discriminate. Similarly, in the case of faces, it may be that people generally do not possess the vocabulary to discriminate faces with the precision our perceptual expertise allows. Indeed, some types of language do appear to improve face memory, such as names (Halberstadt, 1996) and personality descriptions (McKelvie, 1976; Stevens & Halberstadt, 2004).

Schooler (2002), however, outlines a number of reasons to consider verbal overshadowing to represent a global shift in processing strategy rather than a deficit in particular verbal content. First, there is no apparent relationship in the face literature between the quality of verbal descriptions and recognition accuracy, as one would expect if verbal overshadowing were due to inadequacy of verbal face representation (Schooler & Engstler-Schooler, 1991). Second, effects of verbalization have been found to generalize to stimuli that have not themselves been verbalized (Brown & Lloyd-Jones, 2002; Fallshore & Schooler, 1995). Third, other manipulations that, independent of verbalization, impair configural processing, such as identifying the components of larger wholes, have been shown to mimic verbal overshadowing effects (Macrae & Lewis, 2002). Conversely, other manipulations that theoretically encourage configural processing, such as listening to music, can undo the negative effects of verbalization (Finger, 2002). Finally, the configural-featural dichotomy maps nicely on to documented hemispheric differences in brain function. Specifically, language is typically associated with the left hemisphere (Springer & Deutsch, 1993), while at least some verbally overshadowed tasks, such as face recognition (Leehey, Carey, Diamond, & Cahn, 1978) and affective judgments (Gardner, Caccioppo, & Crites, 1995), are associated with the right. While far from conclusive, such associations make plausible a general shift in processing strategy, associated with language, that particularly affects configural stimuli and tasks.

SOCIAL INTERACTIONS AS CONFIGURATIONS

Halberstadt and colleagues have demonstrated that there are biasing effects of explanation on the encoding of individuals' emotional expressions, arguing that these effects are mediated by generalized verbal interference in configural processing. Yet encoding emotional expressions is only a special case of the general problem of how emotions are attributed in social situations. Furthermore, although emotional expressions are relatively discrete, emotional behavior more typically takes place within a complex social context that includes situational information, other people's behaviour, cultural and idiosyncratic expectations, goals, and prior knowledge, among many other factors. To the extent that these factors are processed configually – that is, as a unitary perceptual experience – then verbal explanation may also influence how emotional situations more generally are encoded and remembered.

Although rarely discussed in such terms, the notion of configural social perception has a long history in both theoretical and applied social psychology. Indeed Kurt Lewin, frequently cited as the father of social psychology, based much of his pioneering "field theory" on Gestalt psychological concepts of holistic perception (themselves precursors to the modern concept of configurality), stressing, for example, the necessity of seeing particular social behaviors in the context in which they occur (e.g., Lewin, 1951). Research on impression formation builds on Lewin's and the Gestaltists' insights. Asch's (1946) pioneering work, for example, similarly suggests that social perception is configural, based not on a simple additive process, but rather on the complex and simulaneous integration of information (see Hinton, 1993, for a review). Asch reported that participants were able not only to form impressions quite easily, but also to generate those impressions from minimal information, suggesting that, as Gestalt psychologists insist, a whole percept is more than the sum of its parts. Social schemas, a modern intellectual descendant of Asch's work, assume fundamentally that social information is not stored in isolation, ensuring that we "see" more in any social interaction than is actually in front of our eyes.

The notion of configurality is also implicit in the attribution literature specifically. Although attributions about an actor's behavior are frequently interpreted in terms of three distinct souces of information, related to the actor himself, the target of his behavior, and the situation in which the interaction takes place (e.g., Kelly, 1967), these factors are integrated in our subjective experience. Winter and Uleman (1984), for example, found that participants exposed to particular social behaviors implicitly and automatically extracted and encoded the personality traits associated with them (as evidenced by the effectiveness of those traits in a subseqent memory test). Targets who perform aggressive behaviors, for example, are "seen" as aggressive, a perception subsequently mitigated only with additional cognitive effort (Gilbert, Pelham, & Krull, 1988). Furthermore such spontaneous impressions are surprisingly accurate (Ambady & Rosenthal, 1993; see Ambady & Rosenthal, 1992 for a review). Ambady and Rosenthal (1993), for example, found that observers' personality judgments of teachers based on a 30-second silent videotape correlated strongly with their students' assessments on the same dimensions. The fact that we can see a brief interaction and efficiently and accurately derive meaning from it points to our ability to integrate multiple sources of information into a configural whole.

EXPLANATION AND EMOTION ATTRIBUTION

If social situations are perceived configurally then, like faces and emotional expressions, verbal explanations of emotion may direct attention to particular components of the situation, making them vulternable to reinterpretation in terms of available categories. Thus, we suggest that participants who are asked to explain an ambiguous social interaction in terms of a particular emotion will encode the situation consistent with their explanation.

Although not interpreted in terms of configural decomposition, a number of studies show that verbalization can bias emotional experience and attributions. For example, talking about particular feelings associated with an emotional experience can intensify the emotion felt immediately after an event. In a study by Mendolia and Kleck (1993), participants viewed an emotion-inducing film about power tool accidents, and then talked to the experimenter for two minutes either about their emotional responses to the film, the sequence of events in the film, or the sequence of events in a neutral filler film. Finally, all participants viewed the emotional film for a second time. Physiological data (i.e., skin conductance, heart rate, and skin temperature) indicated that participants who talked about their emotional reactions were more aroused than the control groups when the second viewing occurred immediately after the talk manipulation (although they were less aroused when it occurred 48 hours later, possibly due to habituation). Similar results have been found on measures of physical pain (Ahles, Blanchard, & Leventhal, 1983; Leventhal, Brown, Schaham, & Engquist, 1979). Ahles et al. (1983), for example, asked participants to plunge their hands into a 45 degree cold water bath and either to talk about their sensory experience, to express any affect they were feeling, or to talk about their high school courses. Results indicated that the sensory group reported less pain and distress, and actually showed greater increases in hand temperature (after an initial decrease) than the other two groups (which did not differ). Thus, the type of language that is used to explain an event can direct attention to specific aspects of the situation and have physiological and emotional effects.

Interestingly, some researchers who report that verbalization can impact the nature, extremity, and duration of emotional responses have characterized those responses themselves as configurations of dimensions. Leventhal's perceptual-motor theory (Leventhal, 1984; Leventhal & Everhart, 1979), for example, assumes three levels of emotion processing - sensory, schematic, and conceptual. Although the levels are normally fused in our subjective experience of emotion, verbal labels can influence the schemata with which sensory experiences are integrated. Brown, Enquist, & Leventhal (1977, cited in Leventhal & Everhart, 1979), for example, gave participants whose hands were immersed in ice water information about the sensations they would experience and, for half of the participants only, a warning that the experience would be painful. Those who received the pain warning reported greater distress, in theory because the label facilitated the integration of the sensory experience with a "pain-distress" schema. Similarly, Tesser, Leone, and Clary (1978) asked participants, immediately prior to delivering a public speech, to explain *why* they felt the way did about giving the speech, to describe *how* they felt (i.e., the emotions and physical sensations they were experiencing), or to talk about a non-self related topic. Both physiological measures and self-reports indicated that anxiety during the speech was lowest for those who explained their feelings, and highest for those who described them (c.f., Wilson & Dunn, 1986).

Even more to the current point, there is also research to suggest that people's explanations of *other's* emotional experience will influence their appraisals of events and the emotions they attribute to the actors in them. McGregor and Holmes (1999, Experiment 1), for example, studied the influence of forming a narrative account on memory for an event. Participants were presented with a vignette of an argument between a heteroseuxal couple. The vignette was ambiguous in that there was enough information to blame either character for the argument. After writing brief points about both characters' responsibility for the event, participants were assigned to write an essay arguing in favour of one of the characters. Participants reduced their assigned character's responsibility for the argument and exaggerated the responsibility of the other character, an effect that remained even when participants were tested two weeks later. The authors argue for a "story telling" effect, such that explanation facilitates a particular interpretation of events (cf., Kahneman & Tversky, 1982).

A PRELIMINARY STUDY

Although studies such as those described above demonstrate that people's verbal explanation of emotional events can affect both their own emotional experience and the experience they attribute to others, they are inconclusive regarding the mechanism by which encoding biases occur, and indeed whether they should be characterized as encoding biases at all. From the current perspective, explanation of emotional events "decompose" those events by directing attention to particular, otherwise integrated factors, facilitating the reinterpretation of the events in terms of available emotion concepts. However in few of the cited studies was the specific content of participants' explanations manipulated, and it is therefore difficult to assess the degree to which interpretations of the events were consistent with their explanation.

Therefore, as an initial test of the explanation effect on the encoding of social interactions we conducted a new study in which participants explained and made emotion attributions about an ambiguous emotional interaction, a short scene from the movie *The Accused*. In this scene, a provocatively dressed woman enters a bar and flirts with one man in particular. The two characters dance before the man starts making sexual advances. She protests but is eventually raped by this man and others. (Participants were only shown the sequence of events leading up to the rape and were not shown the rape itself.) Before viewing the scene, (or, in a second experiment, after) some participants were asked to explain why the female character they were about to see was feeling several specified positive emotions (e.g., strong; confident). Other participants were asked to explain why she was feeling negative (e.g., scared; sad). A control group was asked to focus on the sequence of events in the video. After viewing the interaction all participants judged the woman's emotional state, as well as their own mood, on the 20-item Positive and Negative Affect Schedule (PANAS; Watson, Tellegan & Clark, 1988). After making these attributions, participants' memory for the scene was assessed on a 20-item multi-choice test.

Next, participants were told that, following the scene they had just seen, the male and female characters had had sex, and participants were asked to assess how much the female character, the male character and the situation were responsible for this outcome. Finally, participants were informed that the male character had been subsequently convicted of rape and were asked what his sentence, if any, should be. The primary prediction was that negative explanations of the target scene would produce more negative emotion attributions of the female character than would positive explanations or factual accounts. Second we expected differential attributions to be associated with differential assignment of responsibility and blame for the interaction, with participants who explained negative emotions ascribing more responsibility for the interaction to the male character and longer sentences for rape.

The results indicated that although all participants thought the female character felt relatively negative (i.e., compared to the male character), their explanations influenced just how negative (see Figure 2). Planned contrasts conducted on men's and women's data separately indicated that, as hypothesised, women who explained *why* the female character felt negative judged her to *be* more negative, compared to women who explained either positive or no emotion. Unexpectedly, however, explanation had no effect on men's attributions, who judged her to express neutral emotion regardless of experimental condition. Interestingly, for particpants who explained the character's emotions *after* seeing the video, neither contrast reached significance. Explanation condition also influenced the accuracy of women's (but not men's) recall of the events they witnessed, with those explaining negative emotions recalling less than the fact group (and nonsignificantly less than the positive emotion group). Again, there was no effect on memory when explanation occurred after viewing the scene, nor any main effect of timing of explanation. Female participants' own mood was influenced by their explanations as well, such that those who gave positive explanations reported the greatest decrease in mood, followed by the negative explanation and then the fact group. Unexpectedly, no effects emerged on the responsibility or blame measures, and rather surprisingly, all participants strongly endorsed the female character's responsibilty for the situation and blamed her significantly more than either the male character or the situation.

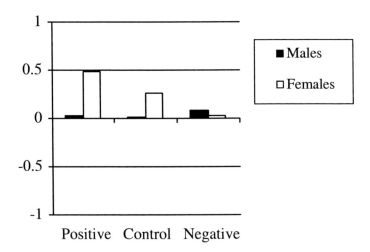

Figure 2. Male and female participants' ratings of the target character's mood as a function of explanation condition. Higher scores indicate more positive mood attribution.

Thus this study, while obviously limited, provides some initial support for the proposed effects of explanation on attribution in emotion-laden social interactions. At least for women, participants' emotion attributions and memory for the facts of the target events were both influenced by how they explained the main character's emotional behavior. In particular, women who explained why the character was feeling negative emotion attributed to her more negative emotion than women who explained why she was feeling positive, or women who recounted the facts of the events they witnessed. Furthermore, the fact that the same bias did not appear when explanation occurred *after* viewing the emotional scene is consistent with an encoding rather than a retrieval effect.

Although not of primary interest in the study, it is also notable that explanations of others' emotions had implications for women's *own* emotional state in a nonobvious way. Women who talked about how positive the female character was feeling actually felt worse than the other two groups as a result. One very plausible (though admittedly speculative) reason lies in the presumed discrepancy between participants' initial impressions of the target situation and how they were asked to explain it. Though intended as an ambiguous situation, if participants were distressed by the beginnings of the sexual assault (as suggested by the fact that participants felt worse after watching it, regardless of condition) the process of explaining the positive aspects of it would have created cognitive dissonance (Festinger, 1957). That is, the positive explanation may have effectively served as a counterattitudinal statement, with predictable effects on participants' own affective state.

LIMITATIONS

Despite their superficial similarity to Halberstadt and Niedenthal's (2001; Halberstadt, 2005) findings in the domain of face perception, it is too early to attribute them to configural decomposition and reintegration at encoding. This is because, first, at this point in time configural processing of social situations remains an untested assumption. Fortunately some indices of object configurality exist that could be used to assess the perception of social interactions. Tanaka and Farah (1993), for example, reported that facial features are easier to recognize in the context of a face than in isolation. They argued that this context advantage can serve as a quantitative measure of configurality because it indicates that features are not represented as independent parts in memory (c.f. Bower & Glass, 1976; Palmer, 1977). An analogous difference between memory for particular aspects of social situations in isolation and in context could similarly provide insight into the extent and moderators of configural processing in these situations. Such research is currently underway in our laboratory.

The memory test in the current study, in fact, provides half of Tanaka and Farah's (1993) measure of configurality, in that participants were asked essentially to remember particular facts in isolation from the social context in which they occurred. Indeed both emotion explanation groups recalled fewer facts under these conditions than the control group, although whether their performance would benefit from reinstatement of the context is unknown. Additional research is also needed to determine whether explanation affects the perception or the interpretation of a scene. Unlike in the previous experiments by Halberstadt and colleagues, emotion attribution, not perceptual memory *per se*, was the dependent variable in this study. The configural decomposition account would predict, however, that participants' recall of the female character's emotional behavior, including her emotional expressions, would be biased in the direction of their explanation.

One unexpected finding in the study was the fact that effects of explanation were limited to female participants. It is not clear whether these data represent a genuine sex difference in participants' vulnerability to explanation biases, or merely half of a gender-congruence effect, such that both men and women are more vulnerable to explanations of same-sex targets. Melcher and Schooler's (1995) work on verbal expertise argues for the former (see also Ryan & Schoolcr, 1998). As noted, the researchers found verbal overshadowing of wine memory only for participants with moderate levels of expertise, arguing that individuals are particularly vulnerable to verbal overshadowing effects if their language abilities are not as developed as their perceptual abilites. It is a frequent finding that women are more empathically accurate than males (Ickes, Gesn & Graham, 2001; Klein & Hodges, 2001), so it is possible that their social perception is more sophisticated than the vocabulary they have to explain it. It is also possible, however, that both women and men are more vulnerable to same-sex emotion attribution because of their greater expertise, attention, motivation, or some other factor associated with gender-congruent judgments. Without additional data from explanations of the male character's emotions, these various explanations cannot be teased apart.

Although explanation influenced women's emotion attributions, it did not affect either their distribution of responsibility for the events or the punishment they meted out to the perpetrator. Recall that the sexual assault itself was omitted from the stimulus materials in an effort to render the situation more ambiguous. Nevertheless it was still surprising to find that, on average, participants assigned significantly more blame to the female character than to the male character or the situation. It is not clear whether the lack of explanation effects reflects a lack of any link between attributions of emotion and attributions of blame, or merely the relative insensitivity of the latter measure. Although a null result would be consistent with literature demonstrating that provocative victims are viewed as responsible for rape (Kanekar & Kolsawalla, 1980; Workman & Freeburg, 1980), a stronger study that, for example, provided more unambiguous evidence of the coercive nature of the interaction, or that increased participants' accountability for their decisions (e.g., Klein & Hodges, 2001) could yet reveal differences on blame and sentencing judgments.

IMPLICATIONS

Despite their limitations our initial data suggest, at a minimum, that verbal explanations can alter attributions about complex social events. Whether due to configural decomposition, priming of emotion schemas at retrieval, reconstructive memory, or some other mechanism, how women explained a target's ambiguous behavior influenced the emotions they believed the target was feeling. The effects, though numerically small, could become more consequential in real social situations, where differential beliefs and behaviors can create self-fulfililng prophecies (Snyder, Tanke, & Berscheid, 1977), particularly when they are believed to be based in perception.

One domain in which explanation effects may be particularly consequential is talk therapy. Talking with others is a natural response following trauma or upheaval (Rime, Mesquita, Philippot, & Boca, 1991; Rime, Philippot, Boca, & Mesquita, 1992; Scherer, Wallbott, & Summerfield, 1986), and many forms of therapy assume that describing and talking about issues is essential for healthful changes to occur (e.g., Beck, 1976). If the current analysis is correct, however, the types of language clients use (or are instructed to use) when describing an event will affect how that event is encoded. In other words, the process of therapeutic (or even informal) introspection is not independent of its content, and two people who use different language to understand the objectively identical social situation may "see" and remember very different events.

In this context it is also noteworthy that verbal explanations had effects on the perceiver's own mood. A goal of spontaneous explanations of emotional events is presumably to feel more positive about those events. Yet our data showed just the opposite effect: participants felt more negative after explaining a target's emotional reactions to an event than when merely describing the facts of the event, especially when they explained positive emotions. We speculated that positive explanations created dissonance because they were inconsistent with participants' spontaneous impressions of the target, who was clearly becoming increasingly distressed. If our effects can be replicated and the presence of dissonance verified with, for example, physiological or misattribution measures of arousal (e.g., Zanna & Cooper, 1974), these data may eventually provide qualifications to cognitive therapeutic efforts to reframe negative events (Beck, 1976). Such reframing may only work when it is close enough to a client's own interpretation (within what Fazio, Zanna, & Cooper (1977) call the "lattitude of acceptance" in the context of attitude change). Otherwise the dissonance the discrepancy causes may produce negative arousal that outweighs affective benefits gained from the reinterpretation of events.

CONCLUSION

Halberstadt (2003) argued that emotion attribution is a "paradox" in that the goal of emotion explanation – to categorize accurately an individual's emotional reaction or state – may be inconsistent with its biasing effects on encoding. Explanations of individuals' ambiguous emotional expressions produce explanation-consistent biases in how the expressions are encoded. Recent theory and data suggest that the bias is related to the configural nature of faces and facial expressions, and if so, it is possible that any configural stimulus will be vulnerable to such biases. We have argued that people typically perceive and process emotional social situations configurally because, among other reasons, emotion attribution is a unitary subjective experience that is not easily separated into its component parts. We reported the results of a preliminary study, modeled after Halberstadt and Niedenthal's (2001) emotion explanation paradigm, in which explanations indeed biased recall for ambiguous emotional events, and unexpectedly the perceivers' own emotional state and memory for the events as well. Whether the results for faces and for social situations are homologous or merely analogous requires further research on the nature and malleability of emotion attribution that more clearly distinguishes effects of encoding, recall, and judgment.

We believe such research is decidedly worth pursuing as a way to understand the interaction of language and attribution – two defining features of human social behavior.

REFERENCES

Ahles, T. A., Blanchard, E. B., & Leventhal, H. (1983). Cognitive control of pain: Attention to the sensory aspects of the cold pressor stimulus. *Cognitive Therapy and Research, 7,* 159-178.

Ambady, N., & Rosenthal, R. (1992). Thin slices of expressive behavior as predictors of interpersonal consequences; A meta-analysis. *Psychological Bulletin, 111,* 256-274.

Ambady, N., & Rosenthal, R. (1993). Half a minute: Predicting teacher evaluations from thin slices of nonverbal behavior and physical attractiveness. *Journal of Personality and Social Psychology, 64,* 431-441.

Asch, S. E. (1946). Forming impressions of personality, *Journal of Abnormal and Social Psychology,* 41, 258-290.

Beck, A. T. (1976). *Cognitive Therapy and the Emotional Disorders.* New York: Meridian.

Bower, G. H., & Glass, A. L. (1976). Structural units and the redintegrative power of picture fragments. *Journal of Experimental Psychology: Human Learning and Memory, 2,* 456-466.

Brown, C., & Lloyd-Jones, T.J. (2002). Verbal overshadowing in a multiple face presentation paradigm: Effects of description instruction. *Applied Cognitive Psychology,* 16, 873-885.

Fallshore, M., & Schooler, J. W. (1995). The verbal vulnerablity of perceptual expertise. *Journal of Experimental Psychology: Learning, Memory, and Cogntiion,* 21, 1608-1623.

Fazio, R. H., Zanna, M. P., & Cooper, J. (1977). Dissonance and self-perception: An integrative view of each theory's proper domain of application.

Festinger, L. (1957). *A theory of cognitive dissonance.* Stanford, CA; Stanford University Press.

Finger, K. (2002). Mazes and music: Using perceptual processing to release verbal overshadowing. *Applied Cognitive Psychology,* 16, 887-896.

Fiske, S. T., & Neuberg, S. L. (1990). A continuum of impression formation, from category-based to individuating processes: Influences of information and motivation on attention and interpretation.In M. P. Zanna (Ed.), *Advances in Experimental Social Psychology* (Vol. 23, pp. 1-74), New York: Academic Press.

Gardner, W.L., Cacioppo, J.T. & Crites, S.L. (1995). *It's your "right" to hold attitudes: Right lateralized brain potentials during evaluative processing.* Paper presented at the Sixty-Seventh Annual Meeting of the Midwestern Psychological Association. Chicago, IL.

Gilbert, D. T., Pelham, B. W., & Krull, D. S. (1988). On cognitive busyness: When person perceivers meet persons perceived. *Journal of Personality and Social Psychology, 54,* 733-739.

Halberstadt, J. B. (1996). Effects of verbalization on configural and featural face recognition. (Doctoral dissertation, University of Indiana, 1996).

Halberstadt, J. B. (2003). The paradox of emotion attribution: Explanation biases perceptual memory for emotional expressions, *Current Directions in Psychological Science,*12, 197-201.

Halberstadt, J. (2005). Featural shift in explanation-biased memory for emotional faces. *Journal of Personality and Social Psychology, 88,* 38-49.

Halberstadt, J. B. & Niedenthal, P. M. (2001). Effects of Emotion Concepts on Perceptual Memory for Emotional Expressions. *Journal of Personality and Social Psychology,* 81, 587-598.

Hastie, R., & Kumar, A. P. (1979). Person memory: Personality traits as organiszing principles in memory for behaviors. *Journal of Personality and Social Psychology,* 37, 25-38.

Hinton, P. R. (1993). *The psychology of interpersonal perception.* London: Routledge.

Houser, T., Fiore, S. M., & Schooler, J. W. (2003). Verbal overshadowing of music memory: What happens when you describe that tune? Unpublished manuscript, University of Pittsburgh.

Ickes, W., Gesn, P. R., & Graham, T. (2000).Gender differences in empathic accuracy: Differential ability or differential motivation? *Personal Relationships,* 7, 95-109.

Kahneman, D., & Tversky, A. (1982). The simulation heuristic. In D. Kahneman, P. Slovic, & A. Tversky (Eds.), Judgment under uncertainty: Heuristics and biases (pp. 201–208). New York: Cambridge Univ. Press.

Kanekar, S., & Kolsawalla, M. B. (1980). Responsibility of a rape victim in relation to her respectability, attractiveness, and provocativeness. *Journal of social psychology,* 112, 153-154.

Kelley, H. H. (1967). Attribution theory in social psychology. *Nebraska symposium on motivation,* 14, 192-241.

Klein, J. K. & Hodges, S. D. (2001). Gender differences, motivation and empathic accuracy; When it pays to understand. *Personality and Social Psychology Bulletin,* 27, 720-730.

Leehey, S. C., Carey, S., Diamond, R., & Cahn, A. (1978). Upright and inverted faces: The right hemisphere knows the difference. *Cortex,* 14, 411-419.

Lewin, K. (1951) *Field Theory in Social Science*; selected theoretical papers. D. Cartwright (ed.). New York: Harper & Brothers.

Leventhal, H. (1984). A perceptual-motor theory of emotion. In L. Berkowitz (Ed.), *Advances in Experimental Social Psychology,* (Vol 17, pp.118-182). Orlando, FL: Academic Press.

Leventhal, H., Brown, D., Schaham, S., & Engquist, C. (1979). Effects of preparatory information about sensations, threat of pain, and attention on cold pressor distress. *Journal of Personality and Social Psychology, 37,* 688-714.

Leventhal, H., & Everhart, D. (1979). Emotion, pain, and physical illness. In C. E.

Macrae, C. N., & Lewis, H. L., (2002). Do I know you? Processing orientation and face recognition. *Psychological Schience,* 13, 194-196.

McGregor, I., & Holmes, J. G. (1999). How storytelling shapes memory and impressions of relationship events over time. *Journal of Personality and Social Psychology,* 68, 403-419.

McKelvie, S. J. (1976). The effects of verbal labelling on recognition memory for schematic faces. *Quarterly Journal of Experimental Psychology,* 28, 459-474.

Melcher, J. M., & Schooler, J. W. (1996). The misremembrance of wines past: Verbal and perceptual expertise differentially mediate verbal overshadowing of taste memory. *Journal of Memory and Language,* 35, 231-245.

Mendolia, M., & Kleck, R.E.,(1993). Effects of talking about a stressful event on arousal: Does what we talk about make a difference? *Journal of Personality and Social Psychology,* 64, 283-292.

Palmer, S. E. (1977). Hierarchical structure in perceptual representation. *Cognitive Psychology,* 9, 441-474.

Rhodes, G., Brake, S., Taylor, K., & Tan, S. (1989). Expertise and configural coding in face recognition. *British Journal of Psychology,* 80, 313-331.

Rime, B. (1994). The social sharing of emotion as a source for the social knowledge of emotion. In J. A. Russell, J. Fernandez-Dols, A.S.R., Manstead & J. C. Wellenkamp (Eds.). Everyday conceptions of emotion (pp. 475 – 495). Boston/London: Kluwer Academic Publishers.

Rime, B., Mesquita, B., Philippot, P., & Boca, S. (1991). Beyond the emotional event: Six studies on the social sharing of emotion. *Cognition and Emotion, 5,* 435-465.

Rime, B., Philippot, P., Boca, S., & Mesquita, B. (1992). Long-lasting consequences of emotion: Social sharing and rumination. In W. Stroebe & M. Hewstone (Eds.), *European Review of Social Psychology,* (Vol. 1, p. 225-258). Chichester: Wiley.

Ryan, R. S., & Schooler, J. W. (1998). Whom do words hurt? Individual differences in susceptibility to verbal overshadowing. *Applied Cognitive Psychology,* 12, S105-S125.

Scherer, K.R. & Tannenbaum, P. H. (1986). Emotional experiences in everyday life: A survey approach. *Motivation and Emotion,* 10,

Scherer, K. R., Wallbott, H. G., & Summerfield, A. B. (Eds.). (1986). *Experiencing Emotion: A Cross-Cultural Study.* Cambridge, England: Cambridge University Press.

Schooler, J. W. (2002). Verbalization produces a transfer-inappropriate processing shift. *Applied Cognitive Psychology,* 16, 989-997.

Schooler, J. W. & Engstler-Schooler, T.Y. (1990). Verbal overshadowing of visual memories: Some things are better left unsaid. *Cognitive Psychology,* 22, 36-71.

Snyder, M., Tanke, E. D., & Berscheid, E. (1977). Social perception and interpersonal behavior: On the self-fulfilling nature of social stereotypes. *Journal of Personality and Social Psychology,* 9, 656-666.

Springer, S. P., & Deutsch, G. (1993). *Left brain, right brain.* New York: W.H. Freeman & Co.

Stevens, M., & Halberstadt, J. (2004). Unpublished data, University of Otago

Tanaka, J. W., & Farah, M. J. (1993). Parts and wholes in face recognition. *The Quarterly Journal of Experimental Psychology, 46A,* 225-245.

Tesser, A., Leone, C., & Clary, E. G. (1978). Affect control: Process constraints versus catharsis. *Cognitive Therapy and Research, 2,* 265-274.

Valentine, T. (1988). Upside-down faces: A review of the effect of inversion upon face recognition, *British Journal of Psychology,* 79, 471-491.

Watson D., Clarke, L. A., & Tellegen, A. (1998). Development and validation of brief measures of positive and negative affect: The PANAS scales. *Journal of Peronality and Social Psychology,* 54, 1063-1070.

Wilson, T. D. & Dunn, D. S. (1986). Effects of introspection on attitude-behavior consistency: Analyzing reasons versus focusing on feelings. *Journal of Experimental Social Psychology, 22,* 249-263.

Winter, L., & Uleman, J. S. (1984). When are social judgments made? Evidence for the spontaneousness of trait inferences. *Journal of Personality and Social Psychology, 47,* 237-252

Workman, J. E. & Freeburg, E. W. (1999). An examination of date rape, victim dress, and perceiver variables within the context of attribution theory. *Sex Roles,* 41(3-4), 261-277.

Young, A. W., Hellawell, D., & Hay, D. C. (1987). Configurational information in face perception. *Perception,* 16, 747-759.

Zanna, M. P., & Cooper, J. (1974). Dissonance and the pill: An attribution approach to studying the arousal properties of dissonance. *Journal of Personality and Social Psychology,* 29, 703-709.

In: Focus on Nonverbal Communication Research
Editor: Finley R. Lewis, pp. 215-236

ISBN 1-59454-790-4
© 2007 Nova Science Publishers, Inc.

Chapter 10

EVALUATION OF OLANZAPINE EFFECTS ON ATTENTION AND EMOTIONAL RECOGNITION PROCESSES THROUGH EVENT RELATED POTENTIALS IN TREATMENT REFRACTORY SCHIZOPHRENICS

[1]Julieta Ramos-Loyo,[*] [2]Luis F. Cerdán and [1]Miguel Angel Guevara
[1]Instituto de Neurociencias, Universidad de Guadalajara, México
[2]Centro Comunitario de Salud Mental No. 1. Instituto Mexicano del Seguro Social, Guadalajara, México

ABSTRACT

Schizophrenics present attentional and emotional disorders. In particular, treatment of refractory schizophrenics (TRS) have shown larger deficits in logical-verbal memory and associative learning as well as in emotional recognition than in good responders. Some evidences point out that olanzapine (OLZ), an atypical neuroleptic, may induce an improvement of attention, memory and depressive symptoms, as well as on the interpretation of positive prosodic affective stimuli. Thus, the main purpose of this study was to determine if OLZ can improve the ability to recognize facial emotional expressions in TRS, regarding differences in performance and in the ERPs amplitude, using an "odd-ball" paradigm. Another objective was to determine the relationship between psychopathology and task performance and P3 amplitude before and after OLZ treatment.

14 TRS and 14 control subjects (CON) participated in the study. Patients were evaluated before (PRE-T) and after 8 weeks of OLZ treatment (POS-T). N2 and P3 were recorded during two "odd-ball" paradigm tasks, a typical attention task and a facial emotional recognition tasks with happiness as the target stimuli. N2 and P3 amplitude, as

---

[*] *Please send correspondence to:* Dra. Julieta Ramos-Loyo. Instituto de Neurociencias, Universidad de Guadalajara, Francisco de Quevedo 180, Col. Arcos Vallarta, Guadalajara, Jal. México. C.P. 44130; Tel-Fax. (05233) 36 47 77 76, Email: jramos@cencar.udg.mx

well as the performance measures were evaluated. Finally, correlations between psychopathology and task performance as well as P3 amplitude were performed.

OLZ did not induce changes in performance nor in ERPs amplitude. However, there were differences between TRS and CON, both on the attention and on the emotional task. TRS showed a lower number of correct responses and higher omissions, as well as a longer reaction time than CON. In addition, N2 and P3 amplitudes were lower in CON than in TRS. There was a correlation between performance and P3 amplitude of both tasks and symptoms related to thought disorders and poor rapport. In the POS-T there was also a correlation of performance with tension and depression in the emotional task. P3 amplitude negatively correlated with anxiety in the attention task and positive (excitement and hostility) and negative (emotional withdrawal) symptoms in the emotional recognition task in the POS-T.

Present results support other findings of attention and emotional disorders in schizophrenics. OLZ did not have a global effect on the performance of the attention nor on the emotional tasks, but there were changes in significant correlations between psychopathology, performance and P3 amplitude after OLZ. Event-related potentials are useful to evaluate deficits in attentional and emotional recognition processes, as well as the effects of neuroleptics in psychiatric populations.

Key words: refractory-schizophrenia, P300, olanzapine, event related potentials, emotional recognition, attention.

INTRODUCTION

Schizophrenia is a chronic illness that effects about 1% of the total population and impairs the person's ability to function cognitively and emotionally in a social environment. In spite of the complexity and diversity of the symptoms, a general classification of positive and negative ones has been made. Among the positive symptoms are: disorders of perception (hallucinations) and in inferential thinking (delusions), disorganized speech and bizarre behavior; meanwhile negative symptoms include: difficulty in logical thinking (alogia), affective blunting, incapacity to feel pleasure (anhedonia) and problems in goal-directed behavior (avolition). More recently, renewed interest in the evaluation of cognitive and emotional symptoms in these patients has been developed. The most consistent deficits in cognitive processes that are reported in schizophrenia are: attention, memory, executive functions, thinking and language.

Especially, the evaluation of specific emotional disorders in schizophrenia represents an important issue because patients' quality of life is related to their ability to establish personal relationships and becoming adapted to their social environment [1].

One can conceive emotional processing as composed by three main subprocesses. In the first place, the recognition of another's emotional expressions, a second aspect is the way in which each person experiences an emotion, both as mood states and as a response to external stimulation and finally, the ability to transmit his own feelings.

Difficulties in the decodification of facial emotional expressions have been reported in schizophrenics as well as failure in their verbal description [2,3,4,5,6].

These difficulties are independent of the sensory modalities since similar deficits are present in emotional prosody. Furthermore, schizophrenics incur social judgment errors because they can´t assign the meaning of expressed emotions in a contextual social situation properly [7,8,9].

Mood and socioemotional disorders are also common in this pathology. Schizophrenics suffer depression, anxiety, tension, hostility, blunted affect, poor rapport, apathetic social withdrawal, guilt feelings and poor impulse control.

Regarding to emotional expression, a reduction in facial expressions of emotion, particularly in joy, has been reported in schizophrenics [10,11].

Moreover, a disassociation of these three aspects of emotional processing, recognition, experience and expression has been proposed [10,12]. There seems to be a lack of congruence between the emotion expressed by other people and the emotion the patient experiences as a response or, between what he feels in relation to what he expresses. This may imply a discoordination of the different neural systems related to emotional processing in schizophrenia. Temporal and frontal lobes, as well as amigdala and anterior cingulate are the main cerebral areas related to emotional disorders in schizophrenia.

The study of emotional disorders in schizophrenics has been done mainly by means of psychopathological scales, some neuropsychological tests and mood states inventories. However, few studies have been conducted with electrophysiology techniques.

In this regard, spontaneous (EEG) and event-related (ERPs) brain electrical activity recording has been a very useful tool for studying brain functioning during cognitive processes in humans. A group of ERPs components have been described to be associated with selective attention (N100, P200, N200 and P300) [13]. Specifically, P300 has been postulated to be involved in new information processing when attention is engaged in updating memory representations [14]. ERPs have the advantage of making it possible to study fast changes in brain functioning temporally coupled with specific stimuli in cognitive tasks.

P300 amplitude has been found to be reduced during selective attention tasks both in auditory and visual modalities [15,16,17]. There exists substantial evidence that these abnormalities are very strong since they are consistently present in schizophrenics [18,19,20], in first grade patients' relatives [21], as well as in children with a high risk of developing schizophrenia [22]. In addition, the P300 amplitude is present before the administration of any pharmachological treatment [23,24] and has been correlated with illness severity [17,25,26,27,28] and with structural superior temporal lobe abnormalities [29].

In regard to emotional recognition, amplitude changes on a positive component of about 450 ms have been found depending on the emotion a normal subject must respond to. Higher amplitude of this component has been found in happiness expressions rather than in neutral ones [30,31,32]. In this respect, Kayser et al. [33] conducted a study of depressed patients in which they found a deficit in late stages of affective evaluation involving dysfunctions of right parietal cortex.

Difficulties in facial emotional recognition could be augmented by typical neuroleptic medication since in a previous study, we found a negative correlation between the P300 amplitude and positive symptoms scores using an "odd-ball" paradigm, only for patients who showed a good response to that kind of medication [34]. In this study, we also found a greater deficit in treatment refractory schizophrenics (TRS) than in non-refractory ones. Schneider et al. [35] have also reported that typical neuroleptics reduce the ability of the patient to express facial emotions and the smiling frequency.

TRS patients manifest positive and negative symptoms in a persistent way and they constitute around 30% of the schizophrenic population [36]. In addition to higher deficits in emotional recognition, TRS have shown smaller efficiency in logic-verbal memory and associative learning tasks [37]. In addition, a different pattern of brain electrical activity (EEG) at rest was observed in these patients in relation to those who did respond to typical medication [38].

Recent growing studies have documented that atypical neuroleptics have been of great relevance in the treatment of TRS, markedly improving, not only positive but also the more resistant negative symptoms of schizophrenia. There also exist some reports pointing out that atypical neuroleptics could improve cognitive functions [39,40] and that risperidone induced an improvement in the performance of an emotional perception task in refractory schizophrenics [41].

Olanzapine (OLZ), one of these atypical neuroleptics, presents the advantages of other atypical neuroleptics as having a greater efficacy spectrum on TRS and less extrapyramidal effects than typical drugs. In addition, it does not cause agranulocytosis as clozapine does. Furthermore, OLZ may improve negative symptoms, attention [39], memory [42,43] and depression [44], although it had no effect on facial expression of emotions [45]. OLZ have also shown its capacity to modify brain electrical activity [46] and to increase auditory P300 amplitude [47].

There is a study of Gallinat et al. [48] conducted in TRS, measuring effects of clozapine and olanzapine in auditory P300 amplitude. No significant differences were found in P300 amplitudes in RT after treatment nor with those antipsychotics. However, changes in P300 amplitude were influenced significantly by changes in positive but not in negative symptoms scores.

Given the importance that a good emotional recognition has in the social adaptation of schizophrenics, its study acquires relevance, as well as the possible effects of pharmachological treatments on emotional processes.

Based on the above mentioned findings, the main purpose of this work was to identify the possible effects of OLZ in TRS' abilities to recognize facial emotions evaluated by means of performance and N2 and P3 amplitudes. Another objective was to examine the possible relationships between attentional and affective disorders measured by clinical scales and the performance and P3 amplitude measures in an attention and an emotional recognition tasks. In order to do this, we evaluated single symptoms scores before and after OLZ treatment instead of global scores for positive and negative symptoms.

METHOD

Subjects

Fourteen male treatment refractory schizophrenics (TRS) were recruited from the outpatient consult of Guadalajara Mental Health Center of the Mexican Social Security Institute. All of them were evaluated by two experienced psychiatrists and diagnosed as paranoid schizophrenics after considering their medical history information, the international criteria of DSM-IV [49] and the International Classification of Mental Diseases [50]. Keefe et al. [51] and Brenner and Merlo [36] criteria for resistant schizophrenia were used to classify the patients as TRS. These include: a) absence of improvement after 6 weeks of treatment; b) a requirement of 40 mg doses of haloperidol or more over 24 hrs; c) Brief Psychiatric Scale (BPRS) changes less than 20% and; d) minimum Clinical Global Impression of two points. The duration of TRS was between 1 and 10 years, a period during which all patients failed to respond to different typical neuroleptics.

Each item of the Positive and Negative Syndromes Scale and General Psychopathology (PANSS, [52]) were evaluated on the pre- and the post-treatment sessions.

In addition to the TRS, a control group was evaluated. All of the subjects were right-handed males and both groups were paired in terms of age (18 – 45 years old) and educational level (at least 9 years). Subjects with neurological diseases or drug abuse were not included in the sample, as well as controls with psychiatric illness antecedents. All subjects gave informed consent to participate in the study after the procedures were fully explained to them. Sample characteristics as well as EEG changes after OLZ treatment in the patients that participated in the present study were reported elsewhere [46].

Procedure

TRS patients were clinically and electrophysiologically evaluated in two sessions: the pre-treatment (PRE-T) under typical neuroleptics and in the post-treatment (POS-T) after 8 weeks of OLZ intake. A group of paired control subjects (CON) was also evaluated in two sessions with 8 weeks in between, without taking medication.

Pharmacotherapy

In the PRE-T, all the patients were medicated with typical neuroleptics (haloperidol, trifluoperazine and fluphenazine decanoate and biperiden as an antiparkinsonic drug). The mean typical neuroleptic dosis was $1,030 \pm 120$ mg chlorpromazine equivalents.

There was a wash out period of typical neuroleptics of one week without any medication. Thereafter, in the first 4 weeks of OLZ the doses were 10 mg/day and in the last 4 weeks, it was increased to 20 mg/day.

Tasks

Two types of tasks were presented to the subjects on a 15 inch computer monitor by means of a specific purpose program [53], in order to evaluate attention and facial emotional recognition in the PRE-T and POS-T. Task designs can be appreciated in Figure 1.

Attention Task

In a visual selective attention task ("odd-ball" XX paradigm) the subject was asked to press a computer key each time the letter "X" only after another "X" (target; probability 20%) appeared on the screen within a series of other nontarget letters (probability 80%). A randomized sequence was made with 450 stimuli. Each stimulus appeared during 100 ms with an interstimuli interval of 1650- 2025 mseg. Subjects were asked to detect the targets as quickly and accurately as possible by pressing a computer key. Subjects were properly trained prior to the beginning of the task.

Tasks Design

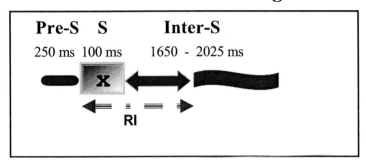

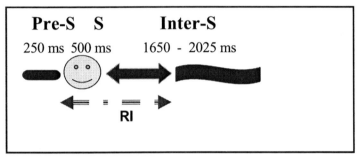

CPT- *XX* Paradigm

Number of stimuli: 450

Target/non-target rate: 20/80

Randomized Presentation

Total duration: 13 –16.5 min

Instructions: speed and accuracy.

S = stimulus
RI = response interval

Figure 1. Tasks design.

Recognition of Facial Emotions

Facial emotional expressions from Ekman and Friesen [1975] were used. Black and white photographs of 10 models (5 men and 5 women) expressing happiness, anger, fear, surprise, disgust, sadness, and a neutral expression were all used. Subjects had to press a keyboard when the expression of happiness (target, 20%) appeared on the screen, whoever expressed it, only in the case that another happiness expression appeared before. Each sequence consisted on 450 photographs that were presented during 500 mseg and the random intertrial interval was between 1250 to 1500 mseg.

The tasks' presentation order was randomized among subjects and each one lasted between 13 and 16.5 min. Performance was evaluated by the number of correct responses and omissions as well as the reaction time (RT).

ERPs Recordings

ERPs recordings in the PRE-T and POS-T sessions took place between 16.30 and 18.30 hrs. Electroencephalographic signals (EEG) were recorded at F3, F4, C3, C4, P3, P4 derivations using linked earlobes as reference according to the International 10/20 System on a 8 Plus Grass polygraph (cutt-off filters 1-35 Hz). Electrodes impedances were kept below 10 Kohms. EEG signals were captured by a PC computer through an analog to digital converter with a sample rate of 256 Hz [54]. Electro-oculogram was also bipolarly recorded to detect eye movement artifacts. A means of 30 artifact-free epochs were selected after visual inspection.

Individual ERPs were obtained during task performance by averaging EEG artifact-free epochs (1375 ms with an additional 250 ms pre-stimulus period). These epochs corresponded only to correct responses and they were equal for both groups (CON and TRS). ERPs baseline was corrected in relation to pre-stimulus EEG prior to the statistical analysis. A window of 600 ms was selected to obtain ERPs.

Due to individual amplitudes of specific ERP components are difficult to define, particularly in clinical populations such as schizophrenics. A Principal Component Analysis (PCA) was performed with individual ERP independently for each task, in order to generate factor loadings which more efficiently describe variance contributions of temporally and spatially overlapping ERP components than conventional ERP components measures do [55]. The temporal sequence of the waveforms obtained in each component offers an advantage of intuitive functional interpretability, since successive time intervals may correspond to the successive stages of information processing [56]. Each component (eigenvector) is formed by combining variables (samples) that are highly interconnected, but relatively uncorrelated with the variables that are included in other components [57]. This method allows isolating independent groups of correlated variables (eigenvectors) that capture most of the information in the original variables. In this work, PCA was performed on a correlation matrix, with orthogonal rotation (Varimax, which keeps the components uncorrelated). The following criteria were used: eigenvectors with eigenvalues (proportional variance that each eigenvector explains of the total variance) that explained 10% or more were considered.

Afterwards, the amplitudes of the major peaks occurring within the defined latency ranges were identified for each individual ERP and these data were considered for statistical analysis.

Statistical Analysis

Differences in psychopathological symptoms between the PRE-T and POS-T sessions were evaluated by means of Wilcoxon Test. Behavioral measures were submitted to an analysis of variance (ANOVAs) for mixed designs. Differences between groups in behavioral measures (reaction time, number of correct responses and omissions) were analyzed using two way ANOVAs (groups: CON and TRS by sessions: PRE-T/POST-T).

Groups and PRE-T/POS-T differences in the resulting PCA component scores were evaluated by T-tests for each principal component that corresponded to N2 and P3 ERP components. Significant level was set at $p < .05$.

Finally, in order to explore the possible relationships between psychopathological symptoms, particularly those related to cognitive and emotional disorders, and performance (RT and number of correct responses) and P3 values a Pearson correlation analyses were performed.

RESULTS

Pychopathology

Positive, negative, as well as general psychopathological symptoms showed a significant reduction (Table 1). The positive symptoms that showed a significant reduction were delusions, hallucinatory behavior excitement and hostility. Blunted affect and poor rapport and apathetic social withdrawal were the negative symptoms that manifested a higher reduction.

Table 1. Significant differences before and after olanzapine treatment in positive, negative and psychopathological symptoms (PANSS) in treatment refractory schizophrenics

Positive Symptoms

Item	p
P1. Delusions	0.01
P2. Conceptual disorganization	0.02
P3. Hallucinatory behavior	0.008
P4. Excitement	0.01
P5. Grandiosity	0.04
P6. Suspiciousness/persecution	0.02
P7. Hostility	0.01

Negative Symptoms

Item	p
N1. Blunted affect	0.008
N2. Emotional withdrawal	0.01
N3. Poor rapport	0.008
N4. Passive/apathetic social withdrawal	0.01
N5. Difficulty in abstract thinking	0.01
N6. Lack of spontaneity and flow of conversation	0.01
N7. Stereotyped thinking	0.01

General Psychopathology

Item	p
G1. Somatic concern	0.01
G2. Anxiety	0.01
G3. Guilt feelings	Ns
G4.Tension	0.008
G5. Mannerism and posturing	Ns
G6. Depression	0.008
G7. Motor retardation	Ns
G8. Uncooperativeness	Ns
G9. Unusual thought content	0.008
G10. Disorientation	Ns
G11. Poor attention	Ns
G12. Lack of judgement and insight	0.04
G13. Disturbance of volition	0.01
G14. Poor impulse control	0.008
G15. Preoccupation	0.01
G16. Active social avoidance	0.01

PANSS general symptoms that showed a higher reduction were tension, depression, unusual thought content and poor impulse control.

Task Performance

Both on the attention and the emotional tasks, TRS showed a lower number of correct responses ($F_{(1,15)}= 6.74$, p=0.01, and ($F_{(1,15)}= 4.25$, p=0.05, respectively) and higher of omissions ($F_{(1,15)}= 6.04$, p=0.02, and ($F_{(1,15)}= 4.25$, p=0.05, respectively) than CON. In addition, significant differences in reaction time (RT) were found between groups in the attention task ($F_{(1,15)}= 5.36$, p=0.03) and in groups by sessions interaction in the emotional task ($F_{(1,15)}= 6.38$, p=0.02) with TRS showing a longer RT than CON. However, there were no significant differences between PRE-T and POST-T. (See Figure 2).

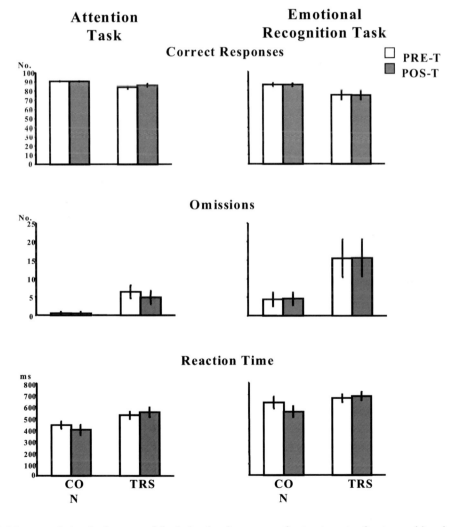

Figure 2. Means and standard errors of the behavioral measures for treatment refractory schizophrenics (TRS) and control (CON) groups in the pre (PRE-T) and the post-treatment sessions (POS-T) for both tasks.

ERPs

Only 10 TRS were considered for ERP analysis because of technical problems with their signals. Grand average ERP waveforms showed a typical N2 and P3 peaks reported in odd-ball paradigms as can be seen in Figures 3 and 4 with the main voltage deflections in parietal derivations. Resulting waveforms from PCA are represented in Figure 5, arranged according to their temporal sequence and their polarity adjusted according to the corresponding original ERPs. In the attention task, the first 4 components account for the 80% of the total variance; according to their latency and waveform the first component may correspond to the P3, the second to the N2, the third to the late positive (LP) and the fourth to the N1.

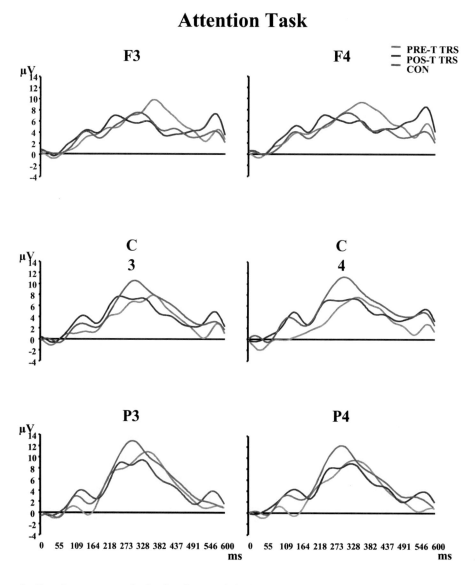

Figure 3. Grand average evoked related potentials (ERPs) in frontal (F3, F4), central (C3, C4) and parietal (P3, P4) areas for the control (CON) group in the initial session and in the pre- (PRE-T) and the post-treatment sessions (POS-T) for the treatment refractory schizophrenics (TRS) in the attention task.

Emotional Recognition Task

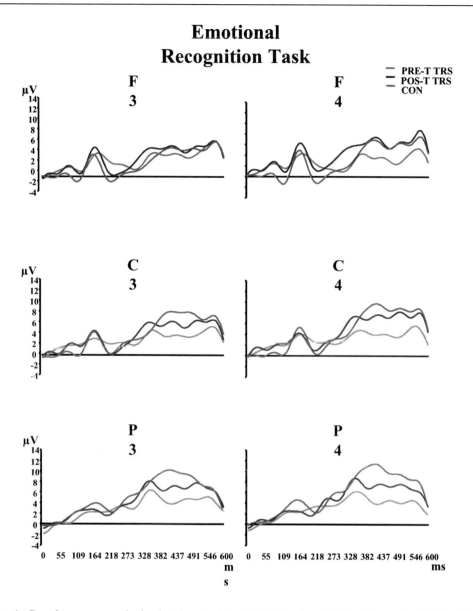

Figure 4. Grand average evoked related potentials (ERPs) in frontal (F3, F4), central (C3, C4) and parietal (P3, P4) areas for the control (CON) group in the initial session and in the pre- (PRE-T) and the post-treatment sessions (POS-T) for the treatment refractory schizophrenics (TRS) in the emotional recognition task.

The PCA components obtained in this study closely corresponded to those found in other works [55,33]. The latency of the N1 peak was at 54 ms, for the N2 at 214 ms, and for the P3 at 355 ms and the LP in 546 ms in the attention task. In the emotional recognition task, the latencies were for N1, 54 ms, for P2, 191 ms, for N2, 296 ms and for the P3, 515 ms.

There were no significant results between PRE-T and POS-T with OLZ neither on N2 nor on P3 latencies or amplitudes. However, significant differences between groups were found in amplitude values. P3 amplitude was higher in CON than in TRS in the right hemisphere in both attention (t = 1.027, p < .01) and emotional recognition tasks (t = 1.66, p< .05). In a similar way, N2 amplitude was also higher in CON than in TRS in the left hemisphere in parietal areas (t = .991, p < .01) and in the right hemisphere in central ones (t = 1.94, p< .03).

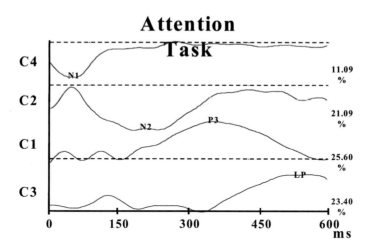

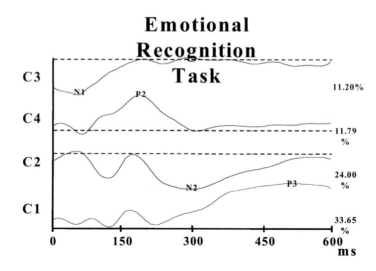

Figure 5. Principal Components extracted from individual ERPs of schizophrenics and controls, arranged according to their temporal sequence and their polarity adjusted in relation to the correspondent original N1, N2, P3 and late positivity (LP) in the attention task and N1, P2, N2 and P3 in the emotional recognition task.

Correlation between Psychopathology and Task Performance

In general terms, a higher level of symptomatology was correlated with a longer reaction time (RT) and a lower number of correct responses in both tasks.

Attention Task

A longer RT showed a significant correlation with poor rapport, poor attention and disturbance of volition; and a lower number of correct responses showed negative correlations with difficulty in abstract thinking and disturbance of volition in the PRE-T session. In the POS-T, a correlation between a longer RT and delusions, conceptual disorganization, blunted affect, tension and poor impulse control was observed. Whereas, lower number of correct responses was negatively correlated with disturbance of volition (see Table 2).

Emotional Recognition Task

A significant positive correlation was obtained between RT, poor rapport and poor attention and a negative one between the number of correct responses and suspiciousness, poor rapport and stereotyped thinking in the PRE-T session. Meanwhile, in the POS-T a longer RT positively correlated with delusions, conceptual disorganization, poor rapport and stereotyped thinking was observed. In addition, a lower number of correct responses negatively correlated with conceptual disorganization, difficulty in abstract thinking, lack of spontaneity and flow of conversation, stereotyped thinking, depression, and disturbance of volition.

Table 2. Significant correlation values between performance measures (RT: reaction time and CR: number of correct responses) of both tasks with positive, negative and general psychopathological symptoms scores before (PRE-T) and after (POS-T) olanzapine in treatment refractory schizophrenics.

	Attention Task				Emotional Task			
	PRE-T		POS-T		PRE-T		POS-T	
	RT	CR	RT	CR	RT	CR	RT	CR
P1			0.61				0.66	
P2			0.64				0.72	-0.71
P6						-0.68		
N5		-0.71						-0.81
N6								-0.68
N7							0.64	-0.65
PG11	0.71				0.82			
PG12	0.62							
PG13		-0.60		-0.62				-0.72
PG14			0.68					
N1			0.61					
N3	0.62				0.60	-0.69	0.68	
PG4			0.63					
PG6								-0.65

P1 = delusions, P2 = conceptual disorganization, P6 = suspiciousness/persecution; N1 = blunted affect, N3 = poor rapport, N5 = difficulty in abstract thinking, N6 = lack of spontaneity and flow of conversation, N7 = stereotyped thinking; PG4 = tension, PG6 = depression, PG11 =poor attention, PG12= lack of judgment and insight, PG13= disturbance of volition, PG14= poor impulse control.

Table 3. Significant correlation values between P3 amplitude with positive, negative and general psychopathological symptoms scores before (PRE-T) and after (POS-T) olanzapine in treatment refractory schizophrenics in both tasks.

	Attention Task				Emotional Task			
	PRE-T		POS -T		PRE-T		POS-T	
	P3	P4	P3	P4	P3	P4	P3	P4
P3								0.61
P4					-0.63	-0.54		
P7					-0.77	-0.67		
N2					-0.60	-0.66		
N3	-0.71							
N5	-0.70	-0.73						
N6	-0.91	-0.88						
N7	-0.77							
PG2			0.66	0.63				
PG16	-0.64							

P3 = hallucinations, P4 = excitement, P7 = hostility; N2 = emotional withdrawal, N3 = poor rapport, N5 = difficulty in abstract thinking, N6 = lack of spontaneity and flow of conversation, N7 = stereotyped thinking; PG2 = anxiety, PG16 = active social avoidance.

Correlation between Psychopathology and P3 Amplitude

Attention Task.

A significant inverse correlation between P3 amplitude and negative symptoms (poor rapport, difficulty in abstract thinking, lack of spontaneity and flow of conversation and stereotyped thinking) was found in the PRE-T; meanwhile in the POS-T higher levels of anxiety was correlated with higher P3 amplitude. (See Table 3).

Emotional Recognition Task.

Higher levels of P3 amplitude were correlated with lower level of excitement, hostility and emotional withdrawal before OLZ. On the contrary, higher levels of hallucinations were associated to higher P3 amplitude in the PRE-T session.

CONCLUSION

As it was expected, significant differences were found between schizophrenics and control subjects in performance and in ERPs amplitude of both tasks. However, no significant differences were observed after olanzapine treatment with respect to the pre-treatment evaluation in these parameters. OLZ did reduce positive, negative and general symptoms. Furthermore, there was a correlation between the level of symptomatology and performance (RT and the number of correct responses) in both tasks in the pre- and the post-treatment conditions, as well as symptomatology and P3 amplitude.

Attentional deficits have been considered a hallmark in schizophrenia. In the present study this was supported by a poorer performance in schizophrenics and a reduction of N2 and P3-like amplitude components. Behavioral results showed that TRS not only had more omissions and fewer correct responses, but they also performed the task slower than controls.

Additionally, a strong relationship between poor performance and items that reflect impairment of thinking processes could be observed in both tasks in the PRE-T. Correlations between these variables included poor attention, disturbance of volition, difficulty in abstract thinking, conceptual disorganization and stereotyped thinking. These cognitive symptoms are related to attention, working memory and executive functions that greatly depend on prefrontal function that are known to be impaired in schizophrenia as core components and not secondary to medication side effects, positive or negative symptoms [58]. Regarding disorganization, severity has been found negatively correlated with ventrolateral prefrontal cortex and parietal association cortex activity, and positively correlated with rCBF in anterior cingulate and thalamus [59]. Yang et al. [60] found that thought disorganization is associated with abnormally low prefrontal dopamine levels.

Other authors have also reported that attention deficits are associated with thought disorders and negative symptoms in schizophrenics [61,62,63,64].

Another item that consistently showed a correlation with poor performance in TRS was poor rapport both in the PRE-T and the POS-T. Poor rapport involves the ability to put oneself in another person's place in order to understand his thoughts and feelings. Underlying this symptom are disorders in working memory, attention, emotional decoding and emotional experience and the inability of representing the external and internal reality in an integral form. In this sense, Sarfati et al. [65] observed that only those schizophrenics with thought and speech disorganization had specific difficulties attributing mental states to others.

Difficulties in facial emotional recognition have also been reported in other studies in schizophrenics [2,3,4,5,6]. Sachs et al. [66] besides finding a worse performance in schizophrenics than in controls on emotional recognition tasks, they reported that these deficits were associated with the severity of negative symptoms and cognition deficits.

The lower performance of TRS may imply that they have poorer neural resources to engage in an attention task, with a less competent executive system in comparison to the control group. This can be reflected in the N2-P3 amplitude.

P3 showed lower amplitude in TRS than in CON, particularly in right parietal derivations. These results are in agreement with those reported by Kayser et al. [33]. They found differences in these regions in normal subjects between neutral and negative emotional stimuli as well as between controls and depressive patients. They support the idea that the late positivity (P3), particularly in right parietal regions, in paradigms where the subject does not have to do a cognitive task, reflects processing of affective stimulus significance. P300 has been postulated to be involved in new information processing when attention is engaged to update memory representations [14]. The reduction of P300 amplitude has been widely reported in literature [15,16,18,19,20], even before any treatment with neuroleptics [23,24].

Nieman et al. [67] reported that P300 amplitude was smaller and latency longer in schizophrenics than in controls and that P300 amplitude reductions was related to poorer performance on neuropsychological tests of memory. They pointed out that the reduction of P300 amplitude could signify a dysfunction in the continuous memory updating of current events.

On the other hand, it has been reported a great inter- and intra-subject variability in ERPs in abnormal populations such as schizophrenia that redound in a difficulty in making a proper evaluation of these parameters. These problems may be underlined by a desynchronization of neuronal populations that may generate ERP components. In this respect, Basar [68] proposed that brain electrical activity (EEG) emerges from the activity of an ensemble of generators producing rhythmic activities in several frequency ranges. Usually, these generators are randomly active, but when sensory stimulation occurs, generators become coupled and act together in a coherent way. He proposed that the superimposition of this coherent activity in particular frequency ranges could, at least partially, determine ERP components. In schizophrenia, the coupling of these generators may be impaired, inducing ERPs abnormalities that are also evident in task performance.

OLZ caused a significant reduction in positive, negative and general psychopathology symptomatology. Positive symptoms that showed a significant reduction were delusions, hallucinatory behavior, excitement and hostility. All the negative symptoms showed a decrease after OLZ treatment, especially blunted affect and poor rapport. Also, a significant reduction of somatic concern, anxiety, tension, depression, unusual thought content, disturbance of volition, poor impulse control, reoccupation and active social avoidance was observed. These results are in agreement with those found in other studies in which a reduction of symptoms scores in TRS after OLZ treatment [69,70] however there is a main difference in the sense that in the present study we evaluated clinical improvement in each of the PANSS items instead of global scores.

OLZ did not improve task performance, maybe because its weak action on D_1 cortical receptors that have been found to be involved in several cognitive functions [71] or because its anticholinergic effects. These results are contrary to those found by Weiser et al. [72] who found a positive effect of OLZ on cognitive functions independent of the improvement in motor abilities. In addition, Nieman et al. [67] observed that patients treated with risperidone showed smaller parietal P300 amplitude than patients using OLZ.

In spite of OLZ, it did not induce changes in task performance nor in P3 amplitude, some changes in the symptoms that correlated with performance and P3 amplitude were observed in both tasks after treatment. In the attention task, there were some symptoms related to thought disorders such as delusions, conceptual disorganization and disturbance of volition, as well as others related to an emotional component –blunted affect, tension and poor impulse control. In the emotional recognition task, significant correlations of performance also implied symptoms related to thought disorders such as delusions, conceptual disorganization, stereotyped thinking, difficulty in abstract thinking, lack of spontaneity and flow of conversation, and disturbance of volition, those related to an emotional component, poor rapport and depression. This may be explained considering that some of the patients may show a good response to OLZ, with an important decrease in these symptoms while others did not. In this sense, it is possible that those patients who improved in delusions, tension and poor impulse control also showed an improvement in task performance. Regarding the emotional task, in the POS-T, a reduction of depression was related to a better performance.

In relation to the correlation between symptomatology and P3 amplitude in the attention task thought disorders negative symptoms were also associated with a lower amplitude, as well as poor rapport in the PRE-T, whereas a positive relationship was found between anxiety and P3 in the POS-T. In the emotional recognition task, P3 amplitude was inversely related to positive (excitement and hostility) and negative (emotional withdrawal) symptoms with an emotional content; also a positive relationship was found with hallucinations in the POS-T.

Controversial results have been presented in relation to correlations between P300 amplitude and psychopathology. While some authors have found inverse correlations between positive symptoms and P300 amplitude [73,74] others haven´t found any correlation [75]. The lack of agreement may be partially due to the fact that global symptoms scores have been used instead of individual items scores to study the mentioned relationship between P300 and psychopathology.

Papageorgiou et al. results [76] suggest that auditory hallucinations, another positive symptom, is related to attention deficits in schizophrenics mediated by a distributed network involving or affecting the left temporoparietal and left prefrontal area. These functions improved after clozapine and OLZ treatment. In the study of Gallinat et al. [48] in TRS, neither P300 amplitude nor RT showed significant differences after clozapine or olanzapine. However, changes in P300 amplitude were significantly influenced by changes in positive but not in negative symptoms scores. In patients who showed a pronounced improvement on positive symptoms, a slight increase in P300 was observed. These authors signal that their results are in line with the idea of a trait character of P300 reduction in schizophrenia, although a state modulation of psychopathology, particularly of positive symptoms, may exist. They propose that this relationship between P300 and positive symptoms may have an inverted U shape, where low or very high levels of positive symptoms may cause a reduction of P300, while moderate scores will redound in good attention processes. This interpretation would correspond with our results of an increased level of anxiety in the attention task and of hallucinations in the emotional task which are related to higher P3 amplitude values in the POS-T.

Present results provide further support for attention and emotional disorders in schizophrenics. OLZ did not have a global effect on the performance of the attention nor the emotional tasks, but there were changes in significant correlations between psychopathology and task performance and P3 amplitude after OLZ. Event-related potentials are useful to evaluate deficits in attentional and emotional recognition processes, as well as the effects of neuroleptics in psychiatric populations.

ACKNOWLEDGEMENTS

This research was supported by CONACyT grant 28590-H. The authors wish to thank to Claudia Amezcua, Miguel Angel Martínez and Juan Pablo Alvarez Tostado for their help in data acquisition and analysis.

REFERENCES

[1]   Mueser, K.T., Doonan, R., Penn, D.L., Blanchard, J.J., Bellack, A.S., Nishith, P. & DeLeon, J. (1996). Emotion recognition and social competence in chronic schizophrenia. *J Abnorm Psychol, 105,* 2271-2275.

[2]   Flack, W.F., Laird, J.D. & Cavallaro, L.A. (1999). Emotional expression and feeling in schizophrenia: effects of specific expressive behaviors on emotional experiences. *J Clin Psycol, 55,* 11-20.

[3]   Garrido-Casas, G. (1997). Especialización hemisférica y procesos emocionales en pacientes esquizofrénicos y depresivos. *(Tesis de Doctorado)*. España: Universidad Autónoma de Madrid.

[4]   Kington, L.A., Jones, L.A. & Hopkin, E. J. (2000). Impaired eye expression recognition in schizophrenia. *J Psychiatric Res, 34,* 314-347.

[5]   Schneider, F., Gur, R.C., Gur, R.E. & Shtasel, D.L. (1995). Emotional processing in schizophrenia: neurobehavioral in relation to psychopathology. *Schizophr Res, 17,* 167-175.

[6]   Walker, E., McGuire, M. & Bettes, B. (1984). Recognition and identification of facial stimuli by schizophrenics and patients with affective disorders. *Br J Clin Psychol, 23,* 37-44.

[7]   Edwards, J., Pattison, P., Jackson, H. & Wales, R. (2001). Facial affect and affective prosody recognition in first –episode schizophrenia. *Schizophr Res, 48,* 235-253.

[8]   Poole, J., Tobias, F. & Vinogradov, S. (2000). The functional relevance of affect recognition error in schizophrenia. *J Int Neuropsy Soc, 6,* 649-658.

[9]   Ibarrarán-Pernas, G.Y., Cerdán, L.F., Guevara, M.A. & Ramos-Loyo, J. (2003). Efectos de la olanzapina sobre el reconocimiento emocional en esquizofrénicos refractarios al tratamiento. *Actas Esp Psiquiatría, 31, 5,* 256-262.

[10]   Kring, AM. & Neale, JM. (1996). Do schizophrenic patients show a disjunctive relationship among expressive, experiential and psychophysiological components of emotion? *J Abnorm Psychol, 102,* 249-257.

[11]   Walter, E.F., Grimes, K.E., Davis, D.M. & Smith, A.J. (1993). Childhood precursors of schizophrenia facial expression of emotion. *Am J Psychiatr, 150,* 1654-1660.

[12]   Kring, A.M. & Neale, JM. (1993). Flat affect in schizophrenia does not reflect diminished subjective experience of emotion. *J Abnorm Psychol, 102,* 507-517.

[13]   Mangun, G.R. & Hillyard, S.A. (1988). Spatial gradients of visual attention: behavioral and electrophysiological evidence. *Electroencephalogr Clin Neurophysiol, 70,* 417-428.

[14]   Donchin, E. & Coles, M.G. (1988). Is the P300 component a manifestation of context updating? *Behav Brain Sci, 113,* 357-374.

[15]   Ford, JM., Pfefferbaum, A., & Roth, W. (1992). P300 Schizophrenia. *Ann NY Acad Sci, 658,* 146-162.

[16]   Friedman, D. & Squires-Wheeler, E. (1994). Evented-related potentials (ERPs) as indicators of risk for schizophrenia. *Schizophr Bull, 20(1),* 63-74.

[17]   Duncan, C.C., Morihisha, J.M., Fawcett, R.W. & Kirch, D.G. (1987). P300 in schizophrenia: State or trait marker? *Psychopharmacol Bull, 23,* 497-501.

[18]   Roth, W.T. & Cannon, E.H. (1972). Some features of the auditory evoked response in schizophrenics. *Arch Gen Psychiatry, 48*, 618-624.

[19]   Turetsky, B.I., Colbath, E.A. & Gur, R.E. (1998). P300 subcomponent abnormalities in schizophrenia I. Physiological evidence for gender and subtype specific differences in regional pathology. *Biol Psychiatry, 43*, 84-96.

[20]   Ford, J.M., White, P., Lin, K.O. & Pfefferbaum, A. (1994). Schizophrenics have fewer and smaller P300s: A single-trial analysis. *Biol Psychiatry, 35*, 96 103.

[21]   Frangou, S., Sharma, T., Alarcon, G., Sigmudsson, T., Takei, N., Binnie, C. & Murray, R.M. (1997). The Maudsley Family Study, II endogenous event-related potentials in familial schizophrenia. *Schizophr Res, 23*, 145-53.

[22]   Schreiber, H., Stolz-Born, G., Kornhuber, H.H. & Born, J. (1992). Event-related potential correlates of impaired selective attention in children at high risk for schizophrenia. *Biol Psychiatry, 32*, 634-651.

[23]   Hirayasu, Y., Asato, N., Ohta, H., Hokama, H., Arakaki, H. & Ogura, C. (1998). Abnormalities of auditory event-potentials in schizophrenia prior to treatment. *Biol Psychiatry, 43*, 244-253.

[24]   Salisbury, D.F., Shenton, M.E., Sherwood, A.R., Fischer, I.A., Yurgelun-Todd, D.A., Tohen, M. & McCarley, R.W. (1998). First-episode schizophrenic psychosis differs from first-episode affective psychosis and controls in P300 amplitude over left temporal lobe. *Arch Gen Psychiatry, 55*, 2173-80.

[25]   Pfefferbaum, A., Ford, J.M., White, P.M. & Roth, W.T.(1989). P3 in schizophrenia is affected by stimulus modality, response requirements, medication status and negative symptoms. *Arch Gen Psychiatry, 46*, 1035-1044.

[26]   McCarley, R.W., Faux, S.F., Shenton, M.E., Nestor, P.G. & Holinger, D.P. (1991). Is there P300 asymmetry in schizophrenia? *Arch Gen Psychiatry, 48*, 4380-3.

[27]   Egan, M.F., Duncan, C.C., Suddath, R.L., Kirch, D.G., Mirsky, A.F. & Wyatt, R.J. (1994). Event-related potential abnormalities correlate with structural brain alterations and clinical features in patients with chronic schizophrenia. *Schizophr Res, 11*, 3259-71.

[28]   Shenton, M.E., Faux, S.F., McCarley, R.W., Ballinger, R., Coleman, M., Torello, M. & Duffy, F.H. (1989). Correlations between abnormal auditory P300 topography and positive symptoms in schizophrenia: A preliminary report. *Biol Psychiatry, 25*, 710-716.

[29]   O'Donnell, B.F., Shenton, M.E., McCarley, R.W., Faux, S.F., Smith, R.S., Salisbury, D.F., Nestor, P.G., Pollak, S.D., Kikinis, R. & Jolesz, F.A. (1993). The auditory N2 component in schizophrenia: Relationship to MRI temporal lobe gray matter and to other ERP abnormalities. *Biol Psychiatry, 34*, 25-40.

[30]   Carretié, L. & Iglesias, J. (1995). An ERP study on the specificity of facial expression processing. *Int J Psychophysiol, 19,*183-192.

[31]   Orozco, S. Y. & Ehlers, C. L. (1998). Gender differences in electrophysiological responses to facial stimuli. *Biol Psychiatry, 44*, 281-279.

[32]   Orozco, S., Wall, T. L. & Ehlers, C. L. (1999). Influence of alcohol on electrophysiological responses to facial stimuli. *Alcohol, 18*, 111-6.

[33]   Kayser, J., Bruder, G.E., Tenke, C.E., Stewart, J.E. & Quitkin, F.M. (2000). Event-related (ERPs) to hemifield presentations of emotional stimuli: differences between

depressed patients and healthy adults in P3 amplitude and asymmetry. *Int J Psychophysiol, 36(3),* 211-236.

[34] Ramos, J., Cerdán, L.F., Guevara, M.A. & Amezcua, C. (2001). Alteraciones en la atención y en el reconocimiento de emociones faciales en ezquizofrénicos refractarios y no refractarios al tratamiento evaluadas a través de un paradigma "odd-ball". *Rev Neurol, 33(11),* 1027-1032.

[35] Schneider, F., Ellgring, H., Friedrich, J., Fus, I., Beyer, T. & Heimann, H. (1992). The effects of neuroleptics on facial action in schizophrenic patients. *Pharmacopsychiatry, 25,* 233-239.

[36] Brenner, H.D. & Merlo, M. C. G. (1995). Definition of therapy resistant schizophrenia, and its assesment. *Eur Psychiatry, 10(1),* 11-18.

[37] Joober, R., Randolph, C. & Green, M. (2002). Neuropsychological impairments in neuroleptic-responder vs. non-responder schizophrenic patients and healthy volunteers. *Schizophr Res, 53,* 229-238.

[38] Ramos, J., Cerdán, L.F., Guevara, M.A., Amezcua, C. & Sanz-Martin, A. (2001). Abnormal EEG Patterns in neuroleptic-resistant schizophrenics. *Int JNeuroscie, 2,* 1-2, 47-59.

[39] Cuesta, M.J., Peralta, V., Zarzuela, A. (2001). Effects of olanzapine and other antipsychotics on cognitive function in chronic schizophrenia: a longitudinal study. *Schizophr Res 48,* 17-28.

[40] Purdon, S.E., Jones, B., Stip, E., Labelle, A., Addington, D., David, S., Breier, A., Tollefson, G. (1999). Cognitive improvement in schizophrenia with novel antipsychotic medications. *Schizophr Res 35,* 551-560.

[41] Kee, K.S., Kern, R., Green, M. (1998). Risperidone versus haloperidol for perception of emotion in treatment-resistant schizophrenia: preliminay findings. *Schizophr Res 31,* 159-3165.

[42] Purdon, S.E. (2000). Measuring neuropsychological change in schizophrenia with novel antipsychotic medications. *Schizophr Res, 25,* 108-116.

[43] Romera, M.I. & Gurpegui, M. (2001). Procesamiento visuo-perceptivo en los pacientes con esquizofrenia tratados con antipsicóticos típicos y los tratados con atípicos. *Actas Esp Psiquiatría, 29,* 19-24.

[44] Tollefson, G., Beasley, C., Tran, P., Street, J., Krueger, J.A. & Tamura, J. (et. al.). (1997). Olanzapine versus haloperidol in the treatment of schizophrenia and schizoaffective and schizophreniform disorders: Results of an international collaborative trial. *Am J Psychiatry, 154,* 457-465.

[45] Wolf, K., Mass, R., Kiefer, F., Eckert, K., Weinhold, N., Wiedermann, K. & Naber, D. (2004). The influence of olanzapine on facial expression of emotions in schizophrenia. An improved facial EMG study. *Reprinted from the German J Psychiatry, 7,* 14-19.

[46] Cerdán, L.F., Guevara, M.A., Sanz, A. Amezcua, C. & Ramos-Loyo, J. Brain electrical activity changes in treatment refractory schizophrenics after olanzapine treatment. *Int J Psychophysiology, in press.*

[47] Schall, U., Catts, S., Chaturvedi, S., Redenbach, J., Karayanidis, F., Ward, P.B. (1995). The effects of clonazepine therapy on pshycometric and event-related potential (ERP) measures on cognitive dysfunction in schizophrenia. *Schizophr Res, 15(1-2),* 164.

[48] Gallinat, J., Riedel, M., Juckel, G., Sokullu, S., Frodl, T. Moukhtieva, R., Mavrogiorgou, P., Nisslé, S., Müller, N., Danker-Hopfe,H. & Hegerl, U. (2001). P300 and symptom improvement in schizophrenia. *Psychopharmacology, 158,* 55-65.

[49] American Psychiatric Association. (1995). DSM-IV. Diagnostic and Statistical Manual of Mental Disorders. Masson, Barcelona.

[50] World Health Organization (WHO). (1992). International Classification of Mental Diseases (ICD-10). Meditor Ed Madrid.

[51] Keefe, R., Mohs, R., Silverman, J.M. (1990). Characteristics of Kraepelinian schizophrenia and their relation to premorbid social functioning. In BO Angrist., CH Schulz, (eds). The neuroleptic nonresponsive patient characterization and treatment. American Psychiatric Press, Washington D.C.

[52] Kay, S.R., Opler, L.A., Fiszbein, A. (1992). The positive and negative syndrome scale PANSS. Manual, Multi-Health systems, Inc, Toronto.

[53] Guevara, M.A., Sanz-Martin, A., Hernández-González, M., Ramos-Loyo, J. (2004). ESTIMVIS: Un sistema computarizado para estimulación visual. *Rev Mex Ing Biomed,* XXV(1).

[54] Guevara, M.A., Ramos, J., Hernández, G.M., Madera, H., Corsi-Cabrera, M. (2000). CAPTUSEN, a system for the computerized acquisition of EEG and event-related potentials. *Rev Mex Psicol 171,* 77-88.

[55] Bruder, G., Kayser, J., Tenke, C., Amador, X., Friedman, M., Sharif, Z. & Gorman, J. (1999). Left temporal lobe Dysfunction in Schizophrenia. *Arch Gen Psychiatry,* 56, 267-276.

[56] John, E.R., Easton, P., Prichep, L.S. & Friedman, J. (1993). Standardized varimax descriptors of event related potentials: basic considerations. *Brain Topography, 6(2),* 143-162.

[57] Arruda, J.E., Weiler, M.D., Valentino, D., Willis, W.G., Rossi, J.S., Stern, R.A., Gold, S.M. & Costa L. (1996). A guide for applying principal-components analysis and confirmatory factor analysis to quantitative electroencephalogram data. *Int J Psychophysiol 23,* 63-81.

[58] Breier, A. (1999). Cognitive deficits in achizophrenia. *Eur Psychiatry, 13,* 219.

[59] Liddle, P.F., (1999). The multidimensional phenotype of schizophrenia. In: Tamminga, C.A., (ed.) Schizophrenia in a molecular age. Review of Psychiatry, American Psychiatric Press, Washington D.C., pp.1-28.

[60] Yang, R.CH., Seamans, J.K., Gorelova, N. (1999). Developing a neuronal model for the pathophysiology of schizophrenia. Based on the nature of electrophysiological actions of dopamine in the prefrontal cortex. *Neuropsychopharmacology. 21,* 161-194.

[61] Kendler, K.S., Ochs, A.L., Gorman, A.M., Hewitt, J.K., Ross, D.E. & Mirsky, A.F. (1991). The structure of schizotypy: a pilot multitrait twin study. *Psychiatr Res, 36,* 19-36.

[62] Lees, S.E., Keefe, R.S.E., Harvey, P.D., Siever, L.J. & Mohs, R.C. (1997). Attentional and eye tracking deficits correlate with negative symptoms in schizophrenia. *Schizophr Res, 26* (2-3), 139-146.

[63] Pandurangi, A.K., Sax, K.W., Pelonero, A.L. & Goldberg, S.C. (1994). Sustained attention and positive formal thought disorder in schizophrenia. *Schizophr Res, 13(2),* 109-16.

[64] Strauss, M.E., Buchanan, R.W. & Hale, J. (1993). Relations between attentional deficits and clinical symptoms in schizophrenic outpatients. *Psychiatr Res, 47(3),* 205-213.

[65] Sarfati, Y., Baylé, M.C., Besche, C. & Widlöcher, D. (1997). Attribution of intentions to others in people with schizophrenia: a non-verbal exploration with comic strips. *Schizophr Res, 20(25),* 3199-209.

[66] Sachs, G., Steger-Wuchse, D., Kryspin-Exner, I., Gur, R.C. & Katschnig, H. (2003). Facial recognition deficits and cognition in schizophrenia. *Schizoph Res.*

[67] Nieman, D.H., Koelman, J.H.T.M., Linszen, D.H., Tour L.J., Dingemans, P.M. and Ongerboer de Visser, B.W. (2002). Clinical and neuropsychological correlatos of the P300 in schizophrenia. *Schizoph Res, 55,* 105-113.

[68] Başar, E. (1992). Brain natural frequencies are causal factors for resonances and induced rhythms [Epilogue]. In: Başar, E., Bullock, T.H. (Eds.), Induced Rhythms in the Brain. Birkhäuser, Boston, pp. 425-467.

[69] Ohaeri, J.U. (2000). Naturalistic study of olanzapine in treatment resistant schizophrenia and acute mania, depression and obsessional disorder. *East African Med J 7,* 286-292.

[70] Chiu, N.Y., Yang, Y.K., Chen, P.S., Chang, C.C., Lee, I.H., Lee, J.R. (2003). Olanzapine in Chinese treatment-resistant patients with schizophrenia: an open-label, prospective trial. *Psychiatry Clin Neurocie 5,* 478-484.

[71] Goldman-Rakic, P.S., Mully, E.C, Williams, G.V. (2000). D1 receptors in prefrontal cells and circuits. *Brain Res Rev 31,* 295-301.

[72] Weiser, M., Schneider-Beeri, M., Nakash, N., Brill, N., Bawnik, O., Reiss, S., Hocherman, S. and Davidson, M. (2000). Improvement in cognition associated with novel antipsychotic drugs: a direct drug effect or reduction of EPS? *Schizophr Res, 46,* 81-89.

[73] Roth, W.T., Pfefferbaum, A. Kelly A, F., Berger, P.A., Kopell, B.S. (1981). Auditory event-related potentials in schizophrenia and depression. *Psychiatry Res, 4,* 199-212.

[74] Kawasaki, Y., Maeda, Y., Higashima, M. Nagasawa, T., Koshino, Y., Susuki,M. Ide, Y. (1997). Reduce auditory P300 amplitude, medial temporal volume reduction and psychopathology in schizophrenia. *Schizophr Res 26,* 107-115.

[75] Pritchard, W.S. (1986). Cognitive event-related potentials correlates of schizophrenia. *Psychol Bull, 89,* 506-540.

[76] Papageorgiou, Ch., Oulis, P., Vasios, Ch., Kontopantelis, E., Uzunoglu, N., Rabavilas, A. and Christodoulou, G.N. (2003). P300 alterations in schizophrenic patients experiencing auditory hallucinations. *Eur Neuropsychopharmacology, 14,* 227-236.

In: Focus on Nonverbal Communication Research   ISBN 1-59454-790-4
Editor: Finley R. Lewis, pp. 237-279   © 2007 Nova Science Publishers, Inc.

Chapter 11

CONVERSATIONAL USE OF SIGN LANGUAGE BY CROSS-FOSTERED CHIMPANZEES

Mary Lee A. Jensvold[1] and R. Allen Gardner[2]
[1]Chimpanzee & Human Communication Institute, Central Washington University
[2]Department of Psychology, University of Nevada, Reno USA

ABSTRACT

Cross-fostered as infants in Reno, chimpanzees Washoe, Moja, Tatu, and Dar freely conversed in signs of American Sign Language with each other as well as with humans in Ellensburg. In this experiment a human interlocutor waited for a chimpanzee to initiate conversations with her and then responded with one of four types of probes; general requests for more information, on topic questions, off topic questions, or negative statements. The responses of the chimpanzees to the probes depended on the type of probe and the particular signs in the probes. They reiterated, adjusted, and shifted the signs in their utterances in conversationally appropriate rejoinders. Their reactions to and interactions with a conversational partner resembled patterns of conversation found in similar studies of human children.

INTRODUCTION

Human verbal behavior is interactive; to proceed smoothly each turn in a conversation must be appropriate to the previous turn. Inappropriate rejoinders disrupt conversation. Successful interaction depends on skills that develop gradually in human children together with vocabulary and other social skills [Brinton, Fujiki, Loeb, & Winkler, 1986; Gallagher, 1977; Roth & Spekman, 1984]. Sign language studies of cross-fostered chimpanzees compare infant chimpanzees with human children. This requires a special sort of laboratory.

CROSS-FOSTERING

Ethologists use the procedure called cross-fostering to study the interaction between environmental and genetic factors by having parents of one genetic stock rear the young of a different genetic stock. It seems as if no form of behavior is so fundamental or so distinctively species-specific that it is not deeply sensitive to the effects of early experience. Ducklings, goslings, lambs, and many other young animals learn to follow the first moving object that they see, whether it is their own mother, a female of another species, or a shoebox. The mating calls of many birds are so species-specific that an ornithologist can identify them by their calls alone without seeing a single feather. Distinctive and species-specific as these calls may be, they, too, depend upon early experience [Slater & Williams, 1994; West, King, & Freeberg, 1997].

How about our own species? How much does our common humanity depend on our common human genetic heritage and how much on the equally species-specific character of a human childhood? The question is as traditional as the story of Romulus and Remus and so tantalizing that even alleged but unverified cases of human cross-fostering, such as the wolf children of India [Singh & Zingg, 1942] and the monkey boy of Burundi [Lane & Pillard, 1978] attract serious scholarly attention. An experimental case of a human infant cross-fostered by nonhuman parents would require an unlikely level of cooperation from both sets of parents. In a few cases, however, chimpanzees have been cross-fostered by human parents [Kellogg, 1968].

Cross-fostering a chimpanzee is very different from keeping one in a home as a pet. Many people keep pets in their homes. They may treat their pets very well, and they may love them dearly, but they do not treat them like children. True cross-fostering -- treating the chimpanzee infant like a human child in all respects, in all living arrangements, 24 hours a day every day of the year -- requires a rigorous experimental regime that has rarely been attempted.

SIBLING SPECIES

Chimpanzees are an obvious first choice for cross-fostering. They look and act remarkably like human beings and recent research reveals closer and deeper biological similarities of all kinds [Goodall, 1986]. In blood chemistry, for example, the chimpanzee is not only the closest species to the human, but the chimpanzee is closer to the human than the chimpanzee is to the gorilla or to the orangutan [Stanyon, Chiarelli, Gottlieb, & Patton, 1986; Ruvolo, 1994] and 98% of human and chimpanzee DNA shares the same structure [Sibley & Ahlquist, 1984].

For cross-fostering, the most important resemblance is that chimpanzees and humans mature very slowly. Infant chimpanzees are quite helpless; adults must provide warmth, bodily care, and food [Plooij, 1984]. In the cross-fostering laboratory in Reno, Moja, Pili, Tatu, and Dar only began to roll over by themselves when they were 4 to 7 weeks old, to sit at 10 to 15 weeks. The change from milk teeth to adult dentition begins at about 5 years. Under natural conditions in Africa, infant chimpanzees depend on their mothers' care almost completely until they are two or three. They cannot survive if their mother dies before they are three, even when older siblings attempt to care for them. Weaning only begins when they are between four and five. In Africa, young chimpanzees usually live with their mothers until they are 7; and females often stay with their mothers until they are 10 or 11. Menarche occurs when wild females are 10 or 11, and their first infant is born when they are between 12 and 15 [Goodall, 1986, pp. 84-88, 443]. Cheeta the chimpanzee who starred in Tarzan movies of the 1930's and 1940's was still alive and well at age 71 in 2003 [Roach, 2003].

Under favorable conditions, their behavioral repertoire continues to expand and develop throughout their long childhood [Goodall, 1967; Hayes & Nissen, 1971; Plooij, 1984]. This gives us a detailed scale of comparative development for measuring the progress of cross-fostered chimpanzees.

SIGN LANGUAGE

Perhaps the most prominent feature of a human childhood is the development of two-way communication in a natural human language. Without conversational give and take in a common language, the cross-fostering conditions could hardly be said to simulate the environment of a human infant. Before Project Washoe, the human foster parents spoke to their adopted chimpanzees as human parents speak to human children. In contrast to the close parallels in all other aspects of development, the chimpanzees acquired hardly any speech. For decades, the failure of a few cross-fostered chimpanzees to learn to speak supported the traditional doctrine of an absolute, unbridgeable discontinuity between human and nonhuman intelligence. There is another possibility; that speech is an inappropriate medium of communication for chimpanzees. In that case we must find a naturally occurring human language that does not require human speech. This was the innovation of Project Washoe. For the first time, the human foster family used a gestural rather than a vocal language.

American Sign Language (ASL) is the naturally-occurring gestural language of the deaf in North America. Word-for-sign translation between English and ASL is about as difficult as word-for-word translation between English and any other spoken language. English has many common words and idiomatic expressions that can only be paraphrased in ASL, and ASL has its own complement of signs and idioms that can only be paraphrased in English. There are also radical differences in grammar. Where English relies heavily on word order, ASL is like the many other human languages that convey most of the same distinctions through inflection. Where English makes heavy use of auxiliary verbs such as the copula, to be, ASL is like the many other human languages that manage without the copula.

Sign language is very different from finger-spelling. The signs of ASL, like the words of English, represent whole concepts. Finger-spelling is based on a manual alphabet in which each letter of a written language is represented by a particular configuration of the fingers. It is a code in which messages of a written language can be spelled out in the air. Literate signers mix finger-spelling with sign language as a way of referring to seldom used proper names and technical terms, and we used finger-spelling for this purpose in our laboratory. We also used finger-spelling from time to time as a code to prevent understanding, the way human parents commonly spell out messages that they want to keep secret from their children. In general, we avoided finger-spelling because our still-illiterate subjects could not understand or copy it, and also because too much finger-spelling could easily lapse into manual English and defeat the objective of a good adult model of ASL.

SIGN LANGUAGE ONLY

Attempting to speak good English while simultaneously signing good ASL is about as difficult as attempting to speak good English while simultaneously writing good Russian. Often, teachers and other helping professionals, who only learn to sign in order to communicate with deaf clients, attempt to speak and sign simultaneously. They soon find that they are speaking English sentences while adding the signs for a few of the key words in each sentence [Bonvillian, Nelson, & Charrow, 1976]. When a native speaker of English practices ASL in this way, the effect is roughly the same as practicing Russian by speaking English sentences and saying some of the key words both in English and in Russian. It is obviously a poor way to teach any language.

It was clear from the start of Project Washoe that the human foster family would provide a poor model of sign language if they spoke and signed at the same time. Signing to the infant chimpanzee and speaking English among ourselves would also be inappropriate. That would lower the status of signs to something suitable for nursery talk, only. In addition, Washoe would lose the opportunity to observe adult models of conversation, and the human newcomers to sign language would lose significant opportunities to practice and to learn from each other.

When the cross-fosterlings were present, all business, all casual conversation was in ASL. Everyone in the foster family had to be fluent enough to make themselves understood under the sometimes hectic conditions of life with these lively youngsters. There were occasional lapses in the rule of sign language only as when outside workmen or the pediatrician entered the laboratory, but such lapses were brief and rare. Visits from nonsigners were strictly limited. Visitors from the deaf community who were fluent in ASL were always welcome.

> The rule of sign-language-only required some of the isolation of a field expedition. We lived and worked with Washoe on that corner of suburban Reno as if at a lonely outpost in a hostile country. We were always avoiding people who might speak to Washoe. On outings in the woods, we were as stealthy and cautious as Indian scouts. On drives in town, we wove through traffic like undercover agents. We could stop at a Dairy Queen or a MacDonald's fast-food restaurant, but only if they had a secluded parking lot in the back. Then one of Washoe's companions could buy the treats while another waited with her in the car. If Washoe was spotted, the car drove off to return later for the missing passenger and the treats, when the coast was clear. [Rimpau, Gardner, & Gardner, 1989, p. 7]

ETHOLOGICAL CONSIDERATIONS

The exquisite development of the human vocal apparatus is matched by the evolution of peculiarly human vocal habits. Human beings are unusually noisy animals. There is a hubbub of voices at almost every social gathering; a great din at the most peaceful cocktail party or restaurant dining room. It is a mark of discipline and respect when an audience settles down in silence to listen to a single speaker. In the rest of the animal kingdom there are very few creatures -- perhaps only whales and dolphins, and some birds -- that make nearly so much vocal racket when they are otherwise undisturbed. Chimpanzees are silent most of the time. A group of ten wild chimpanzees of assorted ages and sexes feeding peacefully in a fig tree at the Gombe stream in Africa may make so little sound that an inexperienced observer passing below can altogether fail to detect them. When chimpanzees use their voices, they are usually too excited to engage in casual conversation. Their vocal habits, much more than the design of their vocal apparatus, keep them from learning to speak.

TEACHING METHODS

In teaching sign language to Washoe, Moja, Pili, Tatu, and Dar we imitated human parents teaching young children in a human home. We called attention to everyday events and objects that might interest the young chimpanzees, e.g., THAT CHAIR. SEE PRETTY BIRD. MY HAT. We often molded their hands in the shape of new signs as deaf parents do [Maestas y Moores, 1980]. They learned many signs by watching adults sign about interesting objects and activities [R. A. Gardner, & Gardner, 1989, pp 17-19]. We asked probing questions to check on communication, and we always tried to answer questions and to comply with requests. We expanded on fragmentary utterances using the fragments to teach and to probe. We also followed the parents of deaf children by using an especially simple and repetitious register of ASL and by making signs on the youngsters' bodies to capture their attention [Maestas y Moores, 1980; Marschark, 1993; Schlesinger & Meadow, 1972].

Washoe, Moja, Pili, Tatu, and Dar signed to friends and to strangers. They signed to themselves and to each other, to dogs, cats, toys, tools, even to trees. We did not have to tempt them with treats or ply them with questions to get them to sign to us. Most of the signing was initiated by the young chimpanzees rather than by the human adults. They commonly named objects and pictures of objects in situations in which we were unlikely to reward them. When Washoe signed to herself in play, she was usually in a private place -- high in a tree or alone in her bedroom before going to sleep. All of the cross-fosterlings signed to themselves when leafing through magazines and picture books, but only Washoe resisted our attempts to join in this activity. If we persisted in joining her or if we watched her too closely, she often abandoned the magazine or picked it up and moved away. Washoe not only named pictures to herself in this situation, she also corrected herself. In a typical example, she indicated a certain advertisement, signed THAT FOOD, then looked at her hand closely and changed the phrase to THAT DRINK, which was correct. The cross-fosterlings also signed to themselves about their own ongoing or impending actions. We sometimes saw Washoe moving stealthily to a forbidden part of the garden signing QUIET to herself, or running pell-mell for the potty chair while signing HURRY.

In most laboratory studies of nonhuman beings, the same procedures serve both for teaching and for testing. A monkey or a rat, for example, learns trial-by-trial to associate one stimulus with the reward and the other with an empty food dish, and the very same trials are scored for correct and incorrect choices and plotted to show learning curves. Washoe, Moja, Pili, Tatu, and Dar spent virtually all of their waking hours in the company of some human member of their foster families. During that time, their exposure to objects and the ASL names for objects was very large compared with the brief periods spent in tests. These tests were as different from the routines of the rest of their daily lives as similar testing would be for young children. For caged subjects, a session of testing is probably the most interesting thing that happens in the course of a laboratory day. For the cross-fosterlings in our laboratory most of the activities of daily life were more attractive than their formal tests. The cross-fostering regime precluded any attempt to starve them like rats or pigeons to make them earn their daily rations by taking tests. Getting free-living, cross-fostered chimpanzees to do their best under stringent, double-blind conditions required ingenuity and patience [R. A. Gardner & Gardner, 1984; 1998].

USES OF THE SIGNS

When teaching a new sign, we usually began with a particular exemplar -- a particular toy for BALL, a particular shoe for SHOE. At first, especially with very young subjects, there would be very few balls and very few shoes. Early in Project Washoe we worried that the signs might become too closely associated with their initial referents. It turned out that this was no more a problem for Washoe or for any of the other cross-fosterlings than it is for human children. The chimpanzees easily transferred the signs they had learned for a few balls, shoes, flowers, or cats to the full range of the concepts wherever found and however represented, as if they divided the world into the same conceptual categories that human beings use.

The human members of the foster families observed the cross-fostered chimpanzees constantly throughout the day and attempted to record all of the significant activities of the day, but particularly the sign language and its verbal and nonverbal contexts. We grouped the signs of Washoe, Moja, Tatu, and Dar at five years of age into functional categories according to the contexts in which they were used, such as names (DAR, ROGER), pronouns (ME, YOU), animates (BABY, DOG), inanimate objects (BALL, TREE), noun/verbs (BRUSH, DRINK), verbs (GO, OPEN), locatives (DOWN, OUT), colors (BLACK, RED), possessives (MINE, YOURS), material (GLASS, WOOD), numbers (ONE, TWO), comparatives (BIG, DIFFERENT), qualities (HOT, SWEET), markers (AGAIN, CAN'T), and traits (SORRY, GOOD) [see B. T. Gardner & Gardner, 1998; B. T. Gardner, Gardner, & Nichols, 1989].

Functional categories of this kind are called sentence constituents because they seem to serve constituent functions in the early fragmentary utterances of human children. One way to demonstrate the functional roles of these categories is to ask a series of questions about the same object. When Greg G. asked Washoe a series of questions about her red boot; her reply to WHAT THAT? was SHOE, to WHAT COLOR THAT? was RED, and to WHOSE THAT? was MINE. Replies to questions can establish the functional character of lexical categories. At the time of this example [filmed in R. A. Gardner & Gardner, 1973; 1974], Washoe had four color signs in her vocabulary, RED, GREEN, WHITE, and BLACK. If her only color sign had been RED, then all she would have had to do was to reply RED whenever anyone asked WHAT COLOR? With a group of color signs in the vocabulary she could reply at different levels of correctness. If she had replied GREEN, when asked WHAT COLOR THAT of the red boot, it would have been an error, but a different sort of error from a reply such as SHOE or HAT or MINE. A reply can be functionally appropriate without being factually correct [R. A. Gardner, Van Cantfort, & Gardner, 1992].

Brown [1968] and others reviewed by Van Cantfort, Gardner, and Gardner [1989] used the replies of human children to Wh-questions of this sort to show that children use different functional categories of words as sentence constituents, even when the children are still so immature that they cannot frame well-formed Wh-questions on their own. Washoe, Moja, Tatu, and Dar also used appropriate sentence constituents in their replies to Wh-questions. As an additional parallel, longitudinal samples of the replies of the chimpanzees show the same developmental pattern that has been found in human children. Children and cross-fostered chimpanzees reply to WHAT questions with nominals and to WHERE questions with locatives before they reply to WHAT DO questions with verbs and to WHO questions with proper names and pronouns, while reliably appropriate replies to HOW questions appear even later [Van Cantfort, et al., 1989].

PHRASES

As soon as Washoe had eight or ten signs in her vocabulary, she began to construct phrases of two or more signs. Before long, multiple-sign constructions were common. The individual terms within these phrases and sentences formed basic meaningful patterns such as agent-action (SUSAN BRUSH, YOU BLOW), action-object (CHASE DAR, OPEN BLANKET), action-location (GO UP, TICKLE THERE), possession (BIB MINE, HAT YOURS), nomination (THAT CAT, THAT SHOE), and recurrence (MORE COOKIE, MORE GO). Longer constructions could specify more than one agent of an action (YOU ME IN, YOU ME GREG GO), or specify agents, actions, and locations (YOU ME DRINK GO, YOU ME OUT SEE), or specify agents, actions, and objects of action (YOU GIVE GUM MOJA, YOU TICKLE ME WASHOE).

Creativity

Without deliberately teaching the chimpanzees to construct multiple-sign utterances, the human signers normally modelled simple phrases and sentences in their daily conversation. Washoe, Moja, Pili, Tatu, and Dar could all invent novel combinations for themselves. Washoe called her refrigerator the OPEN FOOD DRINK and her toilet the DIRTY GOOD even though her human companions referred to these as the COLD BOX and the POTTY CHAIR. When asked WHAT THAT? of assorted unnamed objects, Moja described a cigarette lighter as a METAL HOT, a Thermos flask as a METAL CUP DRINK COFFEE, and a glass of Alkaseltzer, as a LISTEN DRINK [B. T. Gardner, Gardner, & Nichols, 1989; R. A. Gardner & Gardner, 1991].

In Oklahoma, Washoe frequently called the swans in the moat around her island WATER BIRD even though Roger Fouts called the swans DUCK. R. Fouts [1975] reported a systematic study of the chimpanzee Lucy in Oklahoma in which he asked Lucy to name a series of fruits and vegetables that no one had ever named for her in ASL. Among the objects that Lucy had to name for herself were radishes which she called CRY HURT FOOD, and watermelon which she called CANDY DRINK. Perhaps, the clearest evidence that the chimpanzees learned signs as meaningful parts of meaningful phrases is the frequency and variety of new, chimpanzee-invented terms.

Development

Exciting as they are, first steps are only the beginning of walking and first words are only the beginning of talking. If the earliest utterances of human infants represent language, then they are best described as primitive, childish language. Gradually and piecemeal, but in an orderly sequence, the language of toddlers develops into the language of their parents. The well documented record of human development provides a scale for measuring the progress of cross-fostered chimpanzees.

In a cross-fostering laboratory, the sign language of chimpanzees grows and develops. B. T. Gardner and Gardner [1994; 1998] studied the growth and development of phrases in the sign language of Moja, Tatu, and Dar, who were cross-fostered from birth for about 5 years. Size of vocabulary, appropriate use of sentence constituents, number of utterances, proportion of phrases, and inflection all grew robustly throughout 5 years of cross-fostering. The growth was patterned growth and the patterns were consistent across chimpanzees. Wherever there are comparable measurements, the patterns of growth for cross-fostered chimpanzees paralleled the characteristic patterns reported for human infants.

Studies of human children generally agree that the major semantic relations appear in a characteristic developmental sequence [Bloom, 1991; Bloom, Lightbown, & Hood, 1975; Braine, 1976; Leonard, 1976; Wells, 1974]. J. G. De Villiers & De Villiers [1986, pp. 50-51] and Reich [1986, p. 83] summarize this agreement. Nominative phrases and action phrases appear first. Next come attributive phrases expressing the properties of objects (attribution, possession, location). Experience/notice phrases are relatively late in child development. With respect to negatives and requests studies of children have so far either failed to report developmental order or reported inconsistent orders. In the development of Moja, Tatu, and Dar, nominative and action phrases appeared first, attributives second, and experience/notice appeared latest in the developmental samples of each chimpanzee -- the same sequence that appears in studies of child development [B. T. Gardner & Gardner, 1998].

REPLICATION

In October 1970, after 51 months in Reno, when Washoe was about five years old, she went to the University of Oklahoma with Roger Fouts [R. Fouts & Fouts, 1989]. In November 1972, we began a second venture in cross-fostering. For the scientific objectives of cross-fostering, the replication with Moja, Pili, Tatu, and Dar was essential to verify the original discoveries with Washoe. The second project also included many improvements over Project Washoe.

The chimpanzees of the second project interacted with each other and this, in itself, added a new dimension to the cross-fostering. In a human household, children help in the care of their younger siblings who, in their turn, learn a great deal from older siblings. Sibling relationships are also a common feature of the family life of chimpanzees in the wild. Older offspring stay with their mothers while their younger siblings are growing up and they share in the care of their little brothers and sisters. Close bonds are established among the older and younger members of the same family who remain allies for life. Equally significant for cross-fostering, the younger siblings follow and imitate their big sisters and big brothers [Goodall, 1986].

In order to capitalize on the relationships between older and younger foster siblings, we started them newborn, but at intervals, so that there would be age differences. Starting the subjects at intervals in this way also had the practical advantage of allowing us to add human participants to the project more gradually. In each family group there was always a core of experienced human participants for the new recruits to consult as well as a stock of records and films to study. This helped us achieve the necessary stability and continuity in the foster families. Fifteen years after the start of Project Washoe there were still five human participants who had been long-term members of Washoe's original foster family. The second project became a fairly extensive enterprise by the time that there were three chimpanzee subjects. At that point, the laboratory moved from the original suburban home to a secluded site that used to be a guest ranch. The chimpanzees lived in the cabins that formerly housed ranch hands. Some members of the human families lived in the guest apartments and the rancher's quarters. The human bedrooms were wired to intercoms in the chimpanzee cabins so that at least one human adult monitored each cross-fosterling throughout each night. There were great old trees and pastures, corrals and barns, to play in. There were also special rooms for observation and testing as well as office and shop facilities. The place was designed to keep the subjects under cross-fostering conditions until they were nearly grown up, perhaps long enough for them to begin to care for their own offspring.

Throughout the second project, several human members of the family were deaf, themselves, or were the offspring of deaf parents. Others had already learned ASL and had used it extensively with members of the deaf community. With the deaf participants it was always "sign language only" whether or not there were chimpanzees present. The native signers were the best models of ASL, for the human participants who were learning ASL as a second language as well as for the chimpanzees who were learning it as a first language. The native signers were also better observers because it was easier for them to recognize babyish forms of ASL. Along with their own fluency they had a background of experience with human infants who were learning their first signs of ASL.

More advanced developments in sign language appeared with each succeeding year of cross-fostering. The proof that Moja, Tatu, and Dar had not yet reached any limit at 3 years is their growth during the fourth year, and the proof that they had not yet reached a limit at 3 years is the growth during the fifth year. Nevertheless, after 3 years of cross-fostering, their sign language had clearly fallen behind human 3-year-olds, and farther behind after 4 years, and still farther behind after 5 years. Chimpanzees should be even farther behind human children in their sign language after 6 years of cross-fostering, but by the same token, they should continue to advance and at 6 years they should be ahead of themselves at 5 years. Sign language studies of cross-fostered chimpanzees reveal robust growth and development. Further intellectual development should continue until sexual maturity which takes more than 12 years.

CONVERSATIONAL INTERACTION

Conversational interaction is a fundamental characteristic of human face-to-face communication in words and signs and has always been a primary objective of sign language studies of cross-fostered chimpanzees.

> At the outset we were quite sure that Washoe could learn to make various signs in order to obtain food, drink, and other things. For the project to be a success, we felt that something more must be developed. We wanted Washoe not only to ask for objects but to answer questions about them and also to ask us questions. We wanted to develop behavior that could be described as conversation. [R. A. Gardner & Gardner, 1969, pp. 665-666]

At the Chimpanzee & Human Communication Institute (CHCI) at Central Washington University in Ellensburg the chimpanzees continued to sign spontaneously and interactively with each other as well as with human familiars [D. Fouts, 1994; Bodamer & Gardner, 2002]. Formal experimental tests of the chimpanzees that loom so large in the scientific literature represent a small fraction of their daily output of signs both in the cross-fostering laboratory and CHCI. In both laboratories the chimpanzees initiated most of their signed interactions with humans.

> After the first year, most of the signed exchanges between the chimpanzees and the human beings in the cross-fostering laboratory were initiated by the chimpanzees, themselves. Thousands upon thousands of incidents of signing appear in the records and in more than half, usually much more than half, of the incidents in any random sample, the signing was initiated by the chimpanzee. It is the spontaneity illustrated in films, video tapes, and written records that most clearly shows that the young cross-fosterlings had made the signs their own and were using them the way human children use words and signs. [B. T. Gardner, Gardner, & Nichols, 1989, p. 63]

This chapter reports an experimental study of conversational interaction in sign language between cross-fostered chimpanzees and a human interlocutor.

CONVERSATIONAL PARTNERS

The four participants described in this chapter were Washoe, Moja, Tatu, and Dar (see Table 1). Washoe was captured wild in Africa. She arrived in Reno on June 21, 1966, when she was about ten months old and lived as a cross-fosterling until October 1, 1970 when she left to become the first chimpanzee in the Fouts laboratory in Oklahoma. Moja, Pili, Tatu, and Dar were born in American laboratories and each arrived in Reno within a few days of birth. Moja was born at the Laboratory for Experimental Medicine and Surgery in Primates, New York, on November 18, 1972, and arrived in Reno on the following day. Cross-fostering continued for Moja until winter 1979 when she left for the Fouts laboratory in Oklahoma. In 1980 Washoe and Moja moved to the Fouts laboratory (which later became the CHCI in 1992) in Ellensburg where the present study took place. Tatu was born at the Institute for Primate Studies, Oklahoma, on December 30, 1975, and arrived in Reno on January 2, 1976.

Dar, a male, was born at Albany Medical College, Holloman AFB, New Mexico, on August 2, 1976, and arrived in Reno on August 6, 1976. Cross-fostering continued for Tatu and Dar until May, 1981 when they left to join Washoe and Moja in Ellensburg. Pili was born October 30, 1973 and arrived in Reno on November 1, 1973. He died of leukemia on October 20, 1975. Moja died at CHCI on June 6, 2002.

Table 1. Biographical Information for Each Chimpanzee

	Washoe	Moja	Tatu	Dar
	female	female	female	male
Birth date:	9/65 (est.)	11/18/72	12/30/75	8/2/76
Univ. of Nevada, Reno*	6/66-10/70	11/72-11/79	1/76-5/81	8/76-5/81
Univ. of Oklahoma†	10/70-9/80	12/79-9/80	-----	-----
Central Wash. Univ.‡	9/80-	9/80-6/02	5/81-	5/81-

*Exposed to ASL only.
†Exposed to ASL and spoken English.
‡As above until 6/86; thereafter exposed to ASL primarily.

Washoe, Moja, Tatu, and Dar were raised like human children at the Gardner cross-fostering laboratory in Reno.

> Washoe was about 10 months old when she arrived in Reno and almost as helpless as a human child of the same age. In the next few years she learned to drink from a cup and to eat at a table with forks and spoons. She also learned to set and clear the table and even to wash the dishes, in a childish way. She learned to dress and undress herself and she learned to use the toilet to the point where she seemed embarrassed when she could not find a toilet on an outing in the woods, eventually using a discarded coffee can that she found on a hike. She had the usual children's toys and was particularly fond of dolls, kissing them, feeding them, and even bathing them. She was attracted to picture books and magazines almost from the first day and she would look through them by herself or with a friend who would name and explain the pictures and tell stories about them. The objects and activities that most attracted her were those that most engaged the grownups. She was fascinated by household tools, eventually acquiring a creditable level of skill with hammers and screwdrivers. [R. A. Gardner & Gardner, 1998, p. 291]

At CHCI the chimpanzees continued to interact with humans throughout each day signing about activities, meals, games, and events. Although now in enclosures, the chimpanzees still had access to picture books, toys, clothing, and other objects that were part of their lives in Reno and of the lives of human children. Human caregivers probed the chimpanzees with questions and expanded on fragmentary utterances as in the Reno laboratory. The chimpanzees continued to sign spontaneously and interactively with their human caregivers.

> We attempted to break the routine of an institution, to make each meal an interesting and enjoyable social event, and each day special, with many different activities and many opportunities for social interaction. We also celebrated the birthdays of Washoe, Loulis, Moja, Tatu, and Dar, as well as most of the holidays on the calendar, which made at least one, and usually more, days of each month extra special. Thus the Christmas celebration started sometime after Thanksgiving, when we set up a tree near the enclosure, and began to make

garlands of edible ornaments for the tree and the hallways. By late December, the tree was covered with different edible treats such as nuts, dried fruit, popcorn, and gum. Throughout this period, the tree was a popular topic of conversation between the chimpanzees and their human caretakers. In 1986, the first snowstorm of the season came on the day after Thanksgiving. The following morning the laboratory seemed especially quiet and serene, with the sprinkle of snow on the ground visible from all of the laboratory windows. As was usual during college vacations the students were away, and only the Foutses were in the lab. Perhaps, all this reminded Tatu of Christmas... During the cleaning routine, she followed them around, signing, SWEET SWEET SWEET TREE. Deborah Fouts assured Tatu, YOU MUST WAIT FOR SANTA. [R. Fouts & Fouts, 1989, pp. 296-297]

It was during these ongoing casual conversations that an interlocutor engaged the chimpanzees for systematic conversations.

SYSTEMATIC CONVERSATIONS

Interlocutors systematically vary input in conversations to examine conversational skill in children. Anselmi, Tomasello, and Acunzo [1986] examined responses of children to general questions such as "What?" versus specific questions such as "What banana?" Wilcox and Webster [1980] presented questions versus statements to children. They found that children were more responsive to questions than statements. Brinton, Fujiki, Loeb, & Winker [1986] presented a succession of general questions to children 2 to 7 years old. In the succession the interlocutor followed the child's response to the first general question with a second general question for a total of three questions. For example,

Child: Gimme ball.
Probe 1: Huh?
Child: Gimme ball.
Probe 2: What?
Child: Gimme that ball.
Probe 3: I don't understand.
Child: That ball there, gimme it.

Younger children had more difficulty responding to questions occurring later in the series than older children. Older children provided more information to the interlocutor than the younger children. General question series show differences between normal versus language impaired children [Brinton, Fujiki, Winkler, et al., 1986] and among mentally retarded adults [Brinton & Fujiki, 1991]. By systematically varying the response of the interlocutor, research showed that responses of children were contingent on the questions of the interlocutor.

Procedure

In the present experiment the interlocutor systematically varied her input during casual interactions with the chimpanzees. A single interlocutor (MLJ) presented one of four types of probes: general requests for more information, on topic questions, off topic questions, or negative statements. At the time of data collection she had 8 years experience caring for and interacting with this group of chimpanzees and 10 years experience communicating in ASL

When she arrived at the interaction area MLJ either approached a chimpanzee or waited for a chimpanzee to approach her as she normally did in the course of a day. The interlocutor then attempted to engage the chimpanzee in a typical conversational interaction on a subject such as looking at a book, eating a meal, playing a game, or some other common activity [R. Fouts, Abshire, Bodamer, & Fouts, 1989]. The chimpanzees were free to interact with the interlocutor or to ignore her. As the participants settled down during this pretrial period, the camera operator positioned the camera and started the tape record.

A second person operated a video camera to record each trial. At the beginning of a trial the interlocutor stood or knelt to the right of the chimpanzee and positioned herself so that she and the chimpanzee were facing each other at an angle of about 90 degrees. The operator positioned the camera so that the hands and faces of both interlocutor and chimpanzee appeared in the view of the camera. The camera operator used a list containing the sequence of conditions to prompt the interlocutor in English to present the correct condition on each trial.

Although ASL was virtually the only language that the human members of their foster families used in the Gardner laboratory, the chimpanzees often heard spoken English at CHCI and understood spoken English [Bodamer, Fouts, & Fouts, 1987; Shaw, 1989; Sloan, 2002]. To avoid the possibility that the camera operator might prompt the chimpanzee as well as the interlocutor by announcing each upcoming condition, the operator used a numerical code rather than English words to specify conditions and changed the code three times during the course of the study.

When ready, the camera operator signaled that the camera was ready and prompted the interlocutor by indicating which condition to present on that trial. The next time that the chimpanzee signed to the interlocutor, she replied with the first probe in the series specified by the condition for that trial. When the chimpanzee signed in response to the first probe, the interlocutor probed again, and so on until the interlocutor completed the series of three planned probes specified for that trial.

The interlocutor waited for the end of each chimpanzee turn before presenting the next probe. Signers normally end an utterance by dropping their hands or holding their hands without movement [Covington, 1973; Grosjean & Lane, 1977; Stokoe, 1972]. The chimpanzees also use these behaviors at the end of an utterance. In the last third of the film, Teaching Sign Language to the Chimpanzee Washoe [R. A. Gardner & Gardner, 1973; 1974] there are several examples of extended utterances. In one example Washoe signs to Susan Nichols.

Washoe: YOU [hold] ME/ YOU ME WASHOE ME [hold] GO/

Between the phrases YOU ME/ and YOU ME WASHOE ME GO/ Washoe holds her hands in the signing space but they are relaxed. After the final GO Washoe drops her hands. These utterance boundary markers are different from the hesitation pauses after the first YOU and the last ME. The hesitation pauses are typical of the halting signing and speech of young children. Judgments on utterance boundaries yield high interobserver agreement [B. T. Gardner & Gardner, 1994, pp. 229-230; Rimpau, et al., 1989, p. 249].

Here and throughout this chapter, transcriptions of signs appear in all capital letters. Signed utterances are transcribed into word-for-sign English because more literal translations would add words and word endings which lack signed equivalents either in the vocabularies of the chimpanzees or in ASL. This mode of transcription makes the utterances appear to be in a crude or pidgin dialect, but the reader should keep in mind the fact that equally literal word-for-word transcriptions between English and say, Russian or Japanese, appear equally crude.

Transcriptions of signs in this chapter indicate three types of modulation. The gloss is the English word equivalent for a sign. An "x" following a gloss indicates immediate reiteration of that sign. A question mark, "?", following a gloss indicates a questioning inflection. A slash (/) indicates an utterance boundary [see B. T. Gardner & Gardner, 1994, p. 230]. B. T. Gardner and Gardner [1994] and Rimpau, et al. [1986] describe how cross-fosterlings inflected signs and phrases in the Reno laboratory.

After each probe the chimpanzee was free to answer with any signs or phrases in his or her vocabulary, to continue to face the interlocutor, to look away, or to leave the scene entirely. If the chimpanzee ended the interaction by leaving the scene, the response to that probe and all remaining probes of that trial were scored as no response. Because the interlocutor never signed to a chimpanzee unless the chimpanzee was facing her, all cases in which she failed to regain the attention of the chimpanzee within 5 s of the last probe or the last chimpanzee response had to be scored as if the chimpanzee had left the scene.

When the chimpanzee failed to respond to a probe in signs within 5 s but continued to face the interlocutor, the interlocutor presented the next probe in the series. Failures to regain attention appeared in two forms. First, when the chimpanzee signed and then looked away, the interlocutor attempted to regain the attention of the chimpanzee by waving her arms or by making a noise such as tongue clicking noise or kissing noise. If the chimpanzee faced the interlocutor again within 5 s, the interlocutor presented the next probe in the series. If the chimpanzee failed to face the interlocutor for 5 s, the trial ended and the response to the next and all the remaining probes of that trial were scored as no response. Second, when the chimpanzee looked away before responding to a probe in signs, the interlocutor also attempted to regain the attention of the chimpanzee by waving her arms or by making a noise such as tongue clicking noise or kissing noise. If the chimpanzee faced the interlocutor again within 5 s without signing, this was scored as a failure to respond, and the interlocutor presented the next probe. If the chimpanzee failed to face the interlocutor for 5 s without responding in signs, the trial ended and the response to that probe and all remaining probes of that trial were scored as no response.

Other chimpanzees near the interaction area were free to observe or to participate in the interactions at any time as usual in daily interactions. If a second chimpanzee interfered with the interaction, then the interlocutor aborted that trial and discarded it from the record. If the second chimpanzee approached without interfering, the interlocutor ignored the second chimpanzee until the end of the trial with the first chimpanzee. At the end of the trial with the first chimpanzee the interlocutor was free to begin a new trial with the second chimpanzee.

Conditions

There were four conditions in this experiment and they are listed in Table 2. The probes in the general condition consisted of a series of three general questions. The probes in the on-topic condition consisted of a series of three on topic questions. The probes in the off-topic condition consisted of a series of three off topic questions. And, the probes in the can't condition consisted of a series of three negative statements.

Table 2. Conditions Presented During Trials

Condition	Probe type
General	Three general questions
On-topic	Three context appropriate Wh- questions
Off-topic	Three context inappropriate Wh- questions
Can't	Three non-question negative probes

General Trials

For each general trial the interlocutor asked three general question probes that indicated failure to understand the chimpanzee. The interlocutor always presented the same three general probes in this order: 1) a questioning facial expression without any signs, 2) the sign WHAT?/ and 3) I NOT UNDERSTAND?/ often signed with a negative headshake which is common usage in ASL [Baker-Shenk, 1985, p. 299; Humphries, Padden, & O'Rourke, 1980]. In her questioning facial expressions the interlocutor pulled her eyebrows together, leaned forward, and held her eyegaze on the chimpanzee. Baker-Shenk describes this as the typical interrogative facial expression of ASL. The only condition in which the sign WHAT?/ appeared alone in a probe was the general condition.

An example of a general trial is:

Trial # 3/1:04:40
    1:04:35 Washoe: ME GIMMEx/
    1:04:40 Probe 1: questioning expression
    1:04:41 Washoe: GIMME/
    1:04:49 Probe 2: WHAT?/
    1:04:51 Washoe: MEx GIMMEx/
    1:04:54 Probe 3: NOT UNDERSTAND?/
    1:04:56 Washoe: FOOD GIMME/

Each videotaped trial between a chimpanzee and a human interlocutor begins with the address of the observation in the videotape record of this study. In this case the address "Trial #3/1:04:40" indicates that this dialogue is a transcription from the third videotape and that the interlocutor's first probe began at 1 hour 4 minutes 40 seconds from the beginning of the videotape.

On-topic Trials

In each on-topic trial the interlocutor asked three Wh-questions that incorporated a relevant sign from the chimpanzee utterance that started the trial and were also appropriate to the context of the interaction. The on-topic condition contained probes such as: WHO WANT FLOWER?/ if the chimpanzee utterance had included FLOWER; WHO EAT?/ if the chimpanzee utterance had included EAT; WHERE CHASE?/ if the chimpanzee utterance had included CHASE. These were typical questions that human familiars asked the chimpanzees in daily signed interactions. If the chimpanzee's reply to an on-topic probe contained an appropriate sentence constituent [Brown, 1968; B. T. Gardner & Gardner, 1975], then the interlocutor probed again with a different on-topic Wh-question. If the chimpanzee's utterance failed to include an appropriate sentence constituent then the next probe repeated the previous probe. As normal in signed interactions of human and nonhuman primates, a questioning facial expression accompanied signed questions.

Two examples of on-topic trials are:

Trial # 2/0:07:51
　　0:07:47 Dar: GUMx GOODx GUMx THERE/
　　0:07:51 Probe 1: WHO WANT GUM?/
　　0:07:52 Dar: DARx HEIDI DAR THERE/
　　0:07:56 Probe 2: WHERE GUM?/
　　0:07:56 Dar: DARx GUM?/
　　0:07:59 Probe 3: WHERE GUM?/
　　0:08:00 Dar: DARx THERE/
Trial # 3/0:38:26
　　0:38:24 Washoe: THATx/
　　0:38:26 Probe 1: WHO WANT THAT?/
　　0:38:28 Washoe: FLOWER GIMMEx/
　　0:38:30 Probe 2: WHO WANT FLOWER?/
　　0:38:32 Washoe: FLOWER GIMMEx FLOWERx ME/
　　0:38:38 Probe 3: WHERE GIVE FLOWER?/
　　0:38:46 Washoe: GIMMEx/

The Wh-sign in an ASL question can appear at the beginning or end of the question without altering the question [Humphries, et al., 1980, pp. 80-82]. For example:

Trial # 1/1:09:45
　　1:09:45 Probe 1: WHERE DOG?/
　　1:10:00 Probe 2: DOG WHERE?/

Off-topic Trials

For each off-topic trial the interlocutor asked a series of three Wh-questions that were unrelated to the chimpanzee's first utterance in the trial as well as inappropriate to the context, as in:

Trial # 2/0:15:12
    0:15:08 Washoe: SHOEx GIMMEx/
    0:15:12 Probe: WHERE ROGER?/
Trial # 3/0:56:08
    0:56:04 Washoe: RED THERE/
    0:56:08 Probe: WHO FUNNY?/

As in the on-topic condition, the interlocutor made the characteristic interrogative facial expression, and probes were typical questions that human familiars asked the chimpanzees in daily signed interactions. Indeed, off-topic probes were often identical to probes that the interlocutor presented in the on-topic condition. If the chimpanzee's reply to an off-topic probe contained a sentence constituent that was appropriate to the question, then the next probe contained a different off-topic Wh-question. If the chimpanzee's reply failed to include a sentence constituent that was appropriate to the question, then the next probe repeated the previous probe. An example of an off-topic trial is:

Trial #5/0:08:49
    0:08:46 Washoe. FRUIT GIMMEx/
    0:08:49 Probe 1: WHO FUNNY?/
    0:08:51 Washoe: ROGER/
    0:08:54 Probe 2: WHERE CAT?/
    0:08:56 Washoe: ROGER GIMMEx/
    0:09:03 Probe 3: WHERE CAT?/
    0:09:05 Washoe: GIMMEx/

Can't Trials

For each can't trial the interlocutor replied with a series of three negative statements indicating that the interlocutor would not or could not comply with the chimpanzee's request or continue the interaction. Typical examples of can't probes were CAN'T/, SORRY CAN'T/, and I MUST GO/. An example of a can't trial is:

Trial # 1/1:26:13
    1:26:06 Tatu: YOUx SMELL YOUx SMELL YOU/
    1:26:13 Probe 1: CAN'T/
    1:26:14 Tatu: YOU SMELL/
    1:26:17 Probe 2: CAN'T NOW/
    1:26:18 Tatu: THAT (towards floor)/
    1:26:20 Probe 3: CAN'T/
    Tatu: No signed response

Each chimpanzee received 20 trials under each of the four conditions yielding a total of 80 trials for each chimpanzee. The maximum number of trials for one chimpanzee in one day was three trials. The sequence of conditions was random without replacement except that the same condition never appeared on two consecutive trials in the same day.

Transcription

Sign language studies of chimpanzees like developmental studies of human children typically use productive tests in which participants are free to use any word or sign in their vocabulary and any number of words or signs in any given utterance [R. A. Gardner & Gardner, 1984; R. A. Gardner, Gardner, & Drumm, 1989; Van Cantfort, et al., 1989; Jensvold & Gardner, 2000; Bodamer & Gardner, 2002]. Moreover, as in studies of human participants, utterances are relatively appropriate or inappropriate rather than precisely correct or incorrect. Many different utterances can be appropriate in any given conversational context and different utterances are appropriate in different conversational contexts. Appropriateness is judged by patterns of responses rather than by high or low scores. To analyze appropriateness in an objective fashion, transcribers first transcribed the utterances of the chimpanzee and the interlocutor. Next, the coder classified the utterances into a fixed number of categories in order to analyze the distribution of the categories.

During all trials in this experiment the interlocutor appeared on the right and the chimpanzee appeared on the left of the television screen. When transcribing the signs of the interlocutor, transcribers occluded the chimpanzee and when transcribing the signs of the chimpanzee, transcribers occluded the interlocutor. There were approximately 75 trials on each 120 minute videotape. It took approximately 10 weeks to fill a videotape with trials.

Interlocutor

After a videotape was filled, MLJ assigned glosses to each sign in each probe on the entire videotape using the PCM (place, configuration, movement) system. The PCM system [B. Gardner, Gardner, & Nichols, 1989] is a description of how the sign is formed using place where the sign is made, configuration of the hand, and movement of the hand. A second transcriber, who had 2 years experience in ASL with humans, assigned glosses to a sample of 20% of the probes. Agreement between the two transcriptions of this sample appears in Table 3.

Chimpanzee

Next MLJ assigned glosses to each sign in each chimpanzee utterance on the entire videotape using the PCM system. With the exception of a few "home" signs, such as POTTY and PEEKABOO all of the signs also appeared in standard dictionaries of ASL as described and explained in B. T. Gardner, Gardner, and Nichols [1989]. Name signs were created by the normal procedures for creating name signs in the deaf community. The only pointing sign on the PCM list is the indexical, THAT/THERE, which is also a pointing sign in ASL (see also sequential analysis of THAT and THERE in B. T. Gardner and Gardner [1998, pp. 182-184]). Two other signs, ME and YOU, are made by pointing to oneself or to an interlocutor in dictionaries of ASL as well as in the vocabularies of Washoe, Moja, Tatu, and Dar. In the published film [R. Gardner & Gardner, 1973] Washoe names her image in a mirror signing both ME and ME WASHOE in response to the question WHO THAT? When she points to herself the gloss is ME, when she makes the name sign WASHOE the gloss is WASHOE. Only when she makes both signs in the same utterance is the gloss ME WASHOE. In any phrase glossed as THAT APPLE or THERE DOG both the indexical and the object sign must appear.

As MLJ recorded glosses, she indicated utterance boundaries with a slash (/). A second transcriber, who had 12 years experience in ASL with humans, assigned glosses to a sample of 20% of the utterances. Agreement between the two transcriptions of this sample appears in Table 3.

Table 3. Reliability of Transcriptions

Transcription	Percent Agreement
Gloss	
Probes	93%
Replies	
Washoe	87%
Moja	87%
Tatu	95%
Dar	92%
Modulation	
Reiteration	93%
Place	93%

Modulation

Dictionaries of ASL, like dictionaries of spoken languages, show signs in citation form - the form that is seen when an informant responds to the question "What is the sign for 'X'?" In normal conversation, fluent signers inflect their signs in a variety of ways. The sign, GIVE, for example, may start near the signer's body and move out toward the addressee to indicate, "I give you". The same sign with the direction of the movement reversed, indicates, "You give me". Inflection makes signs more versatile and more expressive; a single lexical item can become several different signs. Typical inflections have parallel effects on many different signs. At least 20 different types of inflection appear in the field records [of the Reno laboratory]. Each type can be characterized by an aspect of sign form - e.g., Place or Movement - and by the way in which this aspect differs from citation form. [B. T. Gardner & Gardner, 1994, p. 230]

In this study the cross-fosterlings modulated their signs as they did in most casual interchanges. As she glossed each utterance MLJ also reported two prominent types of modulation; reiteration, in which the signer repeats a sign one or more times and placement in which the signer forms a sign on a place that differs from the citation form [Rimpau, et al., 1989].

A chimpanzee could reiterate the sign APPLE by signing APPLE APPLE APPLE APPLE instead of a single APPLE. Both human children [Keenan, 1977; Keenan & Klein, 1975] and cross-fostered chimpanzees [R. A. Gardner, Gardner, & Drumm, 1989, p. 46; Van Cantfort, et al., 1989, p. 211; Rimpau, et al., 1989, p. 249; B. T. Gardner & Gardner, 1994, p. 231] commonly reiterate words or signs within an utterance. R. A. Gardner, Gardner, and Drumm found that Tatu and Dar, like the human children studied by Keenan [1977] and Keenan and Klein [1975], were likely to reiterate signs in their response to positive announcements and unlikely to reiterate signs in responding to neutral or negative announcements. This indicates that reiteration within an utterance serves as a pragmatic device expressing emphasis or assent. We use reiteration here rather than repetition following R. A. Gardner, Gardner, and Drumm.

> When used in this context, the term repetition leads to confusion since it is also used to refer to incorporation [Keenan, 1977, p. 125]. This confusion is compounded by the practice of classifying some incorporations as repetitions and some as imitations, depending upon adult inferences about the intention of the child. Terminological confusion is still further compounded by the widespread disagreement as to the criteria that might distinguish repetition from imitation in human children's replies [Keenan, 1977, pp. 125-129]. It is for this reason that we recommend the terms; incorporation, for items also found in the preceding utterance of an interlocutor, and reiteration, for items that recurred within a single utterance. [R. A. Gardner, Gardner, & Drumm, 1989, p. 47]

In this chapter we used reiteration across turns for items that recurred across adjacent utterances.

Both human signers [Wilbur, 1980] and cross-fostered chimpanzees vary the place of a sign to express person, place, and instrument [Rimpau, et al., 1989]. For example in its citation form the place for TICKLE is the back of the hand. In the Gardner laboratory, Rimpau, et al. [p. 257] found that Dar also signed TICKLE on the addressee to indicate that the addressee should tickle him, and on objects to indicate that the addressee should tickle Dar with the object.

A second transcriber who had 14 years experience using ASL received a written transcription of the glosses of 20% of the trials without notes for reiteration or place modulation. The second transcriber viewed the corresponding segments of videotape and scored whether each gloss was reiterated or modulated for place. Percent agreement between MLJ and the second transcriber was calculated separately for reiteration and place modulation and appears in Table 3.

Categorization

For convenience this analysis designates each chimpanzee utterance as cn, where the chimpanzee utterance that initiated each trial is $c0$ and the sequence of replies to the interlocutor is $c1$, $c2$, and $c3$. Similarly, this analysis designates each interlocutor probe as pn, where the sequence of three probes is $p1$, $p2$, $p3$. The first analysis measures the *reaction* of the chimpanzees to each probe by comparing the signs in each chimpanzee utterance to the signs in the immediately preceding utterance, $c1{:}c0$, $c2{:}c1$, and $c3{:}c2$. The second analysis measures the *interaction* of the chimpanzees with each probe of the interlocutor by comparing the signs in each reply to the signs in the immediately preceding probe, $c1{:}p1$, $c2{:}p2$, and $c3{:}p3$.

Using the gloss transcriptions, MLJ classified the reaction of each chimpanzee utterance, $c1{:}c0$, $c2{:}c1$, and $c3{:}c2$, according to the scheme in Table 4 and the interaction of each chimpanzee utterance, $c1{:}p1$, $c2{:}p2$, and $c3{:}p3$, according to the scheme in Table 5.

Reaction. *(cn:cn-1)*

1. S (same): The signs in cn were the same as the signs in cn-1 in both gloss and modulation. An example of S is:

Trial # 3/0:26:03
    0:26:07 Moja: CLOTHESx/
    0:26:09 Probe: NOT UNDERSTAND?/
    0:26:11 Moja: CLOTHESx/

2. S-: The signs in cn contained some but not all of the same signs in cn-1 without additional signs or changes in modulation . An example of S- is:

Trial # 3/1:39:45
    1:39:42 Moja: YOU SHOEx/
    1:39:45 Probe: SHOE CAN'T HAVE/
    1:38:48 Moja: YOU/

Table 4. Reaction to Interlocutor Probe

Category	Relation of signs in turn to signs in previous turn		
	Same	Novel	Changed Modulation
S	All	None	None
S-	Some	None	None
Sc			
(S*)	All	None	Some
(S+)	All	Some	None
(S+/-)	Some	Some	None
Dc	None	All	N/A
NR	N/A	N/A	N/A

Note: Modulation was only scored if the glosses in the two replies were exactly the same.

3. S^*: The signs in cn were the same as the signs in cn-1 except that the modulation changed.

a) Reiteration. A shift from single iteration to one or more reiterations or from one or more reiterations to single iteration. An example of change in reiteration is:

Trial # 0:47:53
    0:47:49 Moja: FLOWER/
    0:47:53 Probe: WHAT?/
    0:47:54 Moja: FLOWERx/

b) Place. The chimpanzee changed the place modulation. An example of place is:

Trial # 2/1:36:14
    1:36:11 Tatu: HURRYx THERE (towards the left with outstretched arm)/
    1:36:14 Probe: CAN'T/
    1:36:19 Tatu: SMELL THERE (towards left, fingertip toward interlocutor)/

While the configuration and movement were the same, Tatu changed the referent by changing the place of the sign.

    4. S+: All of the signs in cn-1 appeared in cn together with new signs. An example of S+ is:

Trial # 3/0:21:29
    0:21:23 Washoe: GIMMEx/
    0:21:29 Probe: questioning expression
    0:21:30 Washoe: FOOD GIMMEx/

    5. S+/-: Some but not all of the signs in cn-1 appeared in cn together with new signs. An example of S+/- is:

Trial # 5/0:07:30
    0:07:28 Washoe: HURRYx GIMMEx/
    0:07:30 Probe: WHO STUPID?/
    0:07:32 Washoe: PERSONx GIMME/

In cases of S+ and S+/- the chimpanzees expanded on their previous utterances [B. T. Gardner & Gardner, 1994, p 231; Bloom, Rocissano, & Hood, 1976; Keenan, 1977].

    6. Dc: All the signs in cn-1 were different from the signs in cn. An example of Dc is:

Trial # 5/0:08:24
    0:08:33 Washoe: GRASSx GIMME/
    0:08:34 Probe: WHO WANT GRASS?/
    0:08:35 Washoe: PERSONx HURRYx/

    7. NR (no response): The chimpanzee failed to respond within 5 s after the probe [Brinton, Fujiki, Loeb, et al., 1986, p. 77]. If the chimpanzee looked away or moved away before the interlocutor could present the next probe, the response was classified as NR.

    A second coder classified 20% of the transcribed responses. Agreement between MLJ and the second coder was 96%.

Table 5. Interaction with Interlocutor probe

Category	Relation of signs in turn to signs in previous probe	
	Same	**Novel**
I	All	None
I+	Some	Some
Dp	None	All
NR	N/A	N/A

Interaction. (cn:pn)

1. I (incorporation): All of the signs in cn appeared in pn [R. A. Gardner, Gardner, & Drumm, 1989, p. 47]. An example of incorporation is:

Trial #1/0:15:56
    1:16:08-11 Probe: WHOSE BERRY?/
    1:16:14 Tatu: BERRYx/

2. I+ (expansion): All of the signs in cn appeared in pn together with new signs. In cases of I+ the chimpanzees expanded on the probes of the interlocutor [B. T. Gardner & Gardner 1994, p. 231; Bloom, et al., 1976; Keenan, 1977]. An example of I+ is:

Trial # 3/0:49:58
    0:49:58 Probe: WHO WANT FLOWER?/
    0:49:59 Washoe: FLOWER ME/

3. Dp: All the signs in cn were different from the signs in pn. An example of Dp is:

Trial # 1/0:38:09
    0:38:09 Probe: CAN'T/
    0:38:09 Moja: YOU BUG/

4. NR (no response): The chimpanzee failed to respond within 5 s after the probe [Brinton, Fujiki, Loeb, et al., 1986, p. 77]. If the chimpanzee looked away or moved away before the interlocutor could present the next probe, the response was classified as NR.

The same second coder who classified reaction categories also classified 20% of the transcribed responses in interaction categories. Agreement between MLJ and the second coder was 96%.

Reaction

Although MLJ and the second observer agreed in more than 96% of their assignments of reactions to the seven categories of Table 4, we combined S^*, S+, and S+/- into a single category Sc for statistical analyses.

We also pooled the reactions of the three successive probes into a single measure on the following grounds. The effect of each probe in a trial on the distribution of reactions yielded 16 chi-squares which, with five categories of reaction versus three probes, each had 8 degrees of freedom. Of these 16 chi-squares, 12 probabilities were greater than .50 and the lowest probability was greater than .08. On the basis of this insignificant difference between probes within a trial we pooled all three probes into a single distribution for each trial. This yielded three times 20 or 60 independent probes for each probe condition in all further analyses of reaction to probe type.

The patterns of reaction to probes for each chimpanzee for each condition appear graphically in Figure 1. A one-way chi-square for each distribution appears below each of the 16 panels of Figure 1 and each of these chi-squares is significant with $p < .006$ with two exceptions which were significant with $p < .05$. The distribution of reactions among categories was significantly different from chance equality for each chimpanzee and for each condition.

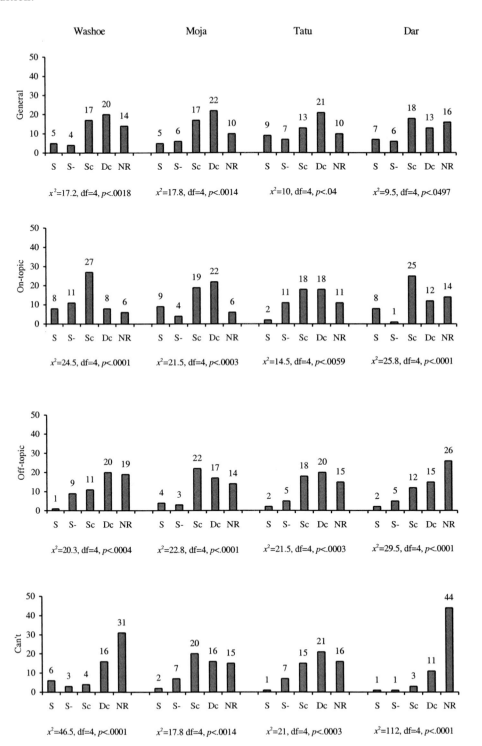

Figure 1. Patterns of reaction to four types of probes; Ns for all chi-squares appear within the bar graphs. See text for definition of terms.

Condition versus Condition

The effect of conditions on the pattern of reaction shown in Figure 1 yielded four chi-squares, one for each chimpanzee. With four conditions and five categories of reaction each test had 12 degrees of freedom. For Washoe the chi-square for conditions was significant ($\chi2$ = 55.85, df = 12, $p < .0001$). Pairwise comparisons showed significant differences ($p < .02$) between each pair of conditions except the general versus off-topic which approached significance with $p < .16$. For Dar also, the chi-square between conditions was significant ($\chi2$ = 55.85, df = 12, $p < .0001$). Pairwise comparisons showed significant differences ($p < .005$) between all of the pairs except the general versus on-topic ($p < .30$) and the general versus off-topic ($p < .16$) which only approached significance. For Moja and for Tatu the chi-squares for conditions only approached significance, for Moja ($\chi2$ = 13.98, df = 12, $p < .3$) and for Tatu ($\chi2$ = 17.7, df = 12, $p < .125$).

General Condition

Figure 1 shows that all four chimpanzees had a similar pattern of reaction. The Dc and Sc categories were the most frequent reactions to the general probes. The chi-square for four chimpanzees by five categories of reaction was insignificant ($\chi2$ = 8.22, df = 12, $p = .7679$) indicating that all four chimpanzees had a similar distribution of reactions to general probes. In an example of the Dc category Moja signed about flowers, something she ate.

    Trial # 1/1:30:30
        1:30:31 Moja: FLOWER/
        1:30:32 Probe: WHAT?/
        1:30:33 Moja: FOOD/

An example of the Sc category

    Trial # 1/1:15:30
        1:15:30 Dar: TOOTHBRUSH/
        1:15:30 Probe: questioning expression
        1:15:32 Dar: TOOTHBRUSHx THERE/

The chimpanzees frequently responded with the Sc category in the general condition as well. Anselmi, et al.; Brinton, Fujiki, Loeb, et al.; Brinton, Fujiki, Winkler, et al.; and Wilcox and Webster found that human children often incorporate and expand across turns when asked questions [1986; 1986; 1986; 1980].

On-topic Condition

Figure 1 shows two patterns of reaction to on-topic probes; one common to Washoe and Dar and the other common to Moja and Tatu. Washoe's and Dar's distributions peaked in the Sc category. Tatu's and Moja's distributions peaked in the Dc and Sc categories. The chi-square for four chimpanzees by five categories of reaction was significant ($\chi2$ = 31.35, df = 12, $p = .0017$) indicating significant individual differences.

Off-topic Condition

Figure 1 shows that all four distributions were similar for all four chimpanzees. The chi-square for four chimpanzees by five categories of reaction was insignificant ($\chi2 = 16.5$, df = 12, $p = .169$) indicating that all four chimpanzees had a similar distribution of reactions to off-topic probes. The chimpanzees' reactions often fell into the Dc and NR categories and rarely fell into the S and S- categories. In example of a Dc response in this condition the interlocutor offered toothbrushes to Washoe and Washoe asked for her choice in color.

> Trial # 2/1:43:54
>   1:43:51 Washoe: REDx/
>   1:43:54 Probe: WHO STUPID?/
>   1:43:56 Washoe: PERSON/

At the time of this study the sign glossed as PERSON in the laboratory was a flat hand with the palm contacting the top of the head. PERSON could be noisy if the signer slapped the top of the head. The chimpanzees used PERSON to gain attention when the addressee was not looking at the signer [Bodamer & Gardner, 2002], as if saying "Hey you" [R. Fouts, Hirsch, & Fouts, 1982, p. 181; R. Fouts, Fouts, & Van Cantfort, 1989].

Can't Condition

Figure 1 shows two patterns of reaction to two patterns of response to can't probes; one common to Washoe and Dar and another common to Moja and Tatu. The chi-square for four chimpanzees by five categories of reaction was significant ($\chi2 = 57.3$, df = 12, $p <.0001$) indicating significant individual differences. Washoe and Dar rarely used S, S-, or Sc in this condition. Instead they used a different sign (Dc) or failed to respond (NR). Moja and Tatu had more Sc responses and more responses than Dar and Washoe. In the can't condition Moja and Tatu were more persistent than Washoe and Dar. In this example before having a meal Tatu had to first enter another area.

> Trial # 1/0:56:18
>   0:56:14 Tatu: EATx?/
>   0:58:18 Probe: CAN'T/.
>   0:56:20 Tatu: IN/

Another example of persistence occurred while Moja was outside and referred to flowers that were beyond her reach.

> Trial # 3/0:24:59
>   0:25:00 Moja: FLOWERx THERE FLOWER THERE/
>   0:25:09 Probe: FLOWER CAN'Tx/
>   0:25:10 Moja FLOWERx YOU/

Moja persisted in the topic she initiated in spite of the negative response of the interlocutor. In contrast Washoe and Dar usually failed to respond to can't probes and when they did respond they mostly reacted with different (Dc) or modified (Sc) utterances.

In summary, in the general condition all four chimpanzees reacted with a similar pattern; their reactions most often fell into the Sc and Dc categories. In the on-topic condition Washoe and Dar had one pattern of reaction and Moja and Tatu had a different pattern of reaction. Washoe's and Dar's reactions often fell into the Sc category while Moja's and Tatu's often fell into both the Sc and Dc categories. In the off-topic condition all four chimpanzees reacted similarly; their reactions most often fell into the Dc and NR categories. In the can't condition, as in the on-topic condition, Washoe and Dar had one pattern of reaction while Moja and Tatu had a different pattern. Washoe and Dar often refused to respond and when they did respond their responses often fell into the Dc category. Moja and Tatu responded more often to the can't condition and their responses fell into the Sc and Dc categories.

Interaction

As in the case of reaction, the effect of each of the three successive probes in each of the 20 trials on the distribution of interactions with each probe condition yielded 16 chi-squares with four categories of reaction versus three probes. Of these 16 chi-squares, 9 probabilities were > 0.50 and the lowest probability was > 0.09. On the basis of this insignificant difference between successive probes within a trial we treated each probe within a trial as independent. This yielded three times 20 or 60 independent probes for each probe condition in all further analyses of interaction with probe type.

The patterns of interaction with probes for each chimpanzee for each condition appear graphically in Figure 2. As in the case of reaction, the effect of repeated probes on the interaction of each utterance with the previous probe yielded 16 chi-squares with four categories of interaction (I, I+, Dp, and NR). A one-way chi-square for each distribution appears below each of the 16 panels of Figure 2 and 14 of these chi-squares are significant with $p < .003$. This indicates that the distribution of interactions among categories was significantly different from chance equality for each chimpanzee and for each condition in all but two cases. The exceptions were the interactions with the on-topic probes for Tatu and Dar which yielded chi-squares of 1.7, $p > .63$ for Tatu and 0.7, $p > .87$ for Dar. As Figure 2 shows, general probes evoked no incorporations at all. Consequently, the chi-squares for this condition omitted these columns of response and had fewer degrees of freedom.

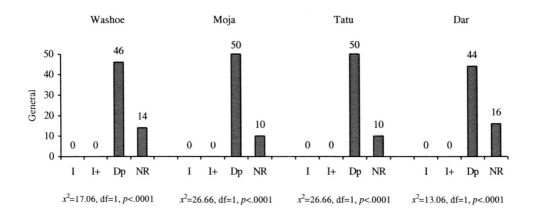

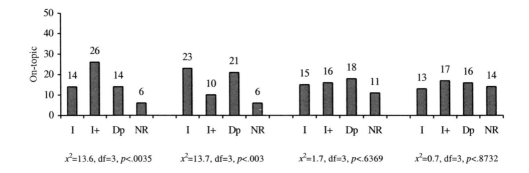

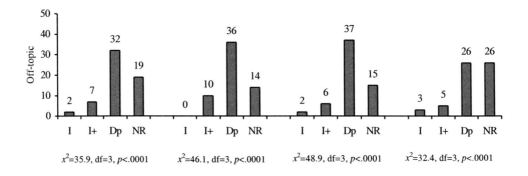

Figure 2. Patterns of interaction with four types of probes; *N*s for all chi-squares appear within the bar graphs. See text for definitions of terms.

Condition versus Condition

The effect of conditions on the pattern of interaction shown in Figure 2 yielded four chi-squares, one for each chimpanzee. With four conditions and four categories of interaction each test had nine degrees of freedom. These tests yielded chi-squares of 115.55 for Washoe, 80.13 for Moja, 67.44 for Tatu, and 104.26 for Dar. All four were significant with $p < 0.0001$. Of the 24 possible pairwise chi-squares 22 were significant with $p < .05$. The pairwise comparisons between can't and off-topic for both Moja and Tatu were insignificant with $p <$

0.21 and 0.75 respectively. In the pairwise comparisons there were three degrees of freedom for two conditions and four categories of interaction. In pairwise comparisons between the can't and general conditions for Washoe and Dar, however, the I and I+ columns had frequencies of less than three and these chi-squares were computed as two by two contingency tables with one degree of freedom. In the pairwise comparison between the general and off-topic condition for Moja the I column had a frequency of zero and this chi-square was computed as a two by three contingency table with two degrees of freedom.

General Condition

Figure 2 shows all four chimpanzees often responded with different (Dp) signs and never responded with incorporations (I) or expansions (I+). Since there were no responses in the I or I+ categories the chi-squares for this condition omitted these columns of response and had fewer degrees of freedom. The chi-square for four chimpanzees by two categories of interaction was insignificant ($\chi 2 = 2.73$, df = 3, $p = .4354$) indicating that all chimpanzees had a similar distribution of reactions to the general probes. Different signs were the most appropriate response in this condition since incorporations and expansions would be like answering a question with a question and would end the conversation. An example of a Dp response in this condition is

> Trial # 3/1:04:40
>   1:04:49 Probe. WHAT?/
>   1:04:51 Washoe: MEx GIMMEx/

On-topic Condition

Figure 2 shows that all four chimpanzees used incorporations (I) and expansions (I+) more in the on-topic condition than in the other conditions. The chi-square for four chimpanzees by four categories of interaction was significant ($\chi 2 = 18.05$, df = 9, $p = .0346$) indicating significant individual differences. In the following example Washoe responded with the I category and incorporated the sign of the interlocutor into her utterance without adding any new signs.

> Trial # 3/0:49:58
>   0:49:58 Probe: WHO WANT FLOWER?/
>   0:49:59 Washoe: FLOWER/

In the following example Tatu responded with the I+ category and she incorporated the sign SMELL into an expanded utterance.

> Trial # 2/0:19:23
>   0:19:26 Probe: WHO SMELL?/
>   0:19:27 Tatu: TATU SMELL YOU/

Off-topic Condition

Figure 2 shows that off-topic probes also depressed responses but less than can't probes. When they did respond to off-topic probes, most of their utterances contained different signs (Dp) or added new signs to incorporations (I+). The chi-square for four chimpanzees by four categories of interaction was insignificant ($\chi2 = 11.81$, df = 9, $p = .2244$) indicating that all chimpanzees had a similar distribution of reactions to the off-topic probes.

In this condition the probes were neither contingent on the chimpanzee's previous utterance nor contingent on the context of the interaction. The interactive effect of this on the chimpanzees was to evoke different signs from them. For example

> Trial # 1/0:19:26
> > 0:19:15 Tatu: CRACKERx/
> > 0:19:26 Probe: WHERE DOG?/
> > 0:19:31 Tatu: EATx TIMEx EATx/

Can't Condition

Figure 2 shows that can't probes depressed responses; the NR category appeared in this condition more often than in other conditions. Since there were few responses in the I or I+ categories the chi-squares for this condition omitted these columns of response and had fewer degrees of freedom. The chi-square for four chimpanzees by four categories of interaction was significant ($\chi2 = 44.86$, df = 9, $p < .0001$) indicating significant individual differences. There were two patterns of response; one common to Washoe and Dar and another common to Moja and Tatu. Most of Washoe's and Dar's responses to can't probes fell into the no response (NR) category but most of the rest of their responses to can't probes fell into the Dp category. Most of Moja's and Tatu's responses to can't probes fell into the Dp category but most of the rest of their responses to can't probes fell into the no response (NR) category. Incorporations (I) and expansions (I+) did appear in responses to can't probes but they were rare. Instead the chimpanzees usually signed something different from the probe (Dp) or failed to respond (NR).

In summary, Washoe's, Moja's, Tatu's, and Dar's responses depended on the probes of their conversational partner. When the interlocutor asked general probes, the chimpanzees responded with different signs. When the interlocutor asked on-topic probes, the chimpanzees responded with incorporations and expansions. When the interlocutor asked off-topic probes, the chimpanzees used fewer incorporations and expansions and often refused to respond. In the can't condition the chimpanzees rarely used incorporations and expansions, instead they used different signs or failed to respond.

CONTINGENT REPLIES

Except, perhaps, for the word-salad of schizophrenia and the speaking-in-tongues of religious ecstasy, verbal behavior depends on context. Conversations between two speakers or signers depend on the verbal give-and-take between conversational partners. Conversational contingency appears in utterances of human children as young as 2 years old (Gallagher, 1977; Wilcox & Webster, 1980; Marcos & Bernicot, 1994; Anselmi, et al., 1986; Bloom, et al., 1976). In this experiment Washoe, Moja, Tatu, and Dar signed to a human familiar whose rejoinders varied according to a systematic experimental design. The responses of the cross-fosterlings were contingent on the rejoinders of the human interlocutor. The cross-fostered chimpanzees reacted to probes appropriately by maintaining or altering the signs in their previous utterance. They interacted with probes appropriately by adjusting their signs in relation to the probes.

Incorporation and Expansion

In conversation both human adults and human children often incorporate all or part of the utterance of a partner into their own next rejoinder. Keenan [1977], Keenan and Klein [1975], and Wilbur and Petitto [1981] suggest that incorporation indicates assent in the utterances of children. They interpreted examples of incorporation as a pragmatic device indicating positive response as in Keenan (p. 130):

Adult: And we're going to have hot dogs.
Child: Hot dogs! (excitedly)

In Reno, Tatu and Dar incorporated signs from the interlocutor's previous utterance and incorporations were more likely to occur in response to announcements of positive events than to neutral or negative announcements. For example, "in response to the statement TIME ICECREAM NOW, Tatu signed ICECREAM ICECREAM ICECREAM ICECREAM ICECREAM ICECREAM" [R. Gardner, Gardner, & Drumm, 1989, p. 47].

Adults and older children interact in conversation by expanding as well as incorporating while younger children tend to incorporate without expanding [Bloom, et al., 1976; Keenan, 1977], as in Bloom, et al., [p. 528].

Adult: Take your shirt off.
Child: Shirt off

As Figure 2 shows, Washoe, Moja, Tatu and Dar often expanded (I+) when they responded to probes in this experiment adding information to the interlocutor's previous utterance as in the following example.

Trial # 2/0:19:23.
    0:19:24 Tatu: SMELL/
    0:19:26 Probe: WHO SMELL?/
    0:19:27 Tatu: TATU SMELL YOU/

As cross-fosterlings in Reno, Washoe, Moja, Tatu, and Dar replied to Wh-questions with expansions [Van Cantfort, et al., 1989, p. 210]. In Reno as in Ellensburg the conversation of these chimpanzees resembled older children rather than younger children.

On-topic and Off-topic Probes

On-topic and off-topic probes had the same Wh-signs combined with signs that were either contingent on or irrelevant to the signs in the previous utterance of the chimpanzee.
On-topic Trial # 2/1:39:59
1:39:57 Moja: EAT/
1:39:59 Probe: WHO EAT?/
Off-topic Trial # 3/0:30:15
0:30:12 Moja: FLOWER/
0:30:15 Probe: WHO IN THERE?/

With on-topic probes the interlocutor followed the conversational lead of the chimpanzee. Off-topic probes created a situation like a dual monologue; the interlocutor's responses ignored the conversational utterances of the chimpanzee.

On-topic probes evoked more response and less failure to respond than any other type of probe. Relative to on-topic probes off-topic probes depressed responses and evoked more failures to respond. On-topic probes evoked more incorporation and expansion (I and I+) than off-topic probes. Off-topic probes evoked more different (Dp) utterances than on-topic probes, although off-topic probes did evoke some I and I+ indicating attempts by the chimpanzees to shift to the new topic introduced by the interlocutor.

P. Dunham and Dunham [1995] examined human children's responses to on-topic and off-topic comments. In an extreme control for non-verbal cues, the researchers used a mechanical robot as the interlocutor. A hidden experimenter observed a child and responded to a child's speech through a speaker in the robot. The effect of on-topic and off-topic probes on the children in Dunham and Dunham's study was similar to the effects found in the cross-fostered chimpanzees in the present study. In both cases on-topic probes evoked more incorporations and expansions and fewer failures to respond than did off-topic probes.

General Probes

WHAT? is a request for general information. Replying WHAT to the question WHAT? is inappropriate because it fails to add any information. Incorporations and expansions never appeared in the replies to general probes although they frequently and appropriately appeared in replies to on-topic probes.

When a child says "Gimme orange," and an adult asks, "What?" the adult has requested general information. The child could answer by repeating "Gimme orange," and this would be appropriate since the adult may have failed to hear or to understand the first time. Suppose instead, the adult asked, "Where is the orange?" This question asks for a specific location. In this case, repeating the first "Gimme orange," would be an inappropriate answer because it fails to provide any new information. On the other hand the child could respond, "Orange there," (pointing toward a fruit bowl) and this would provide appropriate new information [Anselmi, et al., 1986]. Human children react to general probes by expanding across turns as in Brinton, Fujiki, Loeb, et al. [1986, p. 77].

Child: A girl's playing on the swing
Adult: Huh?
Child: A girl and boy are playing on the swing.

Expanding across turns maintains the topic [Garvey, 1977; Wilcox & Webster, 1980] and also adds information. As human children develop they are more likely to expand across turns [Brinton, Fujiki, Loeb, et al., 1986; Anselmi, et al. 1986].

The cross-fostered chimpanzees often reacted to probes by expanding across turns (Sc). This maintained their original topic while adding more information.

Trial # 3/1:04:40
    1:04:51 Washoe: ME GIMME (toward edible plants beyond her reach)/
    1:04:54 Probe: NOT UNDERSTAND/
    1:04:56 Washoe: FOOD GIMME/

It was also appropriate to react to a general probe by repeating the signs in the previous utterance thus emphasizing or clarifying something that the interlocutor may have missed.

Trial # 4/0:22:27
    0:22:28 Dar: FLOWER THERE/
    0:22:29 Probe: WHAT?/
    0:22:30 Dar: FLOWER THERE/

Washoe, Moja, Tatu, and Dar were more likely to expand across turns. In Bodamer and Gardner [2002] Washoe, Moja, Tatu, and Dar also reacted to general probes by expanding on the signs in their previous utterance.

Can't Probes

The can't condition evoked the least response and the most failures to respond of all the conditions of this experiment. Moja and Tatu responded slightly more often than Washoe and Dar showing more persistence since they also expanded on their previous utterances thus staying with their original topic. Marcos and Bernicot [1994] examined reactions of 18 to 30 month old human children to an interlocutor who refused to cooperate with requests for objects. Like the chimpanzees in this experiment, the children sometimes persisted in their original request, sometimes they switched to a different topic, but more often they failed to respond.

Successive Questions

Brinton, Fujiki, Loeb, et al. [1986] asked human children age 2 years 7 months to 9 years 10 months a series of questions like the general questions in the present study. When the interlocutor probed with "Huh?", "What?", "I don't understand." a child could end the conversation or persist. Older children continued to respond after the second and third questions, while younger children often failed to respond or responded inappropriately to the second and third questions. Like older children, Washoe, Moja, Tatu, and Dar continued to respond after each of the three probes in the trial. Likewise in the other three conditions, on-topic, off-topic, and can't, they also continued to respond after each of the probes in the trial regardless of the probe's order in the trial.

When an utterance fails, human children may repeat themselves or shift to something different. Young children with smaller vocabularies are more likely to repeat the same utterance from turn to turn. The younger children in Brinton, Fujiki, Loeb, et al. [1986] often repeated the same utterance throughout the series of questions, while the older children often expanded and also shifted to different utterances. Ciocci and Baran [1998] compared the responses of signing deaf and speaking hearing children age 4 years 6 months to 7 years 6 months to three general questions. They found that the hearing children were more likely to repeat the same utterance from turn to turn than the deaf children. Like older children and deaf children the cross-fostered chimpanzees usually reacted to general probes by expanding their previous utterance or shifting to new utterances. They seldom reacted by repeating their previous utterance without expanding.

The first probe in the general condition was a questioning facial expression without any signs. Pearl, Donahue, and Bryan [1981] found that only older children responded to questioning facial expressions. Moja responded to the questioning facial expression 90% of the time, Tatu 75% of the time and Washoe and Dar 70% of the time. The chimpanzees reacted contingently and appropriately to those non-verbal probes. Future research could vary facial expression while keeping signs constant. For example, an interlocutor could sign TIME EAT/ as the declarative versus TIME EAT?/ with the questioning facial expression [see R. A. Gardner & Gardner, 1973].

Topic Maintenance

The effect of incorporation and expansion on topic maintenance seems fairly clear. Nonoverlapping utterances can maintain the topic, but they also can introduce a new topic.

Pilot data videotape #1 Tatu and interlocutor are looking at a picture of a hamburger.
Tatu: FOODx/
Probe: NOT UNDERSTAND/
Tatu: SANDWICHx/

SANDWICH still refers to a food item even though it is different from Tatu's earlier utterance.

Trial # 4/0:31:00 Moja and interlocutor explore the vegetable garden outside.
    0:31:05 Moja: ONIONx/
    0:31:09 Probe: NOT UNDERSTAND/
    0:31:09 Moja: LOOK THERE (toward the onions in the garden)/

Trial # 4/0:43:22
    0:43:18 Dar: GUMx/
    0:43:22 Probe: WHO WANT GUM?/
    0:43:24 Dar: DARx/

In these three examples it seems clear that the chimpanzee maintained the topic with nonoverlapping utterances. Other cases are less clear.

Trial # 4/1:38:39
    1:38:31 Washoe: GIMMEx (towards plants beyond her reach)/
    1:38:39 Probe: questioning facial expression
    1:38:40 Washoe: HURRYx/
Trial # 2/0:13:16
    0:13:15 Tatu: BLACK/
    0:13:16 Probe: questioning facial expression
    0:13:23 Tatu: CRACKER/

Initiation

The chimpanzee-human dialogues in this experiment were embedded in the casual interactions of daily life at CHCI. For experimental purposes the interlocutor always waited for the chimpanzee to initiate a dialogue, but Washoe, Moja, Tatu, and Dar normally initiated chimpanzee-human dialogues in Reno and in Ellensburg. In a systematic test of initiation Bodamer and Gardner [2002] found that when Washoe, Moja, Tatu, and Dar encountered an interlocutor sitting with his back turned to them, the chimpanzees often made attention getting sounds. The only signs to his back were noisy. When he turned and faced them, they signed to him and rarely made sounds. These behaviors show that, like hearing and deaf human children and adults, the chimpanzees initiated conversations with attention getting devices [Baker, 1977; Foster, 1990; Golinkoff, 1986; Kennan & Schieffelin, 1976; McKirdy & Blank, 1982; McTear, 1979; Mueller, 1972; Prinz & Prinz, 1985; Vandell & George, 1981; Woodward, 1980].

Contingency

This experiment varied conversational input to chimpanzees and showed that systematic variations in input from a familiar conversational partner resulted in systematic variations in the content and the quality of the responses of four cross-fostered chimpanzees, Washoe, Moja, Tatu, and Dar. The responses of the chimpanzees were conversational responses that were contingent on conversational probes of the interlocutor. The responses of the chimpanzees resembled the conversational responses of human children in similar studies and resembled older children more than very young children. Like human children, Washoe, Moja, Tatu, and Dar varied among themselves. They showed patterns of individual differences in their conversational styles.

COMPARATIVE INTELLIGENCE AND INTELLIGENT COMPARISONS

The cross-fosterlings developed into conversational partners because interlocutors had always treated them as conversational partners. Interactive sign language had always been an integral part of their daily lives, beginning at an infantile level and rising to gradually more sophisticated levels as they matured. The development of human children also depends on adults treating them as conversational partners.

In our time the significant interaction between natural endowment and nurturing environment appears very clear, but this is a historically recent development. Early in the twentieth century, infants were supposed to develop according to an inexorable species-specific plan. Provided with sufficient food, water, and shelter, each child should develop into a typical child, each chimpanzee into a typical chimpanzee, and so on. It was in those days that B. F. Skinner recommended a small, sterile, climatically controlled chamber as the best place to raise a human infant. Many hated Skinner for this proposal, but few questioned its scientific and practical merit.

Mounting evidence revealed dramatic contrasts between individual and institutional child rearing that contradicted the traditional view. In institutions, Dennis [1960] and Hunt, Mohandess, Ghodessi, and Akiyama [1976], for example, reported profound retardation, especially in institutions with a high infant to caretaker ratio. Some infants could neither sit alone nor creep at age 1, and many could not walk at age 2. Interventions that lowered the infant to caretaker ratio produced dramatic effects. The mean age for sitting alone dropped from 39 weeks to 27 weeks, and for standing and cruising while holding onto the crib edge, from 69 weeks down to 41 [Hunt, et al., pp. 207-208].

Effects of the behavioral environment begin very soon. Respected authorities once taught that only the most basic postural and locomotor functions develop during the first year of human infancy, and these develop almost independently of the nurturing environment.

> Maturational factors (with the spontaneous exercise and practice derived from them) are sufficient to ensure the early development of typical postural [and locomotor] behavior as long as nutrition, shelter, space for practice, and perhaps a minimum of kindness from mother substitutes for infants not left with their mothers are provided [Riesen & Kinder, 1952, p. 173].

B. T. Gardner and Gardner [1989] compares the age of onset of 50 early postural, locomotor, manipulative, perceptual, and social behaviors in the cross-fostered chimpanzees, Moja, Pili, Tatu, and Dar with norms established for human infants by W. Dennis and Dennis [1937], Shirley [1931/1933], and Cohen and Gross [1979]. The cross-fosterlings were ahead of human infants on many items such as fixating objects and playing with own hands, but the sequences of chimpanzee and human development were highly correlated (rho = .77). Fixating objects and following moving objects came before bringing objects to mouth and playing with own hands, while sitting unsupported and patting, beating, and striking objects came later still, both for human infants and for cross-fostered chimpanzees [B. T. Gardner & Gardner, 1989, pp. 439-441, Tables 1 and 2].

Riesen and Kinder [1952] used the items of Gesell and Thompson's [1929] test for human infants to measure the age of onset of motor milestones for 14 infant chimpanzees reared at Yerkes Laboratories. They found a parallel pattern of development with laboratory infants somewhat ahead of human infants. B. T. Gardner and Gardner [1989] compared the cage-reared chimpanzees of Riesen and Kinder with wild chimpanzees reared by their own mothers and observed by Goodall [1967] and Plooij [1984]. Just as human infants reared by their own mothers are ahead of human infants reared in institutions, so chimpanzee infants reared in the wild are well ahead of chimpanzee infants reared in cages: e.g., sit when propped at 10 weeks for wild, 19 weeks for caged infants; stand alone at 12 weeks for wild, 39 weeks for caged infants.

Table 3 of B. T. Gardner and Gardner [1989] compares cage-reared, wild-reared, and cross-fostered chimpanzees on the overlapping items that provide observations for all three groups. On these milestones of development the cross-fostered chimpanzees are close to wild chimpanzees reared by their own mothers, while both wild and cross-fostered infants are distinctly advanced compared with cage-reared infants. With respect to these milestones of the first year, then, cross-fostering successfully brought Moja, Pili, Tatu, and Dar close to the full potential of their species.

To this day comparisons between human children and other animals often overlook the contribution of behavioral environments. Experiments compare chimpanzees that live in cages – lucky if they have a rubber tire to play with or a rope to swing from – with human children that live in the rich environment of suburban homes. In many so called "developmental studies" of captive animals the developmental variable is the number of years that the animal has lived under deprived conditions. Most modern psychologists would expect human children to lose rather than develop intelligent behavior under comparable conditions. Indeed, older captives often score lower than younger captives at tests of intelligence [e.g. Povinelli, Rulf, Landau, & Bierschwale, 1993; Tomasello, Davis-Dasilva, Camak, & Bard, 1987].

CONCLUSION

Systematic variations in input from a familiar conversational partner resulted in systematic variations in the contents and the quality of the responses of four cross-fostered chimpanzees. The responses of the chimpanzees were conversational responses that were contingent on conversational probes of the interlocutor. When appropriate, they incorporated signs from the interlocutor's responses into their own turns in the conversation and expanded on the signs they incorporated. When appropriate, they also clarified and amplified their own previous responses with suitable expansion. They responded contingently to maintain the interaction and the topic of the interaction. The responses of the chimpanzees resembled the conversational responses of human children in similar studies and resembled older children more than very young children. Like human children, Washoe, Moja, Tatu, and Dar varied among themselves. They showed patterns of individual differences in their conversational styles. The resulting dialogues have the quality of human conversations because they took place in an appropriate environment. They are comparable to dialogues in similar research with human children because cross-fostered chimpanzees and human children carry on conversations under similar conditions.

REFERENCES

Anselmi, D., Tomasello, M., & Acunzo, M. (1986). Young children's responses to neutral and specific contingent queries. *Journal of Child Language, 13,* 135-144.

Baker, C. (1977). Regulators and turn-taking in American Sign Language discourse. In L. Friedman (Ed.), *On the other hand: New perspectives on American Sign Language* (pp. 215-241). New York: Academic Press.

Baker-Shenk, C. (October, 1985). The facial behavior of deaf signers: Evidence of complex language. *American Annals of the Deaf,* 297-304.

Bloom, L. (1991). *Language development from two to three.* New York: Cambridge University Press.

Bloom, L., Lightbown, P., & Hood, L. (1975). Structure and variation in child language. *Monographs of the Society for Research in Child Development, 40* (2, Serial No. 160).

Bloom, L., Rocissano, L., & Hood, L. (1976). Adult-child discourse: Developmental interaction between information processing and linguistic knowledge. *Cognitive Psychology, 8,* 521-552.

Bodamer, M., Fouts, R., & Fouts, D. (1987, April). *Comprehension of vocal English and ASL translation by a chimpanzee.* Paper presented at the meeting of the Western Psychological Association, Long Beach, CA.

Bodamer, M. D., & Gardner, R. A. (2002). How cross-fostered chimpanzees (*Pan troglodytes*) initiate and maintain conversations. *Journal of Comparative Psychology, 116,* 12-26.

Bonvillian, J. D., Nelson, K. E., & Charrow, V. D. (1976). Language and language-related skills in deaf and hearing children. *Sign Language Studies, 12,* 211-250.

Braine, M. D. (1976). Children's first word combinations. *Monographs of the Society for Research in Child Development, 11* (1, Serial No. 164), 1-96.

Brinton, B., & Fujiki, M. (1984). Development of topic manipulation skills in discourse. *Journal of Speech and Hearing Research, 27,* 350-358.

Brinton, B., & Fujiki, M. (1991). Responses to requests for conversational repair by adults with mental retardation. *Journal of Speech and Hearing Research, 34,* 1087-1095.

Brinton, B., Fujiki, M., Loeb, D. F., & Winkler, E. (1986). Development of conversational repair strategies in response to requests for clarification. *Journal of Speech and Hearing Research, 29,* 75-81.

Brinton, B., Fujiki, M., Winkler, E., & Loeb, D. (1986). Responses to requests for clarification in linguistically normal and language-impaired children. *Journal of Speech and Hearing Disorders, 51,* 370-378.

Brown, R. (1968). The development of Wh questions in child speech. *Journal of Verbal Learning and Verbal Behavior, 7,* 277-290.

Brown, R. (1980). The maintenance of conversation. In D. Olson (Ed.), *The social foundation of language and thought* (pp. 187-210). New York: W. W. Norton.

Ciocci, S. R., & Baran, J. A. (1998). The use of conversational repair strategies by children who are deaf. *American Annals of the Deaf, 143,* 235-245.

Cohen, M. A., & Gross, P. J. (1979). *The developmental resource: Behavioral sequences for assessment and program planning.* New York: Grune & Stratton.

Covington, V. (1973). Juncture in American Sign Language. *Sign Language Studies, 2*, 29-38.

De Villiers, J. G., & De Villiers, P. A. (1986). The acquisition of English. In D.I. Slobin (Ed.), *The crosslinguistic study of language acquisition* (Vol. 1). Hillsdale, NJ: Lawrence Erlbaum.

Dennis, W. (1960). Causes of retardation among institutional children: Iran. *Journal of Genetic Psychology, 96*, 47-59.

Dennis, W., & Dennis, M. G. (1937). Behavioral development in the first year as shown by forty biographies. *Psychological Record, 1*, 349-361.

Dunham, P. J., & Dunham, F. (1995). Optimal social structures and adaptive infant development. In C. Moore, & P. J. Dunham (Eds.), *Joint attention: Its origins and role in development* (pp. 159-188). Hillsdale, NJ: Lawrence Erlbaum Associates.

Foster, S. H. (1990). Developmental pragmatics. In H. Winitz (Ed.), *Human communication and its disorders: A review 1990* (pp. 64-134). Stamford, CT: Ablex.

Fouts, D. H. (1994). The use of remote video recordings to study the use of American Sign Language by chimpanzees when no humans are present. In R. A. Gardner, B. T. Gardner, B. Chiarelli, & F. X. Plooij (Eds.), *The ethological roots of culture* (pp. 271-284). Netherlands: Kluwer.

Fouts, R. S. (1975). Communication with chimpanzees. In G. Kurth & I. Eible-Eibesfeldt (Eds.), *Hominisation und verhalten* (pp. 137-158). Suttgart: Gustav Fischer Verlag.

Fouts, R. S., Abshire, M. L., Bodamer, M. D., & Fouts, D. H. (1989). Signs of enrichment: Toward the psychological well-being of chimpanzees. In E. Segal (Ed.), *Housing, care and psychological wellbeing of captive and laboratory primates* (pp. 376-388). Park Ridge, NJ: Noyes.

Fouts, R. S., & Fouts, D. H. (1989). Loulis in conversation with the cross-fostered chimpanzees. In R. A. Gardner, B. T. Gardner, & T. E. Van Cantfort (Eds.), *Teaching sign language to chimpanzees* (pp. 293-307). Albany, NY: State University of New York Press.

Fouts, R. S., Fouts, D. H., & Van Cantfort, T. E. (1989). The infant Loulis learns signs from cross-fostered chimpanzees. In R. A. Gardner, B. T. Gardner, & T. E. Van Cantfort (Eds.), *Teaching sign language to chimpanzees* (pp. 280-292). Albany, NY: State University of New York Press.

Fouts, R. S., Hirsch, A. D., & Fouts, D. H. (1982). Cultural transmission of a human language in a chimpanzee mother-infant relationship. In H. E. Fitzgerald, J. A. Mullins, and P. Page (Eds.), *Psychobiological perspectives: Child nurturance* (Vol. 3, pp. 159-196). New York: Plenum Press.

Gallagher, T. M. (1977). Revision behaviors in the speech of normal children developing language. *Journal of Speech and Hearing Research, 20*, 293-302.

Gardner, B. T., & Gardner, R. A. (1975). Evidence for sentence constituents in the early utterances of child and chimpanzee. *Journal of Experimental Psychology, 104*, 244-267.

Gardner, B. T., & Gardner, R. A. (1989). Prelinguistic development of children and chimpanzees. *Journal of Human Evolution, 4*, 433-460.

Gardner, B. T., & Gardner, R. A. (1994). Development of phrases in the utterances of children and cross-fostered chimpanzees. In R. A. Gardner, B. T. Gardner, B. Chiarelli, & F. X. Plooij (Eds.), *The ethological roots of culture* (pp. 223-256). Netherlands: Kluwer.

Gardner, B. T., & Gardner, R. A. (1998). Development of phrases in the utterances of children and cross-fostered chimpanzees. *Human Evolution, 13*, 161-188.

Gardner, B. T., Gardner, R. A., & Nichols, S. G. (1989). The shapes and uses of signs in a cross-fostering laboratory. In R. A. Gardner, B. T. Gardner, & T. E. Van Cantfort (Eds.), *Teaching sign language to chimpanzees* (pp. 55-180). Albany, NY: State University of New York Press.

Gardner, R. A., & Gardner, B. T. (1969). Teaching sign language to a chimpanzee. *Science, 165*, 664-672.

Gardner, R. A., & Gardner, B. T. (1973). *Teaching sign language to the chimpanzee, Washoe* [Film]. (Available from Psychological Cinema Register, State College, PA).

Gardner, R. A., & Gardner, B. T. (1974). Teaching sign language to the chimpanzee, Washoe. *Bulletin D'Audio Phonologie, 4(5)*, 145-173.

Gardner, R. A., & Gardner, B. T. (1984). A vocabulary test for chimpanzees. *Journal of Comparative Psychology, 98*, 381-404.

Gardner, R. A., & Gardner, B. T. (1989). A cross-fostering laboratory. In R. A. Gardner, B. T. Gardner, & T. E. Van Cantfort (Eds.), *Teaching sign language to chimpanzees* (pp. 1-28). Albany, NY: State University of New York Press.

Gardner, R. A., & Gardner, B. T. (1991). Absence of evidence and evidence of absence. *Behavioral and Brain Sciences, 14*, 558-560.

Gardner, R. A., & Gardner, B. T. (1998). *The structure of learning.* Mahwah, NJ: Lawrence Erlbaum Associates.

Gardner, R. A., Gardner, B. T., & Drumm, P. (1989). Voiced and signed responses in cross-fostered chimpanzees. In R. A. Gardner, B. T. Gardner, & T. E. Van Cantfort (Eds.), *Teaching sign language to chimpanzees* (pp. 29-54). Albany, NY: State University of New York Press.

Gardner, R. A., Van Cantfort, T. E., & Gardner, B. T. (1992). Categorical replies to categorical questions by cross-fostered chimpanzees. *American Journal of Psychology, 105*, 27-57.

Garvey, C. (1977). Contingent queries and their relations in discourse. In E. Ochs, & B. Schieffelin (Eds.), *Developmental pragmatics* (pp. 363-372). New York: Academic Press.

Gesell, A., & Thompson, H. (1929). Learning and growth in identical infant twins: An experimental study by the method of co-twin control. *Genetic Psychology Monographs, 6*, 3-32.

Golinkoff, R. M. (1986). "I beg your pardon?": The preverbal negotiation of failed messages. *Journal of Child Language, 13*, 455-476.

Goodall, J. van Lawick (1967). Mother-offspring relationships in free-ranging chimpanzees. In D. Morris (Ed.), *Primate ethology* (pp. 287-346). London: Weidenfeld and Nicolson.

Goodall, J. (1986). *The chimpanzees of Gombe.* Cambridge, MA: Harvard University Press.

Grosjean, F., & Lane, H. (1977). Pauses and syntax in American Sign Language. *Cognition, 5*, 101-117.

Hayes, K. J., & Nissen, C. H. (1971). Higher mental functions of a home-raised chimpanzee. In A. M. Schrier & F. Stollnitz (Eds.), *Behavior of nonhuman primates* (Vol. 4, pp. 59-115). New York: Academic Press.

Humphries, T., Padden, C., & O'Rourke, T. J. (1980). *A basic course in American Sign Language.* Silver Spring, MD: T. J. Publishers.

Hunt, J. McV., Mohandessi, D., Ghodssi, M., & Akiyama, M. (1976). The psychological development of orphanage-reared infants: Interventions with outcomes (Tehran). *Genetic Psychology Monographs, 94,* 177-226.

Jensvold, M. L. A., & Gardner, R. A. (2000). Interactive use of sign language by cross-fostered chimpanzees. *Journal of Comparative Psychology, 114,* 335-346.

Keenan, E. O. (1977). Making it last: Repetition in children's discourse. In S. Ervin-Tripp & C. Mitchell-Kernan (Eds.), *Child discourse* (pp. 125-138). New York: Academic.

Keenan, E., & Klein, E. (1975). Coherency in children's discourse. *Journal of Psycholinguistic Research, 4,* 365-380.

Keenan, E., & Schieffelin, B. (1976). Topic as a discourse notion: A study of topic in the conversations of children and adults. In C. Li (Ed.), *Subject and topic* (pp. 335-384). New York: Academic Press.

Kellogg, W. N. (1968). Communication and language in the home-raised chimpanzees. *Science, 162,* 423-427.

Lane, H., & Pillard, R. (1978). *The wild boy of Burundi.* New York: Random House.

Leonard, L. B. (1976). *Meaning in child language.* New York: Grune & Stratton.

Maestas y Moores, J. (1980). Early linguistic environment: Interactions of deaf parents with their infants. *Sign Language Studies, 26,* 1-13.

Marcos, H., & Bernicot, J. (1994). Addressee co-operation and request reformulation in young children. *Journal of Child Language, 21,* 677-692.

Marschark, M. (1993). *Psychological development of deaf children.* New York: Oxford University Press.

McKirdy, L. S., & Blank, M. (1982). Dialogue in deaf and hearing preschoolers. *Journal of Speech and Hearing Research, 25,* 487-499.

McTear, M. F. (1979). "Hey! I've got something to tell you": A study of the initiation of conversational exchanges of preschool children. *Journal of Pragmatics, 3,* 21-36.

Mueller, E. (1972). The maintenance of verbal exchanges between young children. *Child Development, 43,* 930-938.

Pearl, R., Donahue, D. M., & Bryan, T. (1981). Children's responses to nonexplicit requests for clarification. *Perceptual and Motor Skills, 55,* 919-925.

Plooij, F. X. (1984). *The behavioural development of free-living chimpanzee babies and infants.* Norwood, NJ: ABLEX.

Povinelli, D. J., Rulf, A. B., Landau, D. R., & Bierschwale, D. T. (1993). Self recognition in chimpanzees: Distribution, ontogeny, and patterns of emergence. *Journal of Comparative Psychology, 107,* 347-372.

Prinz. P. M., & Prinz, E. A. (1985). If only you could hear what I see: Discourse development in sign language. *Discourse Process, 8,* 1-19.

Reich, P. A. (1986). *Language development.* Englewood Cliffs, NJ: Prentice Hall.

Riesen, A. H., & Kinder, E. F. (1952). *Postural development of infant chimpanzees: A comparative and normative study based on the Gesell behavioral examination.* New Haven: Yale University Press.

Rimpau, J. B., Gardner, R. A., & Gardner, B. T. (1989). Expression of person, place, and instrument in ASL utterances of children and chimpanzees. In R. A. Gardner, B. T. Gardner, & T. E. Van Cantfort (Eds.), *Teaching sign language to chimpanzees* (pp. 240-268). Albany, NY: State University of New York Press.

Roach, J. (2003, May 9). Tarzan's Cheeta's life as a retired movie star. *National Geographic News*. http://news.nationalgeographic.com/news/2003/05/0509_030509_cheeta.html

Roth, F. P., & Spekman, N. J. (1984). Assessing the pragmatic abilities of children: Part 1. Organizational framework and assessment parameters. *Journal of Speech and Hearing Disorders, 49,* 2-11.

Ruvolo, M. (1994). Molecular evolutionary processes and conflicting gene trees: The hominoid case. *American Journal of Physical Anthropology, 94,* 89-113.

Schlesinger, H. S., & Meadow, K. P. (1972). *Sound and sign: Childhood deafness and mental health.* Berkeley: University of California Press.

Shaw, H. L. (1989). *Comprehension of the spoken word and ASL translation by chimpanzees.* Unpublished master's thesis, Central Washington University, Ellensburg.

Shirley, M. M. (1931/1933). *The first two years: A study of twenty-five babies* (Vol 1 & Vol II). Minneapolis: University of Minnesota Press.

Short-Meyerson, K. J., & Abbeduto, L. J. (1997). Preschoolers' communication during scripted interactions. *Journal of Child Language, 24,* 469-493.

Sibley, C. G., & Ahlquist, T. E. (1984). The phylogeny of the hominoid primates indicated by DNA-DNA hybridization. *Journal of Molecular Evolution, 20,* 2-15.

Singh, J. A. L., & Zingg, R. M. (1942). *Wolf children and feral man.* Hamden, CT: Shoe String Press (Reprinted in 1966 by Harper & Row).

Slater, P. J. B., & Williams, J. M. (1994). Bird song learning: A model of cultural transmission? In R. A. Gardner, B. T. Gardner, A. B. Chiarelli, & F. X. Plooij (Eds.), *The ethological roots of culture* (pp. 95-106). Dordrecht: Kluwer.

Sloan, A. (2002). *Bilingual conversations between chimpanzees and humans.* Unpublished master's thesis, Central Washington University, Ellensburg.

Stanyon, R., Chiarelli, B., Gottlieb, D., & Patton, W. H. (1986). The phylogenetic and taxonomic status of *Pan paniscus*: A chromosomal perspective. *American Journal of Physical Anthropology, 69,* 489-498.

Stokoe, W. (1972). *Semiotics and human sign languages.* The Hague: Mouton.

Tomasello, M., Davis-Dasilva, M., Camak, L., & Bard, D. (1987). Observational learning of tool use by young chimpanzees. *Human Evolution, 2,* 175-183.

Van Cantfort, T. E., Gardner, B. T., & Gardner, R. A. (1989). Developmental trends in replies to Wh-questions by children and chimpanzees. In R. A. Gardner, B. T. Gardner, & T. E. Van Cantfort (Eds.), *Teaching sign language to chimpanzees* (pp. 198-239). Albany, NY: State University of New York Press.

Vandell, D. L., & George, L. B. (1981). Social interaction in hearing and deaf preschoolers: Successes and failures in initiations. *Child Development, 52,* 627-635.

Wells, G. (1974). Learning to code experience through language. *Journal of Child Language, 1,* 243-269.

West, M. J., King, A. P., & Freeberg, T. M. (1997). Building a social agenda for the study of bird song. In C. T. Snowdon, & M. Hausberger (Eds), *Social influences on vocal development* (pp. 41-56). Cambridge: University Press.

Wilbur, R. (1980). The linguistic description of American Sign Language. In H. Lane, & F. Grosjean (Eds.), *Recent perspective on American Sign Language* (pp. 7-31). Hillsdale, NJ: Lawrence Erlbaum Associates.

Wilbur, R. B., & Petitto, L. A. (1981). How to know a conversation when you see one: Discourse structure in American Sign Language conversations. *Journal of the National Student Speech-Language-Hearing Association, 9,* 66-81.

Wilcox, M. J., & Webster, E. J. (1980). Early discourse behavior: An analysis of children's responses to listener feedback. *Child Development, 51,* 1120-1125.

Woodward, J. (1980). Some sociolinguist aspects of French and American Sign Language. In H. Lane & F. Grosjeans (Eds.), *Recent perspectives on American Sign Language* (pp. 215-237). Hillsdale, NJ: Lawrence Erlbaum Associates.

INDEX

D

F

G

H

Q

R

S

stages, 5, 6, 7, 10, 20, 105, 151, 152, 154, 172, 176, 217, 221
standard deviation, 178
standard error, 223
statistical inference, 167
statistics, 53, 109
statolith, 196
stereotypes, 212
sterile, 272
stimulus, 2, 6, 7, 8, 10, 11, 16, 17, 19, 20, 21, 23, 26, 27, 33, 34, 35, 40, 43, 45, 47, 48, 58, 68, 86, 184, 185, 187, 208, 209, 210, 219, 221, 229, 233, 241
stock, 238, 245
stomach, 117
strain, 150, 154, 158
strategies, ix, x, 102, 105, 121, 123, 126, 143, 166, 193, 274
streams, 183
stress, vii, 31, 72, 90, 92, 98, 99, 133, 154, 158, 160
stridor, 60
stroke, ix, 5, 89, 92, 93, 95, 96
stroke volume, ix, 89, 92, 93, 95, 96
students, 22, 71, 79, 132, 248
subjective experience, 203, 204, 209, 232
subjectivity, 95
substitutes, 272
substrates, 4, 25
superimposition, 230
superior parietal cortex, 183, 193
superior vena cava, 118
superior vena cava syndrome, 118
superiority, 19
suppression, 158, 166, 178, 179, 192
surprise, 67, 111, 134, 200, 220
survey design, x, 126
susceptibility, 181, 189, 191, 197, 212
symbols, 32, 133
symptom, 59, 60, 61, 229, 231, 235
symptoms, xi, 41, 52, 122, 127, 149, 152, 157, 180, 181, 192, 216, 217, 218, 221, 222, 223, 227, 228, 229, 230, 231, 233, 235, 236
syndrome, 23, 48, 50, 52, 59, 62, 235
synthesis, 86
systems, 6, 22, 103, 118, 119, 151, 158, 162, 175, 176, 235
systolic blood pressure, 92, 94, 96, 97

T

T cell, 90, 92
target stimuli, xi, 215
targets, xi, 190, 199, 201, 208, 219
task difficulty, 27
task interference, 182, 183, 184, 185, 193

task performance, xi, 120, 196, 215, 216, 221, 230, 231
tau, 172
teachers, 132, 140, 203, 240
teaching, 241, 242, 243
team members, 127, 128
technology, 70, 102, 103, 118, 119, 122, 138
teeth, 132, 238
telephone, 129
television, 92, 96, 132, 254
temperament, 52, 61
temperature, 32, 93, 204
temporal lobe, 217, 233, 235
tension, ix, xi, 52, 89, 90, 92, 95, 97, 98, 216, 217, 223, 227, 230
textbooks, 48
thalamus, 229
theft, 22
theory, x, 27, 67, 85, 86, 88, 149, 163, 167, 172, 179, 180, 185, 188, 194, 195, 197, 200, 201, 204, 209, 210, 211
therapeutic interventions, 107
therapists, 120
therapy, viii, 32, 89, 90, 91, 94, 98, 159, 209, 234
thinking, 90, 91, 154, 216, 222, 227, 228, 229, 230
thought disorders, xi, 216, 229, 230
threat, 20, 211
threats, 141
threshold, 19, 34, 176, 178
thresholds, 61, 178, 179, 191
time, viii, 8, 17, 19, 20, 32, 33, 34, 35, 41, 52, 53, 54, 57, 58, 62, 87, 88, 91, 93, 98, 105, 107, 111, 112, 116, 117, 120, 121, 153, 155, 166, 168, 169, 170, 172, 180, 182, 183, 184, 185, 188, 204, 207, 211, 219, 221, 239, 240, 241, 242, 245, 249, 250, 262, 268, 270, 272
time constraints, 117
time series, 88
timing, 20, 27, 197, 202, 206
tissue, 95, 97
toddlers, 244
Togo, 78, 88
tonic, 177
toys, 241, 247
tracheostomy, 111, 112, 115
tracking, 196, 235
traffic, 240
training, 94, 97, 119, 126, 140, 155, 156, 158, 178, 187
traits, 203, 211, 242
trajectory, 67, 75, 82, 163, 164, 165, 166, 169, 170, 172, 193
transactions, 24